SECRET ALLIANCES

SPECIAL OPERATIONS AND
INTELLIGENCE IN NORWAY 1940–1945
– THE BRITISH PERSPECTIVE

SECRET ALLIANCES

TONY INSALL

Biteback Publishing

First published in Great Britain in 2019 by
Biteback Publishing Ltd
Westminster Tower
3 Albert Embankment
London SE1 7SP
Copyright © Tony Insall 2019

ISBN 978-1-78590-477-6

10 9 8 7 6 5 4 3 2 1

A CIP catalogue record for this book is available from the British Library.

Set in Adobe Caslon Pro

Printed and bound in Great Britain by
CPI Group (UK) Ltd, Croydon CR0 4YY

CONTENTS

LIST OF ABBREVIATIONS

ANCC	Anglo-Norwegian Collaboration Committee
BBC	British Broadcasting Corporation
BSS	Bayswater Security Section of SOE
C or CSS	Chief of the Secret Intelligence Service SIS
CCO	Chief of Combined Operations
CCS	Combined Chiefs of Staff
CO	Combined Operations
COHQ	Combined Operations Headquarters
COS	Chiefs of Staff
COSSAC	Chief of Staff Supreme Allied Commander
D	Sabotage Section of SIS
DCO	Directorate of Combined Operations
DDNI	Deputy Director of Naval Intelligence
DMI	Director of Military Intelligence
DNA	Det Norske Arbeiderpartiet (the Norwegian Labour Party)
DNI	Director of Naval Intelligence
DSIR	Department for Scientific and Industrial Research
FO	Forsvarets Overkommando (Norwegian Defence High Command)
FO.II	Norwegian Intelligence Office
FO.IV	The office responsible for resistance and military operations in Norway
GC&CS	Government Code and Cypher School

GRU	Main Intelligence Directorate (Russian Military Intelligence Service)
ISK	Illicit Signals Knox
ISOS	Illicit Signals Oliver Strachey
JIC	Joint Intelligence Committee
LO	Landsorganisasjonen i Norge (the Norwegian equivalent of the TUC)
MEW	Ministry of Economic Warfare
MI1c	An early name for the Secret Intelligence Service
MI5	Security Service
MI6	Another name for the Secret Intelligence Service
MI.II	Norwegian intelligence office in Stockholm
MILORG	Norwegian military resistance organisation
MI(R)	Military Intelligence Section for Irregular Warfare
NID	Naval Intelligence Division
NKVD	People's Commissariat for Internal Affairs (Russia's intelligence service)
NOK	Norwegian kroner
NS	Nasjonal Samling
OIC	Operational Intelligence Centre
POW	Prisoner of War
RVPS	Royal Victoria Patriotic School
SD	Sicherheitsdienst (the Nazi Party's intelligence service)
SF HQ	Special Forces headquarters
SHAEF	Supreme Headquarters Allied Expeditionary Force
SIS	Secret Intelligence Service
SEK	Swedish kroner
SOE	Special Operations Executive
STAPO	Norwegian NS secret police
USAAF	American Air Force
W/T	Wireless transmitter
XU	Norwegian resistance intelligence organisation

MAPS

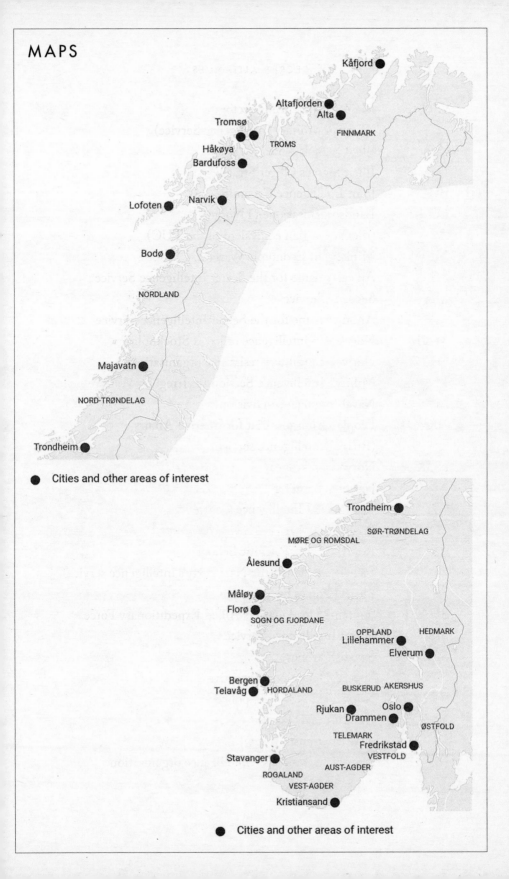

Kåfjord

Altafjorden
Alta

Tromsø
FINNMARK

Håkøya
Bardufoss
TROMS

Lofoten   Narvik

Bodø

NORDLAND

Majavatn

NORD-TRØNDELAG

Trondheim

● Cities and other areas of interest

Trondheim

SØR-TRØNDELAG

MØRE OG ROMSDAL

Ålesund

Måløy
Florø
SOGN OG FJORDANE

OPPLAND   HEDMARK
Lillehammer

Elverum

Bergen
Telavåg   HORDALAND   BUSKERUD   AKERSHUS

Rjukan   Oslo
Drammen
ØSTFOLD

TELEMARK
Fredrikstad
VESTFOLD

Stavanger
AUST-AGDER
ROGALAND
VEST-AGDER

Kristiansand

● Cities and other areas of interest

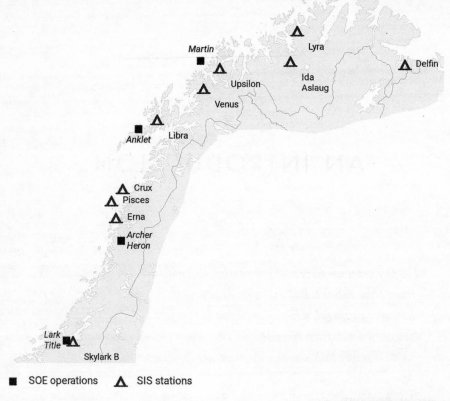

Martin

Lyra

Delfin

Upsilon

Ida
Aslaug

Venus

Anklet

Libra

Crux
Pisces

Erna

Archer
Heron

Lark
Title

Skylark B

■ SOE operations   △ SIS stations

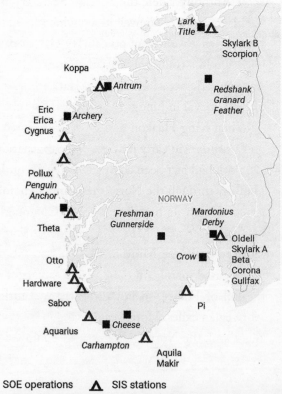

Lark
Title

Skylark B
Scorpion

Koppa

Antrum

Redshank
Granard
Feather

Eric
Erica
Cygnus

Archery

Pollux
Penguin
Anchor

NORWAY

Mardonius
Derby

Theta

Freshman
Gunnerside

Oldell
Skylark A
Beta
Corona
Gullfax

Crow

Otto

Hardware

Sabor

Pi

Aquarius

Cheese

Carhampton

Aquila
Makir

■ SOE operations   △ SIS stations

CHAPTER 1

AN INTRODUCTION

For five years we have worked together, in conditions which have some-times been difficult. But I should like to say that we have had no allies, however powerful, with whom it has been a greater privilege to work than our friends from Norway. They have responded to every call – often heavy calls – which we have had to make upon them.[1]

Sir Anthony Eden, the Foreign Secretary, paid this compliment to his guests at a farewell lunch which he hosted for members of the Norwegian government on 23 May 1945, as they prepared to return to Oslo and to a country liberated after five years of German occupation. The euphoric occasion marked a stark contrast with the circumstances of their arrival in June 1940. How was this change achieved?

When King Haakon and most of his government reached Britain on *Devonshire* in early June 1940, the evacuation of British forces from Dunkirk had just been completed and the outlook was very uncertain. Halfway through the Norwegian campaign, following growing dissat-isfaction with its handling, Neville Chamberlain lost the support of many Conservative MPs in a confidence vote in Parliament. He was replaced as Prime Minister by Winston Churchill. British attention was focused mainly on the possible threats of a German invasion and the fall of France, so initially there was little time to spare for the Norwegian exiles. Moreover, arriving in what was for many of them an alien land, the Norwegians were ill-equipped to establish themselves and work out what they wished to do or where to do it, and even whether to remain in Britain or to move to somewhere safer, such as Canada. The British minister to Norway, Cecil Dormer,* had offered the well-meaning but impractical suggestion that they should consider setting up their administration either in Cornwall or the west coast of Scotland, and the Foreign Office offered to arrange accommodation for them in Exeter. The Norwegian Prime Minister, Johan Nygaardsvold, decided to settle in London to begin with, but left open the possibility of moving elsewhere if German bombing made this too dangerous.

The Norwegians were bitterly disappointed by the lack of support they considered that they had received from the British during the Norwegian campaign. Feeling powerless and lacking all but the most intermittent contact with Norway, they had no realistic option but to accept an alliance with Britain. Nonetheless, there were differences of opinion over what the nature of that alliance should be. Halvdan Koht, the Foreign Minister who had been a strong advocate of Norwegian neutrality – and who had been unwilling to accept and act on growing evidence in early April 1940 which pointed to an imminent German invasion – wanted to limit the new relationship with Britain to practical cooperation without any political commitments. (Perhaps he was still affected by the memory of the boarding of the *Altmark* by the Royal Navy in Jøssingfjord in early 1940, leading to the release of 299 British prisoners, which was a significant violation of Norwegian sovereignty.) Moreover, he preferred not to live or work in London, but settled in Bracknell, some 30 miles west of London, which created further difficulties for the limited staff of his Foreign Ministry who were initially obliged to work there. And to compound the problems faced by the government, quite a few ministers spoke little or no English and needed to have language lessons.[2]

---

* At the beginning of the war, Britain was represented by a legation in Norway, headed by a minister. Its representation was upgraded to an embassy in May 1942, and the then minister Laurence Collier became ambassador to the government in exile.

It would not be an easy process for the Norwegians to resolve their main internal differences and to start to establish closer political and military relations with the British. Their initial numbers were small, and they lacked organisation. Moreover, on the military side, the British were looking not just to develop resistance operations, but also to retain control of them. So they preferred to recruit and train Norwegians themselves, with as little interference as possible. Their insistence on high levels of restrictive security also meant that they did not want to disclose in advance their plans for operations on the Norwegian mainland. Not exactly a promising position for the Norwegians to start from. How did they set about it, and achieve the relationship – crucial to the development of the resistance movement – which Eden later described in such glowing terms?

A new appraisal

Much has been written – and continues to be written – by Norwegian authors about the German occupation and Norwegian resistance. There has been very little from the British side. The most recent book which provides a comprehensive account of this subject is a collection of papers presented at a colloquium in Oxford in 1991 by British and Norwegian academics together with some of those who had taken part in the resistance.[3] We can now add significantly to that picture. In recent years, there has been a wealth of new material released to the National Archives in Kew describing the work of the Special Operations Executive (SOE) responsible for sabotage and subversion, the Government Code and Cypher School (GC&CS) and the Security Service, all of which played significant roles in supporting the Norwegian resistance. The papers now available in the HS series of the archive give new insights into many of the major SOE operations in Norway, including the well-known attack on the heavy water plant at Vemork and the ill-fated Operation MARTIN where only one man, Jan Baalsrud, survived after enduring the most extraordinary hardships. GC&CS made good use of intelligence obtained during raids on Norway to develop its knowledge of German codes and to break many of them. The files show the extent to which Combined Operations raids mounted on the Norwegian coast also had the objective of obtaining German cypher equipment and codes. This greatly assisted GC&CS in decyphering Abwehr (German military intelligence) traffic. It enabled the Security Service to arrest a good number of the Norwegians whom the Abwehr sent to Britain, although intelligence from other sources, particularly the Secret Intelligence Service (SIS), was also crucial. Security Service files show how much the Germans used Norway as a base to try to infiltrate their agents into Britain, especially in the early part of the war. They mounted nearly twenty operations from there, including one with limited success and another which came very close to succeeding. In addition, one Norwegian only escaped a treason trial (where he would certainly have been found guilty and hanged) because of procedural errors during his interrogation, and another managed to commit suicide soon after he had been detained and confronted with the extensive evidence against him. There are also new documents in other series covering the Prime Minister's activities and the Cabinet Office, as well as Foreign Office files.

Some of the recently released material also touches on the role of SIS, whose archives have not been released in Britain – and there is plenty more about their activities available on other files, particularly those of the Naval Intelligence Division in the Admiralty (ADM) series. These include, for example, the Distinguished Service Order (DSO) citations for two of SIS's star agents in Norway, Bjørn Rørholt and Torstein Raaby, which provide comprehensive accounts of their activities.* However, the Norwegian SIS archive is available to researchers in Oslo, as is their SOE archive. The SIS archive is not quite complete. It contains more information on operations than it

---

* The text of their citations is contained in the Appendix. There will be fairly frequent references to medal awards, so it may be helpful to explain their precedence. The highest award after a Victoria Cross is a DSO, followed by a Distinguished Service Cross (DSC), Military Cross (MC), Conspicuous Gallantry Medal (CGM), Distinguished Service Medal (DSM), Military Medal (MM) and a mention in despatches.

does on policy matters, which the British would not necessarily have shared with their Norwegian counterparts. Nonetheless, it complements significantly our knowledge of their Norwegian work, which concentrated on coast-watching stations providing intelligence about German naval and merchant shipping movements. The SOE archives in London and in Oslo are not complete either. The British archive lacks documents which were destroyed after the war and later because of a lack of space, though fire may have destroyed some as well.* The Norwegian archive also lacks policy documents. These omissions have led to a few gaps. For example, the SOE Norwegian section history contains a brief reference to the unsuccessful attempt in March 1941 to assassinate Himmler during his visit to Oslo, but there are no further details elsewhere. (We will look at this in more detail in Chapter 2.) However, they do not significantly affect the overall picture which is presented here.

It has also been possible to draw on some material obtained from the archives of the Russian intelligence service, then known as the NKVD, in Moscow. These are handwritten documents from Kim Philby, the SIS officer who was a Soviet spy who spent part of the war working in the SIS counter-intelligence section. They provide evidence of an Abwehr agent in Norway with whom SIS was in touch throughout the German occupation.

Drawing on this new material the book sets out to provide, from the British perspective, a reappraisal of resistance activities in occupied Norway. It will describe how, initially, with approval from the Norwegian government, both SIS and SOE carried out their operations quite independently. These methods did not always prove successful, especially when things went as wrong as they did after the second Lofoten raid and the death of Martin Linge, the charismatic leader of the Norwegian group working with SOE. This led to some serious disagreements, but effective changes were made which led to closer

---

* The SOE historian M. R. D. Foot estimated that seven-eighths of SOE's papers have not survived.

cooperation. The Norwegians set up a new command structure under General Hansteen with separate offices working as closely as possible with their British Allies. SIS liaised with FO.II (the Norwegian intelligence office) and, together with them, also provided support to XU, a home-grown Norwegian intelligence organisation. After a bumpy start, SOE developed an effective partnership with FO.IV (the office responsible for resistance and military operations in Norway) and Milorg, the military resistance movement in Norway. The establishment of the Anglo-Norwegian Collaboration Committee (ANCC) provided an effective means of sharing information and consultation about SOE operations. Still better, SOE and FO.IV were eventually co-located in 1944 and shared offices. While Norwegian ministers were not directly involved, they were kept closely informed about what became increasingly joint activities. This, and their pragmatism, enabled them to be both stoical and supportive when things went wrong, as they inevitably did sometimes, and there were German reprisals. These attitudes were also reflected in their relations with other British government departments, especially the Foreign Office, which enabled frank exchanges and generally satisfactory results.

The book will not attempt to describe the purely military aspects, particularly the campaign between April and June 1940 which has been well described elsewhere – although it will consider the intelligence available beforehand, and why it was misinterpreted or ignored. Nor will it explore in much detail the naval or commando raids on the Norwegian coast, except insofar as the latter provided opportunities for the discreet acquisition of German cyphers or led to bilateral problems. But it will examine the political links which were developed after a beginning in such unpromising circumstances and which supported resistance activities. The Norwegians were one among many exiled governments trying to establish themselves in London in the summer of 1940. What did they have to offer to help build up their relations, and how did they capitalise on their advantages?

Norwegian assets

By far the most important Norwegian contribution to Britain was the provision of a large part of its extensive merchant fleet. Given the income-earning potential of the merchant marine and its value to the Norwegian economy, it was never likely to be a straightforward matter for the two sides to negotiate agreements (for there were several) which met desperate British needs for tonnage at times when the Germans had sunk considerable numbers of ships crucial to the continued supply of vital war materials across the Atlantic, while also meeting Norwegian concerns to retain a degree of independence, to protect their post-war interests and to earn a reasonable income from their charters, especially in dollars. Not surprisingly given both the importance of these interests, and the strong characters of those involved in the negotiations and also within Nortraship (the Norwegian organisation administering the fleet), negotiations were never easy. Nortraship was controlled by the government but run by ship owners: it had two main offices in London and New York which frequently had conflicting interests. In the course of the war, the fleet lost nearly 2,000,000 tons of its ships, as well as more than 3,200 seamen and passengers. In addition, in the period before the German invasion, there had also been a further loss of more than 100,000 tons of shipping and nearly 400 seamen from vessels which had been chartered to Britain. There had already been discussions about a shipping agreement and in November 1939 one was signed which made available to Britain 150 large tankers – a critically important benefit.

Shipping agreements brought the Norwegians the prospect of significant earnings which would be paid to them in London and ensure that the government remained solvent. But, in addition to that, as the result of a truly remarkable operation carried out by a small group of resourceful and determined Norwegians overseen by Nicolai Rygg, the director of Norges Bank, Norway was able to remove nearly 50 tons of gold bullion from its central bank and transfer it to England from under the noses of the occupying German forces. Their arrival in Oslo had fortuitously been delayed by the sinking of the *Blücher* as she led the invasion fleet up the Oslo Fjord.* The Norwegian group, soldiers as well as a diverse group of enthusiastic volunteers who included such people as the poet Nordahl Grieg, moved the gold out of Oslo on 9 April, the day of the invasion. It was transported by lorry and railway on a tortuous journey, carefully concealed from the Germans who were known to be searching for it. The consignment was eventually divided into three parts, which were loaded onto British naval warships in Åndalsnes and Tromsø. It arrived almost intact in Britain – 'almost' intact because a bag of gold coins had been removed by a sticky-fingered British commando who had helped to load one of the consignments onto HMS *Glasgow*. (Although most were later found by the police, 296 gold coins were never recovered.) The Norwegian government resisted the best efforts of the British to persuade them to make over their gold holdings for the purchase of war materials, and transferred most of the bullion to the United States and Canada for safekeeping. As a result of this, and earnings from shipping, Norway was able to remain financially self-sufficient throughout the war, which provided a considerable advantage.[4] Several other governments, including the French, Dutch and Belgian, managed to transport some of their gold abroad to safer destinations, but were not able to retain control over all of it. Most of the other exiled governments arrived in Britain without significant assets (and in some cases quite impoverished), so were obliged to go into debt and borrow from Britain in order to finance their activities.

Another factor, which did not have the immediate impact of the merchant fleet or gold bullion, but which was of enduring significance throughout the war, was the role played by King Haakon, the Danish prince who had been chosen as monarch when Norway gained its

---

* Before the German invasion, the far-sighted Rygg had already arranged for more than half of Norway's gold reserves to be shipped directly to New York.

independence from Sweden in 1905.* The German failure to capture or kill him during the invasion enabled him to escape to Britain where he became a focal point for the expression of resistance. His frequent broadcasts to occupied Norway were a boost to morale and his speeches were printed and widely circulated by the underground press after the German confiscation of most radios prevented many Norwegians from listening for themselves. He was also a welcome source of advice not only to his own government, but also to senior British officials and ministers.

King Haakon kept in touch not only with Norwegians who had come to Britain to join the armed forces or to support the war effort by other means, but also, wherever possible, with members of the resistance who had returned from occupied Norway. Bjørn Rørholt describes what happened when Dagfinn Ulriksen and Atle Svardal returned to Britain after spending months manning the SIS coast-watching station Eric, north of Florø, living in a sheepfold without being able to wash or change their clothes. The King heard of their return and asked for them to come down to London exactly as they were. When he met the filthy and bedraggled pair, the King held his nose and said something in Danish which might be better imagined than translated – and then proceeded to question them keenly about their activities. Such gestures counted for a great deal among those working for the resistance.[5] They were also invited to a meeting with Stewart Menzies, the head of SIS (known as CSS), a rare honour.[6] When Ulriksen returned to Norway in late 1943 to man Cygnus, another SIS station in the same area, he took advantage of a supply delivery by a Shetlands-based submarine chaser to send back a Christmas tree which SIS was able to deliver to King Haakon on Christmas Eve.[7] It is tempting to speculate

---

* According to Dormer, two days before his departure from Tromsø, King Haakon had sent a note to inform him that he had changed his mind and thought he should remain with his people in Norway. Dormer was able to persuade him that he would become a virtual prisoner of the Germans and that this would play into their hands: in Britain he would be a free agent. The King accepted these arguments and agreed to continue with his journey to Britain. As Dormer was leaving, Crown Prince Olav expressed the same views. Dormer was able to persuade him to carry on, too. (The National Archives, hereafter TNA, FO 371/32835. See also François Kersaudy, *Norway 1940* (London: Arrow, 1990), p. 222.)

that this symbolic gesture might have planted the seed which led to the decision in 1947 by the city of Oslo to donate a Christmas tree every year to Britain in gratitude for wartime support.

Dagfinn Ulriksen (left) and Atle Svardal (right) after six months manning SIS hermit station Eric. They had just met King Haakon. © NHM

Trygve Lie's relations with Eden and the Foreign Office

When Koht took leave in November 1940 before resigning three months later, his successor, the ebullient and more dynamic Trygve Lie, took steps to build better relations with Britain. He made clear that he wanted closer collaboration than Koht had done. He hoped that the British would take the Norwegian government more into their confidence, rather than just informing them of decisions made without prior discussion – a theme to which he would need to return quite frequently, especially in the early years. The Northern Department of the Foreign Office were supportive, pointing out how little the Norwegians were being treated as equals and Allies, citing as evidence a cut imposed by the Ministry of Information on broadcasts to Norway without any prior consultation. Eden agreed. When he first met Lie on 28 December, he suggested they should meet fortnightly in future, and that Lie might bring Prime Minister Nygaardsvold with him whenever he wished. He also proposed monthly meetings with a larger Norwegian ministerial attendance – a suggestion which caused Foreign Office anxieties that this special arrangement might create jealousy among other Allied governments who had not been so favoured.[8] In the event, such regular appointments did not survive diary pressures for very long, though the meeting did lead to a Foreign Office circular to other government departments requesting they provide more ready access to Norwegian ministers in future. Lie built up a close relationship with Eden, both personally as well as officially, and played tennis with him quite frequently. The confidence they established was so great that after Lie had been confronted by Soviet Foreign Minister Vyacheslav Molotov during his visit to Moscow in November 1944, with demands for considerable concessions over Svalbard, as well as the right to establish an air base on Bjørnøya (Bear Island), he decided that on his return he wished to discuss this with Eden before he briefed his own government.[9]

Lie was an effective advocate of Norwegian interests, if occasionally a little too active for the comfort of his hosts. Orme Sargent, a senior Foreign Office official, once wearily reported a visit by Lie 'who had preached him two sermons' about the need for a British plan to occupy northern Norway, and his concerns if this did not happen.[10] King Haakon, who shared with the ambassador to the Norwegian government in exile, Sir Laurence Collier, the view that Lie was the backbone of the Norwegian government, once asked him whether the British found Lie to be pushing his case too hard. Would Collier like him to have a quiet word with Lie? Collier replied that this was not necessary.[11] It was inevitable that there would be bilateral difficulties, often caused in the early part of the war by a British insistence on restrictive security which left the Norwegians ignorant of planned commando raids or other operations in Norway. Lie's handling of many of these issues – though vigorous – produced results which generally improved cooperation thereafter. (Though not always. As Chapter 9 outlines, the decision of senior British officials not to inform Leif Tronstad – a key member of the resistance in London – of the decision to bomb the heavy water plant at Vemork in November 1943 was a significant exception, not least because Tronstad thought he had been given an assurance that this would not happen. His opposition to bombing this target was well known, and he was angry and disappointed by what he saw as bad faith.) And, while Norway may have been the junior partner in the alliance, Lie was also sometimes able to win the argument. For example, his handling of propaganda matters enabled Norway to establish primacy in making arrangements for BBC broadcasting to Norway, and to retain control of all propaganda except that directed at occupation forces. No other occupied country managed to obtain such advantageous treatment. Oscar Torp, especially as defence minister, was also an influential member of the government and an effective complement to Lie in developing pragmatic cooperation with the British – though they achieved little success in their attempts to adjust British policy towards the end of the war when it came to prioritising the liberation of Norway. It is quite possible that they would have become aware of Operation JUPITER, a plan favoured by Churchill (but not by the Chiefs of Staff) for an Allied invasion of Norway which was considered by the planning staff on several occasions between 1941 and 1944. Awareness of this would certainly have raised Norwegian expectations. But the final decision to concentrate on OVERLORD, the invasion of Normandy, was never going to be a subject for compromise.

Close cooperation also extended beyond the two governments. It also included members of the Norwegian Labour Party (Det Norske Arbeiderpartiet, DNA). In 1941 Hugh Dalton, the Minister of Economic Warfare, asked for some prominent DNA members to travel to Britain to help their planning, as his ministry needed more specialist information about Norway than could be provided from their existing sources. They were Konrad Nordahl, the leader of Landsorganisasjonen i Norge (LO), the Norwegian equivalent of the TUC, and Haakon Lie, later secretary of DNA from 1945 to 1969, who provided initial assistance. Both also worked closely with Ernest Bevin, Minister of Labour, and established extremely close links with the British Labour Party which remained effective after the war.[12]

The British perspective

In June 1940 when the Norwegian government arrived in Britain, there was probably a rather greater awareness among their British hosts about conditions in Norway and Scandinavia generally than among the Norwegians about Britain, even though the Norwegian neutrality policy in the later 1930s meant that bilateral relations had not been close. Eden had visited Norway in 1934 when Lord Privy Seal, and in April 1940 was appointed Secretary of State for War before returning to the Foreign Office in December. R. A. Butler, a junior Foreign Office minister in 1940, had also visited Scandinavia to study the development of social democracy. Leading members of the British Labour Party (including Hugh Dalton, responsible for establishing SOE) were also interested in Scandinavia and especially Sweden: several of them had written *Democratic Sweden* for the Fabian Society in 1938.[13] Throughout the war, nearly half the members of the War Cabinet came from the Labour Party. Halvdan Koht had been less interested in visiting London during this period. Although he initially responded positively to a proposal for a visit from the Norwegian minister in London, Erik Colban, in early 1938, he later decided that this could be misconstrued and jeopardise Norwegian neutrality, and turned it down. He rejected a further suggestion the following year, too.[14]

The British agencies involved: background

How much knowledge did the British intelligence and security services have about Norway before the German invasion? SIS (then known as MI1c) had established a station in the Norwegian capital (then known as Kristiania) as early as September 1915 to provide information on the German war effort. It produced frequent reports on this subject throughout the rest of the war.* By early 1918, it also provided detailed reporting on the growing influence of Bolshevism in Norway, which

---

* There are a number of SIS reports in the MUN series in the National Archive, providing information on German attempts to acquire raw materials for their munitions industry, or to develop new weapons, or on other aspects of their munitions production.

was becoming a concern in Britain.[15] The station remained in existence for some time after the war. In March 1920 the chief of SIS, Sir Mansfield Cumming, was instructed to close down eight stations, including Kristiania (renamed Oslo in 1925) as an economy measure – though the order was countermanded very shortly afterwards.[16] However, for much of the interwar period, between 1924 and September 1938, there was no full-time station representative in Norway, and the station was staffed by a very competent multilingual secretary. A permanent representative, Joseph Newill, was sent there at the end of 1938. He was reinforced a year later when Frank Foley (previously head of the SIS station in Berlin) was posted to Norway to try to re-establish contact with some of his German agents and to take overall charge of Scandinavian operations.[17] In this he had only limited success – for example, as Chapter 2 explains, setting up a rudimentary coast-watching system, but little else. He was also able to use SIS communications to provide secure contact with London during the evacuation from Oslo after the German invasion. Once back in London, he remained in charge of Scandinavian operations until the arrival of Rudolf Hess, Hitler's deputy, in May 1941, when his German expertise was required.

After the First World War, the Security Service concentrated much of its effort on the threat from communist activities. Several Norwegians came to its attention.* The first was Aksel Zachariassen, who delivered £300 and messages from Béla Kun, the leader of the short-lived Soviet in Hungary, to Sylvia Pankhurst, the Bolshevik editor of the *Workers' Dreadnought* in 1919. It was known that Zachariassen was coming: a testament to the effectiveness of the coverage of Bolsheviks at that time. He was arrested soon after his arrival, and deported.[18] Then in 1920, another Norwegian, Anker Pettersen, was arrested in Newcastle on a charge of attempting to smuggle several thousand Bolshevik leaflets into the country,[19] and sentenced to three months hard labour. Another

---

* Between 1919 and 1923, DNA was affiliated to the Communist International, or Comintern, the only European socialist party to be so linked. The activities of Norwegian Bolsheviks in Britain were therefore of considerable concern to the Security Service.

was Leonard Aspaas, a Norwegian Comintern courier in Shanghai between 1935 and 1937. The most remarkable case, both because of his prominence and the length of time he remained a subject of investigation, involved Arne Ording, an influential academic, party activist, anglophile and post-war adviser to the Norwegian Foreign Minister Halvard Lange. The Security Service suspected that he might have had a Russian intelligence role because he and his sister had close links to two known or suspected GRU agents (from Russia's Military Intelligence Service). The files show that he was of interest to the Security Service from 1935 (when they obtained a Home Office warrant to intercept his mail) until 1978, some ten years after his death. During the war, they were sufficiently concerned to warn the BBC against allowing Ording to broadcast on the Norwegian service of the BBC. Since they admitted that they could not at that stage justify their suspicions of him, their advice was ignored – and the files show clearly that their suspicions were never substantiated.[20] This curious story shows that after September 1939, while the predominant focus of the Security Service was on the threat from German espionage, they never entirely gave up their coverage of potential communist activities – even if, as in this, case their concerns were misplaced.*

SOE, the agency responsible for sabotage and subversion, did not exist at the beginning of the war. It was formally established in August 1940, based on a directive drafted at Churchill's request by Neville Chamberlain in what was his last political act before his death. It was created out of three separate organisations: Section D of SIS,

---

* For example, T. F. Turner of the Security Service wrote to Ward in Northern Department in July 1940 about Kornelius Støstad, the Norwegian Minister for Social Affairs, who, according to their records, had an extensive history of communist links and on more than one occasion visited Moscow in connection with the Third International. 'As he does not appear to have very arduous duties with the Norwegian government, we wonder whether they might dispense with him.' Ward consulted Dormer, who stated that Støstad had been a prominent member of DNA for some years, had much influence in trade union circles and was close to Nygaardsvold. He added that everyone in the Norwegian government had previous connections with the Third International and they could ill afford to lose him. Turner backed down. (TNA, FO 371/24372.)

under Colonel Lawrence Grand, which had been in existence for two years and was responsible mainly for researching and implementing sabotage and subversion operations; Electra House, which dealt with propaganda; and MI(R) of the War Office, run by Major J. F. C. Holland, which had broadly the same responsibilities as Section D. Both Section D and MI(R) had been active in Norway before the German invasion. Section D (rather better known in Scandinavia because of its ill-fated attempt to sabotage Swedish iron ore exports, which was exposed in April 1940) had commissioned detailed surveys of the Norwegian coastline north of Trondheim in the summer of 1939 to identify suitable beaches for clandestine landings. In March 1940 it sent Gerry Holdsworth (who had previously participated in beach reconnaissances and who had also been in touch with the Swedish saboteurs) back to Norway to explore suitable methods of receiving clandestine shipments of Section D supplies. He came under threat following the German invasion and to justify his continued presence in Sweden or unoccupied Norway, established a 'Fund for the Relief of Distress in Norway' sponsored by reputable benefactors in Britain. It was organised under the auspices of the Lord Mayor of London and was launched on 30 April. As the SOE historian commented, 'it continued to function blamelessly and efficiently throughout the war'.[21] Holdsworth, however, had to leave Sweden shortly afterwards because of his connection with the iron ore sabotage attempt.

MI(R) was involved in organising secret reconnaissances in northern Norway in March 1940, and in the despatch shortly afterwards of several officers loosely described as 'assistant consuls' to Narvik, Trondheim, Bergen and Stavanger to help with further reconnaissance to support offensive operations and the laying of a minefield in Norwegian waters. They were barely in place before the German invasion. One of them was captured, the others escaped with some difficulty and three of them (James Chaworth-Musters, Andrew Croft and Malcolm Munthe) later ended up in SOE. There were other small MI(R) deployments of limited value. It quickly became clear that the overlap between Section D and MI(R) was both inefficient and a potential source of confusion. It was decided to amalgamate them and to put the new organisation under civilian control, with Dalton in charge. Section D was transferred to him from SIS on 16 August – though by bureaucratic oversight Menzies, the chief of SIS, was not informed and only found out about the transfer of control three weeks later. Propaganda responsibilities were also transferred to this new organisation: SO2 dealt with sabotage while SO1 dealt with propaganda.*

Relations with other governments

The nature of the relationship with Norway certainly stands comparison alongside British links with the governments of the other occupied countries of Europe and their resistance movements. Relations with France were complicated initially by the difficulties of dealing with Vichy France and then with General de Gaulle, whose desire to maintain French independence was a constant complication, even if he sometimes aroused respect in SOE as an effective symbol of French resistance. SOE's relations with the Belgian government in London were disrupted by the fact that it contained two separate bodies which claimed primacy over resistance matters. Attempts to resolve this were so unsuccessful that at one stage Paul-Henri Spaak, the Foreign Minister, broke off relations with SOE. In the Netherlands, the successful German *Englandspiel* led to the capture and death of a substantial number of SOE's Dutch agents. The fact that Denmark remained formally neutral until August 1943 limited the development of an effective resistance there for much of the war, though SOE made up for this by providing a reporting service to SIS in a country where for much of the war it did not operate, and by stimulating a rapid growth in the numbers of the resistance from a hundred or two in 1943 to over 10,000 by late 1944. Separate communist resistance movements working to different strategies also created complications, as

---

* Responsibility for propaganda was later transferred to the Political Warfare Executive (PWE) which was established in September 1941.

they were liable to spark German reactions or reprisals at times when British-supported movements were seeking to avoid them (as was the case in Norway). Sometimes, they formed the dominant resistance movement. The most striking example was in Yugoslavia, where the deputy head of the SOE Yugoslav section, James Klugmann, was a communist who played a significant role in the selection of agents to be sent into Yugoslavia, briefed them in such a way as to get them to produce the intelligence he wanted, and manipulated some of their reporting so as to gain support for the communist partisans and to discredit the Chetniks. His actions appear to have helped to influence Churchill's decision to switch support to Tito's partisans.[22] There were also issues with the communist resistance in Greece. This is not to say that resistance movements in all these countries were ineffective: far from it. But dealing with them was rarely straightforward.[23]

It will become clear how, during the German occupation, Britain contributed to the development of the different resistance organisations in Norway, dealt with setbacks and shortcomings and negotiated improvements with Milorg, the military resistance movement, and also the Norwegian government. However, the issues were not always bilateral ones. What about relations on the British side? It was never likely to be easy for SIS and SOE to cooperate with each other, for their objectives were too often mutually exclusive. There were certainly plenty of sharp differences, but while they squabbled a lot over their interests in Norway, there is evidence to show that some – particularly Norwegians who worked for them – were also able to achieve a greater degree of pragmatic cooperation than was possible elsewhere. The chapter on the work of GC&CS, in addition to demonstrating the extent to which their reporting illuminated Abwehr activities in Norway, will also show how much they understood about (and read) Norwegian cyphers in Norway *before* the war. The Security Service depended heavily, though not entirely, on GC&CS reporting for their work against quite extensive German attempts at penetration in Britain, and SIS did occasionally allow their reports to be used to warn SOE agents in Norway who were under threat.

Much of our focus will be on the operations carried out by both SIS and SOE in Norway. The most important achievement of SIS was the provision of intelligence from its coast-watching stations describing the movements of all the major German warships. At the end of the war Finn Nagell, head of FO.II, the Norwegian intelligence office, claimed that SIS agents provided reporting which, to a greater or lesser extent, contributed to the sinking of the *Bismarck*, *Scharnhorst* and *Tirpitz*, and also to the damage caused to the *Prinz Eugen*, *Hipper* and *Admiral Scheer*.[24] However, SIS also provided intelligence on a range of other targets in Norway too.

While the main task of SOE was sabotage, their stations and networks were also encouraged to provide reporting to SIS if it was readily available – and their files show that they provided a fairly consistent and often valuable service for large parts of the war. Although the technical limitations of equipment led to the failures of some operations (particularly the performance of the gliders in mountainous conditions during Operation FRESHMAN, and faulty limpet mines which detached from the ships they were targeting during the Operation MARDONIUS attack) the range of successful SOE operations was extensive. They included GUNNERSIDE (sabotage of the heavy water plant at Vemork), MARDONIUS and BUNDLE (attacks against shipping), Cheese (a variety of activities including the hijacking of a ship to get back to the Shetlands), the destructive activities of the Oslo gang and SOE's anti-U-boat campaign – which was so successful that it earned a warm letter of appreciation from the Assistant Chief of the Naval Staff responsible for operations against U-boats, highlighting the effectiveness of SOE's work in Norway.

The Oslo report and civil resistance

There are two other subjects worthy of mention here, because they do not directly belong in the narrative which follows. The first is the Oslo report, described by Hinsley as 'one of the most remarkable intelligence reports of the war'.[25] Though it was provided in Norway, it owed nothing to British cooperation with the Norwegians and indeed preceded it. The Oslo report was a document sent anonymously to the British legation in Oslo in November 1939 and delivered to the naval attaché. He forwarded it to London where it reached Professor R. V. Jones, the principal scientific adviser at SIS. It contained a considerable quantity of scientific and technical intelligence, on such diverse subjects as German radar development, rocket and glider bombs being worked on at Peenemünde which were the predecessors of the V-1s and V-2s, close-proximity fuses and much more. The fact that it dealt with so many different topics on which no information had previously been collected led some experts to doubt its credibility. However, despite their adverse comments Jones was impressed by its general air of authority and technical competence and it proved to be accurate in all significant respects – and over time was an extremely valuable source of information. Once the existence of the Oslo report became publicly known after the war, much diligent research (and speculative journalism) led to a variety of claims about the authorship of the report, with plenty of imaginative but inaccurate conclusions. Remarkably, it was Jones himself who, by a mixture of detective work and coincidence, was able in 1954 to establish that the author was Hans Mayer, a German scientist who had been touched by the kindness of Frank Foley. When serving in Berlin, Foley had provided, through a British intermediary whose help Mayer had solicited, a visa for a half-Jewish girl who was thus able to escape from Germany. After war broke out, Mayer found an opportunity to repay this kindness by providing the intelligence during a trip to Norway.[26] So, indirectly at least, SIS had played a part in the process which led to the production of the Oslo report.

Norwegian civil resistance, or non-violent action in the form of civil disobedience, also played a significant part in resistance to the Germans. It was an effective means of demonstrating opposition to the German occupation, and provided a considerable boost to morale and helped further to increase the will to resist. For most of the war, the British services who were supporting Milorg, the military resistance, had minimal contact with it. They had little understanding of how it was organised and played virtually no part in providing it with assistance – though there were occasional exceptions. But we should not overlook the importance of the role which it played in demonstrating unwillingness to accept attempts by Vidkun Quisling's Nasjonal Samling party to force political leaders on them, or to sign declarations or give undertakings to support the 'New Order'. This opposition found expression in different forms: from a very active underground press which defeated German censorship by providing information about the progress of the war, through individuals wearing small symbols in their lapels, to widespread disobedience by professional organisations who refused to comply with demands to show their loyalty to NS ideology. Norwegian athletic organisations stopped their activities completely rather than accept political leaders being foisted upon them, and the medical association made similar protests. But the most celebrated examples were provided by teachers and clergy who refused to conform. More than 1,000 teachers were arrested in March 1942, and many of them were eventually deported to Kirkenes, in the far north of Norway, where they did forced labour and lived in the most appalling conditions. A few were eventually obliged to compromise because of ill-health caused by their treatment, but the remainder were eventually released when the NS regime had to accept defeat.

Clergymen were similarly ill-treated when the bishops openly criticised many abuses of power by the NS regime. In February 1942, when *Reichskommissar* Josef Terboven inaugurated Quisling's national government, it was planned that an NS clergyman would hold a mass in the cathedral in Trondheim. The dean, Arne Fjellbu, announced that he would hold a regular service later the same day. Many of the congregation were prevented from entering by the police, and Fjellbu ignored their order not to hold a mass. He was dismissed, whereupon all the bishops announced that they were resigning their offices, followed soon afterwards by all the clergy. Thereafter, there was no state church in Norway, though the churches continued to function unofficially and to criticise the policies and actions of the NS. In 1944, at the request of the Norwegian government, SIS became involved in attempting to help Fjellbu leave Norway and travel to Britain, where it was thought that his influence could be significant. By then he had been compelled to move to the Vesterålen Islands in the far north of Norway. An initial attempt to move him by sea involving station Libra failed because of the disruption caused by German arrests in the area. A later attempt, Operation GUARANTOR, also had to be abandoned because other British naval commitments following the Normandy invasion meant that a ship could only be made available to pick him up on a date before the necessary arrangements could be put in place. Fjellbu was able to get to Sweden in the autumn and was appointed bishop of the liberated parts of northern Norway by the government in London.[27]

All of these activities had a powerful and positive effect on boosting morale. The resistance was also involved in a variety of humanitarian actions. Perhaps the most important was the assistance provided to refugees to facilitate their escape from Norway, usually into Sweden, where escape routes were organised by both civilian and military resistance organisations. They helped not only active resistance members and sometimes their families who needed to escape because they were being sought by the Germans, but also those who wanted to get to Britain to join the armed forces, as well as political refugees and Jews. Unlike Denmark, where early warning had enabled Danish patriots to hide almost all the Jews who were at risk of imminent deportation, there was insufficient warning in Norway. About a third of the total population of 774 Jews was deported, of whom only a handful survived. However, the resistance was subsequently able to smuggle over 1,000 Norwegian and foreign Jews to Sweden. The post-war Norwegian government tried to make some amends by permitting the immigration of 660 Jews into Norway, and the first group arrived on 10 May 1947. This gesture was judged to be insufficient by some senior members of DNA, who later took matters into their own hands. Haakon Lie, the secretary of DNA, was approached by the Israeli ambassador for assistance to help a number of Jews in Poland and Rumania where their conditions were dire: they wanted to emigrate to Israel. He sought help from Asbjørn Bryhn, head of the Norwegian Security Service. Bryhn agreed to provide genuine Norwegian passports to facilitate their travel, into which the necessary details and photograph of the passport bearer could be inserted, provided they were returned after the Jews had arrived safely in Israel.[28]

Sources

A word about sources and their accuracy: much of this book is based on new material, previously unpublished, which has either come to light or recently been released to the archives. It also draws on some excellent histories written (mainly) by prominent Norwegian academics. However, even the primary material is not completely accurate, for sometimes in original documents there are errors in dates and other details, and still more in summaries which were compiled after the event. The most egregious of these errors is to be found in the citation for Leif Larsen's DSO, for which he was put up in late 1945 by Colonel John Wilson, head of the Scandinavian section of SOE. Larsen was a skipper on boats based in the Shetlands which carried both SIS and SOE agents, and their supplies, over to Norway and back. His citation contained details of four meritorious actions towards the end of the war in which he was stated to have taken part. However, three of them had actually been carried out by his colleague Ingvald Eidsheim, who had only been put forward for a mention in despatches.* Moreover, the relevant source material is so extensive, and some of it so carefully (or craftily) hidden that it is extremely difficult for a historian to find it all. For example, in his history of SOE, William Mackenzie describes Rubin Langmo (known as Rubin Larsen) as 'one of SOE's best men'.

---

* This only came to light when the citation for Larsen's DSO was published in Norway. The error was eventually corrected, and both Larsen and Eidsheim received DSOs in 1948. See Chapter 14.

He was indeed a brave and dedicated member of the Linge Company, who took part in the first Norwegian expedition in June 1940 and played an active part in operations throughout the war, including participation as one of only two Norwegians in the Dieppe raid. Perhaps the strain got to him, for Milorg asked for him to be withdrawn from the VESTIGE XIV party* in December 1944 on the grounds of his drunkenness, and insecure and inappropriate behaviour. He was sent to Sweden.[29]

Sometimes, the SOE Norwegian section's historian may also not have had all the facts. For example, there is a reference to an early SOE operation in Norway, which described how Alf Konrad Lindeberg and Frithjof Kviljo Pedersen were sent back by boat to establish communications with Britain in November 1940. 'They were safely landed, but nothing further was heard from them. It later emerged that their set was faulty and they could not establish contact. Soon after landing they were arrested by the Germans in unknown circumstances and executed.'[30] In fact, there were three agents – the third was Melankton Rasmussen, and they were lured back from Shetland by two Norwegian Abwehr agents. The Security Service and Section V of SIS became aware of what had happened, but if news of their fate was passed to SOE, it must have been very tightly held.[†] The memoirs of those who were involved in resistance work also need to be treated with some care, for they were generally written without the benefit of reference to contemporary reports. Even Wilson was affected by this problem. In his unpublished memoir he repeats a statement in the SOE Norwegian section history describing how Cheese (Odd Starheim) had reported in May 1941 that *Bismarck* had broken cover, and commented that this news played a part in the later destruction of the battleship.[31] This claim was repeated in a paper prepared for the War Cabinet in May 1945 on SOE activities in Scandinavia, which also asserted that

---

*   VESTIGE parties were small groups equipped with kayaks for the purpose of attacking shipping.

†   See Chapter 5.

across one of Cheese's reports, a British admiral had written 'who is this boy? I would serve with him anywhere.'[32] Examination of Cheese's file reveals no evidence of any such message, and it would anyway have been physically impossible for such a report to have been conveyed to him and transmitted from his location in the time which was available. No doubt Wilson was drawing on an account which had been given to him orally.* A further warning for the unwary historian of the dangers of relying on personal memoirs is to be found in an article published in 1973 to mark the thirtieth anniversary of the Vemork raid. The author conducted interviews with Claus Helberg and Knut Haugland, two of the participants in GUNNERSIDE, and showed Helberg a book written about the raid by one of his colleagues. 'He began to read. "Nonsense... No, no, no... Nonsense!" he said, and began to tell us how it really happened.'[33] It is not always easy to determine whose memory is likely to be the more accurate. There were strict (and sensible) security regulations designed to prevent members of the resistance from keeping diaries or any personal records during the war, especially when they were on active service. Therefore it would not have been easy for those involved in stressful and demanding operations to be able to remember years afterwards the detail of events they were involved in. There was one significant exception during the Norwegian campaign: Leif Tronstad ignored the rules and kept a diary both while he was in London and also after his return to Norway in October 1944 – a cavalier disregard for discipline which has since been much appreciated by Norwegian historians, including myself. His detailed contemporary accounts have been of great value.

---

* The first report about the movement of the *Bismarck* was passed to the British naval attaché in Stockholm, Henry Denham, by the Norwegian military attaché, Ragnvald Roscher Lund. See Chapter 6.

CHAPTER 2

THE RESISTANCE BEGINS
9 APRIL 1940: GERMAN INVASION

*He considered Operation Weserübung to be particularly daring – in fact
one of the rashest undertakings in the history of modern warfare. Precisely that would ensure its success ... He described the state of anxiety he
would feel until the success of the operation as one of the strongest nervous
tensions of his life ... He pointed out that the strictest secrecy was vital to
the success of the surprise attack.*

EXTRACT FROM GERMAN NAVAL STAFF DIARY, QUOTING AN ADDRESS
BY ADOLF HITLER TO A CONFERENCE OF THE SENIOR GERMAN
COMMANDERS RESPONSIBLE FOR PLANNING THE INVASION
OF NORWAY AND DENMARK, I APRIL 1940.[1]

Many of the German commanders who attended this conference
with Hitler, to go over the final details of the plan for the invasion of Norway and Denmark which began on 9 April, were similarly
apprehensive about the risks involved. One admiral considered that
50 per cent losses were to be expected unless there were especially favourable conditions, while the army chief General von Brauchitsch
declined to attend the final day of the conference because he did
not wish to be too directly associated with such a venture. Including
reinforcements, the size of the force was to be about 100,000 men,
using most of the German surface fleet as well as transports and some
one thousand aircraft.[2] Surprise was the element which was key to

success. The Germans certainly achieved that. But given the scale of the preparations which it required, as well as the size of the fleet and the length of the journey to the furthest of its Norwegian destinations, how did they manage to achieve success without either the British or the Norwegians learning of the intended invasion and reacting before it started? The shortcomings of the Allied campaign which failed to prevent the German occupation of Norway have been forensically examined and well documented. But was the invasion also preceded by a failure of intelligence, as has sometimes been alleged?[3]

There were certainly plenty of indications of German preparations for an offensive. The problem was that no single body existed at that time which received all the reports and was responsible for assessing their significance. One author lists as many as thirty-three between December 1939 and April 1940. These comprised a mixture of pointers mainly from intelligence sources including some Norwegian signals intercepts, as well as service attaché and diplomatic reporting.[4] In fact, there were significantly more than these. For example, GC&CS intercepted a Norwegian report of an overflight of Oslo by a German Heinkel III, and of two further German aircraft overflying Bergen later the same day, 29 March. On 1 April the Foreign Ministry instructed its minister in Berlin to protest: GC&CS circulated the details three days later on 4 April.[*5] An even more telling series of reports were listed in a letter sent by Menzies on 14 April to Lord Hankey, former Cabinet Secretary and a member of the War Cabinet, who had asked him to provide details of SIS intelligence which had warned of the possibility of a German attack on Norway. Menzies summarised the reports which had been sent to a variety of recipients, mainly to the Naval Intelligence Division of the Admiralty, but also to the other service departments and the Foreign Office, between 17 November 1939 and early on 9 April.[6] His letter also referred to other indications, stating that in May 1939 SIS had sent a copy of *Die Seestrategie des*

---

* The extent to which GC&CS was reading Norwegian diplomatic cyphers during this period will be examined in more detail in Chapter 4.

Weltkrieges (*The Sea Strategy of the World War*), published as early as 1929 by the German Admiral Wolfgang Wegener, to the director of naval intelligence, Rear-Admiral John Godfrey. Menzies commented that it was said at the time to be regarded almost as 'Sea Gospel' by Hitler. Wegener criticised German policy in the First World War, arguing that Germany had made a serious mistake in not occupying Norway, so breaking the blockade of Germany and gaining important naval bases which could have been used to attack trade routes.*

SIS reporting about a possible German invasion

Among the most striking of the seventeen reports listed by Menzies, was one entitled 'Germany and Scandinavia – Preparations on the Baltic Coast' which was circulated to the Foreign Office and the Service Departments on 3 January 1940. Menzies commented that these preparations were being made to intimidate the Scandinavian states but drew attention to the caveat which had deliberately been inserted: 'there may be more than mere intimidation in these measures, because careful observation has disclosed a complete readiness for action at short notice'. There were several more which quoted Grand Admiral Raeder, the head of the German Navy. One, dated 15 January, described a pre-war conversation in which he had outlined his intention to operate from Norwegian bases during the next war, so as to destroy the British blockade. Another described a conference which he had attended in late March, where he had strongly argued the case for a forward naval policy. A fuller version of this report, circulated after the invasion, stated that:

> The naval representatives described the encroachment of the British fleet in the North Sea and the repeat attacks of the British Air Force against the German coastal bases as 'serious operations directed against

---

* In fact, Sir Robert Vansittart, the former Permanent Under-Secretary in the Foreign Office, had already drawn the Admiralty's attention to this book in April 1939. The Norwegian naval authorities had been aware of it since at least 1936.

the nerve centres of the German Naval and Air Force advance headquarters and a menace to German war supplies'.[7]

The conference requested Raeder to draw Hitler's attention to the
possibility of Germany finding herself completely deprived of supplies
from Norway, as a result of British countermeasures taken against the
constant use of neutral waters by German warships. There were other
reports describing different aspects of German preparations, such as
cargo and passenger ships being fitted out as transports, troops being
trained in embarkation and disembarkation from launches and large
troop movements near northern German ports. There was also a reference to preparations for a state of *spannung* (maximum preparedness)
which was to come into operation from 17 March. Hankey passed
Menzies' letter to Sir Horace Wilson, head of the civil service and
seconded to Downing Street to work for Chamberlain, and observed
that he considered that it exonerated SIS:

> Most of Menzies' information seems to have been sent to DNI as it was
> naval business, but we did not get any warnings as far as I can recollect
> from the Admiralty except the general warnings that came from many
> sources besides S.S.* that ships were being prepared for embarkation
> purposes and that troops were being practised in embarkation and dis-
> embarkation. It is, of course, not the business of S.S. to comment on
> these facts. They merely furnish them to the Directors of Intelligence
> of the Service Departments whose business it is to send them to the
> appropriate authorities. I am not satisfied that the Services have done
> their job very effectively.[8]

But SIS had also provided even more information than this. In late
March, Menzies had written to Gladwyn Jebb, Private Secretary
to Cadogan, Permanent Under-Secretary in the Foreign Office, to

---

* Secret Service, i.e. SIS.

address the question of what the Germans knew of Allied intentions to send an expeditionary force to Scandinavia and Finland. He quoted a report of mid-March describing Swedish concerns about a rumour which might have come from the Germans, of just such an Allied force being prepared for intervention in Finland, which would be ready to deploy in early April. He referred to a report of a member of Himmler's staff stating in mid-January that the Allies were believed to have a plan ready for armed intervention in Scandinavia. He also described a report which had been sent to the War Office stating that at a conference of service chiefs in Berlin on 4 March there was a discussion of measures to prevent an extension of the war to Scandinavia, when it was recorded that plans had already been completed for the concentration of a large German expeditionary force in the Baltic coast area. He included further details of German preparations which were not mentioned in his later letter to Hankey. The most interesting aspect of these reports is that they describe German concerns about the possibility of an Allied intervention in the region, and preparations to anticipate it.[9] We now know that it was an earlier British intervention on 16 February, the boarding by the Royal Navy of the *Altmark* in the Jøssingfjord, to secure the release of British prisoners, which convinced Hitler that Norway could no longer enforce its neutrality, and that Britain would not respect it.* This led him to order that plans for *Weserübung* should be speeded up.[10] It is not clear why Menzies did not include these details in his letter to Hankey.

It could be expected that SIS and the service departments would try to avoid or at least reduce the extent to which they could be held responsible for the failure to predict or respond effectively to the German threat. The reader might wonder whether SIS had deliberately omitted from Menzies' list any reporting which they had previously circulated, but which did *not* point to the German intention to invade. There were certainly some reports of this nature, but the way in which they were

---

* During the occupation, the term 'jøssing' (from Jøssingfjord) came to be used as a complimentary term for a patriotic Norwegian, the opposite of a 'quisling'.

handled is of interest. For example, an SIS report circulated in January 1940 and seen by Cadogan described a rumour circulating in Berlin of a German offensive on the Western Front, and another of an attack through Switzerland. The source reported that these rumours were deliberately inspired so as to create a sense of uncertainty in Allied countries. The intention was that the Allies would become so used to them, they would be more inclined to discount genuine plans for an offensive.[11] A further report, sent to Jebb on 28 March, stated that the Germans were changing their strategy and abandoning plans for an offensive in the west, apart from air and sea operations against Britain. This would give time to develop Russia's resources undisturbed, which would reduce the effectiveness of the British blockade. SIS added that they thought it undesirable to give formal circulation to this report, which might prove misleading. Nonetheless, the Foreign Office judged it was probably accurate. On the following day, Cadogan commented to Lord Halifax, the Foreign Secretary, that he had had a growing conviction for some time that the Germans would not undertake a large-scale land offensive. Halifax replied that he would like to mention this in Cabinet, but was dissuaded when Cadogan explained that Menzies was concerned lest the report proved to be misleading. He suggested instead that it should be submitted to the Joint Intelligence Committee (JIC), which could give a balanced estimate of its value. The position of the JIC at this time was such that the Foreign Office could not directly commission such work, so Halifax had to write to General Ironside, the Chief of the Imperial General Staff, to request it. The draft letter was not submitted to him until 9 April, by which time, of course, it was too late.[12]

Lack of other indications: shortcomings in assessment
At this early stage of the war, there was only very limited access to signals intelligence – none of which might have given a more precise indication of German planning. GC&CS had achieved limited readability of some low-level Enigma traffic, mainly used for operational

and administrative communications by the German Air Force – but it included nothing which could have given a clue to German intentions.[13] Aerial reconnaissance too was of limited value because of the restricted opportunities for its use, which prevented an overall and developing picture from being built up. As we have seen, though, there was a good range of other intelligence available – and considerably more than has generally been realised. But the intelligence branches in the different service departments were not yet accustomed to dealing with information received from different sources, and it was not generally shared. Thus,

> In the Admiralty, NID 1 [Naval Intelligence Division 1], the geographical section dealing with Germany, was responsible for interpreting the SIS and diplomatic reports bearing on German intentions in Scandinavia, but the OIC [Operational Intelligence Centre], which was responsible for operational intelligence, including that of studying German ships and aircraft, received by no means all of the SIS and diplomatic information. To make matters worse, relations between NID 1 and the OIC were not good, and NID 17* was not properly coordinating their output.[14]

The situation in the other departments was little different. Moreover, they did not find it easy to make assessments independently of the operational branches which they served, and tended to reach conclusions dictated by their expectations. While the intelligence which described aspects of German plans and preparations for an invasion of Norway was plentiful, none of it pointed unambiguously towards a specific plan. This made the lack of any central government body equipped to carry out an assessment of intelligence and other reporting all the more acute. The JIC was not at this time capable of carrying out such a role. So from the British point of view, the failure to anticipate the German invasion was caused not so much by a failure to provide

---

* The executive office of the director for naval intelligence.

relevant intelligence, as by a widespread failure to distribute and assess it adequately.

During the period immediately after the German invasion, it was recognised that changes needed to be made to make the JIC more authoritative, and to give it broader responsibilities which would help to ensure that the handling and assessment of intelligence was more effective in future. Chamberlain signed off the recommendations on 8 May, two days before he resigned, and they were endorsed by Churchill shortly after he took office.[15] Apart from the replacement of Chamberlain by Churchill, the one positive outcome of the German invasion of Norway, therefore, was that it forced changes on the central government machinery for dealing with intelligence, which left it better equipped to make proper use of the growing volume of intelligence which became available during the rest of the war.*

Norwegian knowledge

And what of the Norwegians? Had the concern to maintain their neutrality led them to underestimate the indications they picked up about the growing threat, at a time when they also had reason to be concerned about the possibility of British and Allied intervention? How could they judge which threat was the most serious? There were violations of Norwegian neutrality at sea and also in the air, committed by both Germany and Britain.†[16] These added to the tensions, and the British action against the *Altmark* was seen as an even more serious breach of Norwegian neutrality.

---

* It is not easy to identify other positive outcomes, though once the war was over and politicians reverted to their more familiar tactics of cut and thrust, the somewhat unpredictable and outspoken Harold Laski tried to find one. When the British Labour party was invited to DNA's national conference for the first time in September 1945 Laski, the chairman of the party's national executive, gave a speech in which he thanked the Norwegians for Narvik, 'because it enabled us to get rid of the Chamberlain government, which is the worst that Britain has had'. (Arbeiderbevegelsens bibliotek, DNA Landsmøteprotokoll 1945.) There is no record of how Laski's Norwegian hosts responded to this questionable compliment.

† And the Soviet Union. A message intercepted by GC&CS records the rejection by the Russian Foreign Ministry of a Norwegian protest concerning two overflights of the Norwegian border by Soviet aircraft on 18 and 31 January 1940.

In September 1939 the British had given the Norwegian foreign minister, Halvdan Koht, a confidential assurance of British support in the event of a German attack on Norway. However, their behaviour over the next six months gave the Norwegians good reason to be more concerned about the possibility of a British plan to land in Norway than a German invasion. There were two main reasons for this. First, the 'Winter War' started by the Soviet invasion of Finland in November 1939 led Britain and France to plan an intervention to support Finland with troops which would have been sent in transit through Norway and Sweden. This would have had the advantage of enabling them to seize control of the iron ore fields in northern Sweden, thereby depriving Germany of a significant part of the iron ore which it needed. The Germans were certainly aware of this plan, which added impetus to their preparations for an invasion of their own to pre-empt Anglo-French landings. The Finnish armistice removed the justification for either side to continue their planning for this reason alone. Secondly, British attention was still centred on Narvik, the port from which much Swedish iron ore was shipped to Germany. After several previously planned attempts had been abandoned Churchill, then First Lord of the Admiralty, obtained agreement to sow mines within Norwegian territorial waters which would obstruct this traffic, in an operation improbably codenamed WILFRED. After providing a warning of their intentions several days earlier, the British Navy did lay some mines and so informed the Norwegians, on 8 April.

Against this background, it is scarcely surprising that the Norwegians devoted less attention to consideration of the possibility of a German invasion. A Norwegian commission of investigation was appointed after the war to consider whether the actions of the wartime government gave grounds for impeachment. It concluded that the warnings which the government had received before 5 April 'were consistent with the threat perception that a British action against the iron ore traffic might trigger a German reaction'.[17] The Norwegians did not receive any specific indications about a German initiative until a message from the Norwegian legation in Berlin on 4 April, which reported an imminent invasion of the Netherlands and mentioned the possibility of an attack on Denmark – but not Norway. A threat to Norway was only mentioned in a subsequent report on the following day, which had also been picked up by the Danish legation.* There were further, more specific, warnings over the next few days giving details of German naval movements, but none provided clarity about the scope of any German action. Some limited measures were taken to increase preparedness, but mobilisation was not ordered until after the invasion had begun – too late to have any chance of making a significant difference.

The German campaign to subdue Norway lasted barely two months. Their landings were virtually unopposed, and British actions to send an expeditionary force were poorly organised. Allied troops were despatched without the proper equipment, so either they could not deploy, or they were unable to fight effectively. However, two events of great significance took place in the early stages. First, the German cruiser *Blücher* was sunk by artillery fire and torpedoes from the Oscarsborg fortress as she led the German task force at night up the Oslofjord. The *Blücher* was carrying a divisional headquarters and specialist troops for the occupation of Oslo and the capture of King Haakon. The rest of the fleet bound for Oslo delayed until the following day, and this pause allowed time for the King and his government to escape from the capital, and also for the gold reserves to be moved. The failure of this part of the plan, as well as of subsequent attempts to kill King Haakon by bombing attacks as the party travelled northwards, meant that he and the government were able to travel to Britain to organise resistance. Secondly, C. J. Hambro, the president of the Storting, the Norwegian parliament, convened a meeting in Elverum soon after they had left

---

* SIS informed the Foreign Office in early 1943 that a Dutch military attaché who had been in Berlin in April 1940 had later told them that he had informed both the Norwegian and Danish legations of German intentions to invade both countries on the night of 8/9 April, and that he had passed on this information five days beforehand, i.e. on 4 April. (TNA, FO 371/36876.)

Oslo. The Storting passed a resolution investing the government with plenary powers, until the legislature was reconvened by agreement between the government and its own presidential body. The purpose of this measure was to enable the government to continue to function with legitimacy wherever it might be, even abroad. It was an act of considerable foresight on Hambro's part.

Hampered by inadequacies in both numbers and equipment and lacking coordination among themselves and with Norwegian forces in whom they were reluctant to confide, the Allied forces were never on equal terms.* Unable to resist the German onslaught, they abandoned the south of Norway on 3 May. They fared rather better in the north, and with effective naval assistance were able to eliminate a force of ten German destroyers which was carrying troops intended to reinforce those which had already landed at Narvik. After a series of engagements carried out mainly by Norwegian troops over several weeks, a combined force succeeded in capturing the port. Many of the port installations were destroyed during the assault, which subsequently hampered and delayed later attempts to export Swedish iron ore to Germany. However, by now the Germans had begun their invasion of France and the Low Countries, so both Britain and France decided to withdraw all their forces to reinforce their own defences.† On 7 June, King Haakon and most of his government left Tromsø for Britain on *Devonshire*. The following day, to the intense disappointment of the Norwegians, the Allies gave up Narvik and left. On the way home the

---

* The lack of confidence extended to London and diplomatic exchanges too. Cadogan recorded in his diary an 'extremely embarrassing meeting' with the Norwegian minister Erik Colban, who had asked about rumours that the British were abandoning their attempt to recapture Trondheim. Cadogan noted that 'he could only evade the question by saying that "we would do our damnedest"'. (David Dilks (ed.) *The Diaries of Alexander Cadogan OM 1938–1945* (London: Cassell, 1971), p. 274.)

† Colin Gubbins, who spent most of the war in SOE and ran it from September 1943, commanded a force of five independent companies, known as Scissorsforce, in Norway during this brief campaign. They played an unorthodox role and did so effectively. Gubbins was one of the few officers acknowledged to have come well out of the Norwegian campaign and his experience of working with such unconventional forces stood him in good stead when he took over SOE.

aircraft carrier *Glorious*, with her escort of two destroyers, were sunk by a German battle group led by the *Scharnhorst* and the *Gneisenau*. More than 1,500 men were lost, the most costly individual action in the whole campaign. The Norwegian commander General Ruge, who had chosen to remain behind with his men, had no choice but to surrender.

Believing that he had the support of Hitler, Vidkun Quisling announced himself as Prime Minister at the head of a national government on the same day as the German invasion, but his take-over was short-lived. Unable to gain popular support, he was removed within a week. The government was replaced by an Administrative Council of officials, following an initiative by the High Court. In overall charge, the Germans appointed Josef Terboven as *Reichskommissar*, a position he held until the end of the war. Soon after the surrender in northern Norway, the Germans sought to use the Storting to vote to remove both the King and the Nygaardsvold government from office, undertaking to nominate a new 'constitutional' government and to withdraw the *Reichskommissar*. Their attempt to exercise control in this way failed. Although the Storting was not in formal session, party groups did pass such a resolution and it was forwarded to London. However, the king broadcast a dignified refusal, and his response was printed and widely circulated within Norway. The process by which the Germans sought to win popular support was protracted but not effective. Eventually, in September, the political parties reacted adversely to the changes which Terboven made to his original proposals, and to his increasing introduction of NS co-optees into positions of power. Terboven therefore announced on 25 September that all political parties other than NS would be dissolved, and the Administrative Council would be replaced by commissary ministers. These were for the most part NS members or sympathisers who ran government departments under direct German supervision. The government of Norway was from then on under the effective control of an administrative organisation comprising several hundred German officials. Over the next few months, German control was extended further. Local government councils lost their powers which were transferred to nominated local 'leaders'. Members of the Supreme Court resigned in protest at measures which reduced the independence of the judiciary. This was truly the darkest period in Norwegian history.

It took time for the Norwegians to establish themselves in London, to find suitable accommodation, work out their priorities and begin to develop relations with the British government. Their attempts were not helped by a degree of disunity and lack of coordination. This was perhaps best illustrated by the meeting which Hambro, the President of the Storting, who held no official government position, held with Halifax on 11 June. Hambro sought confirmation that Britain recognised the Norwegian government in exile (which was immediately forthcoming) and raised concerns about extraterritoriality, providing exemption from British laws. The Foreign Office found a flexible way of dealing with this for the Norwegians as for other exiled governments, and never allowed it to become a problem. Hambro then referred in very disparaging terms to the 'criminal lack of preparation' for defence in Norway, and the naivety of the whole Cabinet, particularly Koht. He complained too about BBC broadcasts to Norway, saying that they made him sick, and he understood that they had a similar effect on all Norwegians, who were exasperated by commonplaces and the doctoring of hard facts.[18] Shortly afterwards, Laurence Collier, the head of Northern Department, reported an approach by Birger Ljungberg (Minister of Defence) and Trygve Lie (Minister of Supply) who asked him to inform the authorities that Hambro was not authorised by the Norwegian government to discuss broadcasting or anything else on their behalf.*[19]

There was also some extensive manoeuvring to remove Koht as

---

* Ljungberg and Lie were careful also to say that Hambro was energetic and meant well, but the British did not consider him to be well-disposed or pro-British. Indeed in 1943 Eden told a meeting of the War Cabinet that 'if any of them should meet Mr Carl Hambro, the President of the Norwegian Parliament, he thought they ought to be aware that certain of his recent activities had shown him to be not very well disposed towards this country'. (TNA, WM (43) War Cabinet 127 (43) meeting 13 September 1943, CAB 63/35.)

Foreign Minister. It was started by a letter from five prominent intellectuals, led by Arne Ording, a professor at Oslo University, who wrote to the government on 5 July 1940 to suggest much more active Norwegian participation in the alliance with Britain. This represented a significant change from the traditional Norwegian preference for neutrality so long espoused by Koht, and it took several months before the sometimes heated debate was resolved. Koht took leave of absence at the end of November, and was replaced by Trygve Lie.* The new alliance policy was announced in December and a formal military agreement, allowing for identifiably Norwegian units to operate under British operational control until the end of the war, was signed in May 1941.

Lie was quick to make an impact. Chapter 1 described how he sought closer cooperation with the British. At his first meeting with the Foreign Secretary, Eden agreed that more consideration should be shown to the Norwegians and suggested they should meet fortnightly. Eden hoped that Nygaardsvold, Lie and Colban (Norwegian minister to Britain) could also meet monthly, to discuss 'a number of matters of all kinds which concerned our countries, and Lie would let me know in advance what they would be'.[20] This marked the beginning of a close personal relationship and demonstrated recognition of the value which Norway could provide as an alliance partner. Lie enjoyed more unrestricted access to Eden than any other Foreign Minister of a government in exile, and certainly used it to Norwegian advantage.

First operations: SIS and Hardware
By the time of Lie's appointment, Koht and Ljungberg had already been responsible for authorising the first Norwegian links with British intelligence and sabotage organisations. However, even before that the British had sent groups over to Norway to begin resistance activities, using recruits whom they had found for themselves. Not surprisingly, these early operations were the result more of spontaneous

---

* Koht subsequently submitted his resignation on 27 January 1941, and Lie's appointment was formally announced in February.

improvisation and a desire to start trying to undermine the German occupation, than of any structured planning. Nonetheless, by early May the Ministry of Economic Warfare had already produced a list of six important minerals produced or available in Norway, which they wished to be denied to the Germans, setting out the actions which they wished to be taken.[21] The first SIS operation was actually instigated by an officer from NID called Ware, sent to Stavanger to deal with the *Altmark*, who returned to Britain in mid-May on a fishing boat procured for him and other British officers by Sigurd Jakobsen, a local journalist who accompanied them back to Scotland. Since SIS was at that time preoccupied elsewhere, NID themselves decided to equip Jakobsen with a radio and return him to Norway to report on ship movements. He was for a while accompanied by a British naval officer, Sub-Lieutenant Peters, and when they landed on 7 June they established station Hardware (a rather insecure pun linked to Ware's surname). Jakobsen found no difficulty in recruiting a group of willing Norwegians to assist him. In two months they sent over eighty messages back to London. However, they had much to learn about security and some got involved in another risky activity, helping refugees to cross the North Sea to Britain, and were betrayed. On 8 August, eighteen of them were arrested. Ten were sentenced to death, though at this early stage of the occupation the Germans wished to appear conciliatory and the sentences were commuted to lengthy prison terms.[22] In fact, only a small number of SIS Norwegian agents were executed for intelligence activities alone during the war, though many were killed when resisting arrest, some died in captivity and one was beaten to death by the notorious turncoat Henry Rinnan, of whom more later. Two of those executed were badly let down by the Russians. Thor Sentzen and Hans Michael Skjervø were flown to northern Russia in August 1942, from where it was intended that they should be sent to Kirkenes to provide a coast-watching service. The Russians did not provide the expected support, and instead detained them for some months before re-equipping them with Russian radio crystals and dropping them in Finland, rather than Norway. They were soon captured, and because they were found in possession of Russian equipment, the Germans believed that they were Russian, rather than British agents. Both Sentzen and Skjervø, as well as other SIS agents with whom they were confronted, followed their instructions and refused to admit their connection with the British. They were shot at Trandum in April 1944.[23] A second SIS station, Oldell, was established in Oslo in early July and provided some prolific and useful reporting on German naval movements. Some of their agents also became involved in facilitating refugee travel back to Britain. As a result, when the Germans tracked them down in March 1941, five of them were executed. The station had reported concerns that its location was being pinpointed by direction finding techniques used by the German radio monitoring service.* After its capture, the Germans found the codebook used for transmission, which enabled them to decypher previous traffic and thus to identify and arrest more contacts.

Shortly after Jakobsen and Peters had departed for Norway, Koht asked Sverre Midtskau, a young lieutenant whom he had met on the way back from Norway, to establish a Norwegian intelligence office in London. It was initially known as UD/E.† In late July, at a meeting with Eden, still at the War Office, and Beaumont-Nesbitt, the director of military intelligence, Koht obtained their agreement for Norwegian contact with SIS. Koht participated in some of their early meetings as they worked out objectives for cooperation. This required some compromise, because SIS was mainly interested in military intelligence with a particular emphasis on naval activities, whereas the Norwegians wanted reliable information about political developments in Norway. Koht and Foley also agreed that the costs would be shared equally between them, and signed a memorandum to that effect.[24] Midtskau and four compatriots participated in the first training course at the SIS school in St James's Street. After its completion, Midtskau and

---

* Direction finding was often known as 'D/Fing'.

† *Utenriksdepartementet Etterretningskontor*, or Foreign Ministry Intelligence Office.

three others were sent back to Norway in September to open two stations, Skylark A in Oslo and Skylark B in Trondheim, though problems with radios and transmission schedules meant that Skylark A never came on the air and Skylark B was inoperative for some time, only making contact with London in January 1941.[25] The fifth officer, Bjørn Holtedahl, remained to man the office and to maintain liaison with SIS. At this time, though, neither SIS nor SOE was interested in an official working relationship with the Norwegians, who at this stage were still so limited in manpower that they had little to offer. As long as they had Norwegian consent for their activities, they worked largely independently and recruited agents from among refugees who had fled from Norway. The situation gradually started to change once Finn Nagell, whose journey was arranged through the ill-fated Oldell station, arrived in Britain in November and took over responsibility.

Rear-Admiral Godfrey, director of naval intelligence (DNI), had set out his operational requirements to SIS in November 1939. He specified the interest of the Naval Intelligence Division (NID) in the activities of the more important German naval units and their movements and those of merchantmen carrying iron ore along the Norwegian coast, as well as the building programmes for the *Bismarck* and other major warships.[26] Both NID and SIS had some small successes even before the German invasion. By February 1940, the Admiralty were aware of the movements of a German trawler operating off the Norwegian coast, and GC&CS were soon able to decypher a few of its transmissions, the first of what became a very significant stream of intercepted messages, as outlined in Chapter 4. SIS had also set up a rudimentary system of coast-watchers, using mainly lighthouse keepers, who were under the impression that their reports went only to Norwegian authorities. They were not always very reliable, and their reports were hard to confirm. Godfrey noted that 'they gave us a bad scare one night by reporting the fishing fleet as a fleet of battleships, cruisers and destroyers steaming northward at 20 knots'. NID were also in discussion with SIS about other ways of enhancing their reporting.

They believed that they would require a sea-going watching service to become really efficient. SIS investigated the purchase of a Norwegian company owning six whalers, which could be used for their normal business of whale-catching outside territorial waters, but routed when necessary through territorial waters. They would have been particularly useful for the area north of Tromsø, because the Operational Intelligence Centre (OIC) at that time was generally satisfied with reporting of the coastal regions south of that point. The scheme was not finalised before the invasion and, afterwards, it fell apart.[27] Moreover, as has been shown, the first few attempts to establish reporting stations had not been very successful either. Nonetheless, Godfrey was initially inclined to be generous about SIS performance. He acknowledged in July 1940 that it took time to train agents and case officers and 'the SIS organisation in Norway, though still in its infancy (since it had to be established *de novo* after the invasion) is already covering large stretches of coast'.[28] However, a comment on SIS achievements up to the end of 1940 observed that there had been an almost complete lack of useful information from CX – or intelligence – reporting. This was disheartening after eight months of war.

Section D and SOE

There was similarly little consultation with the Norwegians by Section D of SIS, and later SOE, in the early stages. The genesis of their first operation was actually a plan put forward by MI(R) in late April, with the idea of landing small forces or organising small detachments at about fifty points to harry the enemy if the German advance enabled them to limit regular operations to a relatively restricted area. In early May Section D developed the idea further, with the specific objective of attacking communications installations in the Voss area behind Bergen. They selected a rather motley group of twelve largely untrained men, led by Simon Fjeld, but his instability meant that the effective leader was a Swede, Karl Kronberg. The party included both Rubin Langmo and Karsten Wang, who had earlier enjoyed a career for four years as a bootlegger, running illegal supplies of alcohol between Bermuda and the Florida coast. They sailed on 25 May. Some of the crew soon became very nervous, and wished to return to Britain, which they did, leaving Kronberg and Langmo to carry out the mission. They were moderately successful, destroying the water supply for a power station at Bjølvefossen, which put a ferrosilicon works out of action for some weeks, as well as some telephone and electricity pylons.[29] They returned to Shetland in mid-June having completed the first Allied raid in occupied Europe.*

It was planned that Langmo and Fjeld would return to Norway on another mission two weeks later. They would be accompanied on a separate operation by Olav Wallin and Otto Aksdal. However, on the night before their departure, after spending the evening in the bar and becoming much the worse for wear, Fjeld attempted to shoot Langmo. Fortunately the gun jammed and he failed. He had a breakdown and was sent abroad, but died when his ship was torpedoed. Langmo continued alone. Although their transport carried plenty of sabotage equipment, the mission of Wallin and Aksdal was mainly to gather intelligence on German activities, particularly troop and naval movements in the area around Bergen, but they did also help to organise some small groups. They had barely a week's training before they left, a further reflection of the improvisation which was so much a feature of that period. It was also unusual that they were tasked with intelligence gathering rather than sabotage, which may partly have reflected their lack of training, but also the demands made on Section D by SIS at that time. Unfortunately their radio failed, but they were able to obtain a spare condenser from Bergen. (This was a recurring problem for both SOE and SIS: at least four radios failed to function during this period.[30]) Becoming concerned about their security, they returned to Britain two months later.[31] They agreed to attend the first SOE

---

* Some of the other participants on this operation had mixed fortunes. Kronberg, the Swede, committed suicide because of personal problems while Olav Leirvåg, the pilot, became the chief chaplain to the Norwegian forces.

training course for Norwegians held at Station 17 at Brickendonbury in Hertfordshire, which specialised in demolitions, but fell out over what SOE considered to be an excessive demand for a bonus. They were taken off the course and interned in Brixton prison for several months. An SOE record noted:

> We should not be blackmailed into paying them exorbitant wages or bonuses. These two men were sent to the training centre, and made such exorbitant demands for money that we had to remove them, and in order to preserve security, the higher authorities decided to have them both interned for the duration of the war.*[32]

In fact, they were released after several months following the intervention of Martin Linge and Chaworth-Musters, and Wallin joined the Norwegian Navy. The SOE section history mistakenly noted that at the end of the war he was still rendering good service there,[33] although he had actually rejoined SOE in April 1945, serving in Force 136 which supported operations in Malaya.[34]

The Shetland base

The first few trips across the North Sea to Norway were organised on a fairly rudimentary basis. Things started to become more organised when a base was established near Lerwick on 11 November 1940 by Leslie Mitchell of SIS, who had served briefly in Oslo before the German invasion. He was sent to Lerwick jointly by SIS and SOE to examine refugee Norwegian fishing boats which had begun to arrive in increasing numbers. Most made for the Shetlands as it was a favourite peacetime fishing ground. Both services agreed that it would be valuable to have an officer present who could obtain intelligence and recruit suitable ships

---

* It is not clear whether there was any particular consideration which prompted their request. By this time, Norwegian seamen had also raised concerns about low rates of pay, as well as the lack of defensive equipment on their ships. And so, later, did the Shetland crews who as civilians provided transport for both SIS and SOE across the North Sea – and were enlisted into the Norwegian Navy as a result.

and crews to take agents back to Norway. Mitchell recommended a suitable anchorage at Catfirth, twelve miles north of Lerwick. At this early stage, German defences were limited and fishing boats could mingle freely with coastal traffic. British defences and screening processes were not well organised either, as Chapter 5 illustrates.

The camouflage of the boats was perfect as they returned to Norway in the state in which they had left – it was only later that they began to be both armed and armoured. The short summer nights meant that the operational season for the Shetland was limited to the period between September and April, when the greatest threat to the crews and their passengers was not always the Germans, but violent and occasionally deadly winter storms. SOE's records for the initial 1940–1941 season are incomplete, but estimated that about twelve operational missions were sailed, taking fifteen agents over to Norway. Both SIS and SOE agents were carried, and they were sometimes transported on the same vessel on their different missions. The number of operational trips increased quite significantly as the war progressed – in the 1941–42 season there were forty-one, which landed forty-seven agents (seven for SIS) and 130 tons of stores.

The tenuous lifeline across the North Sea. *Heland* waiting to transport an SOE agent back to Shetland after a reconnaissance mission in the Lofoten Islands. © Scalloway Museum

The development of an SOE policy towards Norwegian operations

During the autumn, SOE started to work out a coherent policy for Norway. Early attempts were directed rather more towards fostering a rebellion, but these were abandoned once a proper overall directive had been worked out by SOE, the Chiefs of Staff and the planning staff. It emphasised the need for sabotage and subversion to undermine German strength, and for organisations to be built up in occupied countries such as Norway to support British-led invasions when the time came. While this appraisal was taking place Charles Hambro, a British banker, was appointed to take over as head of an expanded Scandinavian section, and began the recruitment of Norwegians.* Chaworth-Musters had obtained agreement from Koht and Ljungberg to the appointment as liaison officer of Martin Linge, who had served in a similar position with British forces during the early part of the Norwegian campaign but was injured and brought to Britain in late April. They also obtained consent from General Fleischer, the Norwegian commander in chief, for Linge to recruit suitable candidates from Norwegian refugees who had arrived in Britain and for them to be released from the Norwegian armed forces. It was not easy to find sufficient people with the qualifications required, and their numbers were often fewer than SOE wanted. Fleischer later agreed that SOE could recruit an intake of twenty-five men a month until they had reached a total of 250 (excluding the crews in the Shetlands providing transport to Norway), though there were occasionally periods when they were prevented from doing so.

The early deliberations before Linge's appointment showed that while SOE wished to have a licence to make use of Norwegian personnel for their operations, they also wished to restrict as far as possible the extent to which the Norwegian government was made aware of, and still less involved in, their activities. They were concerned about the risks of insecurity. SOE accepted that 'we might get into very

---

* Hambro was a merchant banker who was distantly related to C. J. Hambro, the Storting President. He became CD, or executive director of SOE, for a year in May 1942.

troubled water if we attempted this without telling the Norwegians. The Norwegians as a people are notoriously ill-disciplined and are great talkers.' There was a reluctance to agree to any closer cooperation with the Norwegians or to any further disclosure of SOE's plans than might be necessary to secure goodwill.

> Since some measure of liaison seems inevitable, I propose to take steps to see that the channel of communication with the Norwegian authorities is the same as in the case of SIS, and to ensure that the channel is as narrow a one as possible – preferably one man appointed by the Norwegian government expressly for the purpose.[35]

From SOE's point of view Linge filled that role admirably.

SOE produced its first paper on Norwegian policy in December 1940. It stated that in the long term, it would aim to train and equip local resistance groups, preparing them to support an Allied landing in Norway when the time came. In the shorter term, it would aim to sustain Norwegian morale by a mixture of sabotage operations mounted from Britain by SOE teams against special targets, and support for the Directorate of Combined Operations (DCO) in their mounting of 'tip and run' operations. A further development of this paper in April 1941 spoke of organising as many tip and run operations against important objectives on the Lofoten model (i.e. coastal raids) as might be practicable. It assessed that because of its long coastline which assisted communications with Britain, as well as the high morale of its population, Norway could become the best field for subversive warfare. The paper concluded: 'it is assumed that the locking up of a number of German divisions in Norway, which will be the result of this short term policy, will be desirable from the strategic point of view'. There is no evidence that either the planning staff or the Norwegians were involved in the preparation of this paper, though in many respects the concentration of German forces in Norway by this means would be a very desirable outcome.[36]

SOE in Stockholm: an uncertain start

It took time to organise a transport system across the North Sea. The first planned operation, involving Odd Starheim (known as Cheese) did not start until January 1941. It was much easier to obtain access to Norway through the land border from Sweden. Malcolm Munthe (one of the MI(R) officers who was sent on a reconnaissance mission to Norway in March 1940) arrived in Stockholm in July 1940 after an arduous two-month journey on foot from Stavanger. He was appointed assistant military attaché and given responsibility for re-establishing an organisation in Sweden, after the Section D disaster in April 1940 when one of its agents was imprisoned.* He was tasked with setting up communications with Norway, and starting resistance activities. At that time, morale in the Norwegian legation was low, and it appeared to the British that few of the staff there had much interest in working against the Germans. Norwegian refugees arriving in Sweden found a more enthusiastic reception in the British legation, and Munthe was quickly able to recruit some willing helpers. For example by mid-October, among other courier activities, Johnny Pevik (later to be involved in SOE activities with Lark and Wagtail) had already made two trips to Trondheim, and established contact with Leif Tronstad.[37]

Later in October, Hambro visited Stockholm to oversee the further development of a section of SOE based in the legation, which would cover Scandinavia. He made Peter Tennant responsible for Sweden and Germany and Ronald Turnbull responsible for Denmark, and instructed that Munthe's work dealing with Norway should also be expanded. Hambro wanted sabotage in Norway to be initiated from Sweden as well as from London, but only on London's approval. The system of communications between Munthe and Hambro at this early stage was quite elementary. It was based on a book code using the

---

* This was an attempt to sabotage some of the port equipment at Oxelösund, which was used for unloading iron ore shipped from Norway. It had been approved by Chamberlain and Halifax, but was disrupted by the Swedes before any action could be taken and a British agent A. F. Rickman was among those who were imprisoned.

works of John Ruskin, a Victorian art critic, known only to the two of them. The first results of Munthe's work were quite encouraging. The Bergen-Oslo railway was sabotaged in November, which put it out of action for a short period, and the following month it was attacked again by the RAF. Their pilots were guided by flares provided by SOE agents. Morton, the Prime Minister's personal assistant and intelligence adviser, informed Churchill of the SOE contribution to this attack. Churchill replied, 'Until I got your memo I had not realised that your people played so prominent a role in the recent successful air operation against the Bergen-Oslo railway. This is very satisfactory.'[38] However, two of Munthe's Norwegian agents were arrested by the Swedes and, following a Swedish protest, the British minister Victor Mallet tried unsuccessfully to have him recalled. This led Munthe to devise an elaborate cover for his work. He set up a non-existent organisation called 'Red Horse', which consisted solely of a mythical wealthy Norwegian refugee who travelled frequently and secretly between Norway, Sweden and Britain carrying orders from King Haakon and Allied war departments. Munthe claimed that Red Horse occasionally used an intermediary to pass messages to him, and that he would then pass them on, typed on special paper, and stamped with a red horse, to various Norwegian addressees. This subterfuge enabled Munthe to present himself simply as a passive recipient of information. We do not know how effective this cover was, but it certainly added to his workload.

Munthe was apparently also involved in organising an attempt to assassinate Himmler when he visited Oslo in January 1941, though the archival evidence consists only of a brief reference in the SOE Norwegian section history. It recorded that the attempt failed because Himmler did not arrive at Oslo East station at the expected platform, the train having taken a different route. Two Norwegians, Tom Wettlesen and Christian Aubert, were arrested carrying weapons provided from Stockholm, but one escaped, and the other was released. Munthe's autobiography gives a slightly different version and states that he consulted Mallet. Given Mallet's views about the work of SOE in Sweden at this time, it would be surprising if he concurred in this plan without first consulting the Foreign Office, and no record has been found which shows that he did so.

Meanwhile, Munthe continued to run into trouble. In January 1941 the Swedes showed Mallet some detailed evidence from the trial of several Norwegians and Swedes who had been jailed for carrying messages from Sweden into Norway to help to foment trouble against Germans there. The material implicated Munthe and the Swedes once again sought his withdrawal. This was avoided, but it led Mallet to review the standing of SOE and the value of its work. In a letter to the Foreign Office, he stated that he believed that the legation was strongly suspect. He anticipated that if there were many more cases of staff being compromised, then he might himself become *persona non grata*. Mallet noted too that the military attaché, Sutton-Pratt, had recently been asked by MI9* to explore the possibility of arranging an escape of prisoners from Germany. Mallet considered this to be a futile venture.

> Here again it will be a case of using neutral Swedish territory for an operation against what Sweden still has to regard as a friendly power. It will be almost impossible to get any Swedish merchant captain to take part in such a venture, which would quite likely land him in jug.

He added that he did not think that the game was worth the candle and suggested that SOE should be closed down in Sweden and its work transferred to SIS:

> In fact, it is a pretty black outlook for SOE if it tries to operate from within Legation or Consulates... If there is no other way of getting

---

* MI9 was a directorate of Military Intelligence formed in December 1939 to facilitate the escape of British forces from prisoner of war camps, and to develop techniques to assist servicemen to evade capture if stranded behind enemy lines. The SOE historian M. R. D. Foot estimated that MI9 and its American sister organisation, MIS-X, helped, between them, over 30,000 prisoners of war to escape back to active duty.

SOE messages to Norway except through this legation or one of its branches, I think it should be seriously considered whether it would not be wiser to do the whole job through the PCO.* I know he would hate it and think it too risky for his other work. The point is however that someone has to take the risk and it is less serious from the point of view of our relations with the Swedish government if Martin† is caught out than if I or my immediate subordinates in the Legation are. The PCO is looked upon by the Swedish authorities as a suspect character, but since the unlucky Rickman affair I believe they have convinced themselves that he is not working against Sweden and are therefore not worrying about him. Although he holds diplomatic rank, I do not think that the Swedish Foreign Ministry really look on him as having much to do with me, and if he burns his fingers they will hardly consider me or other members of my staff to be *au courant* with his activities or seriously compromised thereby. I have not mentioned this to him, as I know he would violently oppose it, but I think you ought seriously to consider it. It is, after all, a less serious matter if a PCO gets blown than if a Legation does – at least that is my perhaps prejudiced view as I happen to think that the information coming from the Legation is more reliable and important than that which reaches you from other sources... If the game really is worth the candle, then of course I shall just have to be sacrificed, but I feel that our other activities ... are really of greater value at the present time.[39]

He received an emollient but firm reply from the Foreign Office stating that they judged the game *was* worth the candle: 'It is our considered opinion that SOE must operate from Swedish territory and that the Scandinavian activities of SOE are more important than any other advantages we can obtain from Sweden'.[40]

However, further SOE operations went wrong. The final straw was when a bomb which had been planted on a train carrying materials to

---

* The PCO, or Passport Control Officer, was often the cover position occupied by members of SIS.
† John Martin had been the head of the SIS station in Stockholm since October 1937.

the Germans in Trondheim exploded prematurely on Swedish territory at Krylbo. Munthe was withdrawn in June, and went to work in SOE headquarters. His successor, Hugh Marks, did not last long either. He undertook some ill-judged activities which aroused the displeasure of both the Swedes and Mallet, and he returned to Britain in October. Mallet continued to find fault with SOE activities, complaining that a visit by a prominent trade union adviser John Price had been organised by SOE and not by the legation. This led the Foreign Office to wonder whether SOE work in Sweden should be carried on with Mallet's consent or without. 'There might be something to be said for the latter'.[41] In the end, it did not come to that. Matters were smoothed over eventually, helped by the fact that thereafter SOE in Stockholm were not so directly involved in the organisation of sabotage activities in Norway. Nonetheless, Stockholm became a very important centre for both British and Norwegians for the development of resistance work.

CHAPTER 3

'DANGEROUS RIVALS'
SIS AND SOE: DID THEIR DIFFERENCES
DAMAGE OPERATIONS IN NORWAY?

No matter how hard the Norwegian section tried, and it tried 'some-thinged' hard, it could never get to grips with and work in accord with its opposite section in SIS. It was a case of personalities. With other sections of SIS, notably Section V, and with the officer in charge of the corresponding region it was all right, and co-operation proceeded on an equable basis. There was frequent intercommunication between the two sections, weekly meetings were tried, but were a total failure.

SOE NORWEGIAN SECTION HISTORY, DESCRIBING RELATIONS WITH SIS.[1]

It is scarcely surprising that relations between SIS and SOE were destined to be fraught. As Menzies told the Secret Service Committee in March 1941, the practice of SO (Special Operations) was frequently inimical to that of SI (Secret Intelligence). Any significant act of sabotage was likely to provoke an intense security response which in turn could jeopardise the less dramatic and more sustained activities necessary to obtain secret intelligence. Moreover, SIS may well have continued to feel some resentment at the way in which SOE had been hived off and formed following the dissolution of Section D, a part of its own organisation – particularly since Menzies was not informed until three weeks afterwards. In this respect, SIS itself may have been partly to blame, because of the poor quality of Section D's leadership and because some of its operations, such as the attempt by Rickman to blow up the iron ore loading cranes at Oxelösund, went badly wrong. The diplomatic problems which this created for Britain in Sweden lasted for some time, and the consequences for Section D were equally unwelcome. By their nature, SIS intelligence gathering operations if they went wrong were unlikely to have such damaging and visible consequences, except perhaps for the agent involved: the Venlo incident was a rare exception.*

So what were the causes of these inter-service differences and, in particular, how great were the problems which they caused in Norway?

After a fairly Byzantine process, Hugh Dalton was made Minister of Economic Warfare with responsibility for SOE. In August 1940 he appointed Sir Frank Nelson, an ex-businessman, former Conservative MP and latterly an SIS officer who had worked in Switzerland from September 1939 to July 1940, as his first director. Gladwyn Jebb, private secretary to Cadogan, was appointed Chief Executive Officer.[2] He drafted a document, signed by both Menzies and Nelson, which defined the nature of the relationship between the two agencies. It stated that D (as the head of SOE was sometimes known) 'is intimately associated with C [i.e. the chief of SIS] both on historical and practical grounds, and if he is to function efficiently, it must be with the friendly cooperation of C'.[3] But the rules to which both sides consented were more advantageous to SIS than they were to SOE, and sowed the seeds of future disputes. The agreement covered projects, transport, communications, spheres of interest and recruitment of agents. The first two subjects were relatively simple, allowing for reference to a higher authority, which would have been the Chiefs of Staff, in the event of a disagreement. But the next three were much less straightforward for SOE. It was agreed that all wireless traffic would be handled by SIS, which would be free to reject it; any intelligence collected by SOE was

---

* Two SIS officers were abducted by the Germans on the German-Dutch border at Venlo on 9 November 1939, when participating in what they thought was a negotiation with German officers planning a coup against Hitler. The Germans exploited this for propaganda purposes.

to be passed to SIS before circulation even within SOE, and while SOE might take the initiative in recruiting agents, it was not to proceed further without the consent of SIS. As their historian pointed out:

> These limitations were very reasonable from the point of view of C, as the advocate of a single centralised Secret Service, in the interests of good administration, good security, and good intelligence; but experience very soon showed that they were incompatible with the licence to grow which had already been given to SOE by the War Cabinet.[4]

As SOE began to recruit and train staff, and to work out how it could effectively play the role which was expected of it, processes which necessarily took time, SIS did not always cooperate and make life easy. The first few months though went reasonably well, because Menzies' liaison officer Colonel Calthrop worked closely with Nelson and regular weekly meetings were arranged between Jebb, Nelson and Menzies. There were a few niggles, such as an SIS complaint about insecure behaviour by an SOE officer in Stockholm, but nothing serious. However, at the end of April 1941, Rear-Admiral Godfrey, the DNI, complained that SIS operations to provide intelligence for the Admiralty were being jeopardised by SOE. Of operations in Norway, he wrote: 'the opportunities for sabotage have led SOE to initiate projects there on a scale which cannot but endanger the permanent intelligence centres which have been established and which are planned for the future'.[5] He sought a directive from the Chiefs of Staff confirming that operations to obtain such intelligence should have priority over other subversive activities. Menzies preferred to avoid the involvement of an outside authority, and it was agreed that his deputy Claude Dansey should act as an arbitrator between the two services. This arrangement worked well for a few months. Soon, though, as SOE planned to expand its operations further, frictions grew and became less easy to resolve. Joseph Newill, then running the Norway section of SIS, commented on the consequence of this increase in the despatch of agents that there were 'many examples of line crossing, which increases the hazard to our agents to such an extent as to make their work almost impossible'.[6] There were quite frequent squabbles over communications as SOE sought to obtain more independence, provoking some testy outbursts from the head of the SIS communications section Gambier-Parry, who wanted to maintain control over all aspects of SOE communications. He belittled SOE's plans to work independently, describing them as 'extravagant, insecure, fatuous and very dangerous'. Menzies supported him, writing to Nelson in February 1942 that he 'viewed with dismay a document on communications plans, DY/TC/187, issued on 22 January 1942, to your Country Sections'.[7] However, SOE maintained their demands and in March 1942 Menzies eventually agreed that they should have autonomy over most of their own communications. Sometimes the inter-service squabbles had to do with primacy – SIS reacted badly to an SOE proposal that the two services be jointly represented in West Africa under an SOE nominee. This disagreement was a primary cause of Dansey's decision to withdraw as the inter-service arbitrator in December 1941.[8]

SOE complains to Eden about SIS behaviour

Relations with SOE continued to deteriorate quite sharply – to such an extent that a few weeks after he had taken over from Dalton as Minister of Economic Warfare, Lord Selborne wrote to Eden in March 1942 to express his concern at the extent of the friction, which he described as a deplorable state of affairs. He was careful not to single out either party for criticism, saying that he expected that SIS could provide a similarly formidable list of grievances to match those of SOE. He felt that the existing measures to resolve problems, consisting largely of weekly meetings between the administrative heads of the two services, were inadequate. He recommended instead a weekly meeting between the two heads of service, presided over by a conciliator, who should be someone of significant stature and authority. He attached a long minute by Jebb summarising how difficult things had become, and an even longer memo (eighteen pages) by Nelson, describing some of what SOE considered the worst examples of SIS behaviour across their common fields of operations. It is a remarkable document, both for its length – which was surely too much for a very busy minister and his senior officials – and also for the frankness with which it described the squabbles and examples of obstructive behaviour and poor faith which were damaging the effectiveness of SOE.

In his covering minute, Jebb noted that several senior members of SOE, himself included, had either worked in SIS or had had a close association with it, so it was unjust to describe them as a bunch of amateurs. He described the extent to which SOE shared information about its activities with SIS, including their progress reports: 'we keep nothing from them, while they keep a very great deal from us'. He criticised the 'false beard' mentality in SIS, acknowledged that SOE had done things which might have earned their legitimate displeasure, and emphasised that an effective liaison between them required a proper two-way exchange of information. It was for this reason that he suggested the appointment of a high-level conciliator who could preside over a weekly meeting between Menzies and Nelson, and give advisory rulings on disputes which would only be binding if accepted by both parties.

Jebb did not go into any detail – though he might have done – about the nature and extent of the intelligence which SOE had passed to SIS in accordance with their original agreement, which would have made some of his arguments even more compelling. He could for example have mentioned the work of one of SOE's star agents in Norway, Odd Starheim (Cheese), who, in just over four months between late February and June 1941, had provided intelligence on oil stocks throughout the whole country including petrol and aviation spirit, German troop movements, shipping, submarines, air intelligence, the Sandefjord cable, the Knaben molybdenum mines, harbour intelligence and coastal fortifications, quislings, the movements of *Tirpitz* and the registering of fishing boats. He also provided precise details of the effectiveness of air raids on Sola and Forus airfields near Stavanger. This followed his initial reporting which had specified the extent of the targets which were available and so led to the attacks. In a fairly unusual example of both feedback and positive comment, SIS confirmed that they were indeed interested in his reporting.[9]

Nelson described the SIS view of SOE as a 'rather ineffective and ridiculous bunch of amateurs', who might endanger SIS and all its works if they were not kept quiet. 'Now their attitude appears to be that we are dangerous rivals and that if we are not squashed quickly, we shall eventually squash them.' He went on to cite a wealth of examples linked to Norway. He described how the SIS station in Stockholm had made several direct attempts to suborn contacts who had been cultivated and trained by SOE, on one occasion advising SOE that their contact was a dangerous German agent who should not be used. SOE dropped him, only to find a few weeks later that his agent network had been picked up and was being used by SIS. He claimed that another SOE agent was successfully inveigled away by SIS, who told him that his former contacts were dangerous and would land him in jail. He referred to a lack of cooperation in issuing visas to contacts whom SOE wanted to get to the UK, to avoid the risk of their arrest by the Swedes. On another occasion in late 1940, SIS had obstructed SOE attempts to interview recently arrived Norwegian refugee fishermen with a view to selecting suitable crew to participate in the first Lofoten raid – this necessitated a meeting between Menzies and Nelson to agree that half a dozen fishermen could be made available. He also quoted an incident in early 1941 when SIS had suppressed an SOE telegram to Stockholm, because they did not think it should be sent. SOE were not informed that this had happened. There were other communications difficulties too, concerning the unreliability of the radio sets provided by SIS, their unwillingness to provide sufficient frequencies and obstructiveness over an SOE request to establish a radio station in the Shetlands to facilitate their traffic with Scandinavia. This might have helped to resolve atmospheric problems which sometimes severely hampered transmissions. There was also an occasion when Linge agreed with Nagell to second an SOE agent to him for a few weeks. After his return, it was discovered that the agent had been sent by SIS to Bergen from Peterhead, at a time when SIS were using Peterhead as a separate base – without SOE being informed. There were also examples of difficulties over agreeing the availability of transport from the Shetland base, and SIS insecurity in the handling of SOE information which led to the unnecessary disclosure of some agent identities.

While SIS and SOE were trying to find a way to resolve their differences, they were subject to a flank attack when the Chiefs of Staff put forward a proposal to amalgamate the two organisations under their control. This was not the first time that they had tried to take over SIS (it had happened during the First World War as well) and on this occasion they attempted some bureaucratic skulduggery by attempting to bypass the JIC. However, the two agencies were able to agree to resist this threat and the Foreign Office took the lead in seeing it off. A senior official, O. A. Scott, warned Brigadier Hollis, secretary of the Chiefs of Staff Committee, that 'if the issue was forced, the Foreign Office would take up the challenge. We had the guns but I hoped that it would not be necessary to open fire.'[10] But a resolution of the dispute between SIS and SOE was not so straightforward. Sir Findlater Stewart, a distinguished senior civil servant, was selected and agreed to take on the task of conciliator. Menzies objected on the grounds that he did not wish to submit to outside arbitration. A compromise was reached, whereby Menzies agreed to attend the fortnightly meeting which Nelson had at the Foreign Office, which could be expected to cover most of the necessary ground. There matters rested. Nelson retired because of ill health in May 1942 and was replaced by Sir Charles Hambro, a rather stronger character. Difficulties and frictions continued at a working level, but there was at least a functioning mechanism at the top by which the most serious problems could be resolved.[11]

The extent of disruption to SIS operations caused by SOE

Selborne was quite right when he wrote in his letter to Eden that he expected that SIS could provide a similarly formidable list of grievances to match those of SOE. In April 1943 Nagell wrote to General Hansteen (who had taken over as Norwegian Commander in Chief in January 1942), giving a list of eight different cases between April 1942 and April 1943 when SIS stations were disrupted and had been forced to close down as a result of SOE activities and operations in their neighbourhood. The stations were located throughout the country from Tromsø in the north down to Kristiansand in the south, and included Oslo and Bergen. There were stations which were affected too by the fallout from serious setbacks in Telavåg and Majavatn, both of which also led to extensive and harsh German reprisals and executions.[12] Moreover, there were other disruptive incidents during this period which were not mentioned by Nagell in his letter, perhaps because they were considered to be misfortunes rather than the result of planned operations. Thus the SIS plan to resuscitate their station Koppa in the Ålesund area in March 1943 was frustrated when the Germans 'bombed an SOE boat in the neighbourhood'.[13] This was in fact the *Bergholm*, skippered by Leif Larsen, which was bombed and strafed while it was on its way back to Shetland after completing a mission for SOE, landing passengers and stores on the edge of the Arctic Circle.[14] Most of the crew were injured, four seriously, and one died. The *Bergholm* sank. Larsen and the survivors rowed ninety miles to Ålesund, and after four days he struck the point at which he was aiming within 100 yards, a remarkable achievement.[15] They landed on an island close to the spot chosen by SIS for the delivery of their own agents.* SIS had to postpone their operation and, after several further delays caused by the short summer nights and other problems, Koppa was never revived. In fact, although neither service was aware of it, their stations had already got in each other's way in this area. For a few months from the autumn of 1941, Koppa was

---

* Larsen and the crew were rescued two weeks later by a boat which was sent from Shetland.

located practically next door to the SOE wireless station Antrum in an isolated area close to the beach.

The villa housing SOE's Antrum radio station near Ålesund. SIS station Koppa is out of sight, just around the corner. © NHM

Neither knew of the presence or activities of the other, and while this must have increased the danger to both because of a greater risk of being located by German direction finding or other investigations, there is nothing to show that it happened. Koppa was later betrayed by an informer in February 1942.

An imaginative hiding place for the SIS Koppa radio, in a grave in Borgund Cemetery near Ålesund. © NHM

SIS progress reports provide further examples from after April 1943 of stations being forced to close so as to avoid unwanted German attention following SOE activities in their area. Some of these incidents will be considered further in due course, but for now they help to explain the lengths to which SIS went to try to ensure that SOE operations were not mounted in areas where there were ongoing operations to obtain intelligence, especially along the Norwegian coast.

The importance attached by the Admiralty's Naval Intelligence Division to the provision of timely reporting about German naval and merchant shipping movements along the Norwegian coast, meant that they became a powerful ally to Menzies in his attempts to ensure that SIS stations were able to operate in the most favourable circumstances for intelligence gathering and that SOE had to take second place. They were not always successful, because sometimes there were oversights leading to a failure by SOE to keep SIS informed of its intentions – as happened with Operation MARTIN in Tromsø (see below). A system of consultation was later developed which, at least until the sinking of the *Tirpitz* in November 1944, gave the Admiralty a chance to judge the risks to SIS operations in allowing SOE operations to take place. This is well illustrated by the discussions which took place when SOE wanted to mount a further series of attacks against shipping targets (Operations SALAMANDER and VESTIGE, using motorised submersible canoes and kayaks respectively) in the area between Ålesund and Egersund in the early autumn of 1944, following some successes the previous year. John Cordeaux, the SIS naval adviser, wrote to the deputy director of naval intelligence (DDNI), setting out what SOE wanted to do. He described in great detail (to DDNI but not to SOE) what SIS equities would be put at risk in each case, and set out which operations SIS would accept, and which it could not agree to. The DDNI accepted his advice, and only SALAMANDER II and VESTIGE V were permitted to go ahead – though even then only on condition that they would be against a large target if one appeared.[16] In the event, SALAMANDER II was unsuccessful – and the coast-watching SIS station Roska, near

Florø, made contact with them and was instrumental in arranging for them to be rescued without endangering its own position.[17]

There was, for the most part, reasonably good cooperation over the arrangements which were made for the transport of agents to and from Norway, and the delivery of supplies. Air drops were unproblematic when weather and lack of daylight permitted them, because there were fewer difficulties in this area over the availability of aircraft or prioritising missions. Occasionally Catalina flying boats were provided at very short notice to carry out rescues of agents from under the noses of the Germans. Sea transport, mainly from the Shetland base, was occasionally more problematic because of a shortage of suitable vessels. This was sometimes resolved by the less secure procedure of delivering both SIS and SOE agents on the same vessel, though to different locations, as once happened to the SIS agent Bjørn Rørholt. Difficulties arose, however, when SIS did not inform SOE of some of the trips it was planning, particularly when it was operating from a different base at Peterhead between July 1941 and November 1943. This led to fatal errors, as happened at Telavåg in April 1942. The *Borghild* from Peterhead delivered an SIS agent on the island of Sotra, and moored there for several days before departing. Soon afterwards the *Olaf* delivered two SOE agents to almost the same spot: they remained in the area instead of moving on straight away. The combination of these activities attracted German attention and led to a raid. There was an exchange of fire between the SOE agents and the Germans, which killed both one of the SOE agents and also two Germans. One of them was a senior Gestapo officer. In retaliation, the Germans blew up the entire village, and deported all the inhabitants, sending many of the men to Sachsenhausen (where thirty-one of them died), and the rest to camps in Norway.* The SIS station Theta, in Bergen, reported on the incident and the fate of the two SOE agents. It received a sharp reproof from SIS: 'there will be the devil to pay when intelligence gets mixed up

---

* See Chapter 7 for further discussion of these actions.

with other organisations'.[18] (This was not an unreasonable attitude. The previous chapter illustrated what could happen when agents became involved in more than one area of activity, leading to the break-up of the Hardware station.) Nothing daunted, Theta reported shortly afterwards that the SOE Arquebus station was unable to report because its set was damaged. On that occasion, they appear to have escaped a rebuke from SIS.[19]

The involvement of Theta here illustrates the other side of the coin. While at almost all levels both the headquarters organisations of both services and their mainly British-staffed stations in Stockholm were engaged in, and distracted by, arguments and ill-feeling from time to time, the same cannot be said for their Norwegian agents. They were focused on their common fight against the German occupiers and generally chose with pragmatism not to get involved in the squabbles and differences between their employers. What is more, they were quite willing to help each other if the need arose, occasionally at some considerable risk to their own safety. For example, in October 1942 the wireless operator of the SOE station Plover took over the set of the SIS station Beta and operated it on behalf of both services at a time when SIS were unable to do so themselves.[20] An even more striking example involved the SIS station Upsilon in Tromsø. In March 1943, SOE despatched Operation MARTIN, a team whose task was to organise and train resistance groups in the area, with the longer-term aim of attacking German airfields which posed a significant threat to Arctic convoys. The team were betrayed and all but one of them, Jan Baalsrud, was captured. Under interrogation, the prisoners revealed the name of Kaare Moursund, the organiser of Upsilon, which led to the arrest of other resistance members. Nonetheless, the remnants of the station were able to pass messages back to SIS in London about the location and circumstances of Baalsrud after he had been caught in a blizzard for several days and was badly affected by exposure and frostbite. They also relayed messages between different SIS agents in separate mountain valleys which enabled them to arrange for him to be rescued and transported to Sweden, and to provide updates to London which SIS forwarded to SOE.[21] This earned the station a warm compliment from SIS: 'The highest British and Norwegian authorities take this opportunity of congratulating you on the calm confidence with which you handled the difficult position in which the arrests in Tromsø placed you.'*[22]

Despite their differences, there were many occasions when both sides behaved responsibly. There are documented examples showing the extent to which they did respect the rules. In October 1942, Welsh wrote to Nagell about a report on Haugen Sigurd Ingold from Ofoten. He thought that it was interesting, and added 'if he has already been recruited by SOE for a special job in that area I am afraid we shall not be able to secure him, but if SOE have recruited him not intending to use him in his own district, we might bring pressure to bear to obtain him for our own coast watching system'.[23]

More significantly, while they may not have received much acknowledgement from SIS, or attracted more than a small amount of information by way of reciprocation, SOE continued to honour their original agreement to pass on to SIS the intelligence which they obtained, and there is nothing to suggest that any of it was withheld. While the example of wide-ranging and high-value reporting from Cheese may have been exceptional, the Norwegian SIS files are littered with plenty of examples of the intelligence passed to it by SOE. There are also examples in Admiralty files, showing aspects of SOE's contribution to the anti-U-boat campaign illustrated by a report from SOE in Voss, quoting a German quartermaster as stating that Bergen would become the main German U-boat base.[24]

What were the practical consequences for Norway?
The impact of German direction finding
There were, fortunately, no other incidents as serious as Telavåg where insecure behaviour by both services contributed to such a tragic outcome.

---

* A more detailed account of this operation is given in Chapter 7.

Nonetheless, there were quite a few cases where the ill-considered actions of one service created problems for the other, even though these were sometimes offset by the pragmatism of Norwegian (usually SIS) agents, who ignored instructions from headquarters. The greater problem was at headquarters level, where too much time needed to be spent attempting to deal with friction, mistrust and a lack of information, all of which would have been distracting and energy-sapping. What might have been achieved with closer cooperation? What were the sorts of opportunities which were foregone? For the most part, we do not know enough to be able to do more than speculate. However, there is one area where there is sufficient evidence to enable us to make a reasonable assessment: security, and the losses which were caused to SIS stations in particular by effective German technical investigations and direction finding (often known as D/Fing for short). SOE knew plenty about German direction finding activities and capabilities – but did not pass their knowledge on to SIS.

The Germans gradually built up extremely effective direction finding organisations throughout occupied Europe. There were two: one military (which covered Denmark among other areas) and the other run by the civil police, whose responsibilities included Norway. Its work was coordinated by a central plotting office in Berlin. Long-range direction finding stations based in Europe often picked up the first signs of transmissions, and were able to provide rough cross-bearings which they passed on to local services for further more detailed investigation. The Germans employed more than 140 people on direction finding in Norway by the end of 1944. They used a range of stations across the country, as well as mobile vehicles and also individual body-borne systems to provide the specific locations of transmitting sets once an investigation was in its final phase. They also sometimes deployed direction finding aircraft and boats, though a post-war report noted that atmospheric and geographical conditions meant that the one Fieseler Storch light aircraft available in Norway for this purpose was never able to get a single cross-bearing for mobile direction finding.[25] Poor

atmospheric conditions also made direction finding work more difficult in northern Norway – though it also caused problems for transmitting stations, with the unwelcome consequence that they had to
come up on the air more often in order to ensure that their messages
were received in London. (In the worst of circumstances, it could take
days or even weeks before a message was able to reach its destination.)

It was never easy for either service to find out about the security
problems affecting their agents in Norway. The Germans tried, where
possible, to conceal the arrests they made, in the hope that a quick and
successful interrogation of captured resistance members would enable
them to capture more people linked to a particular network who had not
yet learned of the danger they were running. When losses and setbacks
were reported to London, the information was often fragmentary and
incomplete, so it could be difficult to work out the likely cause of the
loss of a station. There might be plenty of other possible explanations for
what had gone wrong, ranging from betrayal to loose talk, inadvisable
contact with another resistance network or sheer bad luck. But as early
as the spring of 1941, SIS stations such as Oldell in Oslo and Skylark B
were reporting that they had detected signs of German direction finding
activity shortly before the Germans made arrests. Cheese reported similar concerns to SOE during his first deployment in June 1941, though
he was able to escape in time. There was a steady increase in the number
of SIS stations which were lost as a result of direction finding. By 1944
it had risen to twelve, and it is estimated that most of the losses in 1945
were due to the same cause. There is little to show that SIS or their
Norwegian colleagues were concerned about the dangers which direction finding posed. In December 1944, General Hansteen and Ragnvald Alfred Roscher Lund wrote to Stockholm that while there was a
possibility that any station could be located through direction finding,
it was unlikely that such interception could actually locate it precisely.
Although it was possible that some stations were lost as a result of direction finding and for no other reason, they were not aware of any such
cases.[26] In his post-war report, Roscher Lund acknowledged:

From Norway, there were sometimes reports that our radio agents had been D/Fed. The information available in England, however, indicated that these stations were taken for other reasons. However, after the end of the war, it was found that a larger number of our stations than we knew about had been located by the German D/Fing organisation. Thus, we learned that twelve Norwegian radio stations were taken in 1944 by German D/Fing.[27]

One of the disadvantages for SIS was that their coast-watching stations were generally static, needing to cover fixed vantage points, and it was difficult for them to move very far. SOE generally did not suffer from the same problem and their wireless operators were able to be more mobile. They were also more aware of the dangers. For example Knut Haugland, who was dropped on the Hardanger plateau with the Grouse party in October 1942 to prepare for the FRESHMAN attack on Vemork and who later worked in Oslo, commented on German use of direction finding. He wrote in September 1943 that he did not believe that the Germans were using small aircraft in the mountains for direction finding purposes. However, Oslo was another matter. There the Germans had mobile vans, which was more dangerous as they could approach quite close to the house or site from which transmissions were being made.[28]

Moreover, when stations were lost, SOE regularly assessed the likelihood that the cause had been direction finding, concluding for example that Crow was located by this means in May 1942, while SOE in Stockholm reported that the same had happened to Lark in December 1942 – indeed the station had been warned about it earlier. SOE advised its radio operators to restrict their transmission times as much as possible, and to move their radios to new locations every three weeks. Although making such a move could be risky, it was considered less dangerous than the risk involved in continuing to operate from the same place for a long period. While this was a counsel of perfection – which could not always be followed – it helped to emphasise the need to take suitable precautions. And, while it did not prevent SOE losses from direction finding, it must certainly have helped to reduce them.

The way in which German direction finding tracked down an SIS station is illustrated by the capture of the Sabor station, which operated near Stavanger between January and April 1945, providing intelligence about the movements of ships from Stavanger and Egersund and activities at Sola airfield. Before their departure the two agents, Ernst Askildsen and Magne Bakka, had been told by SIS that the Germans would not be able to identify the frequency which they would be using. In fact, after it started transmitting on 9 January, sometimes several times a day, it was picked up in mid-February by a long-range direction finding station in Konstanz, southern Germany. Further bearings were obtained shortly afterwards by German stations in Vienna and Berlin. On 21 February, local fixed stations in Norway began work to narrow down its location, and then started to deploy mobile and body-borne equipment, using bearings from seven different points, to establish that, by then, it was based on an island in Lutsi Lake. A large number of Germans raided the base on 4 April, in the course of which Askildsen was killed and Bakka captured.*

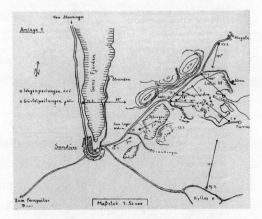

German map showing the final stage of the direction finding operation which located Sabor, giving details of the bearings used to find it. © NHM

---

* Bakka was harshly interrogated and beaten after his capture. Rørholt writes that in the last days of the war the German responsible, Sturmscharführer Hölscher, promised Bakka that he would shoot him before killing himself. On 7 May, when very drunk, he started to go to the jail to carry out this undertaking, but became distracted and forgot, before he committed suicide. So Bakka survived. (Rørholt, *Usynlige soldater*, p. 321.) Bakka was also awarded a DSC after the war.

Gestapo conference before the operation to capture SIS station Sabor in April 1945. *SS-Obersturmführer* Friedrich Wilkens, second from the right, was killed during the attack. © NHM

Magne Bakka, captured and handcuffed after the raid on Sabor. He survived the war. © NHM

While it has not been possible to establish precisely how many stations were lost to direction finding, there are good grounds for concluding that SIS losses were much greater than those of SOE. SOE's post-war Norwegian section history concludes rather optimistically that the Germans were never really successful with their direction finding of SOE stations and that although some stations were troubled, there were only a few located and captured.*[29] But it is certainly clear that SOE were well aware of the threat from German direction finding from some of their own agents. For example, Gunvald Tomstad, who worked closely with Cheese and was for a time his radio operator, joined Quisling's NS especially on SOE instructions. He became highly regarded and was well placed to be able to ingratiate himself so thoroughly with the police and Gestapo that they confided in him many of their suspicions about local Norwegians. They finally even informed him of their attempts to locate the radio station from which he was transmitting. After months of unsuccessful direction finding, they involved Tomstad himself more directly in their investigations. As a condition for his cooperation, he requested that they should brief him on the various direction finding systems they were using. He continued to operate his set, while taking appropriate precautions. On one occasion, when they got quite close to locating it, he persuaded the Germans to strip the panelling from the whole house next door to his, which was occupied by a German official, thereby distracting them and also causing them extra work.[30] After his arrival in England in April 1943, Tomstad provided a more detailed report on the direction finding systems used by the Germans.[31]

In August 1944, Norwegians working for SOE produced a paper on German direction finding, and ways of countering it, which was based on information obtained mainly from Norway, but also from other

---

* Though Berit Nøkleby points out that the head of the Gestapo in Norway, Siegfried Fehmer, stated that all the SIS and SOE stations in the Oslo region captured by the Germans after 1943 were taken as a result of direction finding. (Berit Nøkleby, *Pass godt på Tirpitz!* (Oslo: Gyldendal, 1988), p. 145.)

occupied countries. While we now know that it was not completely accurate, it described quite precisely in outline how German direction finding worked, and how quickly investigators might be able to detect an illicit signal. It considered that if a station transmitted three times a week, it would not take long before a direction finding service would be able to identify it. (In the case of Sabor, it was about five weeks.) It also drew attention to some German investigative techniques when they were close to a transmitting station, but not yet sure of its precise location – such as cutting off the electricity to certain houses but not others, to see whether a station was still receiving power and continuing to transmit.[32]

There is no evidence to show that SOE passed on any of the information about German direction finding capabilities in Norway to SIS, or to explain why it failed to do so. Moreover, despite prompts from some of their Norwegian agents,[33] there is nothing which shows either that SIS ever considered this threat seriously or took steps to deal with it. Why they did not, and how much of a difference some preventive action might have made to the safety and survival of SIS stations in Norway, are now likely to continue to remain unresolved mysteries.

CHAPTER 4

CRACKING ABWEHR CODES
HOW BLETCHLEY PARK MADE
THE BREAKTHROUGH

Gentlemen don't read each other's mail

Writing in his memoirs,[1] Henry Stimson, who had been appointed Secretary of State by Herbert Hoover in 1929, used this aphorism to explain his decision, shortly after he took office, to withdraw funding from the Black Chamber,* America's leading cryptographic agency.[2] The Black Chamber closed soon afterwards, and it took years for American cryptographic work to recover from this setback. European cryptographers were not constrained by any similar concerns about ungentlemanly behaviour and, while limited by their budgets, were able to develop their activities during the interwar period, reading a wide variety of cyphers, without necessarily discriminating too much about whose cyphers they broke.

The extent of codebreaking in the interwar period
In Britain, the Government Code and Cypher School (GC&CS) was formed in November 1919 out of the remnants of the wartime

---

* Its greatest achievement was the breaking of Japanese diplomatic codes which gave a remarkable advantage to the American delegation to the Washington Conference on the Limitation of Armaments in 1921–1922, revealing the Japanese fallback position, and thus enabling the Americans to obtain a significant reduction in the number of battleships which Japan would be permitted to build.

Admiralty and War Office cryptographic branches. After some bureaucratic wrangling about where it was to be housed (the Foreign Office staked a claim), it was agreed that it should be based in the Admiralty, but the Foreign Office soon assumed administrative responsibility for it because of the extent of the diplomatic decrypts which it was producing. This division of responsibility proved unsatisfactory and in 1923 it was agreed that GC&CS should be placed under the authority of Sir Hugh Sinclair, the new head of SIS, an arrangement which lasted for more than twenty years. GC&CS was responsible for cryptography, while SIS circulated the intelligence which was thereby produced. Financial stringency limited the activities of GC&CS as much as it restricted those of SIS in the interwar years, but growing awareness of the threat from Germany enabled this obstacle to be reduced from early 1938 onwards as budgets expanded. By the beginning of the war, the range of diplomatic telegrams which GC&CS was able to read included American, Japanese, French, Italian, Ethiopian, Spanish, Saudi, Turkish – and Norwegian. GC&CS began to move to its wartime location at Bletchley Park in August 1939, and at the same time Alastair Denniston, its head, started the process of recruiting the remarkable range of very talented academics who were to play key roles in the successes of GC&CS in the next few years.

But it was not only GC&CS which was successful in cryptography during this period. A conversation in November 1941 between Roscher Lund, who possessed some knowledge about Swedish cryptographic work and who had just returned from Stockholm, and David Rees of GC&CS, provides a good illustration of the extent to which it had developed in Scandinavia. Roscher Lund told Rees that the Swedes had enjoyed much success in their attacks on French cyphers (reading about 95 per cent of them), Italian military cyphers (85 per cent) and had made fair progress on German cyphers. The Germans were sending many messages by teleprinter to their troops in northern Norway, and the telephone manufacturing firm of L. M. Ericsson had developed a machine which could decypher them. He said nothing about any Swedish success against British cyphers, but added that the Finns had broken Russian military cyphers and were reading about 95 per cent of their traffic.[3]

GC&CS seems to have had fairly extensive coverage of Norwegian diplomatic and commercial traffic during the interwar period. Most of the diplomatic material relates to Norwegian relations with other countries, and there was little on bilateral relations with Britain. GC&CS was already aware that Roscher Lund had started a cypher bureau in Oslo in 1936, knew plenty about Swedish cryptography and was concerned about Norwegian cypher security. He explained to Rees that he was most anxious to have the opinion of British experts on the security of the Hagelin cypher machine, as he had heard rumours from British sources that it was unsafe and the traffic it generated was being read. When he asked Rees if he knew anything about this, Rees was less than honest in his reply, stating that it was news to him and that in his twenty years of cryptographic work, to his knowledge no work had been done on Scandinavian cyphers. This was far from the truth. In further discussion, Roscher Lund told Rees that he had been interested in cryptography for some years but that he had found it hard to get the Norwegian authorities interested in their security. He quoted an example of a code compiled in 1922 which was still being used in 1938. In his report, and revealing the extent of his knowledge, Rees commented on this statement: 'That is correct, but the code was used only for outlying posts'![4]

Steps were subsequently taken to provide advice to the Norwegians on the security of their cypher machines.[5] GC&CS continued to collect Norwegian traffic, though without registering or analysing it, and later circulated material from the Quisling government. No further attempts were made to read traffic from their ally, though a minute to Denniston in January 1942 noted that a Norwegian commercial cypher was available and asked whether it should be provided. There is nothing to show that this offer was taken up.[6] GC&CS also circulated decyphered traffic from wireless stations operated by members of the Norwegian communist resistance in the north of Norway. Many of the messages were terse, and related to the need for supplies by both submarine and aircraft, with occasional requests for reports on the outcome of operations. There were also messages marking the celebration of significant revolutionary anniversaries, but in general they were quite didactic and impersonal. 'Nr 92 received. Your decision is right. Be alive and energetic'. 'Investigate the results of our air attack on a German convoy on 21 April in Kongsfjord'. 'Greetings on the occasion of the 1 May to the unconquerable and persevering reconnaissance troops and tanks for their work. We wish them good health and excellent results in their operations'. They were circulated quite widely within SIS, but it is not clear what other use was made of them.[7]

Mention should also be made of Russian diplomatic and intelligence traffic, which continued to be collected during this period, even though it was indecypherable. However, lengthy and painstaking work by American cryptologists working on the Venona project eventually discovered a vulnerability: wartime pressures caused by the German invasion of the Soviet Union caused the Soviet company making one-time pads to produce thousands of pages of key numbers which were duplicates. This enabled a proportion to be read. The successful decryption of several thousand messages after the war provided clues which led to the identification and arrest of a range of Soviet spies including the British diplomat Donald Maclean and the atom spies Julius and Ethel Rosenberg and Klaus Fuchs.[8] They also provided details of instructions sent in June 1944 to Norwegian communist resistance leader Asbjørn Sunde, telling him to cease sabotage operations immediately and giving other details of Sunde's activities.*

Apart from the Soviet Union, at this time there was no country that had cyphers which were completely invulnerable. Britain had its weaknesses too. The Germans managed to break certain British naval

---

* The key message is a report of 16 February 1945, which states that Sunde had been summoned to Stockholm in accordance with instructions from the centre and that in a conversation with 'Valentin' (Fedor Chernov), he confirmed that he and his group had ceased their sabotage work on receipt of their instructions in June 1944.

cyphers both during the Norwegian campaign and afterwards, causing much damage. After the war Henry Denham, the British naval attaché in Stockholm who had sent the first report about the movement of the *Bismarck* through the Kattegat on 20 May 1941 (based on intelligence which he had obtained from Roscher Lund), was mortified to find in German archives a copy of a message from the Abwehr to the Kriegsmarine dated 21 May, giving details of this message which he had sent to the Admiralty just the day before.*[9] Similarly, GC&CS made a breakthrough with German Air Force cyphers in May 1940 and this series, known as 'Red Enigma', continued to be read with few interruptions until the end of the war.[10] They were also able to make extensive progress in reading an Enigma key used during the Norwegian campaign but, as Hinsley points out, this did not have great practical value for British commanders because of the lack of effective communication, security procedures and expertise.[11]

The value of Ultra (the signals intelligence obtained through the breaking of a range of the German Enigma cyphers) and the impact which it had in key areas of the war has been comprehensively documented, and the fragmentary way in which knowledge was acquired and exploited has been well described. Hinsley judges that its greatest contribution to the war at sea was obtained from the help it provided in enabling Britain to defeat German U-boats in the Battle of the Atlantic in late 1941, mainly by enabling the Admiralty's Operational Intelligence Centre to direct convoys to take routes which avoided the waiting German patrols,[12] although there were other later periods which also came close to matching that. Much of the work of GC&CS

---

* Denham's codes were vulnerable following the German capture of naval code books in Bergen in 1940. But other German work before that time enabled them to learn virtually everything connected with British operations in and off Norway following their invasion, by reading between 30 and 50 per cent of the naval traffic. They were thus able to estimate accurately the correct dispositions of the British Home Fleet. This was by no means their only achievement. German naval intelligence had some significant success against a variety of British naval codes: for example in the autumn of 1941 they were able to read much of the main Royal Navy cypher, as well as a special cypher which was being used for communications in the Atlantic between Britain, the United States and Canada.

is outside the scope of this book, but there are two aspects which are of particular relevance to us.

Successful cypher acquisition operations off the Norwegian coast

The first concerns the extent to which Enigma naval codebooks and cyphers were acquired during 'pinch' operations, which, after some initial fortuitous successes, were mounted for the purpose in Norwegian waters in 1940 and 1941.* The first success occurred on 26 April 1940 when the British destroyer *Griffin* intercepted what appeared to be a trawler, *Polares*, flying a Dutch flag near Åndalsnes, south-west of Trondheim. A boarding party discovered that it was a German ship carrying weapons and ammunition to Trondheim. The frightened crew did not resist and cooperated with the boarding party, who found some cypher tables and messages, and were also able to retrieve one of two weighted bags containing cypher materials which had been thrown overboard. These finds enabled the GC&CS cryptographers in Hut 8 at Bletchley Park, who dealt with German naval Enigma, to break the code for the first time and to read messages for the last few days of April.[13]

There were other important Enigma-related acquisitions during this period, taken as a result of the sinking of two German U-boats, *U-33* and *U-110*. The next success in Norwegian waters came during Operation CLAYMORE, a commando attack in the Lofoten Islands in March 1941. The raid destroyed some fish oil factories and substantial quantities of oil as well as sinking nearly 20,000 tons of shipping. However, a potentially greater prize was found by a boarding party from the destroyer *Somali* after she had attacked and disabled the German trawler *Krebs*. Crew members recovered two cypher machine wheels, along with – and even more significantly – the details of Enigma settings,

---

* I have a personal interest in the acquisition of Enigma equipment and cyphers by 'pinches'. My father-in-law Peter Meryon, when serving in the Mediterranean in October 1940 as a young sub-lieutenant on *Wrestler*, led a boarding party onto the Italian submarine *Durbo* as it was sinking, and grabbed cyphers and cypher tables, as well as recognition signals and details of swept channels into Italian and North African ports. On *Wrestler*'s return to Gibraltar, he was awarded an immediate DSC.

which were the item the GC&CS cryptographers most needed. When these arrived at Bletchley Park, they enabled some Enigma messages from the previous month to be read almost straight away and, by developing knowledge of German processes, provided assistance for future work.[14] But successes such as this did not have lasting benefits, because the tables which had been acquired were only valid for a limited period of time and when they were replaced, Enigma became unreadable again because the cryptographers had not yet developed a means of recreating the tables. So GC&CS asked the Admiralty for assistance, and suggested as a target for another pinch the *Lauenburg*, a German weather ship which was then operating further north off Jan Mayen Island. The Admiralty, while concerned at the danger that the Germans might conclude the capture of such ships was aimed at acquiring cypher material (a constant and prominent worry), decided that the risk was worthwhile. A small group of four ships set off in late June 1941, carrying Allon Bacon, a GC&CS cryptologist, a sensible step as on previous occasions potentially valuable documents had probably been overlooked during searches. The *Lauenburg* was located and some warning shots were sufficient to persuade the crew to abandon ship. Bacon oversaw the search, and his haul included some cypher wheel settings which were of critical importance, enabling German naval messages to be read within hours, rather than within days. When the settings from the *Lauenburg* ran out at the end of July 1941, the average time taken to read naval Enigma signals increased to about fifty hours.[15]

In November 1941, changes in German operating procedures again hampered the work of the GC&CS cryptologists. It happened that further raids were being planned against the Norwegian coast. While the capture of German cyphers was only a subsidiary objective, Bacon was involved in the planning of both Operation ARCHERY against Måløy, and Operation ANKLET in the Lofoten Islands, in December. He identified some likely German ships as targets, and accompanied the fleet which sailed to Måløy as he thought that this, rather than Lofoten, offered the best chance of finding what they were seeking.

His judgement was correct. First, during ARCHERY he accompanied a boarding party onto the *Föhn*, an armed trawler, and found a wealth of material including the tables which he was looking for as well as some Enigma settings and five cypher wheels. Soon afterwards, another German trawler, the *Donner*, was attacked and boarded. This time the booty included an Enigma cypher machine, as well as a further five wheels and another copy of the tables.* ANKLET also produced some worthwhile results, comprising another cypher machine, a further set of the much-prized tables and some code manuals. These finds gave GC&CS so much material that thereafter they were always able to deal with any German changes which might be made for security reasons. The settings used by German surface ships in home waters, and also by U-boats in the Arctic, were broken every day thereafter for the rest of the war.[16]

A rather broader example of the effectiveness of GC&CS by this stage in the war is provided by a vivid report showing the most remarkably detailed description of German reactions to an Allied operation in Norway. Produced in mid-January 1942, it shows how much GC&CS had been able to establish about the way in which the German Air Force reacted to the Måløy raid: a composite report of this nature would have been of considerable value in facilitating planning for other attacks on the coast of German-occupied Europe. German Air Force units in southern Norway were under the command of Fliegerführer Nord (Flg. Nord) at Stavanger. The report explained that the Allied attack started at 0742, aircraft took off at 0820, and the first orders were issued at 0855. However, it became apparent that Flg. Nord did not know what was happening. He sent the main strike force to Vågsøy, but he instructed his reconnaissance aircraft to cover increasingly long stretches of coastline. His instructions, and the increasingly frantic tone in which they were issued, indicate that he

---

* There was a further, unexpected bonus from the Måløy raid in May 1942 when the SOE station Mallard, in the Bergen area, reported that a sack with German documents and codes which had been dropped into the sea during the raid, had later been dredged up by fishermen and was undamaged. SOE quickly replied that they would send a special courier to collect the consignment, but the file thereafter is silent, so we do not know what happened. (TNA, HS 2/154.)

could not be sure that Vågsøy was the only point at which a landing had been made, and he seems to have assumed the worst. So at 0925, he sent a message to all the air and naval operational commands in the west, down to the English Channel, that British forces were landing between 59 and 64 degrees north.

No signal from an outside station was intercepted before Flg. Nord issued instructions at 0855. GC&CS concluded that this suggested that the first intimation of an attack came from the observer post on Vågsøy. The fact that he could not be sure that there were no landings at other points suggested to them that he was relying on visual reports from shore stations. The general atmosphere of panic during the morning indicated that Flg. Nord had little faith in the reliability of his reporting service. Moreover, a German aircraft flying over Ålesund was fired on by the German anti-aircraft defence. The pilot understandably jumped to the conclusion that the vessels firing on him were British, and reported that Ålesund harbour was occupied by a British naval force. Flg. Nord may have known that this was nonsense, but the report can hardly have clarified the situation. During the afternoon of that day reinforcement squadrons were flown to Stavanger from Holland, though they did not arrive until after British forces had left, and they remained there for at least a fortnight afterwards.[17]

ISOS and ISK, and their value

One of the key patterns in the Abwehr's use of communications was discovered by accident. In February 1940, when a Security Service radio operator was monitoring the traffic sent by Snow, their first double agent, he noticed that it was being received and forwarded to the Abwehr station in Hamburg by *Theseus*, a trawler which was sailing up and down off the coast of Norway. He observed that there was other traffic originating from *Theseus* around the time of his transmission periods. 'After considerable disbelief and research, this led to the German agent wireless (or W/T) network being gradually detected and decyphered' until GC&CS eventually picked up (by means of RSS stations* at home and abroad) a network of German traffic channels which covered Europe, with strands going to Asia (as far as China), the United States and South America – of which GC&CS had previously been largely unaware.[18] At this time, the Abwehr were using not only Enigma machines, but also the more old-fashioned and more familiar hand cyphers. In January 1940, GC&CS set up a special section under Oliver Strachey to break these hand cyphers and to report the de-crypted material. They succeeded in doing so in March 1940.[19] When they were first issued, the reports were called 'IS1' (Intelligence Series 1), and a total of 1,384 messages were distributed.[20] On 20 October 1940, messages sent in the particular types of cyphers originally broken were renamed ISOS (Illicit Signals Oliver Strachey).[21] The first ISOS reports were passed to SIS in July 1940. Section V of SIS, which dealt with counter-espionage, took over responsibility for their exploita-tion.† Although GC&CS continued to distribute the reports to service departments and to the Security Service, it was accepted that no action on them was permissible without reference to SIS. Dilly Knox was given responsibility for breaking the more difficult machine cypher used by the Abwehr for all its main European communications, and succeeded in December 1941, when the material produced was known as ISK (i.e. Illicit Signals Knox).‡ For security reasons, to protect the fact that the complicated machine cyphers had become readable, both ISOS and ISK reports were circulated as ISOS and only a very few knew of the difference. They were described to customer departments as MSS (Most Secret Sources) rather than ISOS.

---

* Radio Security Stations were born out of a rather amateur organisation set up in 1928 and run by the War Office to monitor illicit radio transmissions in the UK. After a brief period when these stations were run by the General Post Office and then by the War Office again, they metamorphosed into a much more professional section which was transferred from MI8 to the Security Service. It covered communications of the Abwehr and associated enemy intel-ligence and security agencies across the whole world. However, it was only able to intercept radio transmissions and could do nothing about telex messages which were sent by land line. This happened in several parts of Europe, but fortunately only rarely in Scandinavia.

† For part of the war, the Soviet spy Kim Philby was working in section V of SIS.

‡ Strachey and Knox were two of the very few survivors of the Admiralty's original codebreak-ing section in Room 40 during the First World War.

Over time, a few other related categories such as ISOSICLE (relating to the hand cyphers of the SD, or *Sicherheitsdienst*, which took over the Abwehr in 1944), also became available in limited quantities. There appears to be a surprising discrepancy in GC&CS histories about the number of ISOS reports which were circulated. One record states that 270,000 such reports were circulated between April 1940 and May 1945, of which there were 100,000 messages reported in the ISOS series, 141,000 in the ISK series, 13,000 in the ISOSICLE series and 16,000 in minor categories.[22] However, an entry in a file on the history of ISOS notes that over 500,000 reports were issued.[23] This distinction is perhaps more one for the statisticians than it is for us, because the figure was in any case substantial and the reports provided a comprehensive picture of many significant Abwehr activities directed against Allied interests. Its systematic study was the task of specialists, for many of the messages were partial and incomplete (because of meteorological problems) or cryptic (because of code names). The card index system, patiently built up and collated from all these sources, was an essential tool for investigators.

Once they were observed, the activities of the *Theseus* attracted considerable interest. On 30 March, Rear-Admiral Godfrey circulated a report about her, recommending that *Theseus* be left alone even if she departed Norwegian waters, because of her value. By 23 April, the Naval Intelligence Division (NID) were receiving, in the same cypher which was now being decrypted, reports from Abwehr HQ in Bergen on military operations in Norway and reports from other mobile stations as well as reports from *Theseus*. With the consent of SIS, these reports were passed in a camouflaged form to the War Office and also to the Admiralty. However at this stage, the organisation did not exist to enable the material to be passed to commanders in the field who could make effective operational use of it. Moreover, Hinsley judges that the significance of the intelligence derived from the earliest of these decrypted messages had been overlooked. He considered that the NID had failed to link the activities of the *Theseus* with other evidence for the German invasion of Norway, since for example some of the Abwehr messages contained enquiries about defences and troop dispositions.[24]

As can be seen in Chapter 5 which considers German attempts to send their Norwegian agents to Britain, the effective exploitation by Section V of SIS and the Security Service of most of the Abwehr's means of communications made it difficult for them to have any chance of mounting a successful operation in Britain. (It was only their land lines which could not be intercepted and these were not much used in Norway.) ISOS traffic provided advance information about most German attempts to send agents to the UK. Such activity was especially prevalent in late 1940 and the spring and summer of 1941. It continued in each 'escaping' season from then on, as a favourite Abwehr method was to mix the agents in with genuine escapers or to disguise them as a whole boatload of escapers. ISOS reports provided a developing picture of German planning, and also gave details about the vessels which were to be used. By April 1941, they had provided reports to NID containing detailed descriptions of five different fishing vessels which either had been used or were possibly going to be used, for the transport of agents to the UK. Some of these operations did not take place, but it enabled the Admiralty to be on the lookout to intercept vessels when they arrived in Scotland.

An extract of a report based on ISOS from a slightly later period gives a flavour of the painstaking way in which information was collected and assessed:

i. The mysterious 'Fisherman O' of the Reidar expedition has now been identified as Johan J Olsbø of Ålesund. He was the former owner of the Reidar and intended to come over to the UK in it, but withdrew at the last moment owing to fear of reprisals on his family. V-mann 'Alex'* (Arnold Evensen) had not time to notify his German masters of the change of plan.

---

*   V-mann was an Abwehr term for one of its agents, short for *Vertrauensmann*, German for one who could be trusted.

ii. A rpt BEN/482 of 14.1.43 at the RVPS* by one of our interrogators enabled us to discover that V-person 'Evelyn' was identical with Sigrund Olsen. Sigrund Olsen @ Evelyn was responsible for penetrating an allied intelligence organisation in the Mosjøen area. This report is yet another instance of an interrogation by our RVPS staff tying up and elucidating the most secret material.

iii. A Norwegian national called Henry Øverby arrived in the UK from Stockholm on 1.2.43. On arrival at the RVPS he named numerous prominent members of the Norwegian intelligence organisations with whom he had worked, and was aware of the names of P9 and Captain Turner.† His story however aroused some suspicion as a wireless operator by the name of Øverby figured in our MSS material in May 1942. This Øverby was given the cover name of Holte by the Germans. Henry Øverby is a wireless operator and is known to have used the alias of Erik Holtemoen in Norway. This name readily lends itself to the construction of Holte. This coincidence was pointed out to the Security Service and it has since transpired that Henry Øverby studied wireless engineering in Dresden and twice returned to Germany via Sweden since the invasion of Norway. He therefore had freedom of movement from the Germans. If Henry Øverby should prove to be the Holte of our MSS, the Abwehr has achieved penetration on a major scale. There is a chance that the whole thing is based on coincidence, but the Security Service agree with our suggestion that further enquiries are essential.[25]

GC&CS files provide a remarkably complete picture of the extent of British knowledge about Abwehr structures, including their organisation in Norway, personnel, buildings and even their telephone directories as well as details of many of their Norwegian agents. They also

---

* Royal Victoria Patriotic School, the reception centre where all refugees arriving from occupied Europe were initially interrogated by the security authorities.
† P9 was the designation of Eric Welsh, the head of the SIS section dealing with Norway. Captain John Turner was one of his subordinates.

describe Abwehr preparations to deal with British raids, sabotage and intelligence operations. A report in April 1942 sets out the extra steps they were taking to obtain early warning of enemy intentions and trace agents equipped with wireless sets – by increasing the number of their own small stations equipped with wireless, recruiting more agents to act as coastal watchers and increasing the number of direction finding stations to track such transmissions.[26]

The first operational use of ISOS

Although much of the value of ISOS and ISK lay in their counter-espionage potential, they first showed their usefulness by enabling a series of operations to be mounted to disrupt German attempts to establish weather stations on Svalbard, Jan Mayen and elsewhere in the Arctic. Information from such stations, together with that from weather trawlers, could be of great importance in supplementing reporting from weather reconnaissance flights. After the Abwehr hand cypher was broken in March 1940, ISOS intelligence provided NID with a very detailed picture of German planning. The NID history states that the reports

> revealed the incompetence and self-seeking nature of the various groups
> of Abwehr personnel as well as their insane jealousy of each other. This
> last trait was manifest right up to the level of Goering himself. He in-
> tervened personally to help get arrangements through and do down a
> rival group who were also planning operations.[27]

ISOS enabled the *Fridtjof Nansen* to capture a group of armed Danes who had landed in East Greenland at the end of April 1940. A few months later the same ship intercepted a second party and forced a third ship to return to Norway. Shortly afterwards, it disrupted another attempt to land an armed party on Greenland. In November, the *Fridtjof Nansen* was herself wrecked when trying to interdict *Heinrich Freese*, a trawler which was taking a group of Germans to Jan Mayen, but the trawler was captured by the cruiser *Naiad*.[28] This group in-cluded Count Ulrich von Finckenstein, an Abwehr officer working in Oslo, who had been involved in some of the previous attempts to land weather reporting stations in the Arctic. He was captured, brought to England and interned. His Abwehr connection was finally confirmed by a Dane, Børresen, whom he had sent to Britain in August 1940, who revealed that von Finckenstein was a member of the Stettin Abwehr. After this von Finckenstein talked freely and provided some valua-ble information.[29] There was a further successful interception, of the *Buskø* in 1941, but after August 1942 further German attempts to land weather stations on Svalbard or Greenland were carried out under naval command. GC&CS could not read those naval cyphers and the landings were successful for the following two years.[30]

ISOS occasionally provided other insights. For example, it revealed that the Germans had been obtaining reports about British activities from the Swedes, which initially appeared to have originated from Denham, the British naval attaché, or from his office. Investigations showed that most of the material would not have been available to Denham, and it was concluded that the Swedish naval attaché in London, Count Oxenstierna, was responsible. He was eventually asked to leave at the end of 1943, and was the only neutral naval at-taché to be expelled from Britain during the war.* In the course of the investigation of the naval attaché, it was discovered in October 1943 that Roscher Lund had been making an arrangement to obtain information from Oxenstierna which he was not directly disclosing to the British. NID did not take this further, because they concluded that there was nothing anti-British about it, and that he was doing it for his own purposes.[31]

Abwehr operations in Germany and other German intelligence and

---

* There is no evidence that Oxenstierna acted improperly or was in collusion with the Germans. He was an effective attaché who managed to collect more information than the British would have wanted a neutral to obtain. Some of his information was subsequently passed to the Ger-mans in Stockholm. His successor, Prince Bertil, was much less effective and the leak dried up.

security agencies were not so vulnerable to GC&CS investigations. In fact, it was only after the war that SIS discovered that the Abwehr had succeeded in penetrating the Swedish legation in Berlin, by recruiting a confidential secretary who passed them copies of reports which were sent by the legation to the Foreign Ministry in Stockholm. These included information obtained by the Swedes on the development of new weapons, German economic and industrial potential, and air raid damage. When passing this information to the Security Service, SIS made no mention of cypher materials. The operation lasted from 1941 until 1944, when presumably the secretary was posted back to Stockholm.[32] There was nothing – in the SIS report at least – to indicate that any cyphers had been compromised.

Warnings to agents

In addition to providing intelligence to help detect German espionage attempts in Britain, ISOS could also help to protect the security of Allied agents operating abroad. If an agent was under suspicion or worse, in danger of arrest, a hint of this could often appear in Abwehr traffic with just enough notice for a warning to be sent to the SIS or SOE agent concerned. There were times, though, when the risk of compromising ISOS had to be weighed against the value of an agent's work, and in some cases an agent would have to be left unwarned and take his chance. (The SOE Security Section history noted that until early 1943, there was not the same collaboration and liaison between SOE, SIS and the Security Service on espionage and the protection of agents in the field, as existed later. The history concluded that the need for this collaboration had not been foreseen. 'If a section had been created in SOE earlier than 1943 to specialise in operational security and to study enemy counter-espionage methods, aided by the information in possession of SIS and the Security Service, some of the later penetration might have been avoided'.[33]) Chapter 5 explores such an example, when a suitably disguised warning was sent to Nagell about the imminent danger to two SOE agents in Bergen, who had been compromised following the confession of a captured SOE agent. But ISOS could also provide more general warnings too, as the following example from a fortnightly update from 1943 shows:[34]

At this time last year, by means of agents in Gothenburg itself and a number of fishing smacks specially equipped to operate in the Kattegat, the enemy kept close watch on the Norwegian ships then preparing to run the gauntlet to England. MSS material shows that the Abwehrstelle at Copenhagen is again using fishing smacks to keep an eye on the Norwegian vessels *Dicto* and *Lionel* lying in Gothenburg. SOE, who were considering an attempt to get these vessels to the UK, have been warned.*

MSS material reported that the *Nordfahrt* had been damaged by an explosion while lying at Thamshavn. The German authorities suspect sabotage and a strict surveillance of all boats in the area has been put into force.†

There were clear indications in the MSS material that German Intelligence are able to decypher the codes used by certain of the SOE agents in Norway. Lark is a specific instance.‡

In late 1944 the Norwegians started to obtain reports based on telephone interception of conversations between the SD, Statspoliti (the NS police) and Gestapo. In a revealing exchange, Keith Liversidge, of Section V of SIS, wrote to Roscher Lund to suggest that the intercept material be given the culturally appropriate codenames of 'Ibsen' and 'Grieg'. He also proposed some fairly wide-ranging restrictions on the use which could be made of the reports. Although they were to be copied to the Norwegian legation in Stockholm, he recommended that no action be taken there on them, and that any action should only be initiated by Roscher Lund in London:

---

* This is a reference to PERFORMANCE, an operation to transport a consignment of ball bearings from Sweden to Britain after a previous attempt, RUBBLE, had been very successful.

† A reference to a successful SOE sabotage operation, GRANARD.

‡ Underlined in the original. Lark was an operation in Trondheim where two SOE agents were arrested. One managed to escape shortly afterwards, but the radio operator remained in prison and died of pneumonia after prolonged and harsh interrogation.

'This suggestion may seem hard on individuals about to be arrested when a warning from Stockholm could possibly save them. But the Home Front as a whole will benefit more from the continuance of this material and I fear, if necessary, that individuals must therefore be sacrificed.'* It was vital that the source should be safeguarded and that the Germans should not become aware of the leakage. In his reply, Roscher Lund accepted most of Liversidge's suggestions, but disagreed with this one, commenting 'we can hardly prevent the people in Norway from taking action when they feel it is necessary to save lives. You must remember that it is not only individuals but possibly the whole organisation which might come in danger [sic] if they do not immediately take the necessary steps.'[35]

The reader might wonder whether there was ever any specific discussion with the Norwegians about the codebreaking activities of GC&CS. Nothing has been found to show that there was, or indeed to confirm that there was not. But there are at least oblique references which show that aspects of the subject were being discussed both with them and with the Swedes, with whom there appeared to be some cooperation in the later stages of the war. In November 1944, Cordeaux of SIS wrote to Roscher Lund to inform him that Denham had asked that he should be briefed on a proposal to cut the Narvik cable, which had already been broached before. He continued:

Apparently the Swedes anticipated that we might reopen the matter and have told Denham that, if we do, we must not take it for granted that they will be able to fulfil their part of the plan, that is the breaking of the German cyphered message passing over the other route. They were very doubtful that they would now be able to do this. They also felt that in fact the Germans would be unlikely to use this other route.

To put it another way, the Swedes felt that if the plan was now embarked upon the British would accomplish their part, the Swedes would

---

* The Home Front was a term sometimes used to describe the resistance organisation.

be unable to accomplish theirs, and that the British might then think that the Swedes had rather let them down.[36]

There is nothing further to show how this matter was resolved. The SIS officer responsible for Norway, Eric Welsh, often used the codename Theodor or Theodore in correspondence with Norwegian contacts. It is possible that he borrowed this name from someone whom he might have considered to be one of his German opposite numbers. A report from Captain Hugh Trevor-Roper* provided the following information about him: 'Theodor is the covername of I T/Lw, a section of Abteilung I of the Abwehr, controlled by Oberst Piekenbeck, Chef I, whose object is the collection of technical air force intelligence from enemy and neutral countries (mainly England, the USA and Turkey).'[37] Was this a complete coincidence?

Eric Welsh, the officer in charge of SIS Norwegian operations. © NHM

---

*   The historian who later became Lord Dacre.

CHAPTER 5

GERMAN SUCCESS, NEAR MISSES AND FAILURES

ABWEHR ESPIONAGE: AGENTS, DOUBLE AGENTS AND DOUBLE-CROSS

The prominent SOE historian M. R. D. Foot wrote that 'every single agent the Germans sent to wartime England bar one, was captured … the one exception committed suicide before he started work'.[1] This is not strictly accurate. There were another two, rather more significant, Norwegian exceptions. Ingvald Johansen, one of the Abwehr's Norwegian agents, was sent over on the *Olav* with two other Norwegian agents in March 1941. All three passed without incident through screening at the London Reception Centre, also known as the Royal Victoria Patriotic School (RVPS) and, on Nagell's recommendation, Johansen was recruited by Martin Linge and sent to Shetland to join the North Sea transport. He worked as skipper of the *Vita* and made five trips to Norway (on one of which he landed near Trondheim to collect his girlfriend, whom he brought back to Shetland and subsequently married) before he was captured by the Germans in September 1941. He and his crew spent the rest of the war in captivity, ending up at Natzweiler concentration camp. After the Security Service finally learned of his Abwehr links through ISOS* in

---

* A word of clarification is needed. The nature of ISOS and ISK, and the differences between them, were explained in the previous chapter. Outside GC&CS, they were generally referred to as MSS (Most Secret Sources) and it is not usually clear which type of intercept produced the intelligence. For our purposes the distinction does not greatly matter, so ISOS, the most common source, will be used as a generic description.

November 1941, they eventually concluded that he had changed sides. This remarkable case will be explored in more detail later in the chapter, as well as another episode where Norwegians working for the Abwehr visited Shetland in November 1940 and succeeded in luring three SOE agents back to Norway, where they were caught and executed.

The Abwehr, and later Himmler's SD which took it over in 1944, mounted a series of operations attempting to send Norwegians to Britain. The first group was sent in October 1940, the last arrived in January 1945. Most came over by fishing boat, some were transported by flying boat and landed in rubber dinghies, some dropped by parachute or came by boat from Spain and one arrived from the United States. The early groups were all quickly detected because of poor preparations such as defective identification papers, suspicious aspects in their behaviour, dress or language – and sometimes simply an unsuitable choice of agent. This changed when ISOS gradually came on stream towards the end of 1940 – which was fortunate because the Abwehr was becoming more skilful in their selection and training of agents, and the means by which they tried to disguise them among other travellers. Thereafter ISOS was generally the source of intelligence which led to their identification, detention and (usually) internment, but there were a couple of cases where SIS provided the crucial tip-off and another where it provided significant background reporting on an agent prior to his arrival.

An assessment of Abwehr activities up to March 1942, compiled by B division of the Security Service, and Section V of SIS, provides a remarkable degree of detail about both the extent of operations from their Norwegian bases, and also about those responsible for carrying them out.[2] Their headquarters was at Klingenberggate 5–7 in Oslo, and there were four further sub-stations covering the rest of the country in Bergen, Trondheim, Tromsø and Kirkenes. All of them apart from Kirkenes sent agents to Britain. The main recruiting centre in Oslo used as a cover the firm Andersen and Andersen, Tordenskjolds Plass 3, which claimed to be shipbrokers. The most active recruiter there was Fritz Angermeyer, who used the alias Karl Andersen. After the First World War, Anger-meyer had been associated with Norwegian seamen who smuggled spirits into Norway. Following the invasion he got in touch with some of them, whom he recruited as agents. Most were provided with money or fishing boats either for going to Britain as agents or acting as spies or counter-espionage agents along the coast of Norway.

The report assessed that apart from the Russian front, there were four Abwehr bases of outstanding importance and of special concern, as they were directed against British interests. These were in Norway, the Balkans, Spain and the United States. It calculated that up to that point, Abwehr activity could be divided into six phases, which started in May 1940. Before then, no Abwehr agents were known to have arrived in Britain. The first phase, between May and July 1940, saw the des-patch of agents from Eire. During the second phase from August 1940 to February 1941, which partly coincided with preparations for a possible German invasion, there were at least two attempts to send agents from Norway. During the third phase, between March 1941 and the end of September 1941, the focus was almost entirely on Norway as the Abwehr concentrated on missions involving Norwegian agents. There were seven different attempts, most of which involved the use of fishing boats with Abwehr agents concealing themselves among parties of refugees, a threat of greater concern as they could be much less easy to detect. Attempts continued to be made to send Norwegian agents throughout the rest of the war, either from Norway or elsewhere, but not on the same scale. Although occasionally the Security Service knew which Abwehr de-partment had sent them, it was not always possible for them to work out what their mission was. Sometimes it was to gather naval intelligence, sometimes counter-espionage, and sometimes sabotage.

The report was dismissive of the calibre of Norwegians who had been selected as agents:

The Norwegians whom the Germans have recruited as spies have on the whole been a miserable collection of thieves, drunkards and blackguards of the last order. In no case, with one possible exception, has any Norwegian come to this country as a German spy because of his Nazi sympathies. The motive has invariably been monetary gain or fear – usually the former. The technique adopted has followed very clear cut lines. The victim is first of all employed as an informer against loyal Norwegians in Norway and at a later stage sent to Britain. If the stories which have been told by the spies whom we have captured are to be believed, which is problematical, although they were all employed as counter-espionage spies in the first place in their own country they never gave the Germans any information of the slightest value to them. Agents of this character who are mere mercenary scoundrels are wholly unreliable, and there is good reason to think that having got the German money in their pockets and got out of physical control of their paymasters, they are unlikely to carry out the missions for which they have been assigned.

Although the Security Service would have felt justified in describing any Abwehr agent as a blackguard and a traitor, by no means all of the Norwegians fitted this generalised description, which reflected an unwarranted degree of complacency. There were certainly a few hard-drinking and unreliable fishermen among their number – but some were quite highly educated and well motivated to work for the Germans, and one later case was judged sufficiently serious for the agent to be charged with treason, although in the event the prosecution was dropped on procedural grounds.

An Abwehr coup

The Germans did have one success in their operations from Norway, though the details of what happened are not entirely clear. We know that *Urd II* arrived in Lerwick in mid-November 1940. Two of the crew were Harry Hagemann and George Furre, who were both working for the Abwehr. They brought with them a party of refugees one of whom, Marius Eriksen, had good references in London, including an adjutant to King Haakon.[3] Perhaps because of this, and also because the reception process for foreign arrivals was not yet properly established, the crew of *Urd II* was not detained or questioned in any detail. They made clear that they wanted to go home. SOE had a group of three agents whom they wished to return to Norway, and it was agreed that they would travel with *Urd II*, which had not stayed long enough that it was likely to have been missed. The agents, Melankton Rasmussen, Alf Konrad Lindeberg and Frithjof Kviljo Pedersen, were arrested by the Germans after their return to the Bergen area, and were executed in August 1941. They were the first members of the resistance to receive a death sentence who were not pardoned. The archival files do not provide any insights into what happened when news of the arrests reached SOE headquarters, or how the Security Service reacted. ISOS reporting was at that time still in its early stages, so was unable to provide any insights.

Dødsdømte spioner skutt i dag morges.

Alle tre var nordmenn.

Oslo, 11. august.

(NTB.) Reisende Melankton Rasmussen fra Bergen, styrmann Alf Konrad Lindeberg, Farsund, og styrmann Frithjof Pedersen, Lista, blev av rikskrigsretten den 1. august 1941 dømt til døden for i fellesskap å ha drevet spionasje, begunstiget fienden og for å ha hatt et våbenlager.

De 3 ovennevnte personer var i hemmelighet reist til England, hvor de lot sig overtale til i fellesskap å bygge op en illegal organisasjon av nordmenn i Norge, rettet mot den tyske forsvarsmakt.

Dessuten skulde det oprettes en hemmelig efterretningsforbindelse med England. For å gjennemføre sin opgave hadde de med sig en radiosender tilbake til Norge. De førte også med sig en koffert med pistoler og ammunisjon.

Dommen blev eksekvert idag morges ved skytning.

Announcement of the executions of three SOE agents who were lured back to Norway from Shetland by Abwehr agents in November 1940. © NHM

Alf Konrad Lindeberg, one of the three SOE agents executed
after being lured back to Norway. © NHM

The German agent who avoided capture by the British

Ingvald Johansen, Thorleif Solem and Sigurd Edvard Alseth, all
Abwehr agents, arrived in Buckie on the *Olav* on 17 March 1941. Johansen's background appears to have been similar to that of Solem,
who was originally recruited in June 1940 for counter-espionage work.
In January 1941 he was handed over to Angermeyer, who organised
the passage to Britain.[4] (Alseth, a man of very limited intelligence,
was brought in to make up the numbers for the crew. He was the
brother of Hildur, whom Johansen subsequently married.) Solem
worked as an unskilled labourer on Lade aerodrome, near Trondheim,
for which he was well paid. During interrogation he admitted that his
first betrayal had been of an arms dump housed by Olav Bokvold at
Glåmos south-east of Trondheim. He was an effective German agent,
penetrating other resistance groups, and betraying at least a further

five Norwegians. He was paid 400 Norwegian kroner (NOK) a month for this work.* Johansen was selected to be the skipper of the *Olav* and Angermeyer planned that they should explain to British authorities that they had come over to buy spirits which they could then sell in Trondheim. Angermeyer's purpose was to establish a regular traffic which could be used for espionage purposes and for the introduction of further agents into Britain. Johansen was given nearly 1,700 Swedish kroner (SEK),† which he divided with Solem, for the purpose of buying whisky, and was issued with a radio receiver for listening to Swedish weather forecasts and a recognition signal which they could show to prevent attack by marauding German aircraft. They were each to be paid NOK 500 for the first month, thereafter NOK 400 a month, NOK 1,000 on completion of first trip whether or not it was successful, and NOK 10,000‡ insurance, all to be paid to next of kin – Solem's wife, Johansen's girlfriend, Hildur, and Alseth's sister. All three signed contracts to this effect. It is not clear how the Germans would disguise to the recipients (unaware of their espionage mission) the source of these payments. Angermeyer also arranged for two innocent Norwegian refugees, Frithjof Cleve and Olaf Tandberg, to travel with them.

After the *Olav* arrived in Buckie, the Security Control Officer in Aberdeen recommended in his report to the RVPS that special attention should be paid to Johansen and Solem as they were each in possession of SEK 840§ and did not have any adequate reason for bringing it to Britain. Moreover, there were found on board three cameras, seven exposed and undeveloped films and four unexposed films. However, these recommendations were ignored, and it is not known what happened to either the cameras or the films. Their interrogation at the RVPS was cursory, and they were released after only two days

---

* Allowing for inflation, the equivalent of about £800 at 2019 prices.
† The equivalent of about £3,600 at 2019 prices.
‡ The equivalent of £1,000, £800, £2,000 and £20,000 respectively at 2019 prices.
§ The equivalent of about £1,800 at 2019 prices.

there, on 25 March. When the Security Service later investigated this, they discovered that there was no record at all of the interrogations of Cleve, Tandberg and Alseth and only fragmentary records for Johansen and Solem – a failing which B1, the section responsible for counter-espionage, described as 'melancholy', adding that comment was 'superfluous'.

Shortly after Johansen was released from the RVPS, at Nagell's recommendation he was recruited as a member of the Shetland crews by Martin Linge and sent north. Since at the age of forty he was significantly older and more experienced than other crew members, he was appointed skipper of the *Vita*. He made his first trip, the delivery of a group of SOE agents to Snilfjord, west of Trondheim, in mid-April. Not long afterwards, Solem, having spent a fortnight serving with the Norwegian Army from which he was discharged as being medically unfit, was also recruited by Linge. SOE later maintained that this was because Johansen had asked for him to join them and that, therefore, despite their reservations about his shiftiness and dependability, they permitted him to do so. He sailed with Johansen on his next trip to pick up a party of SOE agents at Sørhunden, near Namsos, in mid-May. The agents were not at the rendezvous, but on the way back the *Vita* rescued the crew and passengers of another vessel in difficulties. Soon afterwards, Solem was sacked by the base commander Leslie Mitchell because he was unsuitable, inquisitive, often drunk and viewed with distrust by companions. It was later reported by other crew members that they had once had to stop him trying to telephone his wife when he was over in Norway. Johansen also stated that he did not like him and would rather he left – quite possibly because he would have seen an indiscreet Solem as a threat to his own security. Back in London Solem approached Nagell and was paid £15* for the one trip he had made.

---

* Approximately £750 at 2019 prices.

The crew of *Vita*. Ingvald Johansen (left) was the Abwehr agent who passed security checks and was recruited to work at the Shetland base. He changed sides, and was later captured by the Germans. © Scalloway Museum

At the end of May, Johansen went over again to collect a party of agents who were going to attend a training course in Scotland, and an SIS agent as well as eight refugees including his girlfriend, Hildur, and his brother. It transpired that he had previously sent her a letter telling her when and where to meet him on his next trip, and asking her to marry him. This was a clear and self-evidently dangerous breach of regulations, but the authorities in Lerwick did not take action against him beyond giving him a ticking off. It may have been easier for Johansen to avoid disciplinary trouble since he was very popular with the other crews. Because of his age he was affectionately known as 'Old Joe'.* After their marriage Hildur was employed as a housekeeper to look after the crews. Following the summer break, he made two further trips to collect SOE agents and to deliver two more on behalf of SIS. He was captured by the Germans in what appears to have been an ambush on his next trip in late September, probably the consequence

---

* David Howarth, *The Shetland Bus* (London: Fontana 1955), p. 43. The fact that Howarth, deputy commander of the Shetland base, wrote about Johansen in these terms is an indication that he was never briefed about his links to the Abwehr, and that this knowledge continued to be tightly held.

of some arrests made by the Germans on 22 September not far from Rekøy, where Johansen was bound. SOE eventually established that after a spell in the Kristiansten Festning prison in Trondheim, he and his crew were moved via a camp in Falstad to Grini prison camp outside Oslo. They went later sent to Germany, first to Oranienburg, and later to Natzweiler concentration camp in France. They all survived the war. Before leaving Norway, Johansen was able to pass a message back that their interrogation had gone well, that they had been forced to admit they had done five trips to Norway, but that they had revealed nothing about their contacts. We do not know when the Abwehr caught up with him and how Johansen dealt with his interrogation by Angermeyer, but it is difficult to believe that it could have gone 'well'. Hildur Johansen remained in her position as housekeeper for a while after Johansen's capture, and slightly longer on Shetland, but then left. The file contains no further information about either of them and concentrates on the equally remarkable story of Solem.

Solem first came to the attention of the Security Service in early June, only a fortnight after he had left Shetland, when he and a Norwegian deserter were found in a prohibited area in Dover and detained. His companion said that Solem wanted to steal a boat and sail to France. During questioning, Solem said that he had been a secret service agent for the Norwegian government and had been paid by Nagell. The Security Service officer who interviewed them concluded that they were both wastrels and liars. They were sentenced to two days' imprisonment each by magistrates for being in a prohibited area, and then released. Solem was transferred to the Norwegian authorities and sent to Bristol on 25 June to report to the Norwegian shipping and trade mission. Later in June, Captain Kristian Gleditsch, responsible to Nagell for security, reported to the Security Service that Sverre Gisvold, a recently arrived refugee from Trondheim, had stated that he had been arrested there by the Germans and that it was Solem who had given him away. Gleditsch said that they were going to bring Solem to London to confront him with Gisvold. There is no direct record of what then happened because the report by Gleditsch has been retained. However, a later Security Service summary recorded that after investigating both Solem and Gisvold, the Norwegians had concluded that 'Solem was only a bit of a rogue who has been indiscreet when drunk, whereas Gisvold was also just a fool, who had no improper connection with the enemy'. Gleditsch also considered that 'since Solem had been in special service with the Norwegian Navy, the matter for the moment may be left there'. He was released to go back to Bristol to work on the tanker *Sandanger*.*

At the end of November 1941, ISOS provided information showing that the crew of the *Olav* were Abwehr agents, and Solem and Alseth (serving in the Norwegian Army in Dumfries) were arrested and brought to Camp 020.† This report also made it plain that the Germans had imprisoned Johansen and his companions, and were proposing to court-martial him.[5] Solem readily admitted his association with the Germans, and gradually revealed the extent of his activities on their behalf. For example, he admitted that he had been briefed on the way to Shetland to observe the mine barrier at Lerwick; the position of any naval units seen on route; the recognition signals used by aircraft; and that it was hoped that they would be permitted to make regular trips between Norway and Scotland. Alseth was of less concern: it was judged that he was of such low mentality as to be almost half-witted, and that he had been recruited more as a crew member than for any specific intelligence purpose.

SOE were of course considerably perturbed to learn the news of Johansen's and Solem's activities. They maintained that Johansen had been loyal to them, because they could find no evidence that any of his expeditions had gone wrong. H. P. Milmo, in the counter-espionage branch B1B, accepted this view, and wrote to Liversidge in late January:

---

* There is no record of what subsequently happened to Gisvold. He continued to be of interest to both the Security Service and SIS, but subsequent records have also been retained.

† The interrogation centre for captured German agents in Latchmere House in Ham, south-west London, run by Colonel Robin 'Tin Eye' Stephens. (He was known as 'Tin Eye' because he wore a monocle.)

I think we can rely with confidence on the crews not taking messages
to Norway and I very much doubt whether any of our crew men are in
the pay of the Germans. My opinion, with which SOE concurs, is that
during the period when Johansen was working for SOE he was not
communicating with the Germans. The reason is that the remainder
of the crew was not known to him before he worked for us and were
in my opinion trustworthy. Furthermore, apart from the trips which
he made himself, Johansen would also know all the other trips made
by our crews. We have no knowledge of any agent having been sent to
Norway via the Shetland base having been caught or any of our arms
dumps having been discovered by the Germans. Apart from information confirming this received from messengers in Norway, we have been
back to the same places on more than one occasion and no indication
has been given to us that the Germans have known that we have been
there in the past.

In late March, Milmo requested that a full summary of the case be
forwarded to Gleditsch. He commented that this 'contained a great
deal of intelligence information which should be of peculiar interest
and we hope use to the Norwegians'. He speculated that the reason for
Johansen's sudden change of allegiance might be found in the fact that
after his discharge from RVPS he and Solem had embarked on a riotous drinking bout, 'during which they appear to have got rid of most of
the money given them by Andersen [i.e. Angermeyer] to buy whisky.
Possibly, after having misappropriated Andersen's money, Johansen
did not feel that he could return to the old fold.' In a later summary in
April, J. P. de C. Day agreed with this evaluation, adding with wit that
since they had conspired together to spend the money given them by
Angermeyer for purchasing whisky for themselves, they had fulfilled
the letter but not the spirit of Angermeyer's instruction. This does
seem a plausible explanation, but given the sum they had available,
to have disposed of it all in a drinking spree within about ten days
would have represented a prodigious feat even for two hard-headed

Norwegian fishermen. It is, however, possible that not all the money which they had been given by Angermeyer was available to them to spend on riotous living. Nagell wrote to SOE on 5 April, complaining that Johansen and Alseth had both had SK 450 in their possession when they arrived, which had been taken from them by the immigration officer. He sought advice on how to recover it. The amounts do not match those in KV files, though Solem did admit under interrogation that he and Johansen had given NOK 170 to Alseth. Perhaps the story became garbled as it was passed to Nagell. [6]

In internal correspondence, Milmo noted the ease with which two German agents were enlisted in SOE. He acknowledged that this was the responsibility of the Security Service, inasmuch as it was discovered, when the case was reopened on the basis of ISOS information, that the security examination of the party on arrival had been inadequate.[7] At the end of Solem's interrogation, the Security Service assessment was extremely disparaging, describing him as stubborn, cunning and a regular drunkard, and the Camp 020 history concluded that 'Solem proved a worthy inmate of Camp 020 since he had a long record of treachery in Norway'. Both Solem and Alseth were interned for the remainder of the war.

It might seem surprising that in the aftermath of this investigation, no action was taken to discourage crews who were delivering agents or landing supplies in remote spots, from entering small ports and allowing their presence to become known to local inhabitants, or to prevent them from sending mail in the way that Johansen had done to his girlfriend. It does not even appear to have been considered. This oversight had some serious consequences, particularly in Telavåg, as highlighted in Chapter 3, after the *Borghild* had landed an SIS agent and the *Olaf* had landed two SOE agents at the same site within days of each other, leading to a German raid and severe reprisals.

The behaviour of the *Borghild* crew in Telavåg was not an isolated instance. There were plenty of other examples. When the SIS agent Kristian Fougner returned to Norway in May 1942, on *Sigalos* commanded by Leif Larsen, he was landed at Vindholmen, just north of Brattvær. He wrote later that the crew wanted some Norwegian salmon so they berthed right inside the harbour and a couple of the men, with Fougner and his suitcase in tow, strolled up to the village shop.

> They didn't even bother to take off their uniforms. There was no doubt that they were in the Norwegian Navy. They got their salmon and after a while I was left standing there with my suitcase. I must admit I didn't feel exactly on top of the world – I might as well have had a baggage tag tied to my hand – 'Handle with care, just arrived from England'. But there wasn't much I could do about it. I rather wished that I had been onboard again as I saw the boat disappearing over the horizon.[8]

It was only in March 1943 that the Admiralty introduced orders prohibiting this behaviour. They instructed the crews of all vessels, including MTBs as well as those operating for SOE and SIS, that no one was to go ashore in Norway except in the course of his duty, and then only if permission had been obtained from the senior officer present. All conversations with the local population were to be recorded in writing. No letters, written or printed papers were to be sent or taken ashore in Norway without authority, and posting of letters by unauthorised persons was also strictly forbidden.[9]

The only agent who committed suicide at Camp 020

The case of Olaf Sætrang was quite different, and had a number of unusual characteristics. In particular, Sætrang had worked for the Abwehr before the war and had been the subject of SIS reporting when he worked in Panama in 1939. He also appeared to have cultivated the wife of Finn Nagell while living in her house in Oslo. Moreover, he was the only detainee who succeeded in committing suicide in Camp 020 which, as the Security Service historian wryly acknowledged, complicated their investigation of his case.[10] Though born in Rotterdam, Sætrang was a Norwegian citizen, a fluent linguist who dabbled in a number of businesses and had spent several periods in South America. He also worked as a purser on cruise ships, often in the Caribbean, and made a number of British contacts. He had retained their addresses, which were found when he was searched on arrival, and it was apparent that he had intended to make use of them.

In March 1939, Sætrang got a job working in the office of a shipping company in Panama. It was thought that he had done this at the behest of the Abwehr. One of his contacts there was Inga Guttman, the secretary of the German consul, who was deported as a spy after she had been found in a prohibited zone. When he left Panama in April 1940, he travelled back with Guttman, going via Italy to Germany, where he spent seven weeks in Berlin. After his return to Norway in June, he made several trips to Stockholm, cultivating the Norwegian military attaché Colonel Oscar Sigvald Strugstad and offering to obtain information on damage to aluminium works in Norway, which the Security Service considered to be evidence of an attempt to penetrate one of the Norwegian services. Sætrang was also found to be in possession of Strugstad's address when he was arrested. In early 1941 he was running a cover business dealing with fire extinguishers based in Klingenberggata 4: right next door to Abwehr HQ! During this period he was living in the house of Nagell's wife. The Security Service concluded that this was either to obtain evidence of his bona fides with which to impress loyal Norwegians on arrival in London, or because he was spying on her. It was also known that he had acted as an agent provocateur, using a letter purported to have been sent to him by Strugstad, as a passport into loyal Norwegian circles. This did not work; the Germans arrested Mads Wiel, the man he had approached asking for assistance to send important information to Britain, before suitable incriminating evidence could be planted on him.

ISOS messages showed that Sætrang was preparing to travel to Britain via Iceland in August 1941, leading a group of passengers who were initially thought to be other agents, but who turned out to be innocent refugees enlisted to provide him with cover. ISOS also revealed that before his departure, Sætrang had been seen by Major Novak, head of the Abwehr in Norway. The party travelled on the *Hornfjell* from Tromsø, but they were all arrested on arrival in Iceland, and reached Britain in September. When Sætrang's possessions were searched, two compromising addresses in Panama and the Netherlands were found, which were linked to the head of Japanese intelligence in Panama and an accommodation address for German agents in Britain and France. Sætrang was taken to Camp 020. He was confronted with the damning information already known about him and his activities, and was told to write a full statement of his life story. He committed suicide that night.

Deprived of the opportunity to interview their suspect, the Security Service were unable to work out what mission Sætrang was expected to perform. Since he had been working for the Abwehr for at least two years and probably rather longer, they concluded that he was intended to perform a much more important mission than the usual type of assignment which had hitherto been given to Norwegian spies sent to Britain. He was known to have been a code and wireless expert, which suggested that he might have been intended to organise some sort of subversive activity in Britain. Furthermore, the fact that he had so many English addresses in his possession indicated that he expected his stay in Britain to be a long one.

Other agents who succeeded in getting through the RVPS

There were two other Norwegian agents who managed to pass through the reception centre at the RVPS and were only picked up later. The first was Helmik Wallem, recruited by the Bergen Abwehr in March 1941 when he was a wireless operator on ships plying to German ports.[11] He refused an initial proposal to go to Britain on their behalf, and instead agreed to spy on Norwegian activities, trying to find out about arms dumps and attempts to escape to Britain. However, in June 1941 his fiancée became pregnant and he needed money, so he agreed to go. He was instructed to familiarise himself with conditions in Britain, and then to offer his services as a wireless operator. The Abwehr hoped that he would be sent back to Bergen with a wireless set, which could be used against the British. He had been paid NOK 100* on his initial recruitment and a further NOK 1,000 when he agreed to go to Britain. His fiancée would receive NOK 300 when he was away, and he would be paid NOK 10,000 on his return. He left Bergen on the *Hernie* on 5 July with two refugees (Georg Lunde and Inge Nilsen) to give him cover, and arrived in Lerwick on 8 July 1941.

After interviews at the RVPS, all three were cleared and released on 17 July. Wallem joined the *Cetus* as a wireless operator and the other two joined the Norwegian Navy. On 25 July, SIS circulated an ISOS report showing that the Abwehr in Bergen had been preparing to send over an agent named Nilsen by boat on 5 July: it proved possible to establish that the *Hernie* was the only boat which had left Bergen on that date. The three were arrested and taken to Camp 020. This was a close call, for by then the *Cetus* had sailed to the Tyne and was preparing to leave as part of an Atlantic convoy. After several interrogations, Wallem eventually made a detailed confession and revealed that his spy name was actually Nilsen, so clearing his fellow passenger. In a report to B1, Stephens revealed that 'Wallem himself states candidly that the object of his mission was to come to England where he would certainly be employed by the British Secret Service to return complete with a wireless transmitter to Bergen, where he was to recontact the German Secret Service'.

Stephens also noted that after his release from the RVPS, Lunde had been interviewed by Commander Smith at Norway House and asked to train as a wireless operator and return to Norway, an offer which he had accepted. A similar offer was made to Wallem by Nagell shortly afterwards: he did not accept – a fact which counted in his favour when he eventually admitted it after his arrest. He may also have helped himself by revealing details of another Abwehr spy, the

---

* Allowing for inflation, the equivalent of about £200 at 2019 prices.

Swede Karl Hanssen, who had arrived on the *Volga* in March 1941 and was already in detention. Summarising this investigation, the Security Service concluded:

> The case illustrates the serious dangers which exist of the Germans pen-
> etrating this country through Norwegian escape parties and the great
> difficulty which is experienced in detecting agents who are sent here
> and who do not carry on them any incriminating property. In this case,
> it must be frankly admitted that had it not been for the information
> from MSS, Wallem would never have been apprehended and would
> have been in a position to do incalculable harm, seated at the key of a
> wireless transmitter aboard a ship proceeding overseas in convoy. The
> technique adopted by the Germans in this case was much superior to
> the usual run of expeditions which they have launched from Norway.

Wallem was detained for the rest of the war and then deported to Norway.

The other agent who passed unhindered through the RVPS, much later in the war, was Henrik Larsen.[12] He had been a deckhand on a Norwegian whaler captured by a German raider in January 1941 and was sent back to Norway. He was recruited by the Abwehr in April 1944 and persuaded to go to sea again. His early missions were to report on shipping in Norwegian coastal waters. Later in 1944 he was sent to Sweden to report on Swedish military organisations and their general state of preparedness. He did this by sending letters to his wife, Ruth, using secret writing. He was paid NOK 400 a month, which was given directly to Ruth. However, he was arrested by a Swedish patrol when trying to cross back into Norway. Larsen gave the Swedes a plausible cover story about attempting to escape from Norway, which he then developed sufficiently to enable him to be flown over to Britain in January 1945. He spent a brief period at the RVPS and was released in early February.

Larsen came to attention when SIS wrote to the Security Service on 19 March, stating that Larsen had worked for the Germans in the past and might still be doing so. A Norwegian counter-intelligence officer in Stockholm had informed them that he occasionally obtained copies of lists compiled in Oslo for use by the German censorship authorities. One stated: 'Hans Larsen, Norwegian refugee in Sweden in contact with Ruth Larsen, Solhagen i Sandar, Sandefjord. Uncensored to 144'.[13] SIS concluded that this suggested that Larsen had accepted employment with German intelligence and was using his wife as a cover address. They suggested that he should be sent to Camp 020. Larsen was first taken to the RVPS as it was initially judged possible that there could be an innocent explanation for the evidence against him. However, in his possession was found a letter from Ruth, in which she complained that his writing was indistinct – a comment which could be construed to mean that his secret writing message was not clear. He was therefore taken to Camp 020.

Following interrogation at Ham, Larsen confessed to his espionage activities and admitted that he had written to his wife on several occasions. As a consequence, action was also taken against her: she was arrested in Oslo on 16 May, after the German surrender. Neither Larsen nor Ruth, who also eventually owned up to her involvement, acknowledged that any of his letters to her had contained secret writing messages – but that may have been because both realised that such an admission would make the case against them much more serious. No trace of secret writing was found in any of the letters which she had retained, though presumably any letters of interest would have been passed to the Germans. Larsen was deported back to Norway in June, and was sentenced to seven years' hard labour.

Brodersen avoids a trial for treason

One lucky Norwegian, Knut Brodersen, came within a whisker of being put on trial for treason at the Old Bailey, where he would have certainly been sentenced to death. (The only Norwegian to have been sentenced to death for espionage in wartime was Alfred Hagn in 1917. He was given a royal pardon by King George V and his sentence was commuted to hard labour.[14]) Brodersen was recruited by Abwehr officer Horst Fanger in Bergen in September 1943 after a black-market deal had gone wrong. He agreed to go Britain, enlist in the Norwegian Army and report by secret writing on preparations for an Allied invasion of Europe. He was also trained in coding and would receive instructions from Fanger by radio. His family would be paid NOK 800 a month, while he could live on what he earned as an officer. Unlike almost all the other Norwegian agents, when he was despatched in December 1943, he was sent to France (where he spent a brief period in the guise of a Todt worker*) before travelling on to Spain, where he contacted the Norwegian embassy.

Reporting his arrival in Madrid in January, Nagell informed the Security Service of Brodersen's Nasjonal Samling background and recommended that he be excluded. SIS then reported in mid-February 1944 that their station in Madrid had confirmed that he had been working for the Germans both in Norway and also in Bayonne. They had known of his mission from ISOS, and there are details of the preparations for his journey contained in ISOS extracts on his file.[15] SIS wanted him brought to Camp 020 for interrogation and so informed Nagell. Milmo agreed and told the Home Office that such interrogation could provide details of the many German agents who had transited Bayonne on their way into Spain. Philby in Section V of SIS wrote to Hart in B1 suggesting that if Brodersen was found to be in possession of secret writing materials when he arrived in Britain, then consideration should be given to using him for deception purposes, an idea which was toyed with for several months.

Brodersen arrived in Leith on 6 May 1944 where he declined under initial questioning to reveal anything about his espionage mission, and was taken to Camp 020. Confronted with detailed knowledge of his activities he confessed, answering all the questions put to him and explaining how the Abwehr would communicate with him. A

---

*   The Todt organisation was a large German civil and military engineering group, responsible during the war for projects in occupied Europe, which relied quite heavily on forced labour.

search of his belongings and person revealed that he was carrying secret writing (SW) materials variously concealed in: a hollow tooth, under a toe nail, in the knee band of his plus fours, under the stud of a boot, in his spongebag and in his suitcase. When reviewing the case, the Security Service considered whether Brodersen could be used for Double-Cross purposes: 'insofar as contre-espionage [*sic*] is concerned, the question arises whether Brodersen's services are worth more than the deterrent effect of a sentence of death for espionage at the present time'. In deciding to recommend prosecution, the Security Service noted that Brodersen had had chances to admit to espionage during meetings with both Norwegian and British authorities, but did not take them, and only did so when he reached Camp 020. They concluded that there were no mitigating circumstances. However, difficulties now arose because SIS had intercepted radio messages in code from Norway which followed the form and times which Brodersen had given as applying to instructions which he and other agents in Britain might expect to receive. Although Brodersen's code had been fully described by him at Camp 020, it was not possible to make sense of the messages. Brodersen, in frantic fear of death, could make nothing of them either. Consideration was given to getting him to send a letter in secret writing demanding clarification. Such contact might lead to a Double-Cross link which might assist in apprehending other spies trained in the same as yet undecyphered code. But this was not a straightforward proposition.

It eventually proved possible to break the code which the Abwehr was using: it was a slightly different system from the one which Brodersen had described. The legal process therefore moved forward and, on 13 June, Sir Edward Atkinson, the Director of Public Prosecutions, recommended that the case should go ahead. The trial was scheduled to start at the Old Bailey on 27 June. Then legal problems arose. Brodersen's solicitor said that they would wish to present evidence showing that Brodersen had been warned by the master of the ship on which he was travelling to Scotland, that he would be sent to jail or detained.

This could have caused him to say nothing to anyone beforehand when he was questioned. Further, he would want at least one of the officers from Camp 020 to be available in court. The Security Service did not agree to this, arguing that half of their information about German intelligence came from interrogations there, and their interests had to be protected. Moreover, on reviewing the statement made to Brodersen which induced him to confess, it was concluded that it was tantamount to a threat. The Attorney General decided that the case should not proceed, and Brodersen was confined to Dartmoor prison for the remainder of the war. Impatient messages continued to arrive from Fanger demanding a response and threatening that his payments to Brodersen's family would soon cease; they were ignored. Brodersen was returned to Norway in June 1945. In May 1947 he was sentenced to fifteen years' hard labour for treason.

Further German attempts to infiltrate agents into Britain from Norway
The Germans also sometimes used Norway as a base to infiltrate their agents into other countries, or to land other nationals in Britain, unsupported by Norwegians. For example, in June 1940, Wilhelm Preetz, a German, was landed in Eire by submarine from Bergen. He was arrested there in August.[16] And in August 1940, F. C. Hansen, a fanatical Danish Nazi working for the Abwehr officer von Finckenstein, transported four Danes including one Børresen, who had been trained in Oslo, from Ålesund to Scotland. The Camp 020 history records that Børresen was picked up and taken to Camp 020, but there are no further details available about him nor any mention of what happened to the other three Danes.

There were plenty of other rather clumsier German attempts to send agents from Norway over to Britain. The first involved Karl Drucke, a German, Werner Walti, a Swiss radio operator, and Vera Eriksen, who was apparently half Danish and half Russian-Polish, who were delivered to the Scottish coast by a flying boat operating from Stavanger and landed by dinghy on 30 September 1940. They were dropped a long way off the coast and had to jettison their bicycles to keep afloat while they rowed for three hours to get ashore. They were ill-prepared, with poor documentation, attracting attention because of their bedraggled appearance and ignorance of their whereabouts, and were quickly arrested. Drucke and Walti were executed. Eriksen did not stand trial, and both the reasons for this and her subsequent fate after wartime internment attracted much colourful, even lurid, speculation. Her Security Service file describes her as a pathological liar, who admitted that she had worked as a Soviet agent in the early 1930s, but contains no reason to explain why she was treated differently at a time before the Double-Cross system was established, when the Security Service would have had good reason to make an example of any German spy whom they caught.[17]

The next party also arrived by dinghy, landing on the Scottish coast on 25 October 1940. It comprised Otto Joost, a German, and two Norwegians – Legvald Lund and Gunnar Edvardsen, a journalist whom the Security Service considered to be a man of intelligence and education. They were even more ill-prepared, with no papers and little training or briefing beyond an instruction to cut telephone wires with the insulated pliers with which each had been provided. At the time of their landing, the Abwehr in Norway expected that the invasion of Britain would take place within three weeks, so did not think any further preparation or precaution was necessary. They were quickly captured, and then claimed that they had intended to give themselves up. Although some Security Service officers wished to invoke the Treachery Act against them, they were treated leniently and interned. After the war Edvardsen was sentenced to two years' hard labour, though Lund was acquitted.[18]

After these early and rather crude attempts, the Abwehr changed their approach and began to attempt to infiltrate their agents among genuine parties of refugees, a tactic which represented a more serious threat. In early March 1941 the *Volga* arrived from Bergen with six people on board, two of whom, the skipper Peder Øien and Karl

August Hanssen, aroused suspicion. It was established that Øien had obtained a briefing from the Germans on his route through the minefields, and did not have a permit to leave port, or even a fishing licence. He appeared to be answerable to Hanssen, a Swede who had been a waiter for fourteen years at the Hotel Norge in Bergen which was a known centre of German espionage prior to the occupation and well used by Germans and quislings. On the journey over, Hanssen's behaviour had aroused the suspicion of other members of the party. Moreover, on arrival in Camp 020 he was denounced by Wallem, who had already confessed to being a German agent. Wallem claimed to have seen Hanssen in Bergen in the company of Martin Hjørnevik who had recruited him, and they had gone together to visit another quisling, Huse. However, despite these adverse indications, the Security Service found insufficient evidence to charge Øien or Hanssen. They were therefore interned for safekeeping instead.[19]

When assessing German espionage planning, the Security Service found worrying parallels between the mission of the *Olav* and that of the *Tånevik*, which arrived in late April 1941 crewed by Bjarne Hansen, Hans Anton Hanssen, Henry Torgersen and Johan Johansen Strandmoen. Identification of these Abwehr agents did not depend on ISOS, but on the chance sighting of Bjarne Hansen at the RVPS by Bjarne Jørgensen, who had recently escaped from Norway and who denounced Hansen as being a man whom he had known in Ålesund as a German agent. Under interrogation, Hansen admitted that the *Tånevik* had been sent to Britain by Angermeyer, with whom he had been associated in smuggling activities over many years. In the summer of 1940 Angermeyer used Hansen as a recruiting agent and asked him to find men for a job on the French coast which would involve taking small craft to Britain to land spies. Hansen put this to Strandmoen who accepted. He acted as crew on a cutter which landed the German spy Charles van den Kieboom on the Kent coast. Van den Kieboom was later executed. In July 1940 Angermeyer also ordered Hansen and Torgersen to go to the Shetlands on the *Boreas* to find out about shipping. Hansen said that they laid up in Norwegian fjords and did not fulfil their mission, although they were well paid for it.

The Security Service had difficulty in working out what they were tasked to do. ISOS messages had merely provided advance warning of the operation, without identifiable details of the crew members. B1 speculated that the powerful wireless receiving set found on board was to be used to receive information about rendezvous for agents at sea. The crew eventually admitted that they had been in German pay for several months and their mission was to return with general information. All four were interned. B1 concluded that the case showed a certain lack of organisation and coordination on the part of the security authorities in Britain, since the similarity of the two expeditions should have drawn attention to the suspicious features of the *Olav* leading to the earlier detection of Johansen and his crew.[20]

The last potentially significant case in 1941 involved Gustav Rønning and Martin Olsen, two seamen who arrived in the Faroes with their families on the *Arnvid* in September. ISOS had given some indications beforehand, but it was only when Rønning admitted during interrogation that his spy name was Frithjof that it was possible, through an examination of ISOS records, to establish the extent of what he had done for the Germans. He had been recruited in July 1940 and tasked to take a German agent to Iceland, though this attempt was thwarted by poor weather and the apparent reluctance of the agent to carry out his mission. Thereafter, Rønning worked quite assiduously, sailing up and down the coast to try to investigate attempts to escape to Britain, and questioning dependants of the men who had managed to get away in an attempt to gather information about who was behind them. Olsen assisted him in these enterprises.

At the end of a protracted investigation, Milmo provided a summary of the case to the Norwegians in November 1942. He concluded that they were a pair of scoundrels. While there was no evidence that they were guilty of any espionage attempt against Britain (and the fact that they had brought their families with them was a point which helped them to prove this), they had, on their own admission, worked for the best part of a year for the Abwehr and had not hesitated to accept money and carry out at least some of the commissions given to them. Since these consisted largely of informing against loyal Norwegians who were trying to escape to Britain or otherwise assist the Allied cause, there was every reason to regard them as traitors against their own country. They were detained for the duration.[21] There was one further Norwegian arrival in 1941. Svend Hammerun, who was Norwegian by birth but an American citizen, arrived from the United States in November 1941. He had been recruited by the Abwehr, who intended to use him as a double-cross agent. However, he developed cold feet and gave up the idea.[22]

The next case, involving Alex Cappelen, did not occur until September 1942, and took a considerable time to resolve. Cappelen arrived in Stockholm earlier in the summer. He admitted to the Norwegian legation at the first opportunity there that he had joined the NS for a period in 1940, though was struck off when he did not pay his dues – but added more significantly that he had been a contact of Astrid Dollis, a notorious informer for the Germans.[23] She had paid him NOK 6,000* and given him a mission to perform in Britain. However, the Security Service was informed that the Norwegian legation had evidence that when in Stockholm Cappelen had written a letter to Dollis, and had also visited some German offices. It was never possible to substantiate either of these allegations, and after a lengthy interrogation at Camp 020 Stephens judged that in the absence of any plausible evidence, there were no longer grounds for keeping him there. However, he could not be released to the Norwegian forces and so Stephens sought advice from Nagell as to what should be done. Nagell recommended that Cappelen should continue to be interned, and SIS took the same view – so he remained in detention until his deportation in June 1945.[24]

It was not always easy for the Security Service to determine whether

---

* Allowing for inflation, £12,000 at 2019 prices.

ISOS material could be depended upon to provide conclusive proof of an intention to commit espionage. One such case involved the *Reidar*, which arrived in Lerwick on 8 January 1943. ISOS information had already reported that a fishing smack of that name was due to leave Ålesund on an Abwehr mission. It strongly suggested that one of those on board was a German agent. Shortly afterwards, a further ISOS report revealed that in October 1942 the Abwehr office in Oslo had approved the expenditure of NOK 13,000* on a ship purchase, and provided confirmation of a notification in late November that *Reidar* had been bought. All three crew members were therefore taken to Camp 020. Arnold Evensen quite quickly confessed that he had been a German agent for some time (actually since August 1942). Although there were initially divided opinions in B1 about the loyalty of the other two, it was eventually accepted that they were innocent and they were released.

Evensen, who was of limited intelligence and had difficulty in telling his story both consistently and coherently, said that he was sent to Britain to be recruited as an agent and sent back to Norway with a transmitter. He maintained that what he really wanted to do was to return with two transmitters, one to hand over to the Germans, and one to operate on his own. He appeared to be trying to make out that he was acting as a sort of freelance double agent. The Security Service might have been inclined to believe this but for other rather fragmentary evidence showing that he had done something similar before, when trying to penetrate another organisation working for the Allies in Norway.† So he remained under suspicion and they considered it quite probable that he was attempting 'some sort of ingenious triple-cross'. This was never resolved, but the Camp 020 authorities eventually concluded that he was innocent, and had intended to declare that he had worked for the Germans, but now wanted to work against them, on arrival in Lerwick. They judged that there was no evidence that he wanted to spy, and that equity demanded that he

---

* Allowing for inflation, approximately £26,000 at 2019 prices.
† The nature of this organisation is not further described, but was most likely SIS.

should be released – but never put in a place from which he could contact the Germans again during the war. There were some strong disagreements about this, but Milmo and director-general Sir David Petrie finally accepted the recommendation. Evensen was found a job in Allardyce Bakeries, to which he was released in August 1943. The Norwegians were given a detailed copy of the final reports prepared by Camp 020, which were as usual sanitised with all indications of ISOS reporting being removed.[25]

Nikolay Hansen, a Norwegian coal miner who spoke almost no English, arrived by parachute in Aberdeenshire on 30 September 1943 with material for secret writing hidden in his teeth, two wireless sets (one German and one British), £120* and a spade. He had been sentenced to twenty-one months in October 1942 for theft from the German naval stores where he was working, and after seven months was visited in prison by Lieutenant Winter of the Abwehr's Bergen office. Hansen agreed to work for him to avoid the rest of his sentence. The original idea was that he should go to Svalbard and transmit weather reports, but then it was decided to send him to Britain. Hansen was not keen on this change of destination, but since the alternative was to go back to prison, he had no choice but to accept. He was told to bury the German set, and give himself up with the British set, saying that he had been trained as a spy but had no intention of working for Germans. Once the British authorities were convinced of his sincerity, he was to get himself a job as a miner, dig up the second transmitter and start reporting. He was tasked to obtain intelligence on military and naval matters, especially those concerning landing craft, convoy movements and aviation. If he had to reveal his second set, he was to report by secret writing to addresses in Sweden, and would receive instructions by radio, which Germans said could be picked up on an ordinary receiver – though Security Service experts said that this was impossible.

On landing, Hansen gave himself up with both sets and because he

---

* Allowing for inflation, worth about £5,160 at 2019 prices.

admitted a connection with the Abwehr, he was sent to Camp 020.[26] He claimed to have no intention of working for the Germans, but did not reveal the secret writing materials in his tooth. Even when this fact (though not the tooth) had been drawn from him, he repeatedly denied having been given a cover address. Under pressure, he eventually revealed this, then later disclosed that he had a second cover address for use with secret writing and, finally, that he had a third, which he claimed to have forgotten. He also admitted at a late stage that he had a further supply of secret writing material hidden elsewhere, and that the Germans had foreseen that he might have to give up both sets and had provided secret writing and cover addresses for this eventuality. Not surprisingly, it was judged that he was still acting on German instructions. He tried to explain away his failure to disclose the details of his secret writing by maintaining that the Germans had threatened to take reprisals against his wife if he did not. Prosecution of Hansen was considered, but it would have been necessary to include testimony from officers serving at Camp 020. The Security Service was of course reluctant to do this, but submitted the case to the Director of Public Prosecutions, who decided against proceedings.[27]

How many Norwegian agents were there?

How many attempts did the Germans make using Norwegians, or Norway as a base, to operate against the British? It is hard to make a conclusive judgement because they are not all easy to categorise. Although ISOS was generally able to provide compelling evidence, some cases were judged to be inconclusive. Moreover, there were others where a full investigation was not possible, but where there was a reasonable presumption of attempted espionage. One such case was described during a post-war interrogation of Horst Fanger, the Bergen-based Abwehr officer who had sent Brodersen to Britain.[28] When he was interrogated in June 1945, Fanger named another of his agents, Henry Amland, stating that he was ready to go to England. However he claimed Amland had disappeared at the last minute.

This was contradicted by Borghild Marie Prestøy, who had worked for Fanger and provided him with facilities such as accommodation addresses. Prestøy said that she had helped Amland to leave by sending him to certain intermediaries who could arrange his passage. The first attempt had failed, but she thought the second in December 1943 had succeeded. He returned early in 1944. Prestøy was then arrested by the Germans for having been in touch with people who had come from Britain, but was held only briefly: she thought that Fanger had arranged her release. Fanger later confirmed to her that Amland had gone to Britain on his behalf. The summary report on the work of the Abwehr Bergen station stated that it had sent two agents to Britain in December 1943. One would have been Brodersen, and there is no ISOS evidence of another agent leaving Bergen in that month. Thus, while the evidence is inconclusive and there is nothing to show how and if Amland got to Britain, what he did there and how he got back, it seems at least quite possible that Fanger's statement that Amland had 'disappeared at the last minute' was an attempt to protect him and that this may have been a case which was not picked up by ISOS.*

There was also Eigil Dag Robr, who arrived in Britain in September 1941, having been given a priority seat to get him out of Sweden, accompanied by warnings from the British military attaché Colonel Reginald Sutton-Pratt and others that he was very suspicious. Robr stated that he had been held in prison by the Germans, but this was not substantiated. During his initial reception at the RVPS Robr's teeth (which he claimed had been badly bashed) were checked, but

---

* A rather less credible case involved Marina Lee, who was Russian by birth, but Norwegian by marriage. According to a statement by Van Wijk, a Dutch agent detained in Camp 020, who obtained the details from von Finckenstein, she was a highly valued and experienced German agent who had worked for the Germans for some five years. The file shows that she apparently somehow managed to gain access to Auchinleck's HQ in Tromsø and by that stage Auchinleck was doing so well that General Dietl was thinking of retreating into Sweden. However, Lee obtained details of his plans, which enabled Dietl to rearrange his defence and to defeat Auchinleck. Lee appears to have spent some of the rest of the war in Spain, and never came into Allied hands. The Security Service merely noted these details and made no attempt to evaluate the credibility of the statement, which seems implausible. They kept records of her in case she was subsequently used by the Russian Intelligence Service: she was put on the ports watch list after the war. (TNA, KV 2/2381.)

little evidence was found of any damage. Moreover, Gleditsch reported on 14 October that he had given sixteen people away to the Germans, all of whom had been arrested. He was sent to Camp 020, where Stephens' conclusion is worth producing in full:

> Over two years many evil people, both traitors and spies have been through here, but I doubt whether there has been a character more vile than that of Eigil Dag Robr. His record is almost beyond belief, for he has confessed to us the names of nineteen fellow Norwegians whom he betrayed to the Germans for a total of NOK 700, or 35/- a head.* The total number may be even greater, but due to pressure of time, and having regard to the fact that we have put the halter 19 times round the neck of this quisling, and the fact that the Gestapo background of this case has been cleared to our intelligence satisfaction, we deem it wise to call a halt to the enquiry. The enquiry was a war of attrition, and for a time Robr was in fear of consequence, but with the resilience of the true gutter-snipe he regained his poise and as quickly turned to duress as an alternative defence and his attitude changed from aggression to that of martyr. He was completely lacking in remorse.

Robr was interned.

Another possible case involved Inge Karl Furre, the son of George Furre, who worked for the Abwehr for over four years and was involved in a number of operations to bring Norwegians over to Britain. He was the subject of much ISOS reporting. Inge Karl was an uneducated seaman who worked for his father and escaped into Sweden in order to avoid compulsory labour under German orders. The Norwegian consular authorities facilitated his travel to Britain as a prospective candidate for the Norwegian Navy. He was identified once he arrived at the RVPS, and transferred to Camp 020. Confronted with the evidence, he confessed and made many admissions about his father's

---

* Allowing for inflation, equivalent to £75 a head at 2019 prices.

work, including that he had been the nominal owner of a German boat in a fleet of six which coasted in Norwegian waters, with German operators and transmitters on board. The authorities concluded that his admissions gave evidence of the extent to which his father had been a spy. They further judged that at that stage of the war, as an espionage case it was of no interest to them.[29] From a treachery point of view, however, it would be of interest to the Norwegians, who could deal with it in due course.*

If we also include two double-agent cases which are described below, then there were nearly twenty cases which could be considered as serious German attempts to plant an agent in Britain. This was a remarkably high number compared with those sent from elsewhere in Occupied Europe. Although the Security Service was probably justified in their disparaging assessment of the quality of some of the first Norwegian agents who were despatched by the Abwehr, a number of the later arrivals were more determined and of a higher calibre. They could have done considerable damage if not uncovered by a mixture of careful investigation and, sometimes, luck.

Double agents

Many readers will be familiar with the Double-Cross operation, where a wide variety of double agents were used to plant misleading intelligence on the Germans, and a celebrated Norwegian example is worth consideration, too. But the Germans also tried it.

Tor Gulbrandsen (Anchor) was trained by SOE and sent back to Norway, through Telavåg, in February 1942. He was surprised by the Germans in Drammen on 3 May, attempted to escape, but was badly wounded and left temporarily paralysed from the waist down. In the course of a lengthy interrogation by the notorious Gestapo chief Siegfried Fehmer, when already weak from his injuries, Gulbrandsen was gradually worn down. Fehmer impressed on him the advantages of

---

* George Furre was shot in error by a German sentry later in the war.

collaboration and allowed him to meet an elderly Swede whose life had been spared because he agreed to work for the Germans.[30] Gulbrandsen agreed to collaborate, and provided a considerable amount of information about the identities of members of the resistance (which led to widespread arrests in Drammen in July) and operations as well as details of SOE, its organisation and its training facilities. He then agreed to return to Britain, having participated in a staged escape, when he was purportedly showing the Germans the location of an arms dump in the woods outside Oslo. He made his way to Sweden and was returned to London.

In the meantime, SOE had been alerted to some of the errors which Gulbrandsen had made before his capture. A refugee in Stockholm stated that Gulbrandsen had made many serious mistakes: he had lived partly with his parents, whose neighbour was a notorious German sympathiser; he got in touch with his fiancée; he dealt with things which were outside his province, even though sometimes successfully; he insisted on using his real name rather than his cover name with direct contacts, and he wrote down their names in a pocket book which was on him when he was arrested.[31] In September, Wilson wrote to Tronstad about Gulbrandsen, observing that although he did not know 'Stor Tor' himself, he had noted reports that he was an intelligent and brave man – but that he suffered from a feeling of self-sufficiency, which made him inclined to resent the advice and warnings of others. He pointed out that this had implications for the selection and handling of others being sent to the field.[32]

When Gulbrandsen returned to London and was interrogated about what happened, there was probably a greater degree of willingness to believe his story in view of the injuries which he had suffered. He maintained that he had managed to destroy his notes and his codes, and had given away only a few names. Wilson was convinced that Gulbrandsen was not withholding information, and Christopher Harmer in the counter-espionage section B1B informed both SIS and SOE that 'one is bound to consider the possibility that this may be a cleverly designed cover to facilitate the entry of an enemy agent into this country. I am however convinced that this is not so in this case.'[33] However, he gradually became less certain and noted that he was unable to avoid the impression that Gulbrandsen was holding something back. But without an admission from Gulbrandsen, it looked as though the case would be closed, and the Security Service would simply recommend that he should not be sent back to Norway. Their investigation was temporarily confused when adverse information was received about someone called Gulbrandsen who appeared to have been operating in another area. On 27 June 1942, Liversidge informed Nagell that SIS had received reliable information that their Bergen operation and some of its agents were in grave danger of imminent arrest, because it had been penetrated by 'an employee, Gulbrandsen, who has reported all their movements to German intelligence'. He suggested that all communication with the organisation should be stopped.*

However, the answer was provided by the return of Ernst Kirkeby Jacobsen (Crow), an SOE wireless operator who had been arrested in Østfold in July 1942, and who had been persuaded by Fehmer to continue to operate his set. SOE knew that he had been arrested, and went along with the Abwehr attempt at deception, so as to help Jacobsen. Remarkably, he was sufficiently trusted by the Germans to be released in November and allowed to live with his family, though he was kept under observation. He took advantage of the Christmas

---

* (Letter from Liversidge to Nagell, 27 June 1942, Riksarkiv, hereafter RA, Nagell box 15.) The file register for KV 2/829 in TNA shows that the first paper on the file, dated 29 June 1942, was a cross-reference to Gulbrandsen, which was dated 29 June 1942, but the document itself has not been released. This may have been the letter from Liversidge. An extract from the second document, a report on German intelligence activities in Norway dated 1 July 1942, states that 'Tor Gulbrandsen, arrested by the Germans has given (probably under coercion) information about an Allied intelligence operation operating in the Kvikne district.' Harmer referred to this latter information, which he described as 'coming from an unimpeachable source', in his report on the first interrogations of Gulbrandsen in later November, but does not refer to the Bergen information. It therefore looks as though by then he had been able to work out that it was a coincidence that another person of the same name had come to adverse attention at almost the same time. It is not clear whether this information came from an Abwehr source which SIS was running in Norway (which will be further described in Chapter 8) or from ISOS.

holiday period, when he knew that German vigilance would be lower, to escape with his family to Sweden and was brought back to Britain. Jacobsen informed the Security Service that the Gestapo had told him that Gulbrandsen had given information to them, and that he had been allowed to escape. Confronted with this at a court of enquiry, Gulbrandsen quickly confessed and admitted the extent of the information which he had given up.[34] The ordeal which he had suffered no doubt contributed significantly to his lenient treatment, and Gulbrandsen was not interned. He continued to be employed by SOE. Although some historians believed that Gulbrandsen was interned for the duration,[35] for much of the rest of the war he was employed as an instructor at STS 26, the Norwegian training school in the Scottish highlands. Indeed, he was so trusted that in July 1944, Bjarne Øen the head of FO.IV, the Norwegian military office which worked with SOE, wrote on behalf of the Norwegian High Command to ask whether he could be used in a scheme to protect hydro-electric facilities in Rjukan and nearby valleys, and whether he could be allowed to leave Britain for such a purpose before Norway was liberated. Although Wilson supported the idea, SOE decided reluctantly that it should not be pursued because it would not be acceptable to the Security Service.[36] There is a curious footnote to this story. In July 1946 Asbjørn Bryhn wrote to the Security Service, asking whether the Norwegians could have a copy of the report of the Court of Enquiry about Gulbrandsen. They were planning to prosecute him and needed the report to help prepare their case. A copy was provided, on condition that it was not published or used during his prosecution. In the event, there was no prosecution and Gulbrandsen went on to enjoy a long career in the Norwegian military.[37]

This was not the only known instance when a captured agent was turned by the Germans and allowed to escape and return to Britain, there were others from France and elsewhere. So it was to be expected that any further agents who claimed to have escaped from German custody would be the objects of extreme suspicion. Herluf Nygaard, who worked for the Lark organisation in Trondheim, was captured on 16 December 1943 and escaped three days later. Despite the absence of any proof, the Security Service, which had had its fingers burned by Gulbrandsen and knew of other unsuccessful cases, was extremely reluctant to accept that he had not cooperated with the Germans. This led to a protracted disagreement with SOE.

Nygaard underwent a series of interviews over a period of several months with members of both SOE and the Security Service. Internal minuting demonstrates the extent to which the latter were determined to find evidence which would show that he had indeed come to some arrangement with the Germans, and that even if this proved impossible, to ensure that he should not be allowed to return to active duty with SOE. This culminated in an interview with Geoffrey Wethered, a Security Service officer on secondment to the security section of SOE, who adopted a bluff technique to try to elicit an admission from Nygaard. It did not work – but the Security Service nonetheless concluded that there remained a sufficient element of doubt in the case to justify their suggesting that he should be posted elsewhere. This proposal incensed Wilson, who wanted to retain Nygaard's services as an adviser for the Trondheim area, believing that it was not for the Security Service to decide how Nygaard should be employed. He added that there was no news of anyone having subsequently been arrested, even some six months after the original capture of Nygaard. At this, the Security Service relented, and Nygaard was permitted to return to training for a future deployment.

However, that was not the end of the matter. In September 1943, Øen obtained a list containing names of people allowed extra rations from the Trondheim *Vinmonopolet* (to the present day the only Norwegian organisation permitted to sell wines and spirits), which appeared to be a reward for services to the Germans. Nygaard's name was included. This provided grounds for further Security Service investigation, and put Nygaard under the spotlight again. He was suspended by SOE. Nygaard, not surprisingly, was unable to provide a sufficiently plausible explanation for the appearance of his name on the list to enable him to be exonerated. SOE's station in Stockholm provided explanatory details, including the fact that the list was dated after March 1943, by which time Nygaard was in England, and that the security police used cards in the name of arrested people in the *Vinmonopolet* as a matter of course. Moreover, the Norwegian High Command pointed out that his family had been arrested and were still detained – unlikely treatment if Nygaard was working for the Abwehr. Despite repeated representations from Wilson, these arguments were insufficient to persuade the Security Service to change its mind.

In early July 1944, Wilson obtained some further evidence in .the form of a report from Reidunn Havnevik Årsæther, who had met the Nygaard family in prison and stated that Nygaard's father and brother had been sent to Nordland to do hard labour. Faced with this additional information, Wethered gave in and replied that the security case would now be closed, and that they would no longer oppose Nygaard's employment in a confidential capacity. He asked how Nygaard would be used. After consulting Øen, Wilson replied that he wished to send Nygaard to reinforce the Grebe party who were covering the railway in the Østerdal valley. The Security Service agreed to this plan, but requested that the officer in charge of the reinforcement should be told to give Nygaard special attention, and to see that as far as possible he was not sent to make local contacts. In the event, he did not go on this mission. Nygaard instead accompanied Tronstad, as leader of a section in the Sunshine party, which was deployed to prepare to protect Norwegian strategic installations, and which left Britain on 4 October 1944. There is nothing to show that Wilson informed the Security Service of this change of plan. Nygaard did have some further contact with the Germans: he was staying in a hotel in Høydalsmo in the west of Telemark in April 1945 when they raided it. Nygaard was forced to shoot his way out, and escaped unharmed.[38]

Compared with the number of attempts they made from elsewhere in occupied Europe, it is remarkable that the Abwehr tried only twice to organise double-cross operations from Norway.* There is no evidence either that they made any attempt to use captured SIS agents for this purpose. There were however a number of cases when SIS agents were captured and managed to escape. A notable example concerned Otto Olsen, responsible for the Otto and Sol networks, who had been involved in setting up all the SIS stations around Stavanger and had much knowledge of operations in the area, who was arrested in September 1944. An SIS attempt to organise his release (Operation HUGORM) proved not to be feasible. A later SIS report noted that Olsen had broken down and was 'furnishing the Gestapo with much assistance' and that the whole SIS organisation from Egersund to the southern approaches to Bergen had collapsed.[39] It is not clear where this information came from: some time after their arrest Olsen and his colleague Ragnar Mack were put in the same cell, and developed a plan to win the trust of the Germans by appearing to cooperate with them so that they could then escape. Someone may have been taken in by their artifice and reported it. They persuaded the Germans to take them out to search for cached equipment and escaped, with Mack even managing to remove the crystals from their radio set which had originally been confiscated, and to take them with him. They spent most of the rest of the war out in the mountains: frozen, ill-clothed and half-starved. They managed to make contact with a member of the Sabor station, and asked him to pass a message to London that they had escaped and were in hiding. SIS replied asking for more information, warning that they were highly suspicious of the genuineness

---

* The other case was a clumsy attempt to use Harald Konrad Aaberg, who was involved in the Workers Sporting Association in Trondheim. Although Aaberg was not involved, the association had a good courier service to Sweden, and the Lark organisation had tried unsuccessfully to use it. In August 1942 Aaberg was arrested by the Germans, for no obvious reason. After six days' interrogation with beatings, when he admitted his interest in money, he was released on condition he would work for them. He invented a story of a contact in Sweden, and was driven to within a mile of the border and released. On crossing, he gave himself up. The Security Service were not satisfied with his story, but he was eventually released and sent to STS 24, where he did poorly on an SOE training course, and in view of this and the lingering Security Service doubts about him, was released to serve in the Norwegian Army. (TNA, HS 9/1/1.)

of their escape. So Olsen and Mack received no help.[40] They took no further part in resistance activities until shortly before the liberation.[41]

Mutt and Jeff

The activities – and the very significant achievements – of the XX Committee (or the Twenty or Double-Cross Committee), have been well described in a range of wartime histories. They do not need to be rehearsed again here,[42] beyond mentioning that the committee worked closely with the Security Service and SIS, and depended heavily on intercept material so as to be able to monitor the progress of their operations, and to adapt them if necessary. The only successful Norwegian agents were John Moe, nicknamed Mutt, and (briefly) Tor Glad, nicknamed Jeff. Mutt was born in London, and was British by birth. Jeff was recruited as an Abwehr agent shortly after the invasion, to do counter-espionage work. When working in Oslo in the censorship department, he met Mutt and got him a job, too. Both agreed that they wanted to pass information to the Allies, though were uncertain about how this could be done. They were recruited to go to England and given training in communications and sabotage. Arriving in Scotland in April 1941, they gave themselves up straight away. On interview, Mutt made a good impression, but Martin Linge, with some prescience, thought that Jeff showed instability and lacked any sustained purpose. Nonetheless, they were judged to be suitable for use together in a deception operation, and the Security Service wrote to the Home Office in May asking for their detention orders to be suspended. In order to prevent their conscription, it was decided to tell the Norwegian government that they were working for the British, but without going into details.

However, Mutt and Jeff did not operate in tandem for very long. Jeff's continued indiscretions caused increasing concern, particularly after an incident in a pub in Aberdeen which led to the police being called. This led to the decision to intern him in August 1941, as it was not judged essential to the continuation of the case that Jeff be at liberty and there were recordings of his wireless transmissions and style of operating. He ended up in Dartmoor, and was returned to Norway in June 1945. He was detained for a further six months, but the case against him was dropped for lack of evidence. It has been suggested that British intelligence intervened to ensure that this happened,[43] but there is nothing in British files which confirms this.* Mutt carried on alone, and his Security Service handlers devised a series of reasons to explain Jeff's absence to the Germans, based on his notional postings to other parts of the country and to places where he could not keep in touch with Mutt.

The Security Service carried out several security reviews of the case, which they did not expect to last for long. So they developed a series of plans designed to push over one more deception before its credibility was destroyed. However, for over two years these deceptions built up, rather than destroyed, the case. Moreover, the Germans continued to respond to requests for further supplies and explosive materials. In February 1943, they dropped another transmitter to Mutt, and a further drop took place at the end of May when they provided money and explosives to be used to blow up an electricity station near Basingstoke. Interestingly, the explosives included six MD1 magnetic clams which had been filled with plastic explosive by SOE and were still in their original SOE wrappers! Mutt told the Abwehr that the consignment had been discovered and asked for another one. This was subsequently provided, and the case continued. However, over the next few months, the Security Service gradually detected a loss of German interest and by 1944 it was no longer productive. Chapter 8 goes into further detail on how an Abwehr source later provided some insights into the reasons for this.

---

* In September 1945, *Morgenbladet* incorrectly reported that Jeff had been sentenced to four months' imprisonment. What is more, the article also revealed that both Jeff and an unnamed Norwegian friend had been released after their initial arrest and given the task of sending to the Germans some false messages which were composed by the British counter-espionage authorities. This was more than twenty-five years before Masterman first wrote publicly about the Double-Cross system!

Not many Double-Cross agents were permitted to undertake sabotage to enhance their credibility with the Germans, though the staged and phony attack on the de Havilland Mosquito factory by Eddie Chapman (Zigzag) in early 1943 is a well-documented exception. However, Mutt was helped to undertake a series of sabotage operations, the first of which was actually genuine. Carried out in November 1941, it was called, with some humour, Operation GUY FAWKES, and involved setting off two bombs in a flour store in Wealdstone. Another example of a staged attack was Operation BUNBURY, where the plan was to sabotage a generating station at Bury St Edmunds in Suffolk. It took place in August 1943, with the prior agreement of the local authorities and the connivance of the manager of the station, and was described as a complete success.

The value of this aspect of Mutt's work is shown in a paper of September 1943, which stated that the counter-sabotage section wanted to obtain information on German sabotage activities. It noted that the only sure sources of intelligence on this subject came from ISOS, the Gibraltar Double-Cross network – and Mutt and Jeff. But while this was an important task it was not their only contribution, for they played a part in deception too. They reported on troop movements and civilian morale, with Mutt purporting to have joined the army and Jeff allegedly being used as an interpreter during the questioning of refugees who had arrived from Norway. They also played a part in deception before Operation TORCH, the invasion of French North Africa in November 1942.

Mutt and Jeff provide the only example of Norwegian involvement in the Double-Cross network. However, there were quite a few other cases where it was considered: several Abwehr agents such as Brodersen were assessed as potential candidates before they were judged unsuitable. Some work was also done to explore the feasibility of sending deception messages to Ernst Kirkeby Jacobsen, passing on rumours of a possible Allied landing in Norway, and to consider whether Gulbrandsen could be used to send misleading messages to his Abwehr contacts. Neither was straightforward: Jacobsen's return scotched the first plan, and Wilson discouraged the use of Gulbrandsen because of his concern about the possibility of misleading the resistance as much as the Germans.

The fertile minds of B1 also came up with at least one other idea using Norwegians, which had not been tried before. This was plan Prudential, where Harmer envisaged the possibility of sending an agent back to Norway to give himself up and offer to work for the Germans. He broached it with Wilson and John Senter (the head of SOE's security section) in April 1943. He discovered, not unexpectedly, that Wilson was not very keen on the idea, and could not think of an agent who might be suitable. Wilson also raised a series of practical difficulties concerning timing (the short summer nights would soon be a hindrance), and the risk of arrest by the Swedes if they tried to send such an agent through Sweden. He did not wish to use one of his existing courier routes because of concerns that it would be given away to the Germans – and also foresaw a problem of devising a safe means of getting a wireless set safely into Norway. The idea was not taken forward.[44]

What did the Abwehr achieve?

So, what was the Abwehr in Norway hoping to achieve through their operations in Britain, and how far did they get? One assessment of their objectives compiled by the Security Service shows that there was a lack of consistency in what they sought from their Norway-based agents, as well as a lack of coordination with tasking given to agents operating from elsewhere. One of the main reasons for this was the lack of central control. Each Abwehrstelle (Ast) or station was independent, and there was no division of targets between them.[45] Thus, while there was considerable interest in obtaining weather reports from Greenland and Svalbard, only one pair of Norwegian agents had been tasked to provide weather data in Britain – though, for example, Gander, the codename of a German who arrived in October 1940 and was briefly used as a double agent, did have such tasking. The main focus appeared to be on penetration of British or Allied services leading to a return to Norway as a British agent, and sometimes the commission of minor acts of sabotage. An updated assessment in June 1942 observed that an earlier prediction that the main German interests would be in supplies coming to Britain from the United States, naval shipping and intelligence on the northern route to Russia, and the strength and equipment of British Army and British food supplies, had been partially correct.

There was a careful examination of the tasking which has been given to double agents Mutt and Jeff: it was noted that they had been asked for a report on the 4.5-inch anti-aircraft (AA) gun and the use of the Kerrison Predictor with the 4cm Bofors gun and had also been asked urgently and in great detail for a report on the organisation of AA command, how many corps were included in it, how many brigades formed a normal AA division, whether the personnel were drawn from the Royal Artillery or also from the Royal Engineers, and whether there were still AA battalions and companies attached to the reserves. It acknowledged that perhaps this flood of questions was produced by the fact that Mutt was ostensibly now in the army and in a good position to report this kind of information, but the persistent recurrence of the same question put month after month to different agents implied a very high level of German interest – and a lack of other well-placed sources too.

Abwehr operations – particularly during the early period in 1940 – were generally quite clumsy. Their main objectives were very short-term and linked to an invasion of Britain, so would have been arranged in a hurry. They gradually acquired a rather greater degree of sophistication, not always necessarily matched in their selection of agents, and took greater care in the methods they used to try to infiltrate their Norwegian agents into Britain, and by equipping them with means of communication, which (especially secret writing materials) had a better chance of success. They were frustrated by two insurmountable disadvantages. First, the success of the Double-Cross operation. Unlike Britain and her Allies in their operations in many parts of occupied Europe, they could not depend on agents in Britain to give them reliable information to help them plan more effectively: their only information came from Double-Cross agents which would have misled them. Secondly, ISOS reporting gave the Security Service an enormous advantage, by alerting them to most of the operations which the Abwehr was planning, and enabling them to be wrapped up before they could cause damage.

In 1945, E. J. Corin, who had spent much of the war in BıB, wrote a report on the work with the Norwegians, Danes and Dutch. He observed that Security Service liaison with the Norwegians was smooth from the outset and was never seriously troubled:

> We had complete confidence in their officers and were able to pass them information which one would have hesitated to give to certain other allied security services. Internal political troubles arose in Norwegian circles, about which we were frequently consulted, and so friendly was the atmosphere that we were invariably able to give advice without committing ourselves and in cases not directly connected with security, were able to tell the Norwegians the British channels through which they should apply for assistance.

He added that the Norwegians were very security minded, and frequently embarrassed them by making requests for the detention of Norwegian nationals who had been connected with NS in Norway. The Home Office, however, were unwilling to detain aliens unless evidence could be brought showing that they had continued their anti-Allied activities in Britain. With the exception of a few very bad cases, which became the subject of detention orders under the Aliens Order, the Security Service had to explain to the Norwegians that any action which they might want to take would have to wait until after the war. Corin also observed that relations with the Norwegians were much more

straightforward than they were with their Dutch and Danish counterparts. Cross-currents and intrigues within the government created
problems for them with the Dutch, and since the Danish king and
government had remained in Denmark, they had to rely on some rather
delicate contacts within the Danish community in London.[46]

It should be pointed out that we have very little information about
the Norwegian view of this relationship. There are notes on most of
the KV case files drawn on here, which show that at least a summary
report was passed to them. These also reveal that in many – though
not all – cases a Norwegian officer was permitted to interview detained Norwegians, though usually at the Oratory schools and never at
Camp 020. However, a diligent search of the likely hiding places in the
Riksarkiv and the Hjemmefrontmuseum has failed so far to unearth
documents describing Norwegian policy or reactions. If the papers
have indeed been retained somewhere, then the most likely explanation was possibly Norwegian awareness in the early post-war period
of British sensitivity to any public mention of Camp 020. This lasted
for some time after the war, and might have influenced a decision that
they should not be released. There would not have been a sensitivity to
ISOS and ISK reporting, as this subject had carefully been excluded
from all material passed to the Norwegian side, so they would not have
been aware of it.

CHAPTER 6

SECRET ALLIANCES
TAKE EFFECT
1941–1942: CREATING A PRODUCTIVE
RELATIONSHIP

I shall be much obliged if your Excellency and M. Lie will help me in
a matter to which I have been giving my personal attention. I am told
that it is the intention of the Norwegian Government to withdraw from
Stockholm their Military Attaché Captain Roscher Lund. This officer has
been of great service to the British intelligence organisation in Sweden,
and his presence there is of special value to Her Majesty's Government and
to the Allied cause as a whole. I realise that the case presents difficulties.
Nevertheless, since this is a question which affects not only the Norwegian
Government but the general war effort, I sincerely hope Your Excellency
and your colleagues may feel able to reverse the decision which has been
taken. It is a matter to which I attach great importance.

Letter from Churchill to Nygaardsvold, requesting him to
overturn his decision to withdraw Roscher Lund, who had
provided the first intelligence about the attempted break-
out of *Bismarck* into the North Sea in May 1941.[1]

In the course of 1941, over 4,000 Norwegians arrived in Britain.
Many of them had successfully completed the often dangerous jour-
ney across the North Sea. Others had travelled much further via the
Middle East or even the Far East and America in order to take part in

the war. These numbers strained the refugee reception facilities at the Royal Victoria Patriotic School, which, in some instances, led to errors being made, as in the case of Ingvald Johansen. In general, though, the arrivals were a welcome addition to the pool of willing volunteers for the Norwegian armed forces from which SIS and SOE were able to recruit. In early 1941, SOE were attempting to recruit between twenty and twenty-five Norwegians a month for their work. Martin Linge approached General Fleischer for permission to form an independent company, whose recruits would all be members of the army and subject to its rules and regulations but not under its command. This was granted and the Norwegian Independent Company No. 1 (NORIC) was formed. After the death of Linge in the Måløy raid in December 1941, it came to be known as the Linge Company. The organisation built up by SOE operated independently – both of Milorg in Norway and also of the Norwegian government in London. Its longer-term objective was to arrange a general uprising in Norway, which did not coincide with the aim of Milorg to slowly build up a secret army which would prepare for the day of liberation. As a result, throughout 1941 and for much of 1942, relations between SOE, the Directorate of Combined Operations, and both the Norwegian government and Milorg were not straightforward. And neither were Norwegian relations always straightforward with the rest of the British government, for example over propaganda – as will be considered in due course.

Naval intelligence requirements for the Admiralty – the value of Roscher Lund

The tide of war was also not going in favour of Britain and her Allies during this period. The Germans were consolidating their control over the extensive areas of Europe which they had occupied, in addition to launching an initially successful attack on Russia in June 1941. In the Far East, the Japanese were also making gains, sinking *Prince of Wales* and *Repulse* in December 1941, to the consternation of Churchill. After the war, he wrote 'in all the war I never received a more direct shock.

As I turned over and twisted in bed the full horror sank in upon me.'[2] Two months later, the Japanese also captured Singapore. The sinking of *Bismarck* in May 1941 had been a rare piece of good news.

Rear-Admiral Godfrey, the DNI, had been critical of SIS achievements up to the end of 1940, observing that there had been an almost complete lack of useful intelligence. He did, however, acknowledge that it took time to establish the kind of coverage which was required. Communications difficulties as well as a shortage of suitably qualified and trained personnel did not help, which meant that for nearly four months between May and August 1941, Skylark B in Trondheim was the only active SIS station in Norway. The naval attaché in Stockholm, Henry Denham, was often producing more valuable reporting than SIS did at this stage. He had an extremely effective relationship with the Norwegian military attaché. Ragnvald Roscher Lund was able to exploit a range of close contacts with members of the Swedish General Staff, who had developed detailed coverage of German naval activities.* He regularly passed their information to Denham. It was Roscher Lund who, on 20 May 1941, provided Denham with intelligence obtained from the Swedes: reporting that two large German warships (which proved to be *Bismarck* and *Prinz Eugen*) had been sighted sailing northwards through the Kattegat, towards the North Sea. Denham's report to the Admiralty started the search which led to the sinking of *Bismarck* on 27 May.[3]

Nonetheless, SIS intelligence subsequently also made an important contribution. Skylark B reported that on 22 May three German destroyers had sailed into Trondheim. The Admiralty was able to work out that these three destroyers had been escorting *Bismarck*. The fact that they were now detached was a clear indication that *Bismarck* was intending to break out into the Atlantic. Shortly afterwards Skylark B received a message from SIS headquarters which read, 'Congratulations

---

* The Swedes covered other significant areas too. For example, they tapped some of the lines between the German High Command in Berlin and their headquarters in Norway, which passed through Swedish waters (TNA, ADM 223/489.)

on the quick transmission of the report on the three destroyers. Keep it up.' It was only some forty years later that one of the members of Skylark B discovered why their report had been so important, when he read a book written by one of the German officers who survived *Bismarck's* sinking, which described the ending of the destroyers' escort duty. Security concerns had prevented Skylark B being told at the time.[4] Such considerations meant that it was rare for an SIS station to be informed about the value of any really significant intelligence which it had provided. An exception occurred when Theta, in Bergen, reported on 23 January 1942 that *Tirpitz* and six destroyers had been observed in a fjord close to Trondheim on 20 January. It was photographed there by RAF reconnaissance a week later. Theta received an enthusiastic response from Eric Welsh in London: 'Our heartiest congratulations. We are proud of you. You have shortened the war.'[5] While Welsh was premature in predicting the consequences, the message marked the beginning of SIS coverage of *Tirpitz* in Norway, which continued regularly until the warship was finally sunk in November 1944.

Unfortunately the productive relationship between Denham and Roscher Lund did not last much longer. In early June 1941, Denham learned that Roscher Lund was being recalled to London. This created a wider problem for the Norwegians. Sweden had decided that legations of foreign countries occupied by the Germans were not to be increased in size, and that new arrivals or replacements would not be recognised. The fact that Roscher Lund's successor Ingvald Smith-Kielland was an old friend of Foreign Minister Christian Günther made no difference. Denham told Mallet that he regarded Roscher Lund's continued presence in Stockholm to be vital to him. The British tried hard to persuade the Norwegians to reverse their decision and to find ways of leaving him in place. Mallet made representations to Günther, and Eden instructed Cadogan (the Permanent Under-Secretary) to approach Lie – but all without effect. Eventually, in early September Eden wrote to Churchill and asked him to meet Lie himself. Churchill went one better and wrote to Nygaardsvold, explaining (more frankly than Eden had advised him to, because the Norwegians in London were not thought to be aware of the extent of Roscher Lund's activities) precisely how Roscher Lund had been of value to British intelligence. He took the unprecedented step of asking that the decision to withdraw him should be reversed. Nygaardsvold replied that although Roscher Lund was urgently needed in London, the Norwegians would be willing to allow him to remain as assistant to Smith-Kielland if the British could ensure that Smith-Kielland was recognised by the Swedish government. Further British attempts to achieve this were unsuccessful, and Roscher Lund left to assume overall responsibility for Norwegian intelligence in Britain. He was replaced instead by Major Ørnulf Dahl, who was already serving in Stockholm.[6] The difficulty in resolving this, and the time it took, caused Churchill to decline a suggestion by Eden, made at the instigation of Lie, that he should meet Nygaardsvold for a general discussion of the progress of the war.[7] They eventually lunched together in February 1942, when Churchill optimistically assured Nygaardsvold that Norway would be the first occupied country to be liberated.[8] The departure of Roscher Lund had an immediate impact in more areas than just the passing of intelligence. For example, Stockholm complained to SOE that land communications with Norway had been disrupted after Roscher Lund had left: the clandestine post boxes which had been established on the Swedish border were no longer working properly.[9]

Chapter 8 examines how the intelligence gap caused by Roscher Lund's departure was filled by the development of reporting from SIS coast-watching stations. For now, it will suffice to say that Godfrey judged that the quality of SIS work gradually improved during the latter part of 1941. In January 1942, he wrote to the Chief of the Naval Staff that 'in the past two years great progress has been made, and a new organisation is flourishing in Norway, Belgium and Holland and France. NID is well served at key points on the Norwegian coast.' SIS work was further improved by the appointment in January 1942 of a senior Marine officer, John Cordeaux, who had been running NID3

covering the Mediterranean. Godfrey hoped he would improve reporting there, but he was given responsibility for Scandinavia instead.[10]

Propaganda problems

It makes sense here on the grounds of coherence to consider problems
with wartime propaganda in one section. Commenting to the Foreign Office in August 1943 about a difficult meeting with Lie when he
and deputy head of SOE Harry Sporborg had discussed propaganda
proposals which proved unwelcome to the Norwegians, Wilson wrote
from SOE that 'it is a curious fact, but true, that it has proved more
difficult to secure cooperation for the distribution of Allied propaganda than it has been to secure cooperation for various enterprises which
are liable to endanger the safety and lives of local people in Norway'.
He referred for example to Operation CARHAMPTON, when in January
and February 1943, an SOE force of forty men was looked after near
Flekkefjord by local Norwegians, who provided them with accommodation, transport and medical attention.[11]

The paradox highlighted by Wilson's comment neatly encapsulat-
ed the difficulty which faced the two governments. The question of
who should exercise control over the dissemination of propaganda
in Norway was for both sides one of the most consistently complex,
difficult and divisive which they had to confront. Although a *modus
vivendi* was eventually achieved, it was one which achieved more for
Norwegian interests than for British objectives. For the Norwegian
government in exile, especially Prime Minister Nygaardsvold, the
question of control over propaganda was essentially a matter of sovereignty. After the disastrous defeat following the German invasion
in 1940, the government was predictably concerned about its standing
back at home. It wanted to be able to regulate the message which was
presented to Norwegians, so as to help to strengthen its position there.
It also needed to manage satisfactorily its relationship with Milorg –
and, for its part, Milorg wanted to be responsible for the conduct of
the propaganda campaign in Norway.

The main propaganda objective of the British government was to ensure coordination of the message which was to be transmitted to enemy countries and countries under German occupation, as well as Allies, to ensure that it was consistent and to prevent the Germans exploiting any discrepancies. A number of factors combined to make this difficult to achieve as far as Norway was concerned. For one thing, there were too many different organisations involved, which did not necessarily all have quite the same aims and which did not always work well with each other – in particular the Ministry of Information, the BBC, the Political Warfare Executive (PWE), SOE and the Foreign Office. There were also some quite sharp clashes of personality. Furthermore, there was an undue emphasis on security which meant that the Norwegian government was not informed about certain propaganda operations affecting their country. This led to significant Norwegian ministerial displeasure when the facts were eventually uncovered. A few select examples will illustrate the difficulties which all these factors caused.

Control over broadcasting

In August 1940, the BBC, Ministry of Information and Norwegian government agreed the arrangements which would govern broadcasts to Norway. PWE did not come into existence until September 1941, and was therefore bound by the terms of a deal which allowed both for Norwegian announcers to be seconded to the BBC without coming under its administrative control, and also for Toralv Øksnevad, the Norwegian government's chief announcer, to advise on all talks in Norwegian. The PWE official historian wrote that:

> Political Warfare [i.e. propaganda] to occupied countries proved ... both far easier and more effective than to Germany, since the majority in every occupied country hated the Germans and respected us for continuing the fight. Nevertheless, there were certain handicaps from which propaganda to the enemy was free. Hasty agreements had been

made with the refugee governments as a result of which they were entitled to carry out their own propaganda to their own peoples. The Norwegian government had exclusive rights, though all governments had 'free time'.[12]

Øksnevad was not an easy colleague, for he was seen by both BBC colleagues and PWE officials as being autocratic and high-handed.[13] Similarly, the Norwegians found Thomas Barman, the PWE official responsible for Scandinavia, equally difficult to deal with. In October 1941 Charles Hambro reported to the director-general of PWE, Robert Bruce Lockhart, that Lie considered that although Barman's parents were Norwegian, the fact that he was born abroad meant that he was neither Norwegian nor British, and was therefore prone to make mistakes in judgement. Lie had suggested to him that Barman no longer be responsible for Norway. At the same time, after Barman had proposed the formation of a committee chaired by Nygaardsvold to discuss propaganda policy, Lie told Laurence Collier that he thought this would give Barman too much importance, and he would rather deal with someone else. Collier advised Lie not to press for Barman's removal unless he had definite proof that it was impossible to work with him.[14] The extent to which differences between Lie and Barman created a problem is illustrated by the fact that the main PWE file for Norway, FO 898/241, contains a folder of papers marked 'Barman–Lie controversy'. Nonetheless, Barman remained at his post until January 1943 – and even then his successor Brinley Thomas proved little more successful in developing an effective working relationship with Lie and his colleagues.

The Norwegians were perhaps as concerned about the quantity of broadcast time as they were about editorial control. It was the only subject raised by Nygaardsvold during his first meeting with Churchill in January 1941, when he complained that the BBC had reduced their main evening broadcast from fifteen to ten minutes.[15] Churchill undertook to look into this.* (This was at a time when Norway was allocated fifty minutes a day, while Denmark was allocated only ten.[16]) There were protracted discussions in the Foreign Office about the extent to which the Norwegians should be allowed responsibility for their own broadcasting, and how much time they should be allowed. They concluded that part of the problem was that Ivone Kirkpatrick in the Ministry of Information was not willing to respect Norwegian wishes. They believed he was concerned that allowing them more responsibility could result in 'an inferior output of news and propaganda' and that the Norwegians could not be trusted to align their broadcasts to the general policy of British government. This led to some tetchy exchanges, with arguments over the extent to which some Norwegian scripts had required censorship. When Kirkpatrick declined to accept Foreign Office suggestions, they invoked the instruction from Churchill. This enabled them to reach an agreement in April which both the Norwegians and Kirkpatrick accepted. It gave Norwegians the time they wanted, and sufficient control over output, while the Ministry of Information and the BBC retained ultimate responsibility for security and general policy. Peace did not last long, however, because the broadcasting section of the Ministry of Information influenced the BBC to change Norwegian broadcasting times to take account of Double Summer Time. Neither the Norwegians nor the Foreign Office were consulted. Christopher Warner, who had taken over Northern Department when Collier left to become minister to the Norwegian government, admitted that they had broken a definite assurance to the Norwegian government. The matter quickly escalated. Lie wrote to Collier to say that his government was seriously dissatisfied with the attitude of the BBC. When matters were not resolved, Lie complained again, saying that the Norwegians were not being

---

* Nygaardsvold brought this up because earlier representations from Colban to Collier in December had not been effective. It transpired that the changes had been made to accommodate more suitable timing for the Hungarians.

given their full entitlement of broadcasting time, allegedly because of a need to service the transmitters. He added that Norwegian engineers did not accept this, and claimed that the arguments being used were 'typical BBC humbug'.[17] This produced an emollient letter from Warner, and the restoration of the time which had been taken away.

The Norwegian Freedom Station

The best example of a British propaganda measure taken without Norwegian knowledge was the Freedom Station set up by SO1 (predecessor to PWE), which started transmitting in February 1941. The PWE historian commented that the need for such a station was strongly felt as the Norwegian government had complete control over talks, and the BBC bulletin was entirely given up to news: 'There was therefore no method of educating the Norwegians in the part they might have to play in liberation.'[18] After its establishment, PWE continued to run it, and the station put out more than 600 programmes before it closed down in December 1942. By a clever feat of wireless subterfuge, the station appeared to be transmitting from within Norway, but was actually located in England. Some of the programmes merely encouraged passive resistance, but a few were more activist. There was speculation that some of its transmissions in August and September 1941 might have incited Norwegian trade unionists to strike, an action which led to the execution of two of their prominent leaders, Viggo Hansteen and Rolf Wickstrøm, though this was denied by Barman. He emphasised that the Freedom Station had consistently refrained from inciting its listeners to greater opposition – maintaining that, on the contrary, they had told listeners to be extremely careful. Lie reacted strongly to the executions and told Hambro that 'if there is anything which can be considered as an effective reply to the Oslo incidents it is bombing, bombing and more bombing – and that immediately'. Hambro asked the Air Ministry whether this could be arranged, and combined with a leaflet drop to explain why the attack was being made, but the response was slow to come.[19] The Norwegians eventually worked out that it was PWE which was responsible for the Freedom Station. This came after a series of transmissions attacking the Norwegian legation in Stockholm because it was failing to do enough to support the Norwegian cause, an accusation which could reasonably be justified at that time. In September 1941 Lie confronted Barman, who admitted that the broadcasts originated in England. He undertook to keep him informed in future about plans for broadcasting. The station was closed in December 1942 because the Norwegian government refused to allow Norwegian staff to continue working there unless it was permitted to assume control over the running of the station.[20]

Despite their personal differences, Barman wrote a handsome (though possibly resigned) compliment about Lie in his autobiography. 'Of all the foreign ministers in London, none was more active or more pugnacious in his country's interest than Trygve Lie. No one resisted pressure, even Churchill's pressure, with greater vigour or determination.'[21]

Propaganda in Norway

PWE was responsible for disseminating white propaganda, which did not hide its origin or nature. SOE accepted responsibility for the distribution of propaganda in enemy-occupied countries – generally described as black propaganda – which disguised its origin to discredit an opposing cause. Its early attempts to cooperate with PWE to organise propaganda activities came to nothing, but progress began to be made when the Norwegian authorities were involved. Discussions took place in the Anglo-Norwegian Collaboration Committee (see below) during the summer of 1942, which led to the creation of the operational propaganda fieldwork scheme. This envisaged dividing southern Norway into ten districts, each of which would have its own three-man propaganda team. It was agreed that Milorg should be consulted about this plan, and Gunnar Fougner (Petrel) was sent to Norway in November 1942 to meet them. He reported that their reaction was positive. However, in February 1943 Milorg reversed its decision, and sent a letter stating that there was no need for such a measure, because they were better equipped to carry out propaganda than anyone who might be sent from Britain. They asked for just one instructor to be supplied.[22] Most of the agents who had been trained for propaganda were reassigned to other tasks. Some, in particular Max Manus and Gregers Gram, returned to Norway to carry out sabotage missions, but retained an interest in propaganda. Manus and Gram produced a series of reports on attitudes among the Norwegian population. Their first highlighted the extent of the apathy shown by many towards taking part in the war effort. Worryingly for SOE and PWE, they also commented on the lack of information about the British war effort, and observed that Russians appeared to be more widely admired in Norway than the British.[23] RAF Bomber Command, and later Coastal Command, did drop leaflets and occasionally small supplies of tobacco and coffee, but competing priorities elsewhere meant that these activities were never extensive enough to generate much attention or achieve a great deal.

After Barman had been replaced by Brinley Thomas, PWE made further unsuccessful attempts to gain Norwegian agreement for their more direct involvement, which, from November 1943 onwards, also included that of the American equivalent of SOE, the Office of Strategic Services (OSS). Although they were still unable to obtain the consent they sought, they did obtain a licence to work to undermine the morale of the German occupying forces. They had been doing some of this already. For example, a poster was put up in Oslo in September 1943. Purporting to have been signed by Terboven, it appealed to German military and civilian personnel to protect the Fuhrer by reporting and quashing any rumours regarding the state of his health and his failing capacity to direct the German war effort. The SOE Norwegian section history noted that it was subsequently sent to most of the large towns in Norway and that 'this particular work was undertaken with some enthusiasm'.[24] In the summer of 1943 SOE had also arranged for a series of posters to be put up, with a forged proclamation from the commander of German forces in Norway, von Falkenhorst, calling on his soldiers not to desert to Sweden in the hour of Germany's greatest need. They were effective, and desertions increased. Von Falkenhorst issued a statement that the posters were forgeries, but this was seized on by some Swedish newspapers which wrote that German denials of this kind deceived nobody, and it prompted derisive editorials.[25] There were other clever ideas to encourage desertion, too. In May 1944, Sefton Delmer of PWE drew attention to an SIS report about a PWE list of streets and towns in Germany which had been bombed, found by a Norwegian in a small town near Oslo. At the same time Delmer received a report of an Austrian soldier who had just deserted from Norway, who had in his possession exactly the same document, which Delmer described as very effective feedback.[26] There were other more hare-brained ideas, for example the spreading of stories about a new type of highly infectious Japanese gonorrhoea capable of being caught from infected clothing or towels, that do not appear to have had much effect.[27]

In early 1944 Manus and Gram developed Operation DERBY to attempt the systematic undermining of German morale, by the circulation of illegal newspapers and posters across the south of Norway. Their organisation grew to nearly 500 people, and they produced two newspapers in German, *Beobachter* and *Im Westen nichts Neues*. A similar operation, DURHAM, was carried out in the Trondheim area, though on a smaller scale. Both these operations were known to the Norwegian government, and to the Milorg leadership, but the latter were not involved in supporting their activities.

It is never easy to judge the effectiveness of propaganda. It is very rare to find out when and how propaganda actually has an effect, and examples of feedback such as those quoted by Delmer are quite unusual. It was dangerous for those involved in circulating propaganda, for they tended to be less well trained and security aware than those involved in sabotage. Many were arrested. Moreover the Germans, not surprisingly, reacted more sharply against those whom they suspected of involvement in spreading anti-German propaganda. There were mixed views within SOE about the value of propaganda work, with or without the assistance of governments in exile. The evaluation of SOE work in Norway concluded that 'owing to circumstances outside the control of the Norwegian section the history of propaganda operations in Norway was not so successful as most other branches of SOE activity'.[28]

Combined Operations raids on the Norwegian coast and Norwegian reactions

The spring of 1941 saw the beginning of Combined Operations raids on the Norwegian coast. The first was CLAYMORE, carried out in the Lofoten Islands in March. Its objective was to damage German controlled industry, to capture Germans and quisling collaborators, and to evacuate Norwegian volunteers back to Britain. The main force consisted of commandos, with some small assistance from the Norwegian Independent Company No. 1 (NORIC). It was judged to have been a complete success. The Norwegian High Command was neither informed about this operation in advance, nor any of the other major Combined Operations raids in Norway.

Combined Operations continued to plan and execute operations in Norway with larger forces which included NORIC participation. HEMISPHERE, in April, was an exception to the practice of excluding the Norwegians from planning, because the Norwegian High Command was briefed. This was a smaller operation which destroyed an important herring oil plant in Øksfjord. The attack was conceived by SOE but carried out by the naval destroyer *Mansfield*. No prisoners were captured, though the local quisling leader escaped. When the destroyer was sighted, he tried to shoot the lock off the door of his house in his haste to get away, but the bullet ricocheted and accidentally killed his wife.[29] December 1941 saw two further operations, ANKLET and ARCHERY. ANKLET was an ambitious plan to establish a temporary base on the Lofoten islands, from which attacks could be launched against German naval communications. The force was landed on 26 December and achieved limited success, but returned after just two days because it lacked air support. The force commander was concerned about his vulnerability to German air attack once he was informed that the Germans had moved a force of dive bombers to Bodø – about 100 miles or thirty-five minutes flying time away, with further reinforcements planned.* ARCHERY was an attack on Måløy on 27 December, which succeeded in destroying fish oil production factories, as well as securing further cypher materials and equipment which were of great value to the codebreakers at Bletchley. However Martin Linge, the inspirational commander of NORIC, was killed during the raid.

These operations helped to convince Hitler of the potential vulnerability of the Norwegian coast to Allied attacks, and led to his decision to send more troops there. They also produced a very strong Norwegian reaction. Lie had already approached Eden in November 1941, requesting that the Norwegian government should be informed in advance if any military operation was planned in Norway. Eden forwarded the request to Lord Louis Mountbatten, who reported that the Chiefs of Staff were strongly opposed on operational grounds, despite Eden's assurance that Lie was reliable. They eventually softened enough to agree that he should be told at the last moment, but only in the most general terms. Orme Sargent, Deputy Under-Secretary at the Foreign Office, was authorised to inform Lie of ANKLET and AR-CHERY a few days beforehand on 11 December. Lie did not take it well. He suspected that not just German bases, but also herring oil factories, would be attacked, and that Norwegian volunteers would be enticed to leave Norway, which would invite German reprisals. When asked,

---

* Churchill was displeased by the speed of the withdrawal, and commented to the Chiefs of Staff that 'ANKLET must be judged a marked failure, as it was abandoned hastily and without any facts being apparent which were not foreseen at the time of its inception and preparation'. When he learned that the First Sea Lord Dudley Pound sent a message supporting the decision to withdraw, he informed him: 'I do not remember that you made any such formal communication to me, and I was not aware that you intended to send such a telegram as this – which taken in conjunction with my telegram ... appears to indicate a relationship between us which I am sure does not exist'. Pound apologised. (TNA, PREM 3/47.)

Sargent also told him that so far as he knew, no Norwegians would take part in these raids. This turned out to be incorrect, as Norwegians from NORIC took part in both operations. The strength of the Norwegian reaction was demonstrated when their naval attaché refused to supply an English-speaking officer for ARCHERY when asked to do so by the Naval Intelligence Division. Jakobsen told SOE that he had explicit instructions not to supply any English-speaking Norwegian, no matter who might request it, unless the purpose for which he was required was set out in detail.[30]

Northern Department suggested that a single Norwegian should be selected to be briefed on all such planned operations in advance in future. The departmental head, Christopher Warner, believed that Norwegian irritation was caused not just because they disliked not being trusted, but also because they were concerned that the British might choose objectives to which they would actively object. To try to make amends, he arranged for Lie to be briefed on the outcome of the Måløy raid. Lie brought Johan Nygaardsvold and Oscar Torp with him. (Torp had replaced Ljungberg as Minister of Defence on 18 November.) Nygaardsvold expressed very strongly the view that such raids were futile, and that they provoked reprisals and involved matters of policy on which the Norwegian government should be consulted.[31] He expressed himself so forcefully that his secretary rang to apologise to the briefing officer for the position he had been put in, though made clear that the Norwegian government felt it had cause for complaint. His remarks certainly made an impact. Warner recommended that in future Torp should be briefed on such operations, and Cadogan wrote accordingly to the Chiefs of Staff. They agreed that Mountbatten would brief Torp, except for those matters in which he was not informed, when Ismay (secretary of the Chief of Staff Committee) would do so himself.[32] In order to try to ensure greater Norwegian participation, Torp also requested that a joint planning committee should be formed to consider future operations. This was agreed, though it did not meet often and never became a very effective tool.

Establishment of the Anglo-Norwegian Collaboration Committee
After the second unsuccessful Lofoten raid, and the death of Linge, morale sank among Norwegians working for SOE. Many of those in the Linge Company were unwilling to carry on without some sort of assurance from their own government that SOE's proposed activities had its approval. In fact, the British had already started to consider this. SOE had prepared a paper on 'Anglo-Norwegian collaboration regarding the Military Organisation in Norway', which was sent to Torp on 25 November. This reflected their growing awareness of the need to work together with Milorg, rather than in parallel with it, and for greater coordination of resistance activities.[33] When Hambro and Torp met to discuss it on 27 November, Torp said that it was essential that the Norwegians should have closer cooperation with the British. He believed this was prevented because the British believed that they could not do so without risk of leakage. Hambro agreed. Torp retorted that working under such a cloud was intolerable and that he would be willing to dismiss staff in order to ensure British trust. This led Hambro to warn Ismay that 'if we do not take the Norwegians to a certain extent into our confidence we shall lose their cooperation and we may lose the benefit of those specially trained Norwegian troops who have been so valuable in the past'. It was this frank exchange which opened the way for negotiations leading to the formation of the Anglo-Norwegian Collaboration Committee (ANCC), a body for the discussion of SOE operations with equal British and Norwegian representation, and with a British chairman. When, on 14 January 1942, Hambro wrote to Torp to confirm in principle their agreement to the ANCC, he provided an undertaking that SOE would not initiate operations in or against Norway without the knowledge and consent of the Norwegian members of the committee. The ANCC first met on 16 February 1942 and, after a short period of fortnightly meetings, met monthly thereafter. It added a welcome degree of coherence and structure to the development of common policies. There were two other significant personnel changes during this period. In January,

John Wilson was appointed as head of a new SOE Norwegian section, which was to be separated from the Scandinavian section to which it had previously belonged.* Also in January, the comparatively junior Major Wilhelm Hansteen was promoted to Major-General and made Commander in Chief of the Norwegian armed forces, which also proved to be an effective appointment.[†]

It was important for the Norwegian government to be able to participate as fully as possible in discussions about future operations in Norway, not just because of concerns over sovereignty, but also to maintain its position as the authority in control over resistance activities. Its standing was still affected by the disastrous campaign in 1940, its relations with Milorg were uncertain, and there were known to be concerns about whether it would seek to use its position to secure its own political future after the liberation of Norway. This latter point was resolved by statements in December 1942 and April 1943 which made clear that on its return to Norway the government would resign and a temporary replacement would arrange for early elections. The creation of the ANCC and the consequent improvement in relations between Milorg and SOE also made a difference. The ANCC did not simply deal with operational matters, but also played an important role in developing policy and resolving the misunderstandings and setbacks which occasionally continued to occur.[‡]

---

* In September 1943, Wilson was promoted to be head of the whole Scandinavian section.
† There were also some significant changes in the hierarchy of SOE at around this time. Dalton was moved and promoted to be President of the Board of Trade. He was succeeded by Lord Selborne. Jebb returned to the Foreign Office. He was replaced by Sporborg, though in a new position approximating to Principal Private Secretary. Sir Frank Nelson retired in May 1942. His position was taken by Hambro, until he was succeeded by Colin Gubbins in September 1943. The most important change on the Norwegian side was the replacement in December 1942 of John Rognes by Bjarne Øen as the head of FO.IV, a post which he held until the end of the war.
‡ Sometimes SOE agents were suspected of being collaborators. For example J. Gunleiksrud, the Anvil organiser, was nearly killed by Milorg who, when reassured about him, wanted to keep him under their control. Sometimes too, operations undisclosed to Milorg had adverse consequences and led to German reprisals and executions, such as those which followed KNOTGRASS/UNICORN, a combined operation mounted with NORIC assistance against Glomfjord power station in September 1942.

In May 1942 Hansteen attended a meeting because he wished to discuss SOE's role in the reconquest of Norway and to start to examine the coordination of activities in London, Stockholm and Norway and the division of responsibility and control between British and Norwegian officers in SOE training camps in Aviemore as well as in the Shetlands. He also stressed the vital need for a greater and better interchange of advance information between SOE and SIS in view of the disaster which had taken place in Telavåg (see Chapter 7).[34] Over the next few months, both Hansteen and SOE worked on longer-term plans for Norway, and reached agreement on policies which would allow for a much closer degree of cooperation between SOE and Milorg, with provision of SOE resources for training and supply of Milorg and its members, as well as direct radio contact with London. SOE would continue with sabotage operations, but with more limited objectives, and they would have a greater degree of freedom in the north, where Milorg had been able to achieve little.[35] Thereafter, there were better relations and better communication, to which the incremental benefits of SOE training would contribute. SOE arranged a visit for Hansteen, Crown Prince Olav and Leif Tronstad to SOE's training camp for Norwegians in Aviemore, STS 26, and also to Shetland, in October 1942. It went well. Hansteen said that he had not previously appreciated quite how much training was being done; he was impressed with the value of their work and the visit helped to inspire confidence.

These improvements were more than overdue. In terms of organisation, planning and effectiveness, none of the parties involved had hitherto achieved as much as they would have liked. For example, SOE's early planning was fairly crude – as sometimes was their grasp of detail. In June 1941, Dalton wrote to Churchill that 'in Norway we have created a trained secret force of considerable strength, to which we intend to supply arms as soon as the nights lengthen. This force, which includes a special company of parachute troops, is controlled by SOE HQ here by secret wireless.'[36] (No such parachute troops existed.

The first SOE agent to be dropped by air was Cheese in January 1942.) Shortly afterwards in July, he provided Churchill with an outline plan for September 1941 to October 1942. He anticipated that by October 1942, SOE would have recruited 500 men for sabotage groups in Norway and would be able to deploy an army of 19,000 men – producing detailed estimates of the large quantities of equipment which would be required. There is nothing, here or elsewhere, to show how these figures were worked out: they were unrealistic for this period.[37] During this time too, Milorg had its problems. Poor security and extensive overcentralisation made it vulnerable to German investigation, which led to many German arrests in the early autumn of 1941, mainly in Oslo, Trondheim and Bergen. Finally, there is a remarkable story of SOE highhandedness when in the summer of 1941 Milorg sent a letter to Britain for King Haakon, which described its views on the role it should play in Norway in keeping a low profile and preparing for liberation. It was not delivered to him but passed instead to SOE by John Rognes. Rognes was a former senior member of Milorg, recalled to London by Torp to work for the Norwegian High Command, who acted as a link between SOE and Milorg. Sporborg drafted a reply, which he called a 'directive', which emphasised the need for continued active resistance. He showed it to Lie and Fleischer. Lie assumed (but did not check) that it had been seen by Nygaardsvold, while Fleischer was quite satisfied with it. Both were content for the 'directive' to be presented to Milorg as an expression of the views of their government.[38] It was sent to Stockholm for delivery to Milorg on 8 August.[39] This was a telling example of Norwegian inability to exercise control of key elements of the resistance – as well as of SOE's rather autocratic assumption of the extent of its authority at that time.

Unlike SOE, SIS was never competing with an organisation based in Norway in this way, and so had a much easier run. There were other indigenous intelligence gathering organisations, but their objectives were different and so the risks of conflict were small. Indeed, from early 1943, SIS provided significant support and training for the largest of them, XU, as it developed. SOE accepted that their relationship with the Norwegians needed to be different from that of SIS. After the arrest of members of Skylark B and Milorg in Trondheim in September 1942 (caused by insecure links between them), Menzies' deputy in SIS commented:

> If we had never passed messages through Skylark B for the Norwegians, the service would probably have still been functioning. It was important and of great value to Admiralty ... If we were only to take bodies of different nationalities, work them ourselves and keep them away from their so-called national governments, things would go much better.

Hambro replied, 'I agree that SIS could and should work without the cooperation of the allied government concerned. I cannot see how SOE can work with the vast organisation that they require without the allied government concerned.'[40] Fortunately, Hansteen was able to develop the Norwegian High Command into a more effective organisation, better equipped to liaise with SIS. Relations between SIS and FO.II, and their respective section chiefs Eric Welsh and Finn Nagell, worked (in general) quite smoothly.

Interventions by Lie
In addition to propaganda and operations on the Norwegian coast, it is worth looking at a selection of the other areas where Lie chose to become involved, to understand the impact of some of his interventions. In May 1941, he suggested that ten Norwegians (including Sigurd Jakobsen, who had run SIS's first station, Hardware) sentenced to death by the Germans, might be exchanged with Germans held by the British. The matter became less urgent when their sentences were commuted, but by then SIS and the Security Service had become involved. The Norwegians still wished to know whether such exchanges might be possible in any future cases involving death sentences. SIS suggested that quislings captured during the Lofoten raids might

be suitable. The Security Service firmly ruled out the release of any Germans, but provided details of just two quislings who might be appropriate choices.[41] The matter was not pursued further. In November 1941, Lie asked Collier to urge the British to stop bombing herring oil factories, as he had evidence to show that the output of these factories no longer went to Germany in any form but was used for feeding Norwegian civilians, whose food situation was getting steadily worse. He argued instead for interfering with other German activities more vigorously than hitherto, such as exports of electrolytic copper, for which the Germans had recently built a new plant. Warner passed this to the Ministry of Economic Warfare.[42] In April 1942, he asked the Foreign Office whether they could arrange with the Admiralty for a warship to be sent to northern Norway to intercept the *Skjerstad*, which had left Trondheim for Finnmark with 500 teachers crammed on board, part of the group which would be forced to live in extreme conditions for a long period. Warner approached the Admiralty to support the request, but was told that it would not be possible to arrange anything in the time available.[43] This was not the only time the Admiralty was requested to intercept a ship on the Norwegian coast. SOE approached them in April 1943 to request assistance when the SIS station Upsilon in Tromsø reported on 10 April that those who had been arrested by the Germans in the aftermath of the ill-fated SOE Operation MARTIN were being transported later that day, under sentence of death, on the *Ragnvald Jarl* from Tromsø to Trondheim.[44] Once again the Admiralty was unable to help in the time available.*

There were other subjects on which Lie expressed himself more forcefully, for example, the extent of uncontrolled sabotage in Norway, which were thought to have been caused by the communists. In September 1942, Lie stressed the need for coordination of these actions to the Soviet ambassador to his government, Bogomolov, because of

---

* For more detail on this operation see Chapter 7.

concerns about German reprisals. He also told the Foreign Office that the Norwegians could not be expected to encourage sabotage so long as there was no British bombing of German installations in Norway. He wanted to see more of it. In the meantime, he thought it wise to go slow on sabotage. SIS were consulted about this, and in order to protect their interests, predictably felt that 'there is little to be said for encouraging the Norwegians to undertake isolated and uncoordinated acts of sabotage and violence ... which frequently cause the arrests of precisely those elements of opposition who would in the future be most useful to the allies'.[45]

Lie sometimes expressed himself more strongly to SOE than he did to the Foreign Office. For example, in November 1942, he told Hambro that he was very negative about Anglo-Norwegian relations. He had sent a message to the Ministry of War Transport saying that unless extra aircraft were made available for the Stockholm service, a key lifeline for both the Norwegian government and the British agencies, and a continuing source of contention, the Norwegian government would refuse to allow the Norwegian ships in Gothenburg to sail to Britain with their valuable cargoes. (These were consignments of ball bearings, used in the manufacture of aircraft engines and important armaments.) Hambro had actually gone to see Lie to try to persuade him not to make this stipulation, but was too late. Lie said he and colleagues thought they had been badly treated by Britain in the past twelve months. They had been promised many things by Churchill, in return for which they had given many concessions. But the promises had not been fulfilled. They needed better transport to bring back more Norwegian refugees to Britain. Hambro mollified Lie to some extent by telling him of the steps which were being taken with the various British ministries, and the constraints under which they were operating. But the lack of aircraft was a critical problem, and it took time before it was even partially resolved. In the meantime, Lie did not carry out his threat about the cargo ships in Gothenburg.[46]

Post-war bases in Norway

But Lie was not only interested in the conduct of the war. With a mixture of optimism and far-sightedness, by January 1941 the Norwegian government had set up a committee to consider what Norway might want from the post-war peace settlement. Lie told Dormer that for the maintenance of peace in the Atlantic it was essential that Britain, the United States and Norway should jointly be responsible for naval, air and military defence of Greenland, Iceland and the Faroes by having bases there – and both Britain and the United States should have bases in Norway. He returned to this theme quite frequently. The initial Admiralty response was lukewarm, but Sargent was much more positive. He noted that one of the major post-war problems would be to enable Britain to maintain its position vis-à-vis the continent. He judged that the failure of France would make American cooperation essential. He thought that Lie's suggestion might offer a practical means of achieving this – and that there might be similar Anglo-American bases in Portugal, Iceland and even Dakar.[47] Lie continued to plug away and spoke about his plan publicly in Oxford in November. By then, Collier concluded that there would be much advantage in committing the Norwegian government to certain principles of post-war collaboration and Lie's approach offered a good chance of achieving this. In December, Lie discussed his plans with Eden who was broadly positive but asked Lie what he thought about possible Russian involvement. Lie replied that he had considered that possibility, and was quite clear that he did not want Russia in the North Atlantic. He added, with further foresight, that part of the reason for suggesting an Anglo-Norwegian alliance was to be prepared if Russia were to present demands.[48] The Foreign Office remained interested, and Lie obtained positive responses when he broached the idea with the Dutch and Belgians. In April 1942 he told Collier though that he was aware that he was regarded as too pro-British – and advised him to avoid emphasising that side of the agreement which would involve the use of Norwegian bases by the British fleet. 'For God's sake don't talk about bases. Talk about mutual defence arrangements.'[49]

There was still a long way to go before the end of the war and, despite his enthusiasm, Lie was unable to maintain momentum for his idea. After the war he was elected the first Secretary-General of the United Nations, and Norway temporarily reverted to a policy of neutrality known as 'bridge-building'. In February 1948, amid growing tension following the takeover of power by communist governments in Eastern Europe, Norway decided to commit to the western defence alliance, which became NATO. But there were no foreign bases in Norway.

This was not the only area where Lie took such a forward position. He also started to suggest more aggressive actions be taken in Norway. For example, he proposed that fish-preserving factories in Trondheim and Bodø should be bombed – though he stressed that he was anxious that it should not get out that this was on his recommendation, because some of his colleagues were opposed to it. When Sargent queried this, he was told that the output of herring oil factories continued to be used exclusively for feeding the Norwegian population, whereas the product of fish-preserving factories went to Germany. Soon afterwards, SOE considered attacking four of these factories, which exported some 25,000 tons of frozen fish to Germany, and considered including an Office of Strategic Services detachment among the raiding parties. However, the mechanics proved to be too difficult, mainly because of the distances involved, and the plans were dropped.[50] Later, in March, Collier reported Lie's request for some bombing attacks in Norway to lift the morale of Norwegians who had been discouraged by the fall of Singapore as well as the undignified conclusion of the Lofoten raid. He thought that a few bombs on a German aerodrome would have a disproportionate effect and demonstrate continued commitment.[51] Sargent passed this on to the Chief of the Air Staff, pointing out that confiscation of radios made it harder for Norwegians to know what was going on. This exchange probably also helped to plant the seed which (following Lie's intervention about sabotage described above) led Wilson, a few months later, to suggest that the RAF should be

asked to bomb Victoria Terrasse, where the Gestapo had its headquarters, to disrupt a large rally planned by Quisling in September
1942 to mark the anniversary of his accession to power.[52] Following a
request by Selborne to Sir Archie Sinclair, the Secretary of State for
Air, the operation was carried out by four Mosquitoes and was very
successful. Hansteen wrote to Selborne to thank him, saying that the
raid would help to keep up the spirit of the Norwegian population.
'They are facing a hard winter and need all the encouragement which
can be given to them.'[53] Lie later told Collier that Quisling had been
furious because the Norwegian victims had been almost exclusively
NS members working for the Germans. The Air Ministry expressed
willingness to carry out further daylight raids with Mosquitoes, as they
saw their value. Wilson so informed Tronstad, but it proved difficult
to find another suitable target which was not too heavily defended.[54]

There was, however, one subject which neither Lie, nor Torp, appears to have raised with the British in London. This concerned the
wish to escape of General Ruge, who was interned in Offlag IV-B in
Königstein, Saxony. The British military attaché in Berne reported in
December 1941 that the Norwegian minister had told him about a
request from Ruge, which had been passed on by a recently released
French general. He stated that the Norwegians wished to discuss with
someone in London the possibility of providing Ruge with appropriate
travel documents and suitable advice on travel by train to Switzerland.
Northern Department noted that SIS had passed this information on
to MI9, the organisation responsible for the escape and evasion of
Allied prisoners of war, which was ready to provide suitable assistance.
They decided not to ask the War Office to raise it with Torp. In the
event, Ruge's circumstances changed and an escape was no longer possible for him.[55]

Foreign Office intelligence requirements for SIS
And what of the Foreign Office? It is sometimes argued that the role of
the Foreign Office is of less importance in wartime. This was generally

not so as far as its relations with the governments in exile of occupied countries were concerned. It was certainly not the case for Norway, where both Eden and senior officials sometimes played an important role in negotiating outcomes which took account of Norwegian concerns. However, in order to be able to do this, the Foreign Office needed to obtain independently as clear an idea as possible of the situation in occupied Norway, to enable it to understand the background to Norwegian requests and to decide how far to go in accommodating them. Even relatively early in the war SIS was sometimes able to help by providing reporting or comment, though it was not always accurate. For example, in April 1941 the American consul in Oslo reported (inaccurately, as it turned out) on German troop numbers in Norway, based on the quantity of ration cards which had been issued, and added that there was evidence that German forces were equipped with gas bombs. SIS was able to dismiss the gas threat, stating that they had investigated it in Oslo, Stavanger and elsewhere. In each case they had established that the supposed bombs were fuel tanks slung under aircraft wings to provide additional range.[56]

A letter to SIS from Anthony Nutting in Northern Department in December 1942 provides a rare contemporary insight into the difficulties which the Foreign Office faced, and the range of its interests. Though long, it is worth quoting in some detail:

> Herewith my questionnaire (14 questions) plus an explanatory footnote in brackets. I fear it is long, but it would be most useful if you could let us have as much information as possible on these lines since we are at present almost entirely dependent for information on the Norwegian 'E' Office* and Ministry of Foreign Affairs, with whom we maintain close collaboration and have no other source with which to check up. We of course realise the difficulties under which your people work with regard to Norway, but as we are constantly burdened with requests for intelligence

---

* *Etterretning*, or intelligence office.

on this country, it is of vital importance that we should have some other
source of information apart from our Norwegian contacts … We attach
considerable importance to information about the state of morale and
about political feeling amongst the population and local authorities in all
parts of Norway, especially in the north, west and south west.

1. General state of morale … with particular reference to pro-British,
    pro-German, pro-Russian, pro-Haakon or pro-Nygaardsvold gov-
    ernment; (there is little evidence of pro-German feeling, except in
    the area between Hedmark and the Trøndelag depression);
2. Opinion towards invasion, commando raids, air raids on towns,
    ports shipping and active or passive sabotage;
3. Any evidence of criticism of allied war strategy and impatience or dis-
    appointment at the long delayed opening of a second front in the west;
4. Any signs of an increase or decrease in underground activity, includ-
    ing communist and illegal press activities; (communist activity has
    been quieter of late. The illegal press suffers much from the difficul-
    ties of communications, which restrictions on travel have increased.)
5. Prevalence of radio sets and the effect of BBC and freedom broad-
    casts (very little is known about this, and we believe that radio sets
    are few and far between, but BBC news does seem to seep through
    especially in populated districts);
6. Feelings towards NS, the army of occupation (including Austrian
    troops), the German civil administration and the Gestapo; (we be-
    lieve … Austrians to be generally regarded as less evil than Germans.)
7. Feelings towards the labour front (especially trade unions), the in-
    tellectuals (i.e. church, teachers etc.) and communists;
8. Attitude of labour, the communists and the intellectuals;
9. Feelings about and any facts obtainable concerning the food situa-
    tion and the question of relief (this is the most knotty problem of
    all, since every report differs slightly from the other. On the whole,
    it is fairly definite that the situation is bad but not critical: the pop-
    ulation would naturally welcome relief but are probably prepared to

face another winter of privation without it, if it will hasten the end of the war);

10. Feeling and percentage of NS amongst the central and local authorities (including Government departments, police and town and county councils); (our information is that on the whole 60–70 per cent of local authorities are either quislings or pro-German. Proportions vary considerably, but in the last year quislings have succeeded in establishing themselves in control in nearly every part of the country.)

11. Any evidence of dissension in NS; (we have little definite information on this.)

12. Relations between the Quisling government and local authorities on the one hand and the German military and civil administration on the other; (bad and not improved by divergence between Gestapo and quislings.)

13. Attitude of German military and civil administration towards Quisling and the NS and any evidence of the former intending to secure Quisling's removal; (we have no concrete information.)

14. Evidence of Germans tightening the screw on the opposition. (it is clear that the Germans have given up their former policy of trying to win over Norwegians by subtle blandishments ... and are resorting to force.)*

There is no evidence to show that this list of requirements was copied to SOE, who were still providing quite regular reporting of their own, and who were by now beginning to be in regular contact with Northern Department. Their contacts were more extensive than those of SIS, which were generally limited to those connected with coast-watching stations. Shortly afterwards, when commenting on the extent to which

---

* Letter of 14 December 1942 from Nutting to G. Pinney, Passport Control Department, i.e. SIS. (TNA, FO 371/32826.) Pinney had been appointed an honorary attaché in Norway in 1930, but his position was terminated in 1931 and he did not thereafter appear in the Diplomatic List. There is, not surprisingly, no record of any reply to this letter.

the Norwegian population still favoured passive resistance – an attitude which was beginning to attract powerful criticism – Nutting observed that he was hoping to obtain further information from SIS on this subject in answer to the questionnaire which he had just sent them.[57]

CHAPTER 7

SOE'S SUCCESSES AND SETBACKS

OPERATIONS AND PROBLEMS 1941–1943

Press here quote official statement from Oslo that two German Secret Service police were shot on an island off Norwegian coast by certain Norwegians who had illegally visited England where they were equipped with explosives arms and sabotage equipment. As a reprisal 18 Norwegians captured some weeks ago when attempting to flee to England from Ålesund were executed. Strongly recommend immediate counter reprisal. Suggest form it might take is to select home town or village of German troops stationed in Norway, identity of certain divisions being known to us, and bomb it heavily irrespective of whether it can be classified as military objective. Fact that such bombing is intended as counter reprisal should be given widest publicity through BBC.

Personal and very restricted circulation telegram from SOE in Stockholm recommending retaliation after the incident at Telavåg, 1 May 1943.[1]

Communications links

While radio provided a vital channel for the passing of intelligence reports and instructions, the main methods of communication between Britain and Norway were by sea and air across the North Sea. The land route into Sweden was also used for agents, refugees and documentary intelligence, but it was slower because air transport facilities between Sweden and Britain were very limited. This was a source of frustration to both sides, particularly the Norwegians, who tried to get the frequency of flights increased but with limited success.* Sea and air transport was generally restricted to the winter months, because the short summer nights increased the dangers of German interception. The extent to which this disrupted resistance work in Norway is illustrated by a minute from Wilson to the head of SOE's naval directorate, Rear-Admiral A. H. Taylor, in January 1943.[2] Wilson wrote that during the previous three years it had been impossible to infiltrate any personnel into Norway by sea between mid-April and mid-September. And, by 1942, the Air Ministry had ruled out flying between mid-May and mid-August. In practice, apart from a couple of Catalina flying boat trips which were arranged unofficially, the non-flying period extended from the end of April to the last week in September.

This was a serious hindrance to SOE. They sought to increase their use of submarines and in December 1941 asked for Admiralty assistance. Unfortunately, an imaginative attempt by Ian Fleming (then working for the Director of Naval Intelligence) to obtain the loan of the French submarine *Surcouf* came to nothing.[3] SOE had to rely instead on occasional use of the Norwegian submarine *Uredd*. In February 1943 she hit a mine while taking the six members of the Seagull party to northern Norway, and was lost with all on board.[4] *Uredd* was also carrying Paul

---

* To give some idea of the problem, which was a continuing irritant, according to SOE figures just 101 passengers were flown to Britain in September 1942. The waiting list for flights was very long indeed, and by then some people had been waiting for two and a half years. The list included SIS and SOE personnel, RAF flight crews, Allied officers and troops from France, Poland, Czechoslovakia, Russia, Holland, Belgium and Yugoslavia, Swedish merchant officers, diplomats from Britain, America, Russia, Poland, Czechoslovakia, Holland and other countries, nearly 3,000 Norwegian refugees, and also vital freight for the Ministry of Supply. A priority system enabled key SOE and SIS personnel to be put at the head of the queue. The basic problems were the inadequate number of aircraft, and that most of those available were unsuitable. Whitleys had very unreliable engines, and could not fly on only one. Lockheed Lodestars had a poor payload and insufficient altitude – and two of them could only carry four passengers. Norwegian frustration at British inability to provide better services grew to such an extent that on several occasions they threatened retaliation. The previous chapter outlined how Lie threatened to prevent the supply of ball bearings from Sweden if the service was not improved. He was only with difficulty dissuaded from this and similar actions. Some Mosquitoes were made available in 1943, but their numbers were still very limited.

Nygaard, an SIS agent who was going to reinforce Upsilon in Tromsø, and also to check the identity of four submariners, two of them French, who had been marooned during an attempt by a French submarine to resupply Upsilon the previous November. This had been abandoned because of a security scare. It had been intended that *Uredd* would recover them.[5] SOE's attempts to procure other air transport fared little better. For example, they had unsuccessfully requested a Sunderland flying boat to take the Seagull party to northern Norway, and were obliged to rely on *Uredd* instead. SIS were more successful in obtaining alternative transport. They were quite frequently able to call on naval vessels and aircraft. Thus Ole Snefjellå was brought back by the submarine *Sea Nymph* from the SIS station Crux in Mo i Rana in January 1944. SIS also made greater use of Catalinas both for despatching agents to Norway and recovering them, and for rescuing them in emergencies. Ole Snefjellå was brought out with four others from station Pi near Stavenes in May 1942 in a rescue in dangerous circumstances.[6] And John Kristoffersen, a stalwart of Pisces and later Erna, both productive stations, managed in May 1944 to escape from the island of Onøya when surrounded by a force of over 200 Germans. He sought assistance from Crux and was flown out with some of them early in June.[7]

A Catalina off the coast of Finnmark during the winter of 1944. They were frequently used to deliver and collect SIS agents. © NHM

The volume of traffic gradually increased, especially from 1944 onwards, with the provision of better boats and greater availability of
aircraft. Despite seasonal disruptions, the statistics tell a remarkable
story of the effectiveness of these supply lines for SOE. There were
over 150 successful trips by sea, landing about 220 agents and collecting
70, while also picking up 360 refugees. The boats also delivered over
320 tons of stores. The RAF, and latterly the USAAF (United States
Army Air Force) too, flew more than 700 missions dropping over 200
agents. We do not have the figures for SIS, but these SOE statistics do
include a number of SIS agents, showing that they landed nearly 40 in
Norway, mainly in 1944–1945.

By sea: Shetland bases
The first base chosen by commandant Leslie Mitchell at Catfirth, described in Chapter 2, did not prove entirely suitable. In the summer of
1941 it was moved to Lunna, about twenty-five miles from Lerwick.
A flotilla of half a dozen Norwegian fishing boats was built up, with
most of the original crews replaced by fishermen from the west coast
of Norway who had been selected and trained for their tasks. Operational demands placed on the base continued to increase, and Lunna
proved to be an inadequately small anchorage for the larger number
of boats which were required, and also too remote from Lerwick for
effective supply and communications. Consequently, in the summer of
the following year the base moved again, this time to Scalloway, where
it remained for the duration of the war. There were periods when both
SIS and SOE set up independent and subordinate bases – SIS in Peterhead from July 1941 until November 1943, and SOE in Burghead
from November 1942 to April 1943.* This separation created problems
– and suspicions – between the two agencies. While SOE was willing
to disclose to SIS the destination of operational trips which it was

---

* It was finally decided to close Burghead after an incident in which the commandant Hugh
Marks (who had been sent home from Stockholm in October 1941) and Andreas Fasting
(who parachuted into Norway with Odd Starheim in January 1942) were drowned.

planning, SIS did not readily reciprocate. This occasionally led to boats landing agents from both services in or near the same place at about the same time. This was an unnecessary security risk, and contributed, for example, to the disaster at Telavåg.

For more than half the war, until they were replaced by larger and much more powerful American submarine chasers, the only means of transport across the North Sea was small Norwegian fishing boats. While they were sturdy and robust, they were not always able to resist the extremities of the winter weather. Between October and March, it was generally expected that the wind in the area between Shetland and Norway would reach gale force about 50 per cent of the time. Each winter, there were generally also a couple of storms which reached hurricane force.

Despite the experience and skill of their skippers, boats were regularly lost without trace. Refugees making their own way to Britain also risked their lives. Oluf Reed Olsen, who worked for SIS, described how he and two comrades escaped from Norway in September 1940 on an eighteen-foot fishing smack. When they had almost reached Scotland, a gale lasting eight days nearly sank the smack and blew them back to the Danish coast. Their journey lasted fourteen and a half days, a remarkable feat of endurance not least because they had lost most of their supplies in the storm.[8] During a hurricane in November 1941 which blew for six days, the *Blia* was sunk with forty-two people on board, and many boats which were laid up in Shetland ports were damaged or destroyed. Apart from the weather, North Sea crossings also became more hazardous as the Germans learned the extent of Shetlands traffic and increased their patrols accordingly. Furthermore, the shortage of fuel and restrictions on coastal fishing off Norway limited the presence of other boats in the area, so Shetlands boats became more visible. The winter of 1942–1943 ended with half the flotilla and nearly half of the crews lost on operations (compared with only three boats lost in 1941–1942).* This led Wilson to visit Shetland, where he

---

* A total of ten boats were lost between 1940 and 1943.

concluded that such a rate of attrition could not continue – and, crucially, to start the process leading to the acquisition of the American submarine chasers which arrived in October.

John Wilson (left), the head of SOE's Scandinavian section, on a trip to the Shetland base. On the right is Leslie Mitchell, the first base commandant. © NHM

After Mitchell's departure in 1942, he was replaced by Arthur Sclater. Sclater, and in particular his deputy David Howarth, oversaw the development of the base. They improved maintenance facilities and built a slipway named after Prince Olav, who visited with his father King Haakon in October 1942. The ships were also adapted, and equipped with weapons, suitable camouflage and defensive armour which more than once came in vitally useful. New crew members received specialised training, too. Handling of the independently minded fishermen was not always straightforward. In 1942 a Norwegian naval officer was appointed by the Norwegian High Command to look after their welfare and discipline, and they were formed into the Norwegian Naval Independent Unit (NNIU). This did not work well. For most of them, their only previous connection with the Norwegian Navy had been limited to contact with fishery patrols and they did not take well to attempts to enforce naval standards of discipline. They expressed a preference for continuing management by the British and refused to act under the orders of their own officer. After some two months of careful discussion, British staff resumed responsibility for certain elements of activity and another Norwegian officer was appointed. A further problem arose when the submarine chasers were introduced, because the crews lost the bonus which had been paid to them for operations using fishing boats. The reason was that motor torpedo boats (MTBs) had been carrying out similar trips from Lerwick without any bonus – and also on Norwegian naval rates of pay considerably lower than the civilian rates which the fishermen received. Against advice, they wrote an ultimatum to Hansteen threatening to resign if retrospective payments were not made. This brought them a further disadvantage, for they were conscripted into the Norwegian Navy and paid at naval rates. None of them resigned, and the only difference was that following conscription it became easier to post in new recruits.

The dry statistics of the losses of valuable crews and their boats give little insight into the risks which they ran and other obstacles which they sometimes had to surmount apart from the weather. Two examples involving Leif Larsen, the most highly decorated Allied naval officer during the war, best illustrate the dangers which Shetland crews faced.* In October 1941 Larsen was the engineer on *Nordsjøen* which was minelaying in the Edøyfjord. The vessel sank in a heavy gale on its return journey, but the crew was able to make their way to land. Some of them, including the skipper, then disappeared, so Larsen took charge of the remainder. He led them over 100 miles through occupied territory to Ålesund. There he stole another fishing vessel, *Arthur*, and sailed it back to Lerwick. For this he received a Distinguished Service Medal (DSM). In March 1943 he sailed *Bergholm* on an even longer mission, landing passengers and stores on the edge of the Arctic Circle. On its return, *Bergholm* was attacked by a series of German

---

* He was awarded the DSO, DSC, CGM, DSM and bar, testimony to some of the remarkable achievements outlined here.

aircraft, which the crew fought off with Lewis guns and a cannon. Larsen stayed in the wheelhouse (which offered little protection) and manoeuvred the boat so as to give the gunners the best field of fire. Most of the seven crew were injured, four seriously. One man had his foot shot off and died shortly afterwards. Damage to *Bergholm* was extensive. The wheelhouse was shot through and its doors torn off, the deckhouse and dinghy were full of holes and the mast nearly shot away. The pumps could not cope with the leaks, and after repairing the dinghy, Larsen abandoned ship. Following various unsuccessful attempts to persuade fishing boat skippers to take them to Shetland (one of which was reported to the Germans by a quisling) they landed on an island near Ålesund. With help from the SOE Antrum station, Larsen sent a message to the Shetland base. He and the surviving crew were picked up and arrived back in Shetland on 12 April. For this he was awarded a bar to his DSM.[9]

The American loan of the three 110-foot submarine chasers, *Hitra*, *Hessa* and *Vigra*, provided a substantial benefit. They were not only faster; they could also operate in any weather. Once they started service, there were no further losses for the rest of the war during nearly 120 operational trips, a remarkable record. Better navigation equipment improved their results too, with seventy-six successful missions sailed out of a total of eighty during 1944 and 1945. The greatest danger they faced was not from the Germans, but from overenthusiastic RAF patrols searching for U-boats which had moved to Norway after the fall of France. They once depth-charged *Hessa*, putting it out of service for fifteen weeks.* Safety lanes were thereafter introduced for their planned routes, within which the RAF would not attack without visual identification.[10] The Americans also briefly posed a threat to continued use of the boats by SOE. They wanted to recover the submarine chasers temporarily, for use by the OSS, SOE's counterpart, in Operation BARTER, which they had been asked to mount against the pyrites mine

---

* The pilot subsequently justified his action by saying that he did not believe that any surface vessel could navigate in the heavy seas which were running, so he assumed that *Hessa* was a U-boat.

north of Bergen. (This would have been a rare American operation on Norwegian soil.) The request was highly inconvenient for SOE, who were planning a series of trips in which they were to be used, and could ill spare them. SOE unwisely pointed this out directly to General Donovan, who ran OSS, stating without much tact that they 'quite realised your moral claim for a share in the vessels' activities'. They added, 'our reluctance to make them available is because they have an extremely full programme of work in connection with our tasks which have been allotted to us in our Norwegian directive from General Eisenhower's staff'. Donovan replied testily:

> I wish you to understand that the US boats now employed in the service of SOE/SO* are, at the present time, and will, in the future, be available, if necessary, for any such operation that is planned, and that their engagement on their present work will not prove an obstacle to the mounting of special operations ... I do not subscribe to your view that we have a 'moral' claim to a share in the SC [submarine chaser] vessels' activities. They are the property of the US Government, assigned to OSS by the US navy, and temporarily allocated by SO to serve SOE/SO Scandinavian work.

However, he was outflanked by SOE who, unchastened by this sharp reply, persuaded the Chiefs of Staff that submarine chasers were not necessary. BARTER was then dropped, and the American requirement fell away.[11]

By air
Air transport was never straightforward. Aircrew had to contend with problems caused by mountain ranges and poor weather, which created difficulties for navigation, as well as snow, which obscured landmarks. All too often, maps were unreliable. A shortwave radio navigation

---

* SO, or Special Operations department, was formed by the OSS to work with SOE.

aid whose components were codenamed Eureka and Rebecca, which helped matters, was only introduced on a large scale in 1944 after limited earlier deployments. Conflicting priorities meant that the RAF was unwilling to provide many aircraft. Until France had been liberated, only two squadrons (138 and 161) were allocated to supply northwest Europe. Conditions on the ground for reception committees were often harsh as well. The sensible choice of isolated dropping points meant that they were usually located in remote valleys. Reception committees endured many long nights in very cold conditions, receiving parachutists trying to land in inhospitable surroundings. Equipment was often lost, being dragged long distances by the wind after landing or deposited on mountain crags.

There is one remarkable story of an agent who ignored SOE's normal reception committee procedure by handling, entirely by himself, the loads dropped by two aircraft, consisting of nine men, twenty-four containers and eight packages. This happened in winter, at a dropping point arranged deep in the mountains, when the snow was soft and skiing conditions very poor. On the night of drop, the agent waited for the alerting message (known as the crack signal) to be broadcast by the BBC. It did not come, because the BBC forgot to send the signal at the normal time. However, they energetically corrected their error at two in the morning when – fortunately – the agent was still listening. By then he had dismissed the reception committee, whom he had no time to recontact. So he skied out alone, carrying on his back three boxes stuffed with petrol-soaked cotton waste and four flashlights. As he finished placing his signals in their normal positions, he heard the sound of the first approaching aircraft. He skied from box to box, lighting each signal, and ended at the position from which he was required to flash his light. The drop was a remarkably good one, with the leader of the party landing a bare ten metres from the middle light.[12]

In certain regions, German spotting aircraft sometimes reconnoitered the area where dropping operations were in progress. In at least one instance, a supply operation to SOE Pipit agents in Buskerud, they dropped their own parachutists on a landing point just after two RAF aircraft had completed their runs. In this case, fortunately, the reception committee was able to escape. SOE judged that pick-ups of agents by sea were almost never likely to be practical because of the lack of suitable landing grounds, though Catalinas were very occasionally used to land stores and even more infrequently to collect agents, usually in emergencies.[13] It was easier for SIS to use seaplanes because, apart from hermit stations, their agents did not require large supplies of stores or equipment to accompany them.

Training – Aviemore

SOE agents were trained in specific skills at specialised training schools (STS), such as STS 17 at Brickendonbury, where they learned the use of explosives. Brickendonbury was run by George Rheam, who commented after the war that of all the exiles whom he had trained, the Norwegians impressed him most. He admired them for their bravery, for their readiness to run risks and for their steadiness in facing the dangers of sabotage.[14] For security reasons, the nationals of each country were allocated their own training school. The initial choice for Norwegians at Fawley Court near Henley, not far from London, was inadequate because the area was unsuitable for realistic exercises. Eventually, three houses were found near Aviemore, in Scotland, which came much nearer to replicating Norwegian conditions for the students under training. These houses, and later a purpose-built log cabin near Glenmore, were designated STS 26 and visited twice by King Haakon, who, on one occasion, also went to Burghead and Shetland. Instructors were both British and Norwegian, and one of the Norwegians was the former Anchor agent Tor Gulbrandsen, who had been released after his appearance before a court of enquiry in 1943. In July 1944 Wilson wrote of him: 'Gulbrandsen has proved of the greatest value as an instructor at STS 26 during the last year, and it is greatly owing to him that the standard of administration, organisation and training at Glenmore Lodge has improved so considerably.'[15]

Visitors watching an SOE training exercise. They include (from left) John Wilson, Carl Gustav
Fleischer, Martin Linge, four unidentified officers, Colin Gubbins, King Haakon and
(in sports gear) Tor Gulbrandsen, captured by the Germans and sent back to Britain
on an unsuccessful double-agent operation. © NHM

As the policies of SOE changed, and their work shifted from raids
towards – in the main – supporting the building up of a countrywide
resistance movement, their recruitment and training processes also
changed. They no longer needed so many of those who would have
fitted well into a commando brigade. They looked instead for recruits
who could fill organising and training roles for the growing numbers
who were joining the resistance. It was not always easy to judge the
suitability of these recruits. The SOE Norwegian section history noted
that no normal course of training could determine a man's character,
observing that it was curious (but true) that some of the best members
of the Linge Company were characterised as not likely to make good
agents. Remarkably, the most outstanding member of the Norwegian
resistance, Gunnar Sønsteby, was very nearly rejected as unsuitable.
Without training, he had already played an important and valuable
role in resistance work. When he came over to Britain, he was sent on
a training course at STS 26 to develop his skills further. He failed to
excel. When Wilson heard that he was likely to fail, he was obliged to

intervene to ensure that this did not happen, travelling up to Scotland himself to explain to his instructors what kind of man Sønsteby was.[*][16]

There were cases where men who were selected were subsequently found to be frail, such as Anders Merkesdal, who deployed on Raven. Merkesdal's training report had described him as 'an excellent type, not easily rattled, keen and energetic, showing marked practical ability'.[17] However, once he was in Norway his organiser, William Waage, reported security concerns about him, relating to unauthorised long-distance telephone calls to his girlfriend, and drunkenness leading to his once being found insensible in a ditch. Unsuccessful attempts were made to repatriate Merkesdal, and he was later arrested in June 1943. Fortunately, such incidences were few. There were also a small number of cases where people, whose records were poor, nonetheless managed to get through the selection process and then distinguished themselves in the field. One such was Bjarne Iversen, who was sent to Canada in 1940 to train as a fighter pilot but showed signs of indiscipline, 'going to bed during parade hours and displaying unmilitary conduct towards his superiors', for which he was punished – and later sacked and drafted into the merchant navy. Commenting on SOE papers which suggested that he had deserted from the air force, Leif Tronstad recommended to Wilson that Iversen did not justify his employment on special service. He was alarmed to discover later that Iversen had been deployed to Norway as a member of Pheasant. The staff officer responsible for Norwegian operations, Joe Adamson, defended Iversen, commenting that he was a man who tended to flout authority from time to time. Moreover, he knew that Iversen had been dismissed from the air force even if the papers did not show it. Wilson described this as regrettable but decided, since Iversen was in Norway, that no action could be taken. Iversen's performance on this and a subsequent

---

[*] The story of this remarkable man is well described in many books. It is worth starting with the autobiographical account of his wartime work *Report from No. 24* (Oslo: Barricade, 1999). Sønsteby describes (pp. 90–91) how he fell out with the officer in charge of his training course, which was the main cause of his problems.

deployment to Norway were beyond reproach, and in 1945 he was awarded the Norwegian War Medal.[18]

The most outstanding SOE operations

During this period, SOE continued to build up a network of separate organisations covering most of the country apart from the far north. In addition, they provided extensive supplies of military equipment which was stored in dumps, usually in outlying areas. The teams responsible for this initially consisted of organisers who took responsibility for building up larger groups, instructors who helped with training in the use of arms and explosives, and wireless operators who maintained contact with Britain. By December 1942 a progress report was able to state that five areas in Norway were now sufficiently well organised to be able to provide small guerrilla bands to attack specific targets under the direction of Milorg and the Norwegian High Command. These were Oslo (Plover), Gudbrandsdalen (Anvil), Telemark (Swallow), Flekkefjord-Kristiansand (Cheese) and Trondheim (Lark).[19] These and other groups achieved some striking successes, although they of course suffered plenty of setbacks, too. The highlights will be examined here, as well as some unsuccessful operations, one of which illustrates an extraordinary example of bravery and fortitude.*

Cheese

Odd Starheim, often known by his codename Cheese, was one of SOE's most distinguished agents. Yet the start to his first operation was distinctly unpromising. In January 1941 he was sent back to Norway by submarine, landing on the southwest coast near Egersund. Before he could leave the submarine, it was spotted by German aircraft who dropped depth charges, so it had to submerge. When the crew was eventually able to launch his canoe, they inadvertently shipped

---

* GUNNERSIDE and the sinking of the *Hydro*, which prevented the Germans obtaining heavy water from Vemork, will be covered in Chapter 9, and SOE contributions to operations against *Tirpitz* will be included in Chapter 11.

a lot of water into it. Starheim had no bailing device, so his progress through choppy seas was difficult and dangerous. He was lucky to get ashore. The weather was bitterly cold; he had a high temperature and was soaked to the skin. He staggered up to the hills and lay there in the fairly open country until the fever had passed. Starheim first came on the air and started sending reports on 25 February 1941. In *The Secret History of SOE*, Mackenzie states that this was the first SOE message to have been received on the air from occupied Europe. However, this achievement probably belonged to Olav Wallin.* After the war, he claimed that once his radio had been repaired, he was able to transmit reports from the Bergen area in the late summer of 1940.[20] Starheim quickly recruited a wide network of informants in Oslo, including Kristiansand and Stavanger, who provided intelligence on topics such as oil, airfields, shipping, and the building of coastal fortifications. He also enlisted the help of Gunvald Tomstad, a local man who provided him with much assistance, playing a part in most of his operations. Moreover, he also joined the Nasjonal Samling so as to ingratiate himself with the Germans and obtain information from them.

On 6 May, Starheim reported intelligence from Stavanger that all the oil tanks on the airfields were full; that their hangars contained approximately 200 planes; and that ships laden with troops and ammunition were going northwards. SOE replied on 9 May, 'Excellent information. Hangers [*sic*] at both aerodromes Stavanger bombed. Ascertain and telegraph results. Do not exaggerate report.' Starheim replied indignantly, 'No exaggeration. Sola: two barracks destroyed and two damaged by incendiary bombs. One hanger [*sic*] heavily damaged, one bomb hit the ground ten metres from it and smashed one wall and damaged eight engines ... Ten Germans killed'. A few days later, he provided details of all the oil stocks in the whole country at the end of April: petrol 23,670 tons; solar 11,787; diesel 4,043; fuel oil

---

* No archival trace of his messages has been found, but his statement is borne out by information on his SOE personal file.

2,502; petroleum 9,054; diesel petroleum 5,177; white spirit 440; lubri-
cating oil 7,446 and aviation spirit 17. In a separate message later the
same day he added that 4,267 tons of aviation spirit had just arrived to
supplement that small amount.

Odd Starheim, famously known as Cheese. © NHM

It is not surprising that SIS, whose reporting resources were very limited at this stage, were grateful to receive his information. And the
Norwegian section of SOE judged with satisfaction that he was 'a
Norwegian of a very superior type … from his intelligence and general
behaviour he is far superior to the normal run of Norwegian merchant
seaman'.[21] However, it did not prove possible to continue this level of
activity. The frequency of his transmissions was probably the cause of
German interest in the area where he was operating. Starheim noticed increasing signs of German attempts to locate his wireless, and
decided to close the station and return to Britain. Before departure,
he arranged with a friend that the station would be reopened after a
month when things had died down, though this did not work as his
friend could not use the cypher. In little more than four months, he
had sent over a hundred reports.[22]

Starheim remained in Britain for six months before returning to
Norway in January 1942. The early stages of this trip were even less

promising than the first had been. Cheese and a companion, Andreas Fasting (imaginatively codenamed Biscuit), were dropped by parachute – the first SOE air operation in Norway. It was nearly a disaster because Fasting, encumbered by a rucksack, was hampered in leaving the aircraft and landed perilously close to a steep mountainous precipice. A few weeks later, Starheim was briefly captured by the Germans when they raided the flat where he was staying in Oslo. Starheim was permitted to use the lavatory, which had two doors. He ran out through the other one and jumped down into the street from a second-floor window. He decided, understandably, that things had temporarily become too hot for him and asked to return to Britain.

His exfiltration proved to be a problem. Starheim himself judged it would be impractical to return via Sweden. There was a serious risk that he would be recognised and interned. The weather was very bad, and the Shetlands crew was also reluctant to make the trip because German air reconnaissance was increasing and – it was now mid-March – much of the trip would need to take place in daylight. When Starheim was informed of these difficulties, he resourcefully resolved matters for himself by hijacking a 600-ton coastal steamer, *Galtesund*, with the assistance of Fasting and four others. (One of them was Einar Skinnarland, who was quickly trained and returned to Norway, where he would play an important part in Swallow/Grouse which supported GUNNERSIDE, the operation against Vemork.) Cheese had earlier arranged for a message to be sent to London, notifying them of his intentions. Fortunately the weather was bad, which facilitated his journey by preventing German air reconnaissance, and he brought *Galtesund*, together with its passengers and a useful cargo, into Aberdeen on 17 March. As a result of this, and what he achieved during his earlier deployment, Starheim was recommended for a Military Cross (MC). This was upgraded and he received a Distinguished Service Order (DSO) instead.[23]

The success of this feat was a contributory factor to the development of a more ambitious plan. This would involve the capture of a small unescorted merchant convoy off the Norwegian coast, which would then be brought back to Britain. Starheim was asked to assess the viability of the operation, and prepared a scheme to achieve it, codenamed CARHAMPTON. He was tasked to lead the attacking party. The force of forty-one men, mainly from the Linge Company, spent longer than anticipated in training at Aviemore. Foul weather prevented their first two attempts to cross the North Sea and they did not reach Norway until they landed at Tellevik on 3 January 1943. The ship which brought them, *Bodø*, hit a mine on her return journey and sank. Almost all the crew, including the accompanying Lieutenant Commander Marstrander, who had been a member of the Anglo-Norwegian Coordination Committee from the early stages, were drowned.

The operation was not successful. Two attempts were made to approach a small convoy lying in Flekkefjord. The first was foiled by bad weather, preventing the timely launch of the boats which were to be used. A further attempt was made three days later. However, the garrison in the guard house protecting the fjord had been increased, and in the resulting skirmish several Germans were killed and a larger number injured. The CARHAMPTON force was obliged to withdraw across Flekkefjord to a secure hideout in the mountains which they reached after a series of forced marches in adverse winter conditions, and without food for much of the time. Communications difficulties delayed their reporting to London and requesting a supply drop. Bad weather prevented this until 16 February, and then only a small part of the drop was recovered. Tightened security and further storms led to the cancellation of other operations planned by Starheim to replace the attack on the convoy. (These were support for a Combined Operations assault against the Titania mine, and an attack on a 10,000-ton freighter.) Poor weather also precluded the possibility of arranging transport from the Shetlands to bring the party back. Starheim decided to split the party and seize another steamer, this time *Tromøysund*, for their return journey. Their action was successful, but in the absence of air cover *Tromøysund* was attacked and sunk by German aircraft the following day. All on board, including Starheim, were drowned. Some survivors were spotted in lifeboats, but a destroyer sent to the area to help was recalled on the instructions of the First Sea Lord because it was on the edge of suspected minefields.[24] Most of the rest of the party successfully made it back to Shetland on a fishing boat, while a small group remained in the mountains with a wireless set.

Wilson concluded that the survival of a force of forty men over nine weeks in winter in occupied Norway was a remarkable achievement. A large enemy force was employed in searching for them. While the force did not achieve its objective, it caused a valuable diversion of German effort. Hambro described it as another epic in the history of SOE, while Selborne rather more realistically observed that the lives of the party had been risked on a plan which had not been worked out like GUNNERSIDE. There were, in truth, no discernible benefits gained, and no wider lessons that could be learned.[25] After the war, when he was travelling through the area of the CARHAMPTON operation, Wilson was taken aback by the difficulty of the terrain. He concluded that the Combined Operations attack against the Titania mine, and the rescue of the CARHAMPTON force in parallel, could not have succeeded – not least because the road was almost precipitous in places and effectively impassable in winter.[26]

Tom

Even before the arrival of Starheim, who recruited him as a valuable assistant, Gunvald Tomstad (known as Tom) had been trying to pass information to Britain. Using a home-made (and not very effective) radio he sent a stream of messages, in plain language or using a commercial code, about the location of German ships in the area around Flekkefjord and Kristiansand. Fortunately he escaped detection, and Starheim trained him to use one of the radio sets which he had brought with him. As a part of their work together, Tom agreed to join the local branch of the NS. He was seen as a trusted member and was soon promoted to be chairman. He arranged to share accommodation for a while with the local NS policeman, who was the chief contact of the Gestapo in Kristiansand. This enabled him to insinuate himself so thoroughly into police and Gestapo organisations and win their confidence that they shared with him their suspicions concerning the local population, and who was thought unreliable. By this means he learned of plans to arrest Tor Njaa, a local organiser for SOE. Tom warned him, but Njaa did not want to leave his mother. He stayed, and was arrested. Tom was called up to serve on the Eastern Front. In order to avoid going, he staged a motorcycle accident to injure himself and required hospitalisation.

Through the monitoring of transmissions the Germans became aware that there was an illegal wireless set operating somewhere in the area. As their attempts to locate the station led them to concentrate on the region in which Tom was living, the Germans finally trusted him enough to inform him that they were searching for what he knew to be his own station. What is more, they handed the case over to him to carry on. Tom persuaded them to explain to him the details of the different direction finding systems which they were using. He used this knowledge (as outlined in Chapter 3) to persuade the Germans to search the house of his German neighbour while looking for his own wireless.

This extraordinary situation could not last, and he received a salutary warning when a German told him that they were looking for an active resistance member called 'Tom', his own code name, and sought his assistance in trying to identify him. Although he did not act immediately on this by trying to escape, Tom became even more exposed because of the active assistance which he provided to the CARHAMPTON force, which further risked drawing attention. He was finally obliged to leave for Sweden in April 1943.

Unfortunately, it did not prove possible to retrain Tom for other work in Norway. The exaggerated sense of security which he had developed when working for Starheim did not serve him well once he arrived in Britain. He was unwilling to share information with anyone else, or to work in any other capacity than as an entirely lone hand.

After completing a training course, he told Wilson that having lived with some ninety other potential agents at STS 26 he did not consider it safe for him to re-enter Norway as an agent. So he left SOE in March 1944 and was transferred to the Norwegian Army.

MARDONIUS and BUNDLE

Max Manus was involved in more attacks against shipping targets than any other member of SOE. His early life was colourful and varied, for he spent time in Cuba, Copenhagen and Chile before travelling in South America for two years. He fought against the Germans when they invaded Norway, and was active in resistance activities, both collecting intelligence and distributing propaganda. Such a combination of activities was risky, and he was arrested in February 1941.* Manus distracted the attention of his captors and jumped out of a first-floor window, breaking his shoulder and damaging his spine. He recovered sufficiently to be able to escape from hospital (even though he was under armed German guard) with assistance from the resistance, and made his way to Britain by a circuitous journey which included Russia, Turkey, Egypt, South Africa, Trinidad, the United States and Canada.

Manus was teamed up with Gregers Gram and they were sent on a series of training courses, and certainly enjoyed themselves while they were preparing in Aviemore. The pair broke into a shooting box (later discovering that it was on the royal estate and so belonged to King George VI) and used it as a base for a series of poaching expeditions. They hunted deer, grouse and hares, and caught salmon too. When they had finished, they left behind £1 as a token payment.[27] After completion of their training, Manus and Gram were despatched to Norway in March 1943 on Operation MARDONIUS. This was an ambitious plan, devised by Manus himself, who had worked out that there

---

* Sverre Midtskau (see Chapter 2) had been in touch with Manus and was also arrested when he visited Manus's flat shortly after this incident, without knowing what had happened. The resistance assisted him to escape from Gestapo headquarters at Møllergata 19. He returned to Britain via Sweden in February 1942.

was generally a significant amount of shipping in Oslo harbour. He recommended training canoeists and using them to attack some of the larger vessels with limpet mines. This would not be a straightforward project, because the narrow waters of the harbour were brightly lit at night and heavily patrolled, making it highly dangerous. Hansteen and Torp were consulted, and gave their consent. Manus and Gram were dropped by parachute – though were fortunate to escape serious injury when Gram's parachute was briefly caught in Manus's static line, leading to a rapid and largely uncontrolled descent that ended in a tree. They recruited some contacts and launched an attack with two canoes on 27 April. The attack itself was not without incident. Working separately, they sometimes had to paddle through floodlit areas while approaching the vessels they were about to attack. Fortunately, those working on deck did not notice them. And, while Manus and his colleague were preparing to fix limpets onto the *Sarpfoss*, they were rudely and unpleasantly interrupted in their task by a man urinating into the harbour, who showered them. They fixed limpets onto six ships, but many of them failed to detonate. A diversionary attack in the nearby Akers shipyard also failed because none of the limpets there exploded either. Nonetheless they succeeded in sinking *Ortelsburg* (3,600 tons), and badly damaging *Tugela* (5,600 tons) and an oil lighter. Three days after the attack, SIS passed a report to SOE with details of the damage which had been done. Manus and Gram returned to Britain via Stockholm. They were awarded the MC and Military Medal (MM) respectively for their work.* A few months later, the Germans executed six Norwegians whom they suspected of complicity in MARDONIUS. One of them was Sigurd Jacobsen, who had planted the limpets in Akers shipyard. SOE carried out extensive experiments to try to discover why the limpets had failed. They could find no conclusive evidence.

---

* When Mockler-Ferryman, AD/E responsible for north-west Europe, put forward these recommendations to Gubbins in July 1943, he wrote that he hoped that they could be dealt with quickly. 'In the past there has been very considerable delay and in many cases men lost their lives in subsequent operations before the awards had come through.' (TNA, HS 9/608/3.) This might otherwise have been the case for Gram, who was killed the following year in Oslo.

Malfunctions continued to be a frustrating problem on subsequent similar operations.[28]

Manus was keen to arrange for further shipping attacks. In September 1943 he outlined a plan for MARDONIUS II, suggesting operations not only in Oslo harbour, but also another half-dozen ports in the region. He wanted to use a larger group of saboteurs, suggesting the inclusion of men such as Gunnar Sønsteby. Wilson supported the idea in principle, but did not wish Sønsteby to be involved, as he was already too busy with other tasks. The operation was renamed BUNDLE, and the team was also asked to undertake some propaganda tasks, examining in particular how best to undermine the Wehrmacht in Norway. Manus and Gram returned to Norway on 11 October. They tried to launch an attack against several ships while swimming in frogman suits, rather than depending on canoes. This was unsuccessful. The diving suits tore very easily, and Manus nearly drowned. So they concentrated for a while on propaganda work instead. Their further operations, including the imaginative use of home-made torpedoes, will be described in Chapter 12.

There were two other series of operations planned against shipping during this period, using kayaks (VESTIGE) and one-man Welman submarines (BARBARA). A total of eight VESTIGE operations took place. Others were abandoned at the planning stage after objections from SIS, who had operational equities in the areas where attacks were intended. Two attacks, VESTIGE I and VESTIGE III, were successful. VESTIGE I badly damaged *Hertmut* (2,700 tons), a modern refrigerated vessel. VESTIGE III severely damaged *Jantze Fritzen* (6,500 tons), which subsequently required substantial repairs. Severe winter weather often made recovery of these teams extremely difficult.[29] There was only one operation involving Welman submarines, when four were deployed to attack a floating dock in Bergen harbour in November 1943. One of them surfaced prematurely and was spotted. The driver, Bjørn Pedersen, came under fire and abandoned it, and the remaining three could not therefore continue with their attack. Other operations were planned, based on intelligence provided by reconnaissance teams sent in specifically for the purpose, and included one party from SIS. However, none proved feasible.

Peter Deinboll: REDSHANK, GRANARD and FEATHER

A Foreign Office history prepared at the end of the war described SOE's campaign to deprive Germany of the benefits of Norwegian pyrites, as largely a personal war between Lieutenant Peter Deinboll and the Germans, who were exploiting the Orkla pyrites mine south-west of Trondheim. During 1941 this mine had produced over 520,000 tons of ore.[30] There were three main battles. For the first, Deinboll received a DSO, for the second an MC and for the third a bar to his DSO – thus becoming the only Norwegian to win this decoration twice. The target of the first, Operation REDSHANK, in May 1942, was the destruction of the Baardshaug converter and transformer station supplying power to the mines, and to the railway carrying the ore to Thamshavn for shipment to Germany. Deinboll had to contend with the fact that in May there were only four hours of darkness and there was a force of 300 Germans quartered only 300 yards from his objective. He and his small party were detected during their preliminary reconnaissance and had to withdraw. However, they returned to carry out the attack on the following night. The explosion completely destroyed the main transformer station and significantly reduced the transport capacity for six months. Deinboll, who had stayed to watch the explosion, was spotted and chased into the hills. He was pursued for seven hours but managed to escape and make his way back to Britain via Sweden. At a meeting of the ANCC shortly afterwards, REDSHANK was described as 'almost a model operation'.*[31]

---

* In his unpublished history, Wilson wrote that he had recommended Deinboll for a DSO. However, the War Office downgraded it to an MC. When the papers were submitted to King George VI, he commented, 'If this citation is correct, this officer deserves a higher award. Resubmit.' So Deinboll received his DSO after all.

As output recovered at Orkla, a further operation was judged necessary, codenamed Operation GRANARD. Since vigilance had been increased, a different target was selected. It was decided to sink an ore ship and destroy the loading tower on the jetty at Thamshavn. Deinboll and his party left in December 1942. They were launched from the *Aksel* some twenty miles off the coast and had many difficulties on their journey to Thamshavn.* The magnets in the limpet mines affected their compass, and therefore their navigation. A night landing on a small island made in a heavy sea severely damaged their boat. On being launched the following day, the boat sank, though all their stores and equipment were recovered. It took them six days to reach the mainland, and a further fortnight to get to the target area. On arrival, they found that German defensive dispositions were stronger than they had anticipated. The loading tower was lit up and so strongly guarded at night that they could not attack it. They also had to wait two months for a suitable ship to target. During this period they were assisted by Deinboll's father, who was the chief engineer at the plant. He concealed them and provided advice on how best to change the plan of attack. In late February, *Nordfahrt* (5,000 tons) appeared. They stole a dinghy and approached the ship. *Nordfahrt* was brightly lit, but an anti-aircraft watch on the stern which appeared to be looking in their direction did not spot them. They successfully attached three limpet mines which detonated and *Nordfahrt*, already loaded with ore, was damaged. However, it proved possible to run her aground and the vessel was later salvaged. As the party withdrew on skis to the Swedish frontier, they became separated in a blizzard. Deinboll fell 200 feet over a precipice, damaged his leg and had to dig himself into snow for thirty hours before he was strong enough to move any further. He lay up in a deserted hut for three days, drinking water from snow melted

---

* *Aksel* and its crew were lost on the return journey.

in a cup between his thighs. He eventually managed to get to Sweden.* His father and family were also obliged to leave for Sweden too, for their own safety.

Production at the mine gradually increased again. A further operation, FEATHER, was launched in October 1943 with the objective of destroying as much ore as possible. This time Deinboll's party was larger, and was dropped by parachute. His reconnaissance showed that the very heavy German presence would prevent them from entering the mine workings to destroy equipment. He decided to blow up the shunting locomotives instead. These were of a special gauge and only available from France. On 31 October the party divided into small groups to attack the locomotives at three different locations. Five locomotives were either destroyed or so badly damaged as to be unserviceable for six months, and Deinboll himself wrecked other essential equipment. The valley thereafter was even more heavily guarded, but Deinboll and his group stayed in the area. Less than three weeks later they made a second attack against the shunting engine at Løkken and the remaining single locomotive. This succeeded, though one saboteur was killed in an accident. The hauling capacity of the railway was considerably reduced. The party remained in Sweden and went back to carry out a further attack the following year, again in the middle of summer. Deinboll returned to Britain and was awarded a bar to his DSO. He was killed in November 1944, when the aircraft carrying him back to Norway disappeared without trace.[32]

---

* The equipment required by the Norwegians for mountain warfare was often unavailable or inadequate. In his report after GRANARD, Deinboll described a bad example of this with studied understatement. He wrote that the only decent ski boots to be found were size ten and upwards. One of his party, Pedersen, required size eight and so had to be content with a pair of old Norwegian ski boots. After they had been in use for a week they began to fall to pieces and after a fortnight, despite constant repairing, they were completely useless. Their soles had to be held on by four straps. 'Ski running with such footwear has little to recommend it. Getting frostbite with 20C of frost is easy even if your toes are not sticking out of your boots as they were in Pedersen's case.' (TNA, HS 2/194.)

Telavåg

As highlighted in Chapter 3, the incident at Telavåg led to one of the worst atrocities committed in Norway during the war. In April 1942, when the *Borghild* landed an SIS agent there, the vessel remained in port for four days and the crew walked around openly wearing Norwegian uniforms, presumably because they thought it would improve their chances of being treated as prisoners of war if they were captured. Shortly afterwards at the same spot, the *Olaf* landed two SOE agents, Emil Hvaal, the Anchor wireless operator, and Arne Værum, the Penguin wireless operator. Unwisely, they remained in the area for a while, were given away, and surprised by the Gestapo. In the subsequent exchange of fire, Værum and two Gestapo officers were killed. In retaliation, the Germans destroyed the village, sent all the able-bodied men to Sachsenhausen concentration camp (where thirty-one out of seventy-two people died), and shot a further eighteen hostages. The subsequent Security Service investigation of this incident did not really address the issue of crew behaviour, apart from recommending that they did not give imported commodities such as white bread, coffee or English cigarettes to the local population as it could attract attention.[33]

Could this atrocity have been prevented? Probably not. But the German raid was the culmination of an unfortunate chain of circumstances. The original plan had been to drop the Anchor team of Tor Gulbrandsen and Hvaal by parachute near Drammen in January 1942. However, there was an incident on the night before their departure, when the pilot of the aircraft which was carrying agents participating in Lark and Anvil decided during the flight that he had insufficient fuel to reach Anvil's dropping point. He suggested that he should drop them both together (which was not normal procedure) on the dropping point which was to be used for Anchor the following evening, a proposal which they declined and which, in any event, was prevented by cloud and icing on the wings. The Anchor party declined to go the following evening, because they believed that Lark and Anvil had been dropped on their point the night before, and no one was able to provide information which would have disabused them. The plan was changed,[34] and the Anchor team travelled separately by sea, with Gulbrandsen being delivered, also to Telavåg, in late February.*

There followed a further instance when SIS did not share information with SOE about its sailings. SOE were not warned that an SIS boat operating from Peterhead had very recently visited Telavåg, where the Anchor team were to be delivered. When they later found out about the activities of the *Borghild* and its crew, SOE complained to SIS. During a conversation between Wilson and SIS a few weeks later in mid-June, to try to resolve some other inter-service difficulties in Bergen, the SIS representative attempted

> to place all the blame on the Telavåg incident for his present troubles in Bergen. I told him that we knew that the German Intelligence Service had rounded on the Gestapo for butting in at Telavåg and thereby spoiling a line [presumably SIS] which they had been carefully nursing for some time.† I also alluded to the fact that his chief had admitted a mistake had been made by allowing the *Borghild* to sail into this area. He then quietened down and realised that we were not perhaps so ignorant as he had assumed us to be.[35]

In May 1942, Finn Nagell of FO.II sent a report on what had happened at Telavåg to General Hansteen, based on information from SIS. Perhaps unsurprisingly, the account laid the responsibility for the incident on SOE's behaviour, though it did contain an admission that the SIS boat had invited a Telavåg resident on board and 'filled him full of rum' – a gesture which could scarcely have passed unnoticed locally. He drew attention to the lack of coordination in choosing landing sites, and suggested that Hansteen should intervene to try to resolve this.[36] Hansteen copied the letter to the Minister of Defence,

---

* The pilot's behaviour was the subject of a written complaint, but this came too late to make any difference.
† It is not clear which operation Wilson was referring to.

Torp, and raised the need for better coordination with SIS at the next meeting of the ANCC, but the problem was not properly resolved until SIS moved its operating base back from Peterhead to Scalloway in November 1943. SOE were, however, certainly more careful on their own account before then. For example, in December 1942, Wilson consulted Øen in FO.IV about the wisdom of landing the Moorhen party at a designated spot so soon after Chough agents had been landed only fifteen miles away. This had stirred up the Germans after the escape of twenty-five men from the district.[37]

When news of the German reprisals became known, it caused widespread outrage and led the SOE station in Stockholm to suggest a retaliatory bombing attack on Germany. Reflecting the sensitivity of the subject, Wilson replied to this controversial suggestion by private cypher, thus limiting the number who saw his message: 'request you make cannot be complied with as it is totally opposed to high policy and would achieve nothing of any value to war effort'. Stockholm were reluctant to accept his decision. They replied that it was of prime importance to keep up the spirits of the Home Front, and to demonstrate to people supporting the work of the resistance in Norway that their sufferings did not pass unobserved. They argued that to allow the executions to go unchallenged would be a fresh confession of impotence where Norway was concerned. Wilson patiently spelt out in more detail the reasons why the policy would not be changed:

> You must appreciate ... that matters of this kind have to be dealt with as questions of major policy involving both the War Cabinet and the Chiefs of Staff committee, and that also the opinions of the Norwegian authorities in this country have to be considered. So far as these are concerned, I am in a position to tell you that the Minister of Defence and General Hansteen have determined that they will allow none of the usual Nazi methods of burning houses and shooting hostages to interfere with our combined activities in Norway ... Their particular anxiety is that Norwegian traitors and informants should be the first objective

rather than the Gestapo leaders themselves. The reason for this is that in this way the supply of information will dry up and reprisals will not normally be taken by the enemy. When any opportunity presents itself by which people like Berenz [sic] and Bernhardt [sic]* can be removed, even at the cost of loyal Norwegians' lives, that opportunity should be taken. Bit by bit we hope to provide you with a sufficiency of material to carry out this line of action, but it is particularly necessary that no direct reference to that material should be made in telegrams, and that reference to it in letters should be veiled, all such letters being written 'off the record' so to speak.[38]

Some of the damaging activities of Norwegian informers, as well as operations against them, will be considered later in the chapter.

Chapter 5 described how Ingvald Johansen, the skipper of the *Vita*, had gone ashore to send a letter to his girlfriend, while his accomplice Solem had tried to telephone his wife, and how Kristian Fougner had been embarrassed by the behaviour of Leif Larsen and his crew when they delivered him to Vindholmen and went ashore to buy salmon. So the behaviour of the *Borghild* crew was not an exception. In fact, such behaviour was remarkably common among crews (including those of naval MTBs) visiting the Norwegian coast, and it is fortunate that it did not lead to more incidents such as that at Telavåg. However, things began to change after Tor Gulbrandsen, the Anchor organiser, confessed that he had agreed to work for the Germans. SOE realised that the behaviour of Shetlands crews in going ashore on operational trips might offer, to a double agent, the means of sending messages back to the Abwehr. In February 1943, Wilson issued an instruction to the Shetland base that they should make sure 'by search of person of both agents and crew and otherwise that no message of any kind is attempted to be smuggled out'.[39] Soon after, the SOE security section wanted to go even further, complaining about the behaviour of

---

* The two Gestapo officers who were killed at Telavåg were Behrens and Bertram.

the SOE crew which had delivered an agent (Pollux) to Norway on behalf of SIS the previous November. They suggested the adoption of more stringent security measures, for example, that a conducting officer should accompany every operational trip. However, this was not accepted.[40]

Worse was to come. In April, an unnamed Norwegian officer who had made a secret visit to Norway on behalf of the Norwegian High Command informed the admiral who was the commanding officer in the Shetlands about the behaviour of the crew of a fishing boat which had taken part in the Operation CARTOON, during the raid on the pyrites mine at Stord in January 1943. One evening, when visiting Godøy, the crew went to a dance where they met some Germans. The skipper was about to draw his revolver and shoot them, but was dissuaded by the others. Before their departure from Godøy the crew wrote letters and asked a local Norwegian to forward them. Although he accepted them, the man was cautious, and subsequently burned them. The same Norwegian officer quoted several other similar examples, including gifts of food and sweets given to local Norwegians, which could only have come from the UK, and which, on occasion, led to arrests. This resulted in strict instructions being issued by the admiral that no one was to go ashore in Norway except in the course of his duty, and then only if permission has been obtained from the senior officer present. All conversations with the local Norwegian population were to be recorded in writing. No letters, written or printed papers were to be sent or taken ashore in Norway without authority, and posting of letters by unauthorised persons was strictly forbidden. Contravention of the order would be treated as a serious offence.[41]

MARTIN

MARTIN was an unsuccessful operation, for almost all those involved were killed by the Germans. However, the experience of the lone survivor, Jan Baalsrud, is a truly epic story of endurance and bloody-minded determination in the most adverse of circumstances. It also shows the remarkable extent to which SIS helped SOE by arranging his return to Britain via Sweden.

The plan for MARTIN involved sending four men to northern Norway to organise the sabotage of German fuel and ammunition depots, particularly those at the airfields of Bardufoss and Harstad. These were used as bases by German aircraft which attacked Arctic convoys taking supplies to Murmansk. The party travelled on the *Brattholm* in late March 1943. After arriving at a small island off Tromsø, they sought to get in touch with a local merchant who was known to be a reliable contact. Unfortunately he had died, and his successor, uncertain whether they were loyal Norwegians or agents provocateurs, reported them to the local magistrate, who informed the Germans. They sent a force to capture the group. The SOE agents managed to destroy the *Brattholm*, but one of them was shot and killed and the rest, apart from Baalsrud, were arrested. Following a brutal interrogation, they gave up the name of their local contact, Kaare Moursund, the head of the local SIS station, Upsilon. He was arrested and this led to further arrests, including another SIS agent, Thor Knudsen.

Through a neighbouring SIS station, Mu, the remnants of Upsilon informed London of these events, quoting a Gestapo officer and other sources as informing them that both Moursund and Knudsen had been forced to make a partial confession. In early April they added that the *Brattholm* survivors, together with Moursund and Knudsen, would be transferred to Trondheim by sea on the *Ragnvald Jarl* on 10 April. The station asked for the *Ragnvald Jarl* to be intercepted by the Royal Navy. SIS passed the message to SOE, who asked the Admiralty to arrange this. The Assistant Chief of Naval Staff declined to do so. A further message from Upsilon stated that the whole group had apparently been sentenced to death, and repeated their request for their transport to be intercepted. Once more SOE approached the Admiralty, but again to no effect – 'I think rightly', commented Wilson later. In the event, the transfer to Trondheim did not take place, and Upsilon reported that the eight SOE survivors had been shot in Tromsø. (Two others died of their injuries.) It added that one survivor was safe and would be sent to Sweden when his frostbitten feet had recovered. Both Moursund and Knudsen were transported to concentration camps and died there in 1944 – Moursund in Melk, a sub-camp of Mauthausen, and Knudsen in Natzweiler.[42] As outlined in Chapter 3, once things settled down in Tromsø and the station was able to restart regular transmissions, SIS sent Upsilon a warm commendation praising their activities.[43] They also grumbled that SOE had not notified them about their planned activity in the Tromsø area. Wilson retorted that SOE had earlier informed them that they had no intention of setting up an organisation in Tromsø itself, but would be confining operations to the hinterland, mentioning specifically the possibilities of operating against Bardufoss. Despite the disruption which it had caused to Upsilon, Wilson later noted that SIS did not appear likely to make a big issue over this case. There is nothing to show that SOE knew in advance that Moursund was working for SIS when his name was given to the MARTIN party as a contact which they might use. It is nonetheless surprising that SIS chose not to criticise SOE for actions which had caused them to lose two of their agents.

In the meantime, Baalsrud managed to escape the large German force which was searching for him, though he lost one of his boots, was hit by a bullet and had most of his big toe shot off. He swam through freezing Arctic waters to a small island, where he waited for a couple of hours until dusk before swimming several hundred yards further to an inhabited island. There he received assistance from several families and was eventually rowed to the mainland and equipped with skis and food sufficient for him to travel to Sweden, some seventy miles away across the mountains. This part of his journey was uneventful, except for an incident when he was skiing through a small village in the early morning and was suddenly confronted by a group of German troops crossing the road. He assumed that they must have been half asleep because they failed to notice his Norwegian uniform and badges, with 'Norway' in English on his shoulders. Soon afterwards, however, he was caught in a blizzard and fell over a cliff, breaking one ski and losing the other, as well as his rucksack containing clothes and food. He wandered around in the blizzard for four days, before he stumbled, snow-blind and with badly frostbitten feet and legs, into a house in Furuflaten, by Lyngenfjord, occupied by the sister of Marius Grønvold, who fortuitously was working for SIS.

It was clear to Grønvold that Baalsrud's condition was too bad for him to be able to continue to Sweden on his own. He would need to be carried. In fact, some of his frostbitten toes turned gangrenous and Baalsrud later amputated them himself with a pocket knife. Grønvold informed his Upsilon colleagues in Tromsø (who reported it to London), and arranged that fellow resistance members in Manndalen, the next valley, would collect Baalsrud and seek assistance from some Samis (in those days described as 'Lapps') who would take him to Sweden. Grønvold and trusted friends strapped Baalsrud to a homemade sledge and carried him up the steep cliff to the top of the mountain range dividing Lyngenfjord from Manndal. When they arrived, there was no one to meet them because a German patrol had just arrived in Manndal and it was not safe for the party to leave the village. The cliff was too precipitous for Baalsrud to be taken back down, so he had to be left in the open, while Grønvold arranged via Tromsø for another attempt to collect him. In the meantime, it snowed, and when the Manndal party arrived several days later, they could not find Baalsrud because he had been buried. A week elapsed before Grønvold could return and establish that Baalsrud was still alive, and the third attempt by the men from Manndal to locate him was finally successful. However, bad weather intervened again, and Baalsrud had to be abandoned in the open or in a cave on several further occasions before there was finally contact with a Sami who agreed to take Baalsrud to Sweden. During this period, when he was on his own, a small German patrol passed by only thirty yards from where Baalsrud was lying, without discovering him. He spent nearly three weeks out in the open, exposed to freezing winter weather. The last part of the journey with the Samis was not uneventful either, because close to the border they were spotted and fired on by a German patrol. Fortunately, the patrol was too far away, and the party crossed into Sweden unscathed. Baalsrud was taken to hospital in Boden, where he was taken out of the sleeping bag in which he had lain for over a month. He spent months in hospital, where medical treatment saved what remained of his feet, and was repatriated to England in late September.[44] He was awarded an MBE and recovered sufficiently to be able to work as an instructor at Glenmore and to deploy back to Norway as the war ended.

A cheerful Jan Baalsrud (right), the only survivor from Operation MARTIN, on his way back to Norway at the end of the war. © NHM

SOE calculated that the total distance which Baalsrud had covered during his escape was approximately 170 miles, which included thirty-five miles by water, seventy miles on foot and by ski, and sixty-five miles when he was being carried on a sledge.[45] SIS wrote to SOE in July, saying that they had heard that Baalsrud was in Sweden. They asked whether it could be arranged for them to interview him once he returned to England. 'He has been looked after in Tromsø district by our men, and we would like to get from him all the local colour we possibly can with regard to our organisation in this district.' SOE duly arranged this, and after they had met him and read his report SIS wrote, 'this is an amazing story of fortitude, devotion and courage on the part of Baalsrud and our Upsilon organisation, and is epic'.[46]

Archer/Heron: further German reprisals

SOE normally took great care to try to avoid the possibility of German reprisals against the local population. Saboteurs were instructed to leave items of British equipment or clothing at the scene of an operation, to encourage the Germans to think that British commandos were responsible. This deception generally worked well, but it was inevitable that there would occasionally be incidents involving SOE personnel which led to harsh German reprisals. One of the worst occurred after the penetration of the Archer/Heron party. The first members of this group landed on Vega Island in Nordland, just south of the Arctic Circle, in December 1941, and were reinforced in the spring of 1942 by two further groups led by a Swede, Birger Sjøberg. Their tasks were to train local groups and set up arms dumps: over six months they received twenty-four tons of supplies, and moved most of them long distances over difficult terrain to safer storage, a prodigious feat. They achieved good success and SOE estimated, with exaggerated optimism, that the team had trained nearly a thousand men. However, they were given away by a mixture of the indiscretions of local supporters, and betrayal by a Norwegian informant. An exchange of fire between some of the group and a German arresting party near Majavatn on 6 September led to the death of two Germans and the accompanying Norwegian sheriff. Archer/Heron broke up.[47] This incident also coincided with two successful raids – Knotgrass/Unicorn – against the Glomfjord power station, and Kestrel against the Fosdalen iron ore mine. (SOE contributed to the former, and carried out the latter.) The Germans reacted very sharply and, as a reprisal, shot thirty-four local hostages and proclaimed a state of emergency in the Trondheim area.*

Other problems faced by SOE

In early September 1942, Wilson reviewed the extent of SOE's progress in establishing its organisation in Norway. He noted that in the previous year SOE had extended its reach by setting up stations from the edge of the Arctic Circle southwards: including Archer and Heron in Nordland; Lark in Sør-Trøndelag; Antrum in Møre og Romsdal; Mallard, Raven and Penguin in Hordaland; Arquebus in Rogaland; Cheese and Swan in Vest-Agder and Aust-Agder; Grouse in Telemark; Anchor in Vestfold, Anvil in Oppland; and Crow in Akershus. While this was an impressive achievement, it had come at a cost. The Arquebus agents had been lost at sea while returning to Britain and the radio was out of action. The Penguin and Anchor wireless operators had both been killed in Telavåg in late April. The Anchor organiser was captured in Drammen in May. Mallard and his assistant were both captured on 30 May after they had been in Norway for only six weeks. The Crow wireless operator had been arrested on 26 July after being in Norway for four months. The Archer wireless operator was arrested on 6 September and there was also information that Heron had come under suspicion and some of his party had been arrested in early September. Wireless operators had experienced the greatest difficulties, and Wilson calculated that a total of sixteen operators had been sent over to Norway with fifteen sets. However, of that number only six stations were still surviving – Heron, Lark, Anvil, Antrum, Raven and Cheese – while two more, Swan and Plover, were not yet on the air.

Wilson concluded that the Norwegian section had achieved a success rate of about 50 per cent. However, this did not take into account

---

* Although the group broke up, Sjøberg remained in the area and continued his work until a further group arrived in May 1943 to replace him and he returned to Britain. He went back to Norway with Falcon in January 1944 and was killed in June that year.

the very severe losses suffered by loyal Norwegians in Norway who might have been implicated in SOE's activities. He noted that the Norwegian government was solid in its support and emphasised that the threat of reprisals could not be permitted to justify the cessation of all aggressive operations. The fact that the Germans used reprisals as a weapon meant that the very greatest care needed to be taken in the preparation and planning of all their activities. This should include the thorough training of personnel, the collection of up-to-date intelligence, the provision of equipment and supplies, transport, the passing of messages, and every detail connected with activities of every nature operated both from Britain and through Stockholm. Equipment needed to be checked carefully to ensure that it worked properly – there were still examples of radios failing to function – and that it contained no compromising materials of British origin, such as toothpaste or British batteries. There had been examples of both – and sometimes even more embarrassing incidents, where supplies were wrapped in British newspapers.

Wilson was frank about the fairly long list of reasons causing failures, which involved shortcomings on both the British and the Norwegian sides, and the steps which should be taken to address them. He pointed out that long-term planning was a foreign concept to many of those who were sent to Norway, as they had hoped for an Allied landing in 1942 and risked being more casual. He also blamed a Norwegian tendency to overrate the loyalty of relatives and friends, carelessness and the combination of separate objectives for the same mission – a characteristic we have seen several times. It would be necessary to ensure in future that personnel were not landed at the same time as arms which were to be stored in dumps. No two arms consignments should be landed in the same neighbourhood. Neither organisers nor wireless operators destined for different areas should be sent on the same trip, as had happened at Telavåg. A series of trips to the same destination should be avoided unless there was certainty that no suspicion had been aroused by a previous trip. A boat carrying out an operation should not visit two separate places on the coast during a single trip. Prior arrangement for the reception of personnel or arms should be made most carefully. And, finally – and perhaps most importantly – it was essential to establish close liaison with other organisations (such as the navy) also conducting operations on the Norwegian coast.[48]

Dealing with Norwegian collaborators

Despite the planning and careful preparation outlined by Wilson to reduce the risks to SOE in Norway, it did not prove possible to eliminate all the risks. There were some aspects which were often beyond their control. In particular, the actions of collaborators, informers and agents provocateurs posed a threat to loyal Norwegians.

The most damage was done by members of the Rinnan gang, led by Henry Rinnan and Ivar Grande, whose activities led to the deaths of many Norwegians. Perhaps Rinnan's most notorious achievement was the successful infiltration of a resistance group based in the Vikna district of Trøndelag, of which one of the leaders was the cleric Thorvald Moe. Rinnan ingratiated himself so successfully that Moe started to trust him with information and to cooperate with him. When Moe was arrested by the Germans, Rinnan staged his release and encouraged him to travel to Sweden. Before his departure, Moe gave Rinnan extensive information about his activities and contacts, which enabled Rinnan to take over the whole organisation, running it from early 1943 until September 1944. The group was eventually broken up, and well over a hundred Norwegians were arrested. Many were tortured, and some were killed.[49] Also in 1943, Rinnan obtained information which enabled him to betray Henry Thingstad, the leader of the youth sports club in Trondheim which was active in resistance. Thingstad and nine others were executed. The Rinnan group was considered so important that they were given their own office in the German headquarters in the Misjonshotell, the Gestapo headquarters in Trondheim. Grande was liquidated after four unsuccessful attempts, while Rinnan was captured, tried and executed after the liberation.

In the wartime conditions which existed in Norway, it was also possible for experienced resistance members to be taken in by people who subsequently sought to betray the organisation. For example, Einar Skinnarland, who played a key role in GUNNERSIDE, later recruited a young lad called Erling Solheim in the winter of 1943. Solheim had been a school friend and was considered to be a good patriot by local acquaintances. He provided the resistance with some quite useful information. In February 1944, a Norwegian working for the Gestapo in Oslo intercepted a letter to the Gestapo from Solheim in which he expressed his willingness (in return for money) to provide information on Milorg activities in Rjukan, Brevik and Moss. This was reported and two resistance members disguised themselves as Norwegian state police and drove to Rjukan in a Norwegian police car, carrying police identification papers. They told Solheim that the Gestapo were most grateful for his offer, which they accepted, and asked him to tell all he knew. Solheim did so, while they took copious notes. He then asked for 100,000 Norwegian kroner, whereupon they shot him, left his body in the middle of the road and arranged for publication of the story in the local clandestine press as a warning to others.[50]

Sometimes there was compassion, or at least understanding, in similar (but less serious) cases. Arthur Pevik, who was one of the early SOE organisers in Trondheim, recruited Nils Lien into his organisation. He had known Lien well before the war; the two of them had fought together against the Germans after the invasion. Lien was wounded and Pevik took over their platoon.[51] For some time Lien worked effectively by disseminating BBC news broadcasts to local patriots. However, he was then seen being driven in a car belonging to the German security police, which led to him being unmasked as an informer. Pevik informed him that he would be liquidated unless he left for Sweden, which he did immediately.

As this problem became more serious, the Norwegian government decided that it was necessary to take action to eliminate informers. Actions to deal with them were approved by Torp and General Hansteen.

However, the first attempt, Bittern, which was mounted by SOE at the request of the Norwegian High Command in October 1942, was not a success.

Milorg were not consulted before the group's arrival about the nature of the tasks which they had been given. They were not at that stage convinced that the policy was justified and did not agree with the selection of those on the list for 'liquidation'. The group was dropped without warning on a site that had been selected by another resistance group, which consequently then had to look for somewhere else. Other aspects of the group's behaviour also upset Milorg, particularly the excessive drinking of some of them. They exhibited other shortcomings too: Johannes Andersen had been a notorious burglar before the war and took little trouble to conceal that fact. Although some of the group did well as instructors, Milorg became alarmed at the risks which Bittern posed, and sent them back to Stockholm after only six weeks. Wilson was told afterwards that 'it is extremely interesting to note that the worst complaint we have ever heard from Norway concerning our agents in the field and our own behaviour in London comes from an operation planned entirely by the Norwegian High Command'. With SOE's own previous problems with Milorg in mind, Wilson retorted that the case had served a useful purpose, 'if for no other reason than that it had made the Norwegian High Command fully alive to the difficulties which we ourselves have experienced in the past'.[52]

In the autumn of 1943, SOE staged a 'rat week' covering all occupied European countries. The intention was to liquidate a range of informers throughout Europe and thereby obtain the maximum effect. The results in Norway were meagre, but gradually Milorg became more accepting of the need for such measures, which were carried out quite extensively in 1944 and 1945. Although SOE helped to support these activities, and to despatch groups such as Goldfinch and Chaffinch (which were among those heavily involved), the decisions about which collaborators should be liquidated were generally resolved between Milorg and the Norwegian High Command. It will never be known exactly how many people were killed in these operations. SOE calculated that there had been fifty-nine, while the Norwegian total was sixty-five. Arnfinn Moland's research has gone further, providing details of eighty-two confirmed cases of liquidations carried out by the resistance, but it is quite possible that there were other instances which will remain unknown.[53]

CHAPTER 8

THE SIS COAST-WATCHERS
DEVELOPMENT OF NAVAL COVERAGE

*The following consists of extracts from reports on German intelligence opera-
tions in Scandinavia. They are chiefly of interest from a technical viewpoint.
The information about the German post at Vardø was obtained from an
agent in the post, and is of such a secret nature that the CSS* has forbidden
its distribution 'in toto'. If found, it will certainly be traced back to me.*

HANDWRITTEN REPORT FROM KIM PHILBY TO THE NKVD
(RUSSIAN INTELLIGENCE), I AUGUST 1941, PASSING ON
INTELLIGENCE OBTAINED FROM AN SIS ABWEHR AGENT
BASED IN VARDØ IN NORTHERN NORWAY.

It has hitherto been thought that at the beginning of August 1941,
Skylark B in Trondheim was the only active SIS station in Norway.
While it provided some valuable information (including details about
heavy water production at Vemork – see Chapter 9 – and *Bismarck*'s
destroyer escort), it was not able to supply more than a small fraction
of the naval intelligence which was urgently required by Naval Intelligence Division (NID). However, SIS did have another source of
intelligence in Norway at this time, even if they chose not to circulate
his reporting outside their own service. This was an Abwehr officer
who, in August 1941, was based in the coastal port of Vardø, in the far

---

* Chief of SIS, Stewart Menzies.

north of Norway, not far from the Russian border. He remained in Norway throughout the war.

British and Norwegian archives provide few details about his work. The best information available comes, ironically enough, from NKVD archives in the form of reporting in August 1941 by Kim Philby, the SIS officer who was a Soviet spy.* Philby was at that time working in Section V, the counter-intelligence section of SIS, a position which gave him access to some of SIS's most sensitive secrets – as these documents show. Since the most detailed of his reports described the location of SIS's Abwehr agent, Philby, with understandable concern for his own safety, pointed out that Menzies had forbidden its circulation outside SIS. It would therefore make him vulnerable if the Russians were to use the material unwisely. The intelligence he sent to the NKVD described the extent of Abwehr activities against the Soviet Union – mostly through the use of fishing vessels, also the identities of cover firms which were used, communications schedules, cypher systems and the identities of Abwehr officers in Vardø, Tromsø and Oslo, as well as the names of Norwegians who were involved in these operations. Although the German invasion of Russia, Operation BARBAROSSA, had started barely seven weeks previously, these Abwehr operations were already well developed – they would of course have known well in advance of what was being planned and so had time to prepare.

A further Philby report provided the names of suspected Norwegian communists who were known to be active in the Kirkenes area near the Russian border, the identities of several more Abwehr officers, and also details of Norwegians working for the Germans. These included George Furre, the skipper of *Urd II*, who had sailed to Lerwick in November 1940 and lured three SOE agents back to Norway – and back to their deaths (see Chapter 5). Although Philby did not make its provenance clear in this report, some of his information almost certainly came from ISOS – Abwehr reports which had been decyphered by GC&CS. In view of the

---

* NKVD records are held in the SVR archives, Moscow.

large number of Abwehr attempts to infiltrate Norwegian agents into Britain, several of whom managed to slip through the refugee screening process, counter-intelligence information from this Abwehr source would have been of considerable value. It usefully supplemented the GC&CS reporting. This evidence shows how Philby was in a position to cause damage to British and Norwegian interests by passing information to the Russians about German and presumably Anglo-Norwegian intelligence operations in northern Norway. But, even greater damage would have been caused by the fact that he was revealing that GC&CS had already broken Abwehr cyphers.

The only information concerning this agent in British archives is contained in a letter of May 1945 from SIS to John Masterman, chairman of the Twenty Committee which ran the successful series of double-agent operations against the Germans. The letter described the agent as 'a reliable source, who has been working in Norway for the Abwehr since 1941'. SIS informed Masterman that he had provided information about the double agents Mutt and Jeff (see Chapter 5), commenting that since they had asked for a new wireless set – the most recent one which the Germans had – the Abwehr had concluded that the pair were under control and that the transmitters were being operated by the British. Their suspicion was strengthened by the fact that their transmissions sometimes lasted for as long as an hour. By the time the request for a new set was made, Mutt had been operating for over three years, so his career had been a pretty successful one. The agent also provided details of Nikolay Hansen, who had been dropped by parachute on 30 September 1943 and given himself up, and of an agent codenamed Beetle, who had been operating in Iceland since 1942. Beetle had been delivered there by submarine, and provided intelligence about convoys as well as weather reports.[*]

---

* The fact that SIS only passed this information to the Security Service right at the end of the war might suggest that they continued to regard his reporting as extremely sensitive and so its circulation remained restricted. However, it is also possible that the agent did not discover these details until a very late stage.

The agent would certainly have provided intelligence about Abwehr operations against SIS stations and activities in Norway. There is no clear evidence in Norwegian archives that SIS shared this intelligence with the Norwegians at any stage during the war, though it is quite possible that they might have done so in a disguised form in circumstances which they judged to be particularly important.

Towards the end of the war, SIS Norwegian agents began to develop contacts with German officers who foresaw the coming German defeat and wanted to trade information in the hope of obtaining better treatment after hostilities ended. These included a senior Abwehr officer, Konrad Gallen, whose original name appears to have been Galuzka, which was Polish. He had served in Norway since the summer of 1944 and started to cooperate with the SIS station Gullfax, which was based outside Oslo, in the spring of 1945. Gullfax reported that through him they had a chance to get in touch with the appropriate German authorities to negotiate a possible capitulation to the Allies. Since Allied policy was to insist on unconditional German surrender and to discourage such initiatives, SIS replied simply that the suggestion had been passed on to the proper authorities.[2] Gallen also offered the station a chance to move from the forest into his house and transmit from there, which he considered would be safer for them. Gullfax reported this to SIS in London, who were suspicious of the offer and instructed the station to remain in the woods.[3]

An example of Gullfax reporting from such a German source on 25 January 1945 is contained in the following extract, which gives something of the atmosphere in which the station was operating:

My head source reports that a German officer in the security police has told him that the German security police are in a state of emergency, ready to take action against a transmitter in the Oslo district.

The Germans know where the transmitter is and that the station is to have supplies dropped.

They also know and can break the station's codes and have [had] the station under complete control for a long time.

Action will be taken when the stores are dropped.

Other details are not known and apparently cannot be obtained. I will do what I can and will await your instructions regarding what you wish I should try to bring to light.

Can these codes be broken?

That was an understandable question. The Germans were generally only able to break SIS and SOE cyphers after they had captured a station and gained possession of the codes. They could then analyse the traffic and recover previous messages. The station referred to was Corona. Poignantly, it was Johanna (the name of the new wireless set provided for Corona), which replied on 28 January:

It is reported from Victoria Terrasse* that a code has been broken, and that BBC message and pinpoint for a proposed parachute drop are known. The Germans are lying in wait.

I propose the following: send all the relevant BBC messages for the Oslo area immediately.† But do not send any aircraft.

Inform all stations of the situation. Use emergency code and let us watch how the Germans react. Send urgent reply today.

There is nothing to show whether this warning was passed on by SIS to the four other stations which were operating in the Oslo area at that time. It only later became known that the Germans had indeed been able to read the cypher which Corona was using after they had surprised some of its members, who dropped a bag and fled. The bag contained transmission schedules and other information which gave the Germans what they needed. They subsequently also managed to locate the station by direction finding.[4] For unknown reasons they did not interfere when stores were dropped on 21 February, but raided the

---

* Gestapo headquarters in Oslo.
† BBC messages were often used to alert stations to drops which were planned for the following night. This suggestion, if followed, could have misled the Germans about what was planned.

site where it was operating on 18 March 1945, and both the wireless operator Arne Eikrem, and his lookout Karl August Nerdrum, resisted arrest and were killed in an exchange of fire.[5]

SIS radio operators were often protected by an armed guard in case of a German raid. © NHM

The early stations

Chapter 4 examined the importance of Norway as a suitable location for operations which recovered significant quantities of German cypher material and equipment. This greatly helped the breaking of Abwehr codes. Some of the material also helped to break other German cypher systems. The part which this intelligence played in winning the Battle of the Atlantic has been well described by Hinsley.[6] It played an important role, too, in charting the movement of German naval units in Norwegian waters, after they began to be based there in force from 1942 onwards, as well as the movements of commercial shipping carrying cargoes of strategic minerals. But as Edward Thomas (who worked in GC&CS for a period in 1942) commented, valuable though this intelligence was, it was seldom complete and often late. The reporting of SIS coast-watching stations was a very important supplement to Ultra, and regularly provided the first intelligence about German naval movements to be received in London.[7] Its value cannot be underestimated.

However, the early attempts to establish coverage were frustratingly slow. Although the director of naval intelligence, Godfrey, told the Chief of Naval Staff in early January 1942 that 'NID is well served at key points on the Norwegian coast', not everyone shared his view. Only three months later, in April, the newly appointed SIS deputy director (Navy), John Cordeaux, complained that SIS coverage in Scandinavia was very limited, with representation only in Oslo (Beta), Bergen (Theta), Trondheim (Lark and Lark II) and Bodø (Deneb, but it did not have two-way communications).[8] In fact, the situation was rather better than that and closer to Godfrey's description. Station Koppa was established in Ålesund the previous October, and had functioned effectively until it was betrayed in February 1942; Eric (north of Florø), manned by the redoubtable Dagfinn Ulriksen and Atle Svardal who performed so well that they were to meet King Haakon on their return (see Chapter 1), had been a prolific source of intelligence for six months between August 1941 and February 1942; Zeta (near Stord between Bergen and Stavanger) was also in action between November 1941 and July 1942, providing a small number of useful reports.

SIS hermit station Eric, manned by Dagfinn Ulriksen and Atle Svardal. It was located on Gåsøy (on the right in the middle distance in the shipping lane). © NHM

Nonetheless, the need for extensive coverage of the Norwegian coast had become strikingly obvious after Theta reported on 23 January 1942 that *Tirpitz* was lying in a fjord near to Trondheim and large elements of the main German fleet began to be based there. By May 1942, the *Tirpitz* and three heavy cruisers *Hipper*, *Lützow* and *Admiral Scheer* together with eight destroyers, four MTBs and twenty U-boats were located between Trondheim and Kirkenes.[9] Their presence represented a very considerable threat to Atlantic and later Arctic convoys. SIS took steps to extend its coverage, recruiting and training more willing Norwegian volunteers, and by July 1942 NID commented that intelligence on Norway was much improved – 'though more information on coast defences would be welcome and certain vital areas are not adequately covered'.*[10] Theta also contributed to Ultra reporting about the passage northwards from Bergen of *Prinz Eugen* and other German warships in late February 1942, which enabled the British submarine *Trident* to damage her with a torpedo off Trondheim shortly afterwards. The station received praise from SIS: 'Congratulations. You are sitting right in a wasp's nest. Be careful and live long.'[11] (This well-meaning advice was insufficient. The Germans arrested members of the group in June 1942, and the station was forced to close.) Moreover, in May 1942, four SIS stations reported on the movements of *Prinz Eugen*, sailing southwards from Trondheim to Kristiansand. They provided sufficient notice that the Admiralty was able to have her located by air reconnaissance and subjected to an air attack. Unfortunately, the attack was unsuccessful.[12]

The scale of the coverage required from SIS agents, and the number of possible hiding places for German ships as well as boats operating from Shetland and supplying the resistance, were much larger than one might think. It gradually became apparent that German ships were adopting the technique of hiding in narrow fjords by day, positioning

---

* As well as providing cryptographic material, documents captured in the Vågsøy raid in December 1941 included full details of German coastal defences from Norway to France. But these needed to be updated.

themselves as close as possible to the sides of steep fjords to avoid detection. It was not easy for the analysts in NID, as it might not be for the reader either, to grasp the complexities of Norwegian coastal geography or to appreciate the distances involved as they struggled to locate some of the place names mentioned in SIS agent reporting or to plan deployments. A baffled Lieutenant Commander W. Todd, responsible for Scandinavia, illustrated the difficulties in 1942:

Norway is God's own jigsaw puzzle. No other coastline in the world is so deeply indented. Fjords, with inner branches like trees in winter, push in between the mountains for ninety miles or more. Islands are counted by the hundred on every chart. Yet every fjord, every point, bay and island must have a name. No language on earth could provide different names for so many places, and Norway has long since abandoned the attempt. Place names repeat themselves unblushingly. But there are other potential causes of confusion … For example, there is a Puddefjord, which was so called by those who lived on one side of the fjord, but it is called Damsgårdfjord by those who lived on the other side, as they did not like the name Puddefjord…* It is 2,100 miles from the Swedish border of Norway in the south to the Finnish frontier in the north, but following the coastline, the distance would be 16,400 miles.[13]

That is two-thirds of the circumference of the earth.

Training

The first SIS training school for Norwegian agents was established by Frank Foley at 5 St James's Street in central London. It was later moved to another location at 14 Brompton Square. The initial training run by the British was quite rudimentary, concentrating on telegraphy, basic security measures and the use of codes. It was gradually developed further and Norwegian instructors started to work there during the

---

* Puddefjord and Damsgårdfjord lie off Byfjord, in the central part of Bergen.

summer of 1941, though SIS retained responsibility for the syllabus. However, the Norwegian students became disillusioned with the quality and breadth of the training – and also the standard of some of the equipment with which they were issued. There were stories of cameras that did not function properly, faulty weapons and equipment which had been wrapped in English newspapers.[14] (A complaint which was also made by SOE agents, see Chapter 7.) Wireless sets, which were large, were provided in identical suitcases. Oluf Reed Olsen (stations Aquila and Makir) described how he once travelled on a train with a German SS officer, who became interested in the bag containing his radio, and could not stop staring at it.[15] There were also incidents when agents were sent to Norway but found on arrival that they could not get in touch with London. They did not know whether they had been inadequately trained, their radio was faulty, or they had been issued with the wrong transmission schedule – there were times when each of those faults was identified. One such example happened in November 1941 when Eivind Viken was sent to Florø to establish station Pi, but could not make contact. He was brought back a few weeks later by Leif Larsen.

Norwegian dissatisfaction grew to such an extent that a letter of complaint, listing shortcomings in training and equipment, was sent to Oscar Torp, the Minister of Defence. This led to some extensive discussion. At a meeting between Cordeaux and Roscher Lund on 9 October 1942 to discuss the future organisation of SIS in Norway, a comprehensive range of changes were agreed. The syllabus was significantly extended, and training responsibilities were fairly evenly divided between British and Norwegian staff. Codes were improved too, and some staff were posted elsewhere.[16] Thereafter the Norwegians were more fully involved in policy regarding training matters, and the quality of training improved greatly. From an early stage, SIS agents were trained to operate as discreetly as possible, and not to become involved in other activities such as sabotage or propaganda. They were instructed not to fight unless in self-defence where silent escape was impossible.

SIS coast-watching operations in Norway

The SIS controlling officer Eric Welsh was keen on establishing what came to be called 'hermit stations' in isolated places on the coast, where SIS agents (usually sent in pairs) would be expected to survive on their own, often for considerable periods of time. They would generally be living in extremely difficult conditions and sheltering from the weather in goat caves or tents or, if they were lucky, in a primitive cabin. Ole Snefjellå, one of SIS's most successful coast-watching agents, worked for a total of eighteen months on three different hermit stations, Pi (near Stavenes) in 1942, Crux (near Mo i Rana) in 1943 and Frey (south of Ålesund) in 1944. He calculated that a station which was expected to operate self-sufficiently for six months would need almost two tons of supplies consisting of food, equipment and a small power plant with fuel to provide electricity for the radio. So the delivery of agents – by whatever means – and the establishment of their stations, was rarely a straightforward matter. Snefjellå provides a vivid description of how he and his fellow agents lived in caves, or primitive dugouts made of turf and stones. These needed to be buried as far as possible below ground level to facilitate camouflage protection, which meant that they were generally very damp. Food quickly became mouldy and deteriorated.

Keeping track of German naval movements. A coast-watcher's vantage point. © NHM

Snefjellå also described the respect in which Welsh was held by SIS's Norwegian agents, noting that while 'he required the agents to endure hazards and if need be, severe conditions', he also 'did his utmost to save agents who were being chased by the Germans or who were in severe difficulties'.[7] (One of Welsh's favourite catchphrases was 'little, but good'.) Snefjellå had particular reason to be grateful to Welsh for his humanity on these grounds. He was first deployed to Pi in April 1942, and his station provided extremely valuable intelligence, for example being one of the four SIS stations to report the southbound journey of *Prinz Eugen* on 17 May, and the northbound journey of *Lützow* two days later. But, shortly afterwards, the Germans began to make arrests locally, and at least one of those taken knew of the activities of the station. Fearing for their safety, on 21 May the members of Pi asked to be rescued and the following night a Catalina collected Snefjellå and four others. This was not a straightforward operation, for there was a German guard boat in the area, and in their haste to escape the agents had to leave a large amount of money and grenades in their boat, though these were later recovered by a sympathiser.[18] Godfrey wrote to Air Chief Marshal Joubert de la Ferté, in charge of Coastal Command, to thank the crew for 'carrying out the hazardous flight so successfully'.[19] The Norwegian crew of the Catalina, and John Turner of SIS who had accompanied them, were decorated with the King's Cross by King Haakon.

Not all SIS attempts to rescue their agents were so successful. In February 1945 Ibsen, a station based in Finnsnes in northern Norway, reported that *Lofoten* was carrying 150 Norwegian prisoners from Tromsø to Trondheim. This number included three SIS head agents, from Lyra, Synnove and Taurus. SIS sought Admiralty assistance in arranging to intercept the vessel and rescue them. This proved to be impossible, because the only ships which could be made available were unsuitable for the stormy weather then prevailing. SIS made considerable further attempts to intervene, contacting another five stations to see whether they could help, but these efforts were also thwarted by poor weather. The agents were taken to Oslo, and survived the war.

It was perhaps unrealistic of Welsh to expect that hermit stations would be able to manage entirely on their own. They needed to rely on assistance provided by the local population for a range of support, from charging accumulators to enable them to work their radio sets, to the occasional provision of fresh food and keeping them in touch with events in the neighbourhood, particularly the effectiveness of German attempts to locate them. Sometimes this support included acting as couriers and delivering information provided by other agents, which could supplement the coast-watching intelligence they sent back to London.* For young and active men, living in such close proximity for extended periods in danger and under stress could cause nervous tensions which led to disagreements and fights and bloodshed. The damage this caused to their hands could then create problems for them when sending in Morse code. Atle Svardal, who had been a part of Eric, the first hermit station, returned with Eivind Viken to its successor, Erica. He and Viken occasionally came to blows. When in August 1944 Svardal was sent back to establish Roska, also in the same area, he asked for boxing gloves to be included in their supplies, to minimise both the damage which they might cause to each other and also the difficulties which they might otherwise have had with their Morse transmissions.[20] This showed a remarkable philosophical acceptance of the pressure and tension which he knew that he and Viken would be facing once again on their mission, as well as an imaginatively pragmatic way of dealing with it.

There were just over a hundred SIS stations active in Norway in contact with London at various times during the German occupation. Some of them lasted only weeks before their agents were arrested by the Germans or disrupted and force to leave their posts. Others were able to last much longer. Beta, in Oslo, held the remarkable record of remaining operative from 14 January 1942 until the end of the war, a period of nearly three and a half years.

---

* Nagell calculated that there were altogether about 1,800 such Norwegians who helped to support SIS stations, while Nøkleby reckons that the figure was closer to 2,000.

Rudsetra, one of the locations of Beta, SIS's longest-surviving station, in the Nordmarka, a large forest to the north of Oslo. © NHM

The various incarnations of Upsilon, in Tromsø, did almost as well. Others achieved notable results in a much shorter space of time. Cygnus, near Florø, sent around three hundred messages in seven months between October 1943 and May 1944. As soon as November, Welsh noted that Cygnus was sending in valuable messages almost every day. The Air Officer Commanding in Scotland commented that the intelligence was of great value and that several operations had already been based on it. Furthermore, the Admiral Commanding Orkneys and Shetland wanted to see such operations extended to the Fleet Air Arm and to submarines: SIS was exploring how this might be done. Cygnus was eventually forced to close when it was located as a result of a German direction finding operation, but the agents were evacuated by a British MTB on 29 May. There were many similar examples. It was not only direction finding which enabled the Germans to identify stations and capture their agents. In one bad month in February 1944, SIS lost a series of stations including Upsilon in Tromsø, and Scorpion and Lark II in Trondheim. Welsh concluded – we do not know how accurately – that all of them had been lost due to German penetration of courier services which were carrying equipment or information to them from Stockholm. Both Welsh and Nagell had long been concerned about the risks of couriers from different services, mainly SIS and SOE, using the same routes and often travelling together, especially to northern Norway. Nagell observed, 'to judge by the not too good security-mindedness of these couriers I am afraid that in some cases this may lead to the ultimate destination and purpose of the journey being made known to the other party'.[21] Two further stations in the north, Libra and Taurus, had been forced to close for a while because of the loss of Upsilon. However, Welsh reported more cheerfully (and exaggeratedly) that the Libra wireless operator, while in the best of health, was taking a holiday at 'the SIS convalescent home' at Blomli in northern Norway!

There were other ambitious plans which did not work. One, in March 1943, was to establish station Andromeda on the island of Stjernøya, which would have controlled the entrance to the Altafjord. This could not be achieved because it proved impossible to arrange delivery of the agents to the island. If it had been in place and had been able to survive detection – which would have been quite a tall order for the area was really quite exposed – then Andromeda should have been able to report the departure of the *Scharnhorst* on 25 December 1943. Ultra did provide coverage of this, but GC&CS decyphering of the critical sailing report was slightly delayed because a new setting had just come into force. *Scharnhorst* sailed to attack an Allied convoy but was sunk by the Royal Navy off the North Cape of Norway. The only SIS station operational in the Altafjord at that time was Ida, manned by Torstein Raaby, which was located too far from *Scharnhorst*'s base in Langfjord to learn of her departure in time.

Skylark B and Lark

Skylark B was one of the first stations to be established in Norway. Erik Welle-Strand led a small team which was trained and sent back to Florø in September 1940. They moved to Trondheim, but difficulties with both the radio and transmission schedules meant that the station did not establish contact until January 1941. The group recruited a range of contacts to help them, including Einar Johansen and Bjørn Rørholt, both of whom did significant work for SIS. Rørholt was a student at the Norwegian Institute of Technology in Trondheim. He was a radio expert and helped to resolve Skylark B's communications problems. He had earlier had contacts with elements of the Norwegian resistance in Oslo. Such links enabled Skylark B to provide reports on German activities not only in Trondheim but elsewhere, too. After Oldell was broken up in Oslo in March, Skylark B was the only station functioning in Norway until August 1941. It was located by German direction finding in September 1941, and many of its members were captured. When this happened Rørholt was in Oslo and the Germans came looking for him. After exchanging shots with an arresting party, he escaped over a garden wall. The pursuing Germans were unable to follow Rørholt's example and lost him.

With the loss of Skylark B, SIS had no coverage of Trondheim. This became a matter of acute concern once *Tirpitz* became operational and Theta reported its arrival there in January 1942. SIS was required to re-establish a station urgently. Despite the fact that he was well known in the area and was still being sought after the earlier abortive attempt to arrest him, Rørholt volunteered to return from Britain. His first journey was unsuccessful because the boat proved to be unserviceable, but he was back in Trondheim early in February and quickly established contact with London. Rørholt decided that it would be necessary to have more than one station to monitor German naval traffic. Showing remarkable courage and resourcefulness, he posed as an insurance salesman and entered the Agdenes Fort, a series of fortified emplacements which guarded the entrance to the Trondheimfjord. While offering insurance policies to German officers, he also reconnoitred a suitable site for locating a wireless station close to the forts. He had recruited Magne Hassel for the task, equipping him with a simple code and initially arranging for him to send (but not to receive) messages, so as to reduce the risks of his transmissions being intercepted. Hassel sent some valuable messages on the movements of *Tirpitz* and other German warships. Within a fortnight in May, for example, he provided intelligence on the movements of *Hipper* (twice), and *Admiral Scheer*, as well as several other reports of cruisers and smaller naval vessels. In March 1943 he reported that *Tirpitz* with her escort had left the Trondheimfjord. This message reached the Admiralty within three hours. It was welcome intelligence because an aerial reconnaissance the previous afternoon had shown *Tirpitz* safely at anchor and they were not aware of her planned deployment.[22] Before he left again, Rørholt established a network with three further stations in Trondheim to extend naval intelligence coverage. These were Leporis, Scorpion and Virgo. All were valuable, and Scorpion was particularly useful.

Rørholt was awarded a DSO on his return, one of three such decorations which were given to SIS Norwegian agents – the others were Einar Johansen and Torstein Raaby. (The citation for Rørholt's award is given in the Appendix.) However, his career in SIS did not last much longer. He felt strongly that SIS radio communications were inadequate, and potentially dangerous to Norwegian agents. Before his departure to set up Lark he had worked with the Poles to develop a better, lighter and more compact wireless set, and took one with him. On his return to London, he sought to persuade SIS to introduce the use of the Polish sets with better cyphers, as well as adopting changes in sending frequencies which would complicate German direction finding activities. SIS refused to accept his recommendations, concluding that they were too complicated for the ordinary agent.[23] Rørholt argued strongly against this judgement, and at a meeting in October 1942 attended by Roscher Lund, Nagell, Cordeaux and Welsh, it was decided to dismiss him.[24] He spent the rest of the war working with SOE.[25]

Eric and Erica

Eric was the first hermit station to be set up in Norway. It was based on Gåsøya, north of Florø, and was manned by Atle Svardal and Dagfinn Ulriksen. Eric started in August 1941, and the two agents stayed there for seven months through a bitter winter, providing regular reporting on German naval movements. They were withdrawn in February 1942 because of concerns about German direction finding. Accompanied by Eivind

Viken, Svardal returned to the area in January 1943 to set up Erica, which has deservedly been described as one of the most successful stations run by SIS in Norway, for both the accuracy as well as the timeliness of its reporting. In a progress report, Welsh described one of their most significant achievements, noting that on 5 February Erica had sent in the following:

> Time of observation 1100: time of transmission 1312: time of receipt at HQ 1342: time of receipt at Admiralty 1348. The essence of this message was that one battle cruiser, one cruiser and three destroyers were travelling south. This signal was amplified on the same date at 1440 (received here at 1617 and passed to Admiralty at 1630). This proved fairly conclusively that the vessels in question were *Hipper*, *Koln* and three destroyers.

The quicker the Admiralty received such reports, the greater the chance that they would be able to arrange for the warships to be intercepted, although all too often such attempts were frustrated by poor weather. Despite the timely warning, that is what happened on this occasion.[26] On 1 May at 0630, Erica reported a sighting of *Nurnberg* going south, a message which was reinforced by one from Pollux (on the Sognefjord) sent at 0910 and received in the Admiralty at 1200.[27] These supplemented Ultra reporting and provided sufficient notice for RAF Coastal Command to search and sight her twice, but their attempted strike came to nothing.[28] Erica was also responsible for reporting which led to the sinking of the German merchant ship *Optima* by two Norwegian naval ships, MTB 619 and MTB 631, in Florø harbour on 14 March 1943.[29] NID was delighted by this intelligence and the deputy director of naval intelligence (D/DNI) wrote to SIS to 'express my appreciation for the invaluable reports which have been received from this station. The reliability of the reports and the speed of transmission make them of great value.'[30] When Viken and Svardal returned to London in September 1943, they met Menzies, who also congratulated them.*

---

* Svardal returned to Norway to run Roska, near Florø, and was killed in March 1945 when the Germans located the station through direction finding and raided it.

Ole Snefjellå: Pi, Crux and Frey

The brief but successful activities of Pi have already been described. When Ole Snefjellå went back to Norway the following year to a different location further north at Renga, near Mo i Rana, he took over the work of Crux with his brother Tore. Almost every progress report circulated by Welsh during the nine months they were based there commented that they were sending in valuable convoy intelligence. In early October 1943 they reported the passage northwards of the 4,000-ton cargo ship *Skramstad*, which was carrying nearly 1,000 German troops. She passed so close that Snefjellå could see the faces of the troops as they stood on deck admiring the passing scenery.[31] *Skramstad* was sunk on 4 October by aircraft operating from the USS *Ranger*.

The Snefjellå brothers returned to Norway in April 1944 to establish Frey on Gurskøy, south of Ålesund. The site they chose enabled them to watch convoys travelling south from Ålesund to Stad. They remained there until January 1945, and for much of this period they lived out in the open, their only shelter being a crude stone hut which they had built for themselves. The Germans had by this stage learned that the predictably precise timings and speeds of their convoys enabled Norwegian agents to forecast their progress along the coast. This facilitated the organisation of Allied attacks. So they mounted a series of intensive but unsuccessful searches to try to find them. On one occasion a German patrol spent the night only fifty feet from the ledge where the two brothers lay concealed. The Germans also tried to confuse matters by slowing down and delaying convoys before they rounded the peninsula at Stad. This did not work because it was right in front of the location where Frey was based. So Snefjellå could sometimes see the results for himself. 'We were located right on the end of the Stad peninsula, and after we reported the passage of a German convoy it would sail round the end of the peninsula. Then it had no chance of escaping. We watched the aircraft going in to attack.'[32] In July 1944, British aircraft attacked a large German ship carrying munitions, which exploded and sank off Kvamsøy. In December, the Snefjellå brothers watched a successful attack on a convoy which left ships in flames, 'and danced with joy'. SIS stations did not very often receive specific feedback on the value of their reporting, though Snefjellå did comment that Welsh credited Crux with responsibility for reporting which led to the sinking of twelve ships. 'But I don't know whether that is true for he was inclined to boast.'[33]

Snefjellå was awarded the Conspicuous Gallantry Medal for his work. He was the only Norwegian in SIS to receive this medal, though it was also given to Leif Larsen in SOE. After the war, he was also awarded the Distinguished Service Cross (DSC).[34]

Upsilon

While *Tirpitz* was based in Trondheimfjord, the Fleet Air Arm attacked it unsuccessfully when it emerged to try to intercept two Atlantic convoys, one sailing to and one returning from Murmansk. The RAF also attacked *Tirpitz* in Trondheim without success on three occasions in March and April, losing twelve aircraft. When elements of the German fleet moved further north to Narvik and Bogenfjord, and *Tirpitz* then moved to Altafjord in June, it became essential for SIS to develop its reporting capacity in the north of Norway.

A resistance photograph of the *Tirpitz*, damaged by the RAF and on its last journey from the Altafjord to Tromsø, where it was sunk in November 1944. © NHM

Torstein Raaby (Ida) and Einar Johansen (Venus) training in south London woods in the summer of 1943. The equipment (an Onan unit) supplied power for a radio transmitter. © NHM

An initial attempt to set up Delta in Bodø in November 1941 had failed because it proved impossible to establish a communications link. (This may have been because the wireless operator used too low a frequency, but atmospheric conditions in the far north frequently interfered with transmissions and telegraphic traffic was often delayed.) The first successful steps were taken when Einar Johansen was landed on Kvaløya west of Tromsø in April 1942. Johansen was among the most active of SIS Norwegian agents. He had started work as a wireless operator with Skylark B in Trondheim and either set up or assisted with the running of a further six stations, all of them in the north of Norway: Upsilon, Libra, Venus, Mu, Denebola and Gudrun. The first, Upsilon, made contact with London on 8 May 1942. It survived a series of disruptions, and was several times obliged to close and move to a new site. The effects of the ill-fated SOE Operation MARTIN, which led to the arrest and death of Kaare Moursund and Thor Knudsen, have already been described in Chapter 7. The following year Upsilon II was raided by the Germans in February 1944. Its successor was moved to the hospital in Tromsø and eventually installed in the attic above the mortuary. Chapter 11 highlights how the wireless operator Egil Lindberg sent reports from there about the sinking of Tirpitz while the bodies of dead German sailors were being carried in below. In its various different incarnations, Upsilon operated almost continuously from May 1942 until the end of the war. Johansen was evacuated back to Britain in January 1943, when it was found that he was suffering from pulmonary tuberculosis in both lungs as a result of the privations he had endured.[35] He recovered and later returned to Norway to continue his work.

Aquila

A progress report of September 1943 provides a flavour of the initiative and spirit with which one particular station coped with an unexpected German attempt to capture it. Aquila had been operating in the south of Norway in the Kristiansand area, and Welsh wrote,

> We are again in contact with this station which has had a most exciting time. It appears that while our stores were successfully dropped on 22 August, on the morning of the 23rd the landing ground and reception committee were surrounded by Germans and the men had to shoot their way out, leaving their stores and equipment behind.
>
> Two days later, the leader of the station returned and stole the wireless gear from beneath the noses of the Germans. Again two days later, he returned to see what else he could pick up and, in his own words, 'regretted that he had to make use of his weapon'.
>
> On getting in touch with him again, we instructed him to proceed immediately to Sweden to return to this country. However, on his way out, he found that he could set up a station in Oslo, believing that he was in a position to tap sources of information with which we were not in contact.
>
> Permission was given to him to do this, and I am pleased to inform you that he has re-established a really magnificent station whose reports are not only prolific, but of great value. He has also re-established his meteorological station and sends in weather reports every morning.[36]

The head agent was Oluf Reed Olsen. The site of Aquila, where the equipment was also stored, was under an overhanging ledge on a steep slope and so well hidden that despite an extensive search of the area, the several hundred searching Germans had not yet been able to find it. The best source of information Reed Olsen established in Oslo was the secretary to the Minister of Justice, who was able to provide intelligence on German future intentions in Norway. He subsequently spent six months running the Makir station near Kristiansand, providing information on shipping and U-boat movements, as well as weather reports.

Oluf Reed Olsen operating the SIS station Makir. © NHM

Another attempt to land agents in the far north

Chapter 2 described the unsuccessful attempt in August 1942 to send agents to the far north of Norway to establish a coast-watching service based in Kirkenes, station Argo. The Russians did not honour the agreement, and equipped Thor Sentzen and Hans Michael Skjervø with their own radio crystals, which proved fatally compromising for them after they were captured, and they were later shot. Moreover, they appeared to be about to intern the escorting SIS officer John Turner and not permit him to travel back with the Catalina which had brought the agents. Turner arranged with the RAF crew (who had permission to leave) to take advantage of confusion caused by a German bombing raid, evade the Russians and slip on board the

Catalina just as it was on the point of departure. They took him home.[37] But, notwithstanding this setback, the need for agent coverage of the German naval anchorage in the Altafjord became so acute that in May 1943 SIS decided to try again. At this time, they were still unaware of the fate of the Argo agents. The operation was codenamed ANTARES.[38] Menzies wrote to Rear-Admiral Rushbrooke, Godfrey's successor as DNI, outlining their plan. SIS first considered sending a Halifax to Murmansk, dropping the agents on the way, but this was ruled out because of the weight involved. An alternative, using a Catalina (carrying agents and stores) and a Halifax flying to Murmansk and then dropping the agents later, was also considered. The Air Ministry was reluctant to take the risk which it calculated only had a 5 per cent chance of success, and was only prepared to do so if the Chiefs of Staff so instructed them. They did not.[39] Nagell therefore wrote to a Russian liaison contact to ask whether the Russian Navy would be willing to make available a submarine or patrol boat to deliver the agents.[40] This was also unsuccessful. The agents were eventually transported by a Norwegian submarine, *Ula*, which in September 1943 delivered several others as well – some of whom would establish the Venus station near Tromsø. The group also included Torstein Raaby, who travelled on to Alta and established station Ida close to Kåfjord, where *Tirpitz* was based.

Finally, it is worth considering the example of an SIS agent who was never formally trained, but who nevertheless provided a remarkable service. When the Crux station was evacuated from Mo i Rana, south of Bodø, in June 1944, a fallback arrangement was made with the farmer on whose land the station had been hidden. It was agreed with him that in the event of necessity, he would receive a message over the BBC, and he would then try to get in touch. The SIS progress report for October 1944 describes what happened:

> Owing to recent activities in North Norway, it was considered necessary
> to try to resuscitate the station, and much to our surprise an immediate

message was received. We are greatly indebted to this 60 year old fisherman (Klaus Lines) who not only during the lives of the various Crux stations taught himself morse and code, but remembered both these and wireless procedures so well after a lapse of nearly six months that contact was achieved when it became necessary again to call on his services.[41]

Lines continued to provide reporting on shipping movements until the end of the war.

German attempts to infiltrate SIS operations

The Germans never succeeded in replicating in Norway the *England-spiel*. This was the operation in the Netherlands where for two years they captured almost all the agents sent by SOE and played radio games with SOE headquarters. They did arrest several SIS Norwegian wireless operators and forced them to send messages back to London. However, SIS was generally able to recognise the signs of this quite quickly, not least because it was difficult for the Abwehr to obtain approval to transmit any significant intelligence which might have enhanced the credibility of what they were trying to achieve. Once they detected them, SIS went along with these deceptions because they hoped that it might prolong the lives of the radio operators. In one particular case involving Lyra, in Vargsund on the Altafjord, the Germans captured the station in June 1944. They found a contact list which enabled them to roll up not only the station's network in Troms and Finnmark, but some of those of other stations in the area as well. Nonetheless, Einar Johansen remained and set up the Denebola station shortly afterwards. The Germans knew of his presence and his activities, and were continually searching for him, but without success. He remained until the end of the war and, having earlier received a DSC, was awarded the DSO.[42] The Lyra wireless operator, Trygve Duklæt, was made to keep up contact with London. SIS was warned what had happened, and kept up the pretence for nearly six months until the

Germans lost interest in December following the sinking of *Tirpitz*.[43] Duklæt was sent to Oslo and confined there until the liberation.

However, the Germans did come close to achieving some successful deception operations, in particular when they infiltrated Canopus. The agents, Arnfinn Grande and Kåre Nøstvold, were originally intended for Leo, near Trondheim. But, when they were dropped in March 1943, they could not find the radio and other equipment which had been sent with them. It was dropped in the wrong place. So they went to Sweden. The Abwehr learned of the drop, and found the equipment. Through a Norwegian agent Karl Adding, who had won the confidence of local resistance members, they sent a message to the Norwegian intelligence office MI.II in Stockholm asking the operator to return. Nøstvold did so, met Adding, and established contact with London in July. The Germans wanted him to establish contact with other resistance groups, but Nøstvold followed the guidance he had been given about avoiding such links, and refused to follow Adding's proposals. He insisted on sending only marine intelligence and – for a period at least – whatever the Germans provided for him passed muster in London.[44] SIS progress reports (which during this period were shown to Prime Minister Nygaardsvold as well as to Torp and Lie) record that he was sending in useful and sometimes valuable information. Without German intervention, Nøstvold went back to Stockholm in October and was supplied with equipment for Canopus as well as two further stations, Leporis and Aries. He returned in November, but did not re-establish contact with London. SIS learned shortly afterwards that the Germans were in touch with the station and so closed it down. They also learned at the same time that the short-lived station Capricorn, also in Trondheim, had been the unwitting recipient of intelligence provided to them by the Germans through an SOE group which they had infiltrated. So Capricorn was closed as well. All the agents, from both stations, escaped and were redeployed elsewhere.[45]

SIS progress reports contain regular references to German disruptions which compelled stations to close to allow things to quieten down. Sometimes they had close shaves. Upsilon II had to close in July 1943 when a German direction finding headquarters was set up barely fifty yards from where the station was based. More frequently the closures were the consequence of German activity following SOE operations in the neighbourhood. In November 1943, the operator manning the SIS Grid station reported that he had been obliged to close his station for a week because he had been given civil guard duty to prevent sabotage. SIS reported that he had complained, 'stop this sabotage nonsense so that I can get on with my work'. This was a sentiment which Menzies might have been tempted to reflect to the Chiefs of Staff![46]

The extent of coast-watching achievements

In addition to their reporting of the movements of German warships, coast-watching stations also provided extremely valuable coverage of merchant shipping along the Norwegian coast. It is not easy to make a reliable estimate of the volume of shipping which was sunk during the war, because of the range of different units involved in such operations – warships, MTBs, submarines, Bomber Command and Coastal Command. However, No. 18 Group of Coastal Command, responsible for this area (and a small part of Denmark), claimed responsibility for sinking 147 ships totalling over 267,000 tons, and damaging ninety ships totalling over 281,000 tons.[47] An equally telling statistic was that iron ore shipments declined from 40,000 tons a month in October 1943 to 12,000 tons in November 1944.[48] By 1943, the extent of successful Allied attacks on shipping in this area was so great that large ships were generally not permitted to sail beyond Tromsø. Most cargoes of strategic value were carried in smaller vessels, and ships were obliged to travel in convoys. Some of these sinkings can be attributed to RAF reconnaissance and signals interception. But the role played by the SIS coast-watchers was of the greatest significance.[49]

It is not often easy to establish from archival sources precisely which intelligence reports led to attacks on which merchant ships – though there is evidence for example that a report from Corona in May 1943 was the direct cause of an MTB sweep 'which resulted in the sinking of a large modern German cargo ship carrying valuable cargo'. The Admiral Commanding, Orkneys and Shetlands, was reported to be particularly pleased with this operation because 'it was carried out through the intelligence, planning and operational stages in the true naval manner'.[50] However, by the end of 1941 the Ministry of Economic Warfare had started to collate intelligence from photographic reconnaissance and SIS reporting to produce a survey of ports used by merchant shipping, to which Oldell and Skylark B made significant contributions.[51] This showed that the southern ports, especially Oslo and Bergen, were most heavily used and that shipping was concentrated in these more heavily defended anchorages until convoys could be formed for passage southward. Ports in northern Norway were used less and for shorter periods. Coastal Command therefore had to choose between attacking well-stocked but more dangerous anchorages in the south or the safer option of attempting to catch shipping further north in fjords and areas between defended anchorages. They chose the latter until much later in the war when German defences were weaker.[52] By the end of 1942 SIS agents were regularly providing intelligence on the movements of ore carriers, tankers, troop transports, flak ships and some larger fishing vessels.[53] Even better, by 1943, stations such as Aquarius were regularly providing intelligence about the planned departures of convoys the day before they took place, which allowed more time for attacks to be planned.[54]

NID had commented in July 1942 that more information on coast defences would be welcome and that certain vital areas were not adequately covered. However, by then SIS had already started to provide reporting on the locations and extent of enemy shore defences. This was reflected in the coastal defence reports which were produced by the Admiralty. In April 1942, for example, it was known to NID that in Norway there were some seventy-one gun emplacements fortified with heavy weapons, and another 137 containing smaller calibres. The locations of all significant fortifications around major ports had also been provided, as well as other important intelligence such as the location of minefields. SIS continued to develop this service throughout the war. It enabled both Coastal Command and Bomber Command to plan routes into Norway which had the best chance of avoiding these defences and thus limiting their losses.[55]

We have seen plenty of evidence of the extent to which the SIS coast-watching stations provided coverage of German naval movements – and Chapter 11 will consider the remarkable extent to which they contributed to coverage of *Tirpitz*, providing support for all of the attempts made to sink it while it was in Norwegian waters. It must sometimes have been as frustrating to SIS as it was to GC&CS that a combination of circumstances (poor weather, distance, unavailability of naval or air force units in the right location and sometimes sheer bad luck) prevented more successful attempts to sink German warships. On one particular occasion in September 1943, Crux reported the passage southwards of *Lützow* past Mo i Rana. Together with a series of Ultra reports, this intelligence helped to provide unusually precise details of its passage as *Lützow* sailed almost the entire length of the Norwegian coast without – on this occasion – being troubled.[56] It was a matter of some concern to SIS that the next four stations who might have seen her were not in a position to report on her passage. She passed Trondheim in the dark, the Erica station had been closed down, Cygnus was not yet properly established and *Lützow* passed the location of Aquarius so early in the morning that she was not observed. It was a reminder of some of the shortcomings of the system which was in place, and an encouragement to develop it further. But such intelligence contributed to other important objectives. In particular it facilitated appreciations by the Admiralty of German naval intentions, which enabled them to plan their own dispositions and quite frequently to take action to protect their own naval resources and convoys – though not, of course, PQ17.*

---

* See Chapter 11.

XU

The network developed by SIS and FO.II to provide intelligence reporting from Norway was not the only intelligence organisation functioning there during the occupation. There were more than a dozen others which were home-grown and operated quite independently. Two groups, known as RMO and SB, provided naval intelligence. Another, 830S, specialised in telephone interception and eavesdropping on Gestapo communications, which was of great value to Milorg. There were a number of smaller regional groups, too, such as the CX group which operated in Bergen until June 1942 when it was penetrated and broken up by the Germans. Most of them found means of sending the information they collected to the Norwegian legation in Sweden, where MI.II was responsible for receiving intelligence and collating then sending it back to London. However, the largest organisation was XU, with approximately 1,500 agents in southern Norway, which had achieved countrywide coverage by 1943, providing a wealth of political and military intelligence. It was formed in the summer of 1940, but its first steps were uncertain, and several of its early leaders were either shot (Arvid Storsveen), arrested or, like John Hagle, forced to escape to Sweden. Quite a number of XU members were also involved in supporting or working with SIS stations, not necessarily wise from a security point of view, but sometimes an unavoidable necessity when one or the other had been disrupted by the Germans. Thus the SIS wireless operator Kristian Fougner briefly used the flat of an XU leader, Bjørn Eriksen, as a transmitting base in Trondheim early in 1943.[57] Eriksen was arrested shortly afterwards and committed suicide by jumping out of a fourth-floor window. Hans Clifton, a very experienced radio operator who manned Njord and Lillemor in Vestfold, also sent many messages on behalf of XU.

We do not know a great deal about the work of XU. All of its members signed a non-disclosure agreement at the end of the war, which was only annulled in 1988. Only a handful have written or spoken publicly about their activities.[58] A few books have been written about its work, notably by Ulstein and Sæter, but archival material, particularly about its work in Germany on behalf of SIS, is relatively scarce. However, it is clear that SIS began to become closely involved in the work of XU in the spring of 1943. In January, General Hansteen suggested that XU should be extended and developed in close collaboration with SIS, who began to work on a plan for a network which would consist of fifteen stations throughout Norway. Soon afterwards, Roscher Lund produced a draft proposal for cooperation between SIS and the Norwegian services. This foresaw that the Norwegian office in Stockholm, MI.II, would have responsibility for all intelligence work originating in Sweden (which would include XU), while SIS would continue to be responsible for operations launched from Britain. There would be a planning council in London consisting of Welsh from SIS, together with representatives from FO.II and XU.[59] Cordeaux initially suggested that 'we should consider our present agents in Norway and the XU organisation as one service, and we should not consider this service separately insofar as it is providing information either by W/T or by courier service'.[60] However, Roscher Lund preferred to keep a closer degree of Norwegian control over XU activities. Cordeaux therefore suggested that the Norwegians should bear the cost for this work: 'As you know we are generally speaking anxious to share and share alike in the question of expenses but ... it seems that the XU ... will remain very much your responsibility and it will hardly be possible for us to have a detailed knowledge of it.'[61] SIS did provide assistance with training though. Matters did not remain so completely one-sided after SIS appreciated and started to exploit the potential of Norwegians studying in Germany either as sources of intelligence in their own right, or as channels of communication to pass on information from German agents who were working there. It is not surprising that such intelligence would have been of considerable interest to SIS, who found it difficult to run sources in Germany. In such cases, they paid all the costs which were involved.[62] The growth of this work, and the scale of XU reporting from Norway, led to a great increase in the activities of MI.II in Stockholm.

Cramped conditions in the MI.II Norwegian military
intelligence office in Stockholm. © NHM

SIS therefore arranged to second a Norwegian-speaking British officer,
John Turner, to work in MI.II with Colonel Dahl and facilitate liaison.
He used the alias John Pettersen and represented himself as a Norwegian.
This arrangement worked well, one might say profitably, until it came to
light that Turner was being paid both by SIS and also by XU. An irritated
Cordeaux told him to stop taking a salary from XU forthwith.[63]

SIS officer Captain John Turner, seconded to the Norwegian military intelligence office MI.II
in Sweden, wearing a mixture of Swedish and Norwegian uniform. © NHM

In November 1943, Cordeaux wrote to Roscher Lund to discuss the establishment of further SIS stations in the interior of Norway to provide reporting on military and air intelligence. He expressed concern that SIS might hitherto have been concentrating on naval matters to the detriment of other important areas. He intended to ask the War Office and Air Ministry whether they thought such intelligence could already be important enough to justify this investment, or whether it might become so in the near future – and if so, where? Cordeaux also asked whether Roscher Lund would want additional stations in Norway to facilitate communication with XU, as long as such an increase did not lead to the country being saturated with transmitting stations. As an interim step, he wanted to increase to twenty the number of agents in training. The service departments saw no immediate necessity for SIS to extend its reporting service, but anticipated that this might change quite quickly in the near future. They therefore welcomed the idea of SIS being in a position to respond without delay. So Cordeaux decided that it would be worth going ahead with additional stations. He asked Roscher Lund to coordinate this so as to fit in with XU requirements. He was very keen to expand the number of stations being worked by XU, which would enable them to provide a better reporting service. Scottish Command, which would be responsible for operations linked to the liberation of Norway, also wanted SIS to consider the formation of a special unit to obtain tactical and strategic intelligence for the Commander in Chief in the period immediately before and after liberation. They doubted whether this would require a large-scale investment. In the event, it proved possible to achieve all that was required through an increase in XU stations and XU reporting.[64]

The most well-known achievements of an XU agent in Germany appear to have been those of Sverre Bergh, a young Norwegian who was studying at the Technical High School in Dresden. He has described how he was recruited in Gothenburg in September 1941 and instructed to make contact with Paul Rosbaud, a German scientist who was already working for SIS.[65] Bergh was not the only Norwegian

XU agent who acted as a link to Rosbaud. There were several. After the war, Rosbaud wrote to an American academic colleague that 'all my messages I sent to England and were received there by old Eric Welsh through my contact with the Norwegian agents who came to see me regularly in Berlin'.[66] Through his wide range of contacts with German scientists, Rosbaud was in a position to provide intelligence on all significant German scientific work, including the progress of research in their atomic weapons programme. He also passed on information about the work being carried out at the experimental research station at Peenemünde on the Baltic coast in northern Germany, into the missiles which were developed as V-1s and the even larger V-2s. Rosbaud gave information on Peenemünde to Bergh during their first meeting in Berlin in September 1941. SIS apparently initially found this difficult to credit, and sent Bergh up to the Baltic coast to make his own inspection. The site was eventually bombed by the RAF in August 1943, and several times thereafter by the USAAF. Bergh's book described how he devised a range of methods to send his reporting back to Stockholm – via a friendly Swedish diplomat based in Berlin or in the handle of a hollowed-out tennis racket. He occasionally carried reports himself when travelling back via Sweden to Norway on holiday.

There are also examples of reports from other XU sources in Germany, exchanged between Welsh and Roscher Lund, on a variety of defence-related subjects. For example, a collated series of reports in February 1944, covering the location of factories for production of synthetic petrol; damage reports of the RAF attack on Peenemünde (not very successful); a detailed description of the V-2 missile, its payload, range and the launch site at Peenemünde; camouflage arrangements to disguise the large chemical works at Leuna near Leipzig, which was hidden by a village made from rushes being built on the roof; anti-aircraft defences on strategic factories near Dresden; dummy landing lights near Wiener Neustadt intended for deception purposes and new equipment for German night fighters enabling them to fly at over 30,000 feet, though not for more than fifteen minutes.[67] This was a remarkably wide range of subjects. Another report, from Roscher Lund to Welsh in December 1944, was also comprehensive, describing V-2s, and providing a specimen of an explosive used in the latest type of German bomb. Welsh commented that he found the report 'extremely interesting'. He wanted to know more about the source.[68] However, such archival references are limited, and there are even fewer details about other Norwegian students in Germany working for XU. The geographical range of subjects covered in the available reporting suggests that there must have been quite a few more.[69]

Bonuses

We saw in Chapter 2 and Chapter 7 how SOE personnel had problems over the amount of the bonuses which they were paid. This led to Wallin and Aksdal being imprisoned in Brixton, and was a contributory cause to the Shetlands crews being conscripted into the Norwegian Navy after they had complained about the loss of their bonus. All Norwegian agents were members of the Norwegian armed forces and seconded to SIS, who were sometimes more generous than SOE. When Rørholt came to Britain in December 1941 after the collapse of Skylark B in Trondheim, he submitted claims for money which he had spent on behalf of the station. Welsh told Nagell that he thought that the group deserved to be rewarded and suggested paying them altogether £700 (worth more than £35,000 today). He reminded Nagell that according to the original agreement drawn up between Frank Foley and Halvdan Koht, costs should be divided equally between the two services. Similarly, when Harald Johannessen returned in March 1942 after working on Beta in Oslo, Welsh suggested a bonus of £100 (worth more than £5,000 today). He also recommended paying bonuses of £200 (worth more than £10,000) to Sverre Midtskau (Skylark A) and of £100 to Erik Welle-Strand (Skylark B).[70] SIS continued to pay similarly generous bonuses throughout the war. Oluf Reed Olsen was paid £150 (worth over £7,500) for his work on Makir.[71] For most of the war, all Norwegian agents, whatever their rank, were paid £10 a week (worth more than £500), though after 1944 the most experienced agents were paid £12 a week.[72]

Transmitting from SIS station Beta in the summer of 1942. © NHM

Results, setbacks and losses

Just over a hundred SIS stations in Norway were able to establish contact with London during the occupation. Another forty stations never managed to function effectively or communicate with SIS. Although it has not been possible to establish precisely the numbers involved, for they can be calculated in different ways, well over a hundred agents were sent to Norway by various routes. Another a hundred who were recruited and trained locally, also worked for SIS. More than thirty stations were captured by the Germans or so disrupted that they had to close. Nearly thirty agents lost their lives, a slightly higher percentage than that of Norwegians working for SOE. Most were either shot by the Germans when resisting arrest, were executed or died in camps in Germany. Some committed suicide after arrest, or were killed in crashes or sinkings on their way to Norway. Some of these deaths were the result of unfortunate and unpredictable accidents. Thus in August 1942, Ewald Knudsen and Peter Andreas Ravik were delivered to Norway by

Catalina to establish Boreas on Skogsøy in northern Norway. However, as the result of a navigational error they were landed at Vornes, not far away from their intended landing site, but on the same beach where Hugo Munthe-Kaas had been landed from another Catalina only five weeks before to set up Libra. As a result of that, the Germans were alert to this site, and ambushed them. Ravik was killed before he could leave the beach, though Knudsen managed to escape.[73]

Ewald Knudsen (left) and Peter Andreas Ravik return to base after an unsuccessful attempt to land in Norway. On their next trip, they were ambushed by the Germans, and Ravik was killed. © NHM

Setbacks sometimes occurred because of other human errors. Ulva was landed from *Hitra* on 4 November 1944, with a large consignment of stores, to establish a station at Os, south of Bergen. The agent supervised the transfer of stores from *Hitra*, but forgot to go down to his bunk in the wardroom to collect two suitcases containing all the documents he needed, including his codes, passes, wireless crystals and money. (When informed about this error, Wilson commented: 'Words fail me!'[74]) SOE sailed another mission with *Hitra* to restore them to him on 8 November. The station sent its first – and only – transmission on 14 November, and was captured by the Germans three days later.[75]

CHAPTER 9

OPERATIONS FRESHMAN
AND GUNNERSIDE
ATTEMPTS TO DESTROY THE HEAVY
WATER PLANT AT VEMORK

At Vemork, I met Dr Brun, whose technical knowledge was so valuable to
Gunnerside ... Among those present were Poulsson, Skinnarland, Helberg
and Lind. I felt that if I had seen the actual terrain, I would have said that
the attack on the heavy water high concentration plant was an impossibility.
I said so to those who had taken part in it, and they grinned.
DIARY ENTRY DESCRIBING WILSON'S TOUR OF NORWAY, JUNE 1945.[1]

Allied attempts to prevent Norsk Hydro's production of heavy
water, which was thought to be a critical ingredient in the
production of a German atomic bomb, are among the best-known
stories of the Second World War. Operation GUNNERSIDE, the daring
and well-executed operation carried out by Norwegian members of
SOE against the heavy water plant at Vemork, stands prominently
among the most successful of SOE's achievements – and in stark
contrast to the tragic outcome of its predecessor, Operation FRESH-
MAN, where the British commandos involved lost their lives, many
of them brutally murdered by the Germans. It is also a good example of a target on which SIS and SOE were able to collaborate
quite effectively.

Norsk Hydro was founded in 1905, shortly after Norway gained its independence from Sweden. Its early development centred on the building of a factory producing fertiliser in Rjukan, which was linked to a hydro-electric plant (the largest in Europe at the time of its construction) in Vemork.* Some of the water from the power station was diverted to a hydrogen plant nearby, which consumed most of the power it generated to produce the hydrogen which was the basis of the fertiliser. A part of the water used in this process was then channelled through a further cascade of more specialised electrolysis cells to produce a very small amount of low-purity deuterium oxide, or heavy water. The process was extremely resource-intensive, requiring the use of much electricity and a considerable volume of water. However, in 1933, Leif Tronstad, a talented young Norwegian scientist, collaborated with Jomar Brun who ran the hydrogen plant at Vemork, to develop a heavy water industrial facility which they hoped would have a commercial value. They designed a system which was much more efficient and produced heavy water of 99.5 per cent purity. There was insufficient commercial demand and production stopped in June 1939, though it restarted again a few months later in November. It was during this period that German scientists working on nuclear fission concluded that heavy water, rather than graphite, offered the best chance of serving as the moderator necessary to separate U-235 and produce a bomb. The plant at Vemork was the only source producing heavy water on any scale. However, German attempts to buy large quantities were unsuccessful because their purchasing agent, I. G.

---

* Lucy Jago, *The Northern Lights* (London: Penguin 2002), pp. 180–193 and 200–201, gives an account of how the first fertiliser plant was initially equipped with two furnaces, one Norwegian and one German, built by the German company, BASF. If the German design had been adopted, it would have had serious consequences for Norsk Hydro, which would probably have remained Norwegian in name only. However, politics intervened. During the Agadir crisis of 1911, the Germans sent a gunboat to protect their interests. After the crisis had been resolved, the French government applied pressure to push the Germans out of Norsk Hydro and thus hinder their access to saltpetre, a key component in explosives. The Norwegian furnace designed by Birkeland and Eyde was then selected for the new fertiliser plant in Rjukan.

Farben, would not reveal the purpose for which it was required. A Norsk Hydro representative informed the French of this German interest in early 1940, for the French bank Paribas owned a large stake in Norsk Hydro, and had done so since 1905. Acting on advice from a French physicist Frédéric Joliot-Curie, and with consent from Axel Aubert, the director-general of Norsk Hydro, the French government took steps to remove the large quantity of heavy water which by now had been produced, some 185 kg. They were able to ship it out of Oslo via Scotland to France, in March 1940. After the German invasion of France in June, it was removed to Britain.[2]

Tronstad and Brun remained in contact, and exchanged visits between Trondheim where Tronstad was working at the Norwegian Technical High School (NTH), and Vemork. Brun told Tronstad about a series of increases in German orders for the production of heavy water. By March 1941, they were demanding 1,500 kg a year. Not long after that, Tronstad was approached by a member of the SIS Skylark B station in Trondheim, who told him that SIS wanted intelligence about Vemork and heavy water, which he provided.[3] In September, Brun visited Trondheim and reported that the Germans had ordered a more than threefold increase in heavy water production to 5,000 kg a year. This coincided with German arrests of several members of the Skylark B station. Tronstad himself was in danger and had to escape from Norway. He made his way to Sweden and arrived in London in October. He briefed SIS and developed contacts with Tube Alloys, a subsidiary of the Department of Scientific and Industrial Research (DSIR), responsible for work on developing an atomic bomb, where he liaised with Wallace Akers and Michael Perrin. He became a close and valued contact of both SIS and SOE and later was closely involved in the planning of the main sabotage Operations, FRESHMAN and GUNNERSIDE, against the heavy water facility at Vemork. In October 1942, Brun was also requested to come over to London, so as to contribute to the planning for these operations.

Leif Tronstad. © NHM

FRESHMAN

The news of the German demand to increase production at Vemork coincided with a meeting chaired by Churchill in early September 1941, which determined that nothing should be spared to promote the development of an atomic weapon, in Britain and not abroad. General Ismay, the secretary of the Chiefs of Staff Committee, wrote to Sir John Anderson, Lord President of the Council (and from September 1943 Chancellor of the Exchequer), and asked him to take charge of the project. Anderson had responsibility not only for work on the development of a bomb, but also for British attempts to prevent the Germans from doing the same.[4] Rjukan was first mentioned in this connection in early December 1941, when the Assistant Chief of Air Staff was informed that during a meeting of the Consultative Council under Sir John Anderson, investigating 'certain scientific developments in this country', it came to light that the Germans were obtaining heavy water from a plant near Rjukan. It was suggested that the facility should be attacked to deny them this substance.[5] The possibility of an attack was discussed shortly afterwards during a meeting of the Air Ministry's German target committee, but it decided that such an attack was not yet merited.[6]

Not long after this, Tronstad was interviewed by R. V. Jones, head of the scientific section at SIS, and Professor F. Lindemann, Churchill's scientific adviser. As a result of his information, Welsh at SIS, himself a scientist, proposed the destruction of the facility by bombing or sabotage. He observed:

> the removal of this source of supply would completely cripple any designs the Germans may have had with regard to this type of weapon and ... the Allies are not in a position to use this type of weapon themselves for at least eighteen months as they are only now considering building a suitable plant in America.[7]

Tronstad himself offered to organise an action to stop or delay production by a means which would minimise harm to the civilian population. He was told that his proposal was not considered relevant.[8]

It took time for planning for the FRESHMAN operation to crystallise. However, SOE took an important step when Einar Skinnarland, who lived in the valley near Vemork and whose brother Torstein was the warden of the dam from which Vemork drew its power, arrived in Scotland on the *Galtesund* with Odd Starheim. In a mere eleven days, he was trained as a radio operator, briefed by Tronstad, and parachuted back onto the Hardangervidda (the plateau above Rjukan), on 28 March 1942. He developed contacts among the Norwegians working at Vemork, and provided regular intelligence reports essential for all the operations which were subsequently planned against the heavy water target. So when on 9 April DSIR contacted SOE to ask for information on this, it did not take them long to respond.[9] In early May, Wilson informed DSIR that while SOE had a small project for an attack on Rjukan, it would really take a major combined operation to deal with the whole supply satisfactorily. In July, Norman Brook, the Deputy Secretary to the War Cabinet, approached the Chief of Combined Operations (CCO) with a request that Vemork be attacked. SOE prepared an outline plan, presented on 15 September, which proposed a combined attack, with an SOE advance party to act as local guides, and the main attack being carried out by airborne troops.

After two false starts, the SOE party, initially codenamed Grouse and led by Jens-Anton Poulsson, was dropped successfully on 18 October. They had to carry their heavy equipment quite long distances in relays during a series of forced marches in slushy and unfavourable conditions before making their base in a cabin on the Hardangervidda plateau. Wireless communications were established on 9 November. They maintained regular contact despite the fact that weather conditions, in particular the extreme cold, were difficult for them. On one occasion Wilson was informed of concerns that the station had been captured because the 'hand' of the wireless operator (i.e. manipulation of the sending key) did not match their records. The operator, Knut Haugland, satisfactorily answered the special security question and SOE's concerns were allayed. Haugland later explained to Wilson that owing to the intense cold, he was forced to operate with only the almost frozen tips of his fingers protruding from his sleeping bag.[10] The success of MUSKETOON, an earlier combined SOE/Combined Operations (CO) attack on Glomfjord power station in September 1942, had put the Germans on a higher alert and the garrison in the Rjukan area had increased by over a hundred men. General von Falkenhorst visited the Vemork plant in early October and briefed the senior management on the increased security precautions he was taking as a result of these attacks. He said that he was also going to mine the area around the factory perimeter, because he could not afford to release the number of troops required for the safe protection of the plant. Commenting on this, Wilson also noted that von Falkenhorst had particularly mentioned the raid at Glomfjord, acknowledging his very great admiration for the British commandos used there, and admitting that the attack had caused a complete standstill of production.[11] SIS station Beta, in Oslo, reported on the extent of these reinforcements on 28 October.[12] This led Gubbins (then D/CD (O) with responsibility for European operations) to write on 30 October to Major-General J. C. Haydon at Combined Operations Headquarters (COHQ) suggesting that, in view of the report, he might decide that the FRESHMAN operation was currently impractical. Haydon passed this to the planners, but the suggestion was not taken up.[13]

The length of time it took to finalise the plan, and the increased priority it had been given, meant that there was relatively little opportunity for the commandos to practise and train for the operation. The timetable was accelerated further when COHQ was informed on 24 September of the Lord President's view that the objective was of the utmost importance and of the greatest urgency. On 30 September, the Chief Air Planner concluded that the only way a military force could be introduced was by parachute. On 13 October, after discussions with Roscher Lund, the use of Catalinas was reconsidered, but it was concluded that the lakes would be frozen by the time the party was ready to move, so this would be impractical. Roscher Lund also thought, based on his memory, that the area at the south-east end of Lake Møsvatn would be suitable as a landing ground for gliders or as a dropping zone for parachutists. The meeting he attended then concluded that gliders should be used, because they would be less likely to cause many casualties than a parachute drop. The Chiefs of Staff Committee approved in principle on 19 October.[14]

It was accepted from the outset that FRESHMAN involved considerable difficulties and a high degree of risk. For this reason, it was decided to use two Horsa gliders and twice as many commandos as were originally thought necessary, to improve the chances of success. The problems facing the planners started with the need to obtain Halifax aircraft to replace Whitleys, which were unsuitable and did not have adequate endurance. The aircraft were dogged by unserviceability and problems with maintenance, which further limited training opportunities. Difficulties with operating the gliders included the duration and length of the tow, much further than anything previously attempted, unpredictable weather, uncertainties about identifying the landing area with only limited technical assistance,* and also inadequate and sometimes inaccurate maps exacerbated by difficulties with map reading over snow-covered terrain at night. Moreover, none of those involved had any operational experience, for this was the first Allied mission of the war in which gliders would be used to transport troops.[15] On the night before their departure, Captain F. Carver, an SOE administrative officer based in the Shetlands, visited the base to pass on a request from Hansteen, approved by COHQ, that only eight of the generators at Vemork should be destroyed. This would leave two intact, which would facilitate the resumption of some work in the power station, judged essential for the livelihood of the civilian population and the production of even a reduced quantity of fertiliser. He spoke to a young subaltern and asked how the gliders were performing. The officer replied that over Salisbury Plain they were quite satisfactory but that they had never used them over mountains and expected a rough passage. 'One of the pilots in the mess said that he had had a bad trip towing a glider over the Highlands, when owing to air currents he found himself dropping at 500 ft a minute when at full climb!'† He continued that he was confident of success, adding poignantly that he was computing his chances of getting back in time to be married late in December.[16] He was, sadly, killed less than a day later. On the day of the operation, the Norwegian meteorologist provided by COHQ, Dr Petterssen, advised delaying the operation by a couple of days because he anticipated that the weather would improve and provide

---

* The aircraft attempted to use a short-range radio navigation system. Rebecca was an airborne transceiver and antenna, while Eureka was the ground-based transponder. Rebecca calculated the range to Eureka based on the timing of the return signals, and its relative position using a highly directional antenna. Both the towing aircraft were fitted with a Rebecca system which should have connected to the Eureka operated by the Grouse reception party. However, the generator lead on the surviving aircraft failed. Grouse heard a tone from Rebecca, but it is not known whether this was reciprocal and transmitted to the crew of the other Halifax, because they did not survive.

† The Hardangervidda, where the gliders were to land, was between 1,100 and 1,700 metres (3,500–5,600 feet) high, much higher than the Scottish Highlands.

better conditions. The senior British officers in command at the base at Skitten, Lieutenant Colonel Henniker and Wing Commander Cooper, decided to ignore this advice because they were concerned about the possibility of deterioration in the weather for the remainder of the November moon period. They decided to proceed that night, 19 November.

The tragic outcome is well known. Both Halifaxes made their landfall in Norway as planned, but despite searching for two hours were unable to find the landing site. They experienced increasing problems with ice, and both tow ropes sheared. One Halifax managed to return to Wick in Scotland, but the other crashed into a mountain at Hæstadfjell, killing all the crew. One glider crashed near Egersund between Helleland and Bjerkreim, the other near Lysefjord.

A *Kommandobefehl*, or Commando Order, had been issued by the German High Command on 18 October 1942, stating that all Allied commandos should be killed immediately without trial, even if they were in proper uniforms or tried to surrender. The commandos captured after FRESHMAN were among the first victims of this Order, which was a direct breach of the laws of war.* There were fourteen survivors from the first crash, three quite badly injured. They were taken to a military camp at Slettebø, where they were briefly and unsuccessfully interrogated by the Gestapo. Later that day, all of them were then taken out to a deserted valley, and spaced out along the road, some fifty metres apart, each guarded by two soldiers. One by one they were taken into a quarry and shot by a firing squad. This took more than an hour. They were buried on a nearby beach by Polish prisoners of war. The nine survivors from the Lysefjord crash, four of them very badly injured, were taken to a jail in Stavanger. A couple of days after their capture, the Germans brought in a Norwegian SOE wireless operator whom they had caught, Ernst Kirkeby Jakobsen, to interpret for them, as they

---

* The first to be executed were the seven commandos captured after MUSKETOON, who were shot in Sachsenhausen concentration camp on 23 October 1942.

were not certain whether their prisoners were Norwegian or British. He confirmed that they were all British.[17] The five uninjured commandos were taken to the camp at Grini, where they were kept in isolation and interrogated at length by the Gestapo. They were unable to avoid giving up some information, but the Germans already knew plenty about their mission from examination of maps and other equipment recovered from the crash sites. On 17 January 1943, they were told that they were going to meet a high-ranking German officer, and would accordingly be blindfolded. They were taken to Trandum, lined up in front of an open trench, and shot without warning. The remaining four injured prisoners were tortured and given a series of morphine and then air injections which only killed two of them. One of the others was strangled with a belt, while the fourth was kicked down stairs and then shot in the back of the head. Their bodies were taken out into the fjord that night, weighted and dumped overboard. Chapter 14 will examine how after the war some of those responsible were charged with war crimes and punished appropriately.

In his post-war history, Wilson wrote of FRESHMAN, 'This was the first occasion on which COHQ were to use gliders, and Norway was hardly the country to experiment on. Our advice and that of others was ignored.'[18] It is not clear what representations he and his unnamed colleagues made, but given the importance which was known to be attached to the operation at the highest level, it was never likely that their views would have carried much weight.

Preparations for GUNNERSIDE

When Wilson heard of the disasters which had befallen FRESHMAN, he contacted Tronstad to discuss what to do next. They concluded that there was a possibility that the operation could be carried out instead by a small number of members of the Linge Company. Wilson rang COHQ to ask whether they would permit SOE to take over responsibility for the task, noting that 'there was a heartfelt "Thank God for that" on the phone'. Only then did Wilson inform Gubbins of what he had done, telling him that they had already selected the leader of the party. Not surprisingly, Gubbins hesitated, but Wilson was able to persuade him and he undertook to seek the consent of the War Cabinet. In the meantime, Wilson gave instructions for Joachim Rønneberg to be informed that he had been selected to lead a very important mission, and to choose a team of five expert skiers to accompany him.[19] Rønneberg selected Birger Strømsheim, Fredrik Kayser, Kasper Idland, Hans Storhaug and Knut Haukelid. Haukelid had originally worked for SIS as a member of the Skylark A station in Oslo, until he had been forced to leave when the station was broken up. He transferred to SOE in December 1941 because he wanted to take a more active part in the war, and joined the Linge Company.* He was due to join the Grouse team, but shot himself in the foot during a training exercise. He was replaced by Claus Helberg on Grouse, but recovered in time to join the GUNNERSIDE party. There is plenty of evidence, not surprisingly, that the members of both GUNNERSIDE and Swallow (as the Grouse party was renamed) were spirited young men. Kasper Idland's SOE file[20] reveals that he was fined £10 (a substantial sum in those days) for unspecified damage which he had caused to an isolated farm used by SOE, while Claus Helberg[21] was fined £2.10/- for fishing in Loch Morlich out of season. Rønneberg was not entirely exempt, either. At Brickendonbury Hall, when examining a new Colt 45 which he had procured for the operation, he accidentally fired a bullet into the ceiling, feigning casual indifference when questioned by an alarmed adjutant shortly afterwards.[22] And other members of the Linge Company just about managed to escape being caught red-handed when found poaching deer up on the hills...

---

* There was a small number of people, both Norwegian and British, who switched from one service to the other, usually from SIS to SOE. Bjørn Rørholt was another. J. L. Chaworth-Musters transferred in the other direction in August 1943.

Joachim Rønneberg, who led the successful GUNNERSIDE operation
against the heavy water plant at Vemork. © NHM

Rønneberg was a perfect choice to lead the party. He was an inspirational leader, well at home and experienced in the mountains, a
consummate professional and extremely thorough in his preparations.*
This was just as well, for when Rønneberg was briefed on GUNNERSIDE
on 24 November, he was told that they were due to leave barely three
weeks later. In fact, they were delayed by poor weather during two
moon periods including an abortive trip when the landing zone could
not be located, and were not dropped by parachute until 16 February.
This allowed him more time for meticulous preparation in the selection of suitable weapons (he did not wish to take Sten guns which
had a reputation for unreliability, preferring Tommy guns instead even
though they were heavier), skis, better watertight boots, warmer clothing and sleeping bags, and the preparation of concentrated, dehydrated
(and therefore lighter) combat rations. In many cases, these items were
made to his specifications. And while the delays were frustrating, they
also allowed time for additional training. At the SOE training school

---

* Rønneberg had been given outstanding reports during training. The commanding officer of
STS 23 wrote to Norwegian High Command to say that he and Martin Linge both considered that he deserved immediate promotion. (TNA, HS 9/1279/5.)

at Brickendonbury, STS 17, guided by advice from Tronstad during his regular visits, they familiarised themselves with scale models of the factory at Vemork. Tronstad also briefed them in detail on the defences around the factory.[23] They also practised with the weapons and explosives they would use, using charges specially prepared by experts. Later, they trained even harder in remote and inhospitable areas of Scotland to make themselves fitter. Rønneberg began to conclude that a party of six men might not be sufficient, and they would need additional cover. This coincided with a message from Swallow (as the Grouse party was renamed for security reasons in November) asking whether it was intended that they should be involved, because they doubted that six men would be enough.[24] This was accepted and, apart from their radio operator Haugland, who remained to look after communications, the rest of the team did take part.

Meanwhile, Wilson wrote to SIS to inform them of the failure of FRESHMAN and plans for GUNNERSIDE. He requested SIS to provide him with any available information about German reinforcements to their garrisons in the Rjukan valley in general, and Vemork in particular. On 9 December Swallow reported the first details of such reinforcements, the extent of hostage taking after FRESHMAN as well as the extensive raids which were being mounted in the area. The SIS station Corona (located near Oslo) transmitted a warning on 15 December, 'If you are going to drop agents in northern parts of Telemark be very careful. The Germans know about the place.'[25]

While Swallow were waiting for the arrival of GUNNERSIDE, their conditions became even more difficult. They all narrowly avoided being discovered by German raiding parties on separate occasions when out searching for food or meeting contacts. They had not expected they would need to survive so long in such an isolated area, and took with them only a month's worth of provisions, so soon ran very short of food and fuel. Semi-starved, all of them became sick. They were reduced to eating a watery soup made largely with reindeer moss, which had practically no nutritional value. Fortunately, on 23 December and after many fruitless hunting expeditions, Poulsson managed to shoot a reindeer, the first of over a dozen which they hunted successfully. Consequently they were able to eat a little better. Soon afterwards, they were joined by Einar Skinnarland, whose brother Torstein had been arrested, a fate which he had only just avoided himself. He provided the party with considerable assistance, fetching stores and helping to operate the hand accumulator for the radio set, which was a very tiring job.

The GUNNERSIDE party was finally dropped on the night of 16 February. A subsequent SOE report noted that 'the party were dropped in accordance with the leader's arrangements made with the pilot before departure', which may have contributed to the fact that they landed near Lake Skrykken, some twenty miles away from the Swallow reception committee. That was not the only reason, though. On 16 December, the senior RAF officer Group Captain Grierson had instructed that the aircraft carrying GUNNERSIDE was to be equipped with Rebecca if possible, to link up with Eureka (a system which had not worked during FRESHMAN). The Swallow team was briefed, and made an arduous journey back to their original landing zone to collect the receiver. However, for reasons which are not entirely clear, the Eureka system was not used when the team was finally dropped – but Swallow were not informed and Poulsson only found out when told by Rønneberg after the war.[26]

When the GUNNERSIDE party landed, they had no idea where they were. They collected the containers holding their stores and equipment and stored most of it in a trench which they dug, carefully marking the site. Soon after they had set off to look for Swallow, weather conditions deteriorated suddenly and very badly, with heavy snow and strong winds. In conditions of almost zero visibility they providentially stumbled upon a cabin they had found earlier, by retracing their steps along a compass bearing. The violent storm lasted for five days, and was so powerful that they were unable to leave the cabin at all. However,

Rønneberg was at least able to identify where they were from a map on the wall. On 22 February, the storm abated, and they prepared to leave. At that point, they were approached by a reindeer hunter. Uncertain whether to trust him or whether to kill him to protect their mission, they decided to take him with them, benefiting from some of the reindeer meat which he had been carrying with him and enlisting his help to pull a sledge. The following day, they came across two members of the Swallow team who were out looking for them. After discussion with Poulsson, Rønneberg decided to release the reindeer hunter, having first given him a very stern warning about the consequences which would follow if he spoke to anyone about their presence. And that evening, benefiting from the supplies which the GUNNERSIDE party had brought with them, the Swallow team had their first decent meal in over four months.

The following day, they discussed the best means of making their attack on the plant, which was in quite a remote and inaccessible location. The presence of new guards, and additional minefields, limited their options to two avenues of attack. They could either approach it via the bridge across the gorge facing the plant, where they would have to dispose of the guard force which could likely warn of their presence. Even if they were successful, they would probably have to carry out their sabotage while fighting off a German reaction – with little chance of escape afterwards. The other way would be to descend into the gorge below Vemork, cross the river and climb what appeared to be a sheer cliff before making their way to the factory. Rønneberg sent Helberg to meet a contact in Rjukan to obtain updated information about German defences, and then to make a reconnaissance assessing the viability of the route through the gorge. He reported that the bridge was better defended than they had expected. The gorge looked more promising, for there was still an ice bridge across the river, and he judged that there was a passable route up the cliff, which they could also use for their retreat back up to the Hardangervidda and thence across country to Sweden. There followed a lively discussion, with a narrow majority in favour of using the route across the gorge. Idland sought a private word with Rønneberg, to tell him that he doubted that he was a good enough skier to be able to keep up with the rest of the team, and that he would escape on his own. Rønneberg dismissed his concerns, and said that they would stay together as a team. Idland came from Stavanger and was not experienced in mountain conditions. In Rønneberg's report on Idland, written after GUNNERSIDE, he noted that Idland 'was no skier at all. However he did a marvellous job in completing the retreat without delaying the party.'[27]

Their route was indeed very difficult and demanding, but with an ice bridge able to withstand their weight as they crossed the river, it was just possible. They walked along the railway, carefully negotiated a minefield and then the demolition party cut through the fence to get into the plant. Haukelid and four others kept watch outside. Although their initial access point was blocked by an unexpectedly locked door, Rønneberg and Kayser found a tunnel giving access into the room with the high-concentration cells. There they detained a Norwegian night watchman. As they laid the charges, weighing barely five kilos, on each of the eighteen cells, they were joined by Strømsheim and Idland, the back-up party. They shortened the fuses from two minutes to thirty seconds and then left. Rønneberg carefully dropped some items of British military equipment, intended to convince the Germans that the sabotage party was British and reduce the chances of their retaliating against Norwegian civilians. The thickness of the walls, the noise of the wind and hum of the power station all helped to dull the noise of the explosion, which was no more than a muffled thud. A German sentry came out twice briefly to look around, but did not investigate further, and the team was able to retrace their route back into the gorge, over the road and up through forest onto the Hardangervidda. Their sabotage was completely successful, for they had destroyed all eighteen of the high-concentration cells – and left again unnoticed, without firing a shot.

General Nikolaus von Falkenhorst and *Reichskommissar* Josef Terboven
visit Vemork, the target of Operation GUNNERSIDE. © NHM

The escape of the sabotage party was helped that night by another
storm, which removed any traces of their ski tracks for the Germans
to find. The group split up. Haukelid, alone of the GUNNERSIDE party,
remained to organise resistance cells in the Telemark area, assisted
by Arne Kjelstrup. Poulsson left for Oslo, where he planned to meet
Helberg. Haugland would also remain, continuing to act as the communications link. Rønneberg led the remaining members of GUN-
NERSIDE on an arduous trip on skis to the Swedish border. He would
leave a message at a prearranged cabin along their route for collection
by Haugland, to report the successful outcome of the mission back
to London. Despite checking regularly, Haugland did not find any
message. Instead, he was told the news in person by Haukelid and
Kjelstrup, and reported to London, where the news was received on
10 March. Rønneberg's journey to Sweden, a distance of well over 300
miles, took more than a fortnight. The Swedish authorities accepted
the cover story which they all told, and the party were able to continue
to Stockholm without much delay. SOE instructed Stockholm that
the whole GUNNERSIDE team should be congratulated, that priority
return flights were being organised, and that no report should be

made to anyone in Stockholm. All the members of both Swallow and GUNNERSIDE continued to carry out important tasks for the resistance during the remainder of the war. After the war, Haugland (and Torstein Raaby, an SIS agent whose activities will be described in Chapter 11) took part in the Kon-Tiki expedition, a journey on a balsawood raft across the Pacific Ocean from South America to Polynesia, which was led by the Norwegian explorer Thor Heyerdahl.

The German reaction to the raid was extensive, as they searched for those who were responsible, and also for those who had helped them. Swallow reported that over 300 civilians had been arrested as part of their search, and as a reprisal. However, when General von Falkenhorst (who commanded the German occupation forces in Norway) arrived to inspect the damage, he was reported to have smiled and said, 'this is the most splendid coup I have seen in this war'.[28] He accepted the evidence of discarded British equipment as a suggestion that only British troops had been involved, and all of those who had been arrested were released. The German hunt continued. The reindeer hunter was subsequently arrested. According to a later report from Helberg after his arrival in Stockholm in June, the hunter helpfully and inaccurately told his captors he had been detained by English soldiers, as he could not understand the regional accent of those who came from Bergen and so thought that they must be British! Helberg also reported that tension among the German troops searching the inhospitable terrain on the Hardangervidda was so great that more than once they ended up opening fire on each other, inflicting a number of casualties on their own side.[29] Helberg had earlier nearly been caught twice. On the first occasion he was surprised by a small German patrol and pursued for hours across the mountains. He eventually managed to shoot and injure the only one who had kept up with him, and make his escape. However, soon afterwards in the darkness he skied over a cliff and broke his arm. He took refuge in a hotel where most of the guests were arrested, following an altercation between a Norwegian woman and Terboven, the *Reichskommissar* who was staying there. They were put on a bus to be taken to prison at Grini. Helberg knew that his identity papers would not stand scrutiny and despite his broken arm managed to leap out of the bus at an opportune moment. He escaped into the woods and fortunately avoided further injury as his German pursuers shot and threw grenades at him. For a while, SOE thought that Helberg had been killed, but after a period of recuperation near Oslo, he turned up in Stockholm.

Estimates varied as to how long the plant at Vemork would remain out of production. On 7 April, the Chief of the Air Staff informed the Military Mission in Washington that it would be out of action for twelve months and 'so the question of bombing the plant does not now arise'.[30] Wilson had been rather more realistic a fortnight earlier, when he predicted that it would take six months to build another high-concentration plant. (The poor weather had prevented the GUNNERSIDE party from taking sufficient explosives with them to be able to attack other parts of the plant, thereby putting it out of commission for longer.[31]) Anderson asked his secretary Gorell Barnes to inform Gubbins that he wanted all the participants to be suitably rewarded, and once he had seen a report on the operation, Churchill famously asked Lord Selborne, 'What rewards are to be given to these heroic men?' Rønneberg and Poulsson, who led GUNNERSIDE and Swallow, received the DSO. The other officers (Haugland, Idland and Haukelid) were given the MC, while the rest each received an MM. Wilson and Tronstad were given the Order of the British Empire (OBE), while Brun was made a Member of the British Empire (MBE). The citation for Brun stated that he had provided complete technical information on the plant and 'his specialist scientific advice was of the greatest value, as it showed that the attack could be carried out by a small party without danger to the lives of loyal Norwegians or the causing of damage which would involve Norway in severe economic loss after the war'.[32]

Members of the GUNNERSIDE and Swallow teams who blew up the heavy water plant.
Leif Tronstad is seated in the middle, to his left is Joachim Rønneberg. © NHM

In mid-April, Boyle, by then assistant to Gubbins, asked Wilson
whether he had received any reporting from SIS about the success of
GUNNERSIDE and German reactions to it. Had the Germans in Stockholm connected the arrival of the GUNNERSIDE party with the operation and increased pressure on the Swedes? In a very rare indication
that SOE may have been aware of the substance of intercepted signals
decyphered by GC&CS, he continued, 'I wonder whether we have
covered adequately these matters by putting C fully into the picture?*
There is a vast amount of enemy traffic to examine and unless section
V and others know what to look for they cannot be expected to keep us
informed.' Wilson replied that he had briefed SIS in detail before the
operation and afterwards, and that Section V fully understood SOE's
interest in this particular area.[33]

Heavy water production restarts:
War Cabinet considers further measures
Initial estimates of the length of time that the heavy water plant would
be out of operation did indeed prove to be overly optimistic. There
were reports in early July that production would be resumed in the

---

* That is, SIS.

middle of August. It actually happened slightly earlier: Swallow reported on 3 August, less than six months after the raid, that it had restarted. Tronstad predicted that it would return to full capacity by the end of August. He suggested a bomber attack on the Skarfoss dam (which fed the power stations at both Vemork and Såheim which separately also provided a small quantity of heavy water), as a means of hampering further production. He also suggested taking steps to contaminate the heavy water with castor oil. Neither suggestion was taken up. Wilson informed Gubbins of the situation, explaining that repairs had been made more quickly than anticipated, and that scientists were unsure of the acuteness of the problem caused by renewed production, as they thought it would take a further two or three years before a weapon might be viable. He concluded that this uncertainty needed further examination by Allied scientists. If another attack was considered necessary, every possibility including air attack should be considered.[34] Rønneberg heard about the resumption of production through a press report. He wrote to Wilson:

It certainly seems as if our work was not thorough enough. May I ask you one favour? If our old target should once again be in the foreground, would you please remember GUNNERSIDE? I know that all my friends would be obliged to get a chance to play the guards at Vemork a new trick.[35]

Wilson replied that it was unlikely that SOE would wish to stage another major operation, but if one was required, then Rønneberg would be given first refusal.

Shortly afterwards, Perrin recommended a fresh attack on the plant. He suggested that destruction could be achieved by a second sabotage operation or by a daylight bombing attack. He thought that bombing was likely to be the most effective, but noted that Tronstad had argued that such drastic measures should not be taken because of the extent of the damage that would be caused to the whole factory and thus to local livelihood, and that he had suggested it might be better to try to protect the plant if there was any chance it might be available for use by the Allies in the near future. If there was to be an attempt to stop production, he noted that SIS judged that only a daylight bombing raid would be really successful in ensuring that production could not be restarted for a long time. He suggested that the USAAF should be approached, adding that 'it would probably be advisable that no decisions should at present be communicated by us to the Norwegian authorities'.[36] However, the Assistant Chief of the Air Staff Frank Inglis did not think that bombing would be a practical proposition, and recommended that SOE should be asked to consider other means of sabotage. Ismay and the Chiefs of Staff agreed. Gorell Barnes accordingly approached SOE and asked for an appreciation of the possibility of a further sabotage operation. He stressed the view of the War Cabinet office that 'we ought not to have regard to Norwegian post-war interests if these form an obstacle to the most effective plan. The appreciation should be prepared with this point in mind.'

On 11 October Joe Adamson, the Norwegian section operations officer, informed Wilson that although there was a dearth of precise information, they knew from Swallow that the guard forces at Vemork and Rjukan had been increased and entry to the plant would now be too difficult to force. Moreover, after the success of GUNNERSIDE, it was unthinkable that the Germans would not have increased their physical defences, blocking entrances and adding landmines and additional lighting. He judged that an attack was out of the question, but if handled with care, contamination could be effective in reducing production quite significantly without direct danger to the perpetrators, if reduction rather than stopping production completely was an acceptable outcome. He took issue with the Air Staff view, considering that a daylight precision bombing attack would be feasible and that it was the only effective answer. He added carefully that he was 'refraining from any expression of opinion as to political repercussions in the event of such an attack'. Adamson's advice was accepted, and Harry

Sporborg so informed Gorell Barnes, explaining that SOE concluded that further sabotage would not be practical,

> unless one could produce a body of at least 40 well trained and heavily armed men, who would have virtually no hope of escape afterwards. An operation of this character could not in present conditions in Norway be carried out on a clandestine basis and could really only be done on the basis of a small commando raid such as that which ended so disastrously on the previous occasion. As regards an attack from the air, we quite realise that no low level attack would be a practical proposition, but would there be no chance of a medium level precision attack in broad daylight by United States aircraft? Although this would be a very difficult operation, it does seem to be the best chance of doing really conclusive damage to the plant. As you will see from our appreciation, we think it would be possible to interfere with production, or at least to reduce it for a month or so, by insaisissable methods.* We are pretty confident that if instructions were given, a fairly satisfactory though of course temporary effect would be created. Perhaps you would let me have instructions about this.[37]

Gorell Barnes rejected the idea of contamination. This was later shown to be a prudent decision. Gunnar Syverstad, an engineer at the plant and a reliable resistance contact, later tried treating two of the vats with oil, but it floated and was quickly noticed. He concluded that such contamination would have a nuisance value, but would not prevent the subsequent use of the heavy water.[38] Sir John Anderson therefore requested that a bombing raid be undertaken. The Chief of the Air Staff, Lord Portal, approached the commander of the US Eighth Air Force, General Eaker, who, after a study of the target, agreed to take on the assignment.

---

* That is, by contamination.

The US Air Force bombing attack on Vemork and its aftermath
Several weeks later on 16 November 1943, Vemork was attacked from
medium altitude by several squadrons of Flying Fortresses from the
Eighth Air Force. Shortly after they had finished bombing, a further
attack was made by a force of Liberators which had been prevented
by cloud from bombing their primary target, an airfield at Kjeller, and
so diverted to their secondary objective. Unfortunately they mistook
the nitrate plant at Rjukan for their target and bombed it instead. The
bombing caused widespread damage, destroying the nitrate plant,
most of the penstocks which supplied water to the power station, and
some of the generators as well. It did not touch the high-concentration
plant producing heavy water which was located in greater safety in the
basement – though loss of the water supply and damage to the rest of
the plant were sufficient to halt production. Of greater significance
to the Norwegians was the number of civilian casualties. Twenty-one
Norwegians, many of them women and children, were killed – most of
them as the result of a direct hit on an air raid shelter.

The attack provoked a very strong reaction from the Norwegian
government, which complained about the loss of a significant supply
of fertiliser to a population which was already very short of food (particularly following the damage to another fertiliser plant by bombing
at Herøya in July), and the fact that they had neither been consulted
nor informed about the attack in advance, as well as about the loss of
Norwegian lives. Lie sought a meeting with Eden (who as a member
of the War Cabinet would probably have been aware of the planned
attack and perhaps wisely declared himself unavailable) and saw ambassador Collier on several occasions instead. He told him that 'the
destruction of the factory was something not far off a national disaster', and he understood that it had been put on a list of exempted
targets. This had been discussed in the Norwegian cabinet and he had
been asked to find out exactly what undertakings had been broken and
who was responsible for breaking them. However, when he questioned
Hansteen, who was ultimately responsible for the Norwegian side of

arrangements with Air Ministry, he was disquieted to discover that there was no written and binding agreement regarding respect for exempted targets. This was a significant admission, for it turned out that there had been different understandings of the nature of any assurances which might have been given. Lie added that the root of the trouble was that 'both on the Norwegian and on the British side the military and air authorities concerned had been reluctant to take the civilians into their confidence, while it was notorious that on the British side the Air Ministry always tried to be a law unto themselves'.*[39] Lie followed this up with a formal written Norwegian protest on 1 December, criticising the attacks on both the fertiliser plants, which were also a potential source of revenue because some of the output was sold to Sweden. He stated that no reason had been given for the attack on Vemork, and that a bombing raid would have been highly unlikely to destroy the heavy water production there. Indeed effective destruction was almost impossible. Stressing the need for effective collaboration in future, to ensure that the nature and extent of any further bombing attacks should be proportionate to their objectives, he sought British assistance in establishing an arrangement which would henceforward permit such collaboration. When handing over the aide-memoire, Lie told Collier that while the Norwegian military authorities could not point to the existence of anything more than a verbal agreement on exempted targets, they had certainly understood and given the Norwegian government to understand, that this agreement precluded action against the Rjukan fertiliser works (as distinct from the heavy water plant close by at Vemork) without prior consultation. Though this was important, the main point for the Norwegians was to have an agreement on a list of accepted targets.

Tronstad was also shocked and bitterly disappointed by the attack on Vemork. He believed that he had been misled because he had been given an assurance by Perrin, Welsh and others that Vemork was a

---

* The final section was underlined by a reader in the Air Ministry.

'starred target' and would not be attacked without prior consultation.[40] Tronstad reemphasised this in a letter to Hansteen, which he also handed to Perrin, stating that 'he had constantly been told that nothing would be done without his knowledge'.[41] Since Tronstad's consistent opposition to the bombing of Vemork was quite widely known, it is surprising that any of his British colleagues in DSIR, SIS or SOE should have given him such an assurance. Some of them would have been in a position to know of the operation which was being considered, and would therefore also have known that any assurances which they might have given would have counted for nothing. It is unsurprising that there is no British record of any of these exchanges.

Although the order for the operation was not given through the usual channels, it is worth taking account of how the Air Ministry's German target committee (the ultimate body normally responsible for target selection) weighed up conflicting considerations when assessing the priority which should be given to Norwegian targets throughout the war. It shows the extent to which the Air Ministry responded to requests from other departments in the selection of targets, and did not necessarily select them itself. There were no discussions about the need for any prior consultation with the exiled governments of countries where targets were being considered for attack. There is only one reference to Vemork, in December 1941, when the committee was told that the 'heavy water' factory in Norway had been suggested as a target. The officer responsible reported that he had been in contact with the experts, who had informed him that such an attack was not yet merited. Shortly afterwards, the MEW representative told the committee that the Norwegian government had complained about RAF attacks on fish oil factories, since this was the sole source from which the population could obtain their fats. He sought the opinion of the Admiralty and Coastal Command. They both stated that these factories were useful alternative targets to aircraft of Coastal Command or the Fleet Air Arm, but were not regarded as of prime importance. After further review it was determined that these targets would not be attacked. There was a discussion about the NS anniversary meeting to be addressed by Quisling in Oslo on 25 September 1942, when it was agreed that it should be attacked. (This was successful.) There were also discussions about an attack on the fertiliser plant at Herøya, but the MEW reported that it would not be completed and therefore constitute a worthwhile target before 1943, so it was taken off the target list. In October 1942 there was consideration of a proposal for bombing cement factories which were wholly engaged in supplying material for German fortifications. It was agreed that the importance of these targets, combined with the tactical difficulty of locating them, did not justify attacking them.

In late 1942 there was discussion of targeting the molybdenum mines at Knaben. The chairman of the target committee concluded that the plant, being small and difficult to locate, constituted a most unsatisfactory bombing target. The committee agreed that the Knaben mine was more suited for action by SOE. However, the subject was raised again in January 1943 because of the increased importance of molybdenum from Knaben to the German economy as a result of the denial of supplies from North Africa. CCO and SOE held out little prospect of a successful attack, and the same applied to bombing by normal methods. It was suggested that Bomber Command might consider the possibility of a low-level attack by Mosquitoes. The subsequent attack did have some success, but insufficient to put it out of production. It was later attacked by a larger USAAF raid on 16 November 1943, the same day as the attack on Vemork, though again damage was limited. There was consideration of a possible attack on the Holmenkollen hotel in Oslo as it was being used by the German Air Force, which was dismissed unless a case could be made that such an attack would have significant political value. There were also reviews of the U-boat pens in Bergen and Trondheim. Although the pens in Trondheim were considered to be less solidly built and therefore more vulnerable to bombing, the RAF preferred Bergen. When the pens there were attacked in October 1944, there was poor visibility. Most of the force did not drop their bombs as they could not identify target markers. However some bombs fell on the central part of the town, causing civilian casualties and damaging buildings of cultural and historical value. In April 1943, there was an assessment of Dutch protests about casualties to civilians, following attacks near Haarlem. It was agreed to re-evaluate targets with a view to eliminating those where attacks might lead to similar results in future.

These records give a useful insight into the way in which important targets were selected (or sometimes discounted), and the attention which was sometimes paid to the concerns of Allied governments. This does not mean that Vemork would have been treated any differently, given the importance which the War Cabinet attached to the destruction of the heavy water plant there, but it shows that while the Air Ministry may have been a law unto itself – after all, it had a job to do – it was quite capable of taking reasonable requests into consideration.[42] But there is nothing in Air Ministry or Cabinet Office files to show that there had been any prior discussion about placing Vemork or any other Norwegian target on a list which would exempt them from aerial attack. There is, though, evidence to show that both were keen to ensure that the Norwegians were not made aware of what was being considered. Moreover, in his unpublished history of the Norwegian section which was written after the war, Wilson stated that the USAAF bombing of Vemork had been carried out by them 'without consultation with their allies'.[43] Unless Wilson was referring to a lack of consultation with Norwegian Allies rather than British Allies, then in view of his involvement in preparing the appreciation which concluded that bombing was the only viable means of destroying the plant and its stocks, which led to Sporborg's recommendation that a USAAF attack should be reconsidered, this assertion is hard to understand.

As a result of the protests over Vemork, there were protracted negotiations about an agreed list of targets in a process which involved the Air Ministry, MEW and later the Admiralty – because of the possibility of the navy shelling coastal targets and the involvement of carrier-launched aircraft. Indeed in June 1944, Lie complained about an attack by naval aircraft on shipping and oil tanks off the Norwegian coast, in the course of which a fish oil factory north-east of Stadlandet was hit. This was not on the draft list of agreed targets which was being discussed. Lie pointed out that it was producing entirely for Norwegian consumption, that it was not a special or urgent case, and that it could not be considered a German military or naval objective. An agreed list, which included Knaben and the mine at Sulitjelma, was eventually finalised on 11 October 1944. It made a number of concessions to take account of Norwegian concerns. The attack on the Bergen U-boat pens (which, as a military target, was outside the scope of the agreement) took place shortly afterwards. However, when making his protest to Collier, Lie acknowledged pragmatically that there was no evidence that there had been any breach of the undertaking and he was complaining only because the Crown Prince had instructed him to do so. He made clear that he wanted to avoid any further recriminations.[44]

The sinking of the Hydro

Shortly after the attack on Vemork, the German scientist Kurt Diebner visited the Norsk Hydro headquarters in Oslo to assess the situation. He was told by Axel Aubert, who had been reappointed as director-general, that Norsk Hydro had decided to discontinue the production of heavy water because of the risks to staff and costs involved. Diebner agreed, saying he intended to move both the plant equipment and heavy water to Germany, where a new factory would be built. This information soon reached Stockholm, who informed London. A message was sent to Swallow asking Skinnarland to find out whether it was true.[45] On 6 February, he confirmed that the factory would not be repaired and that existing stocks of heavy water would be transported to Germany within a week or so.[46] They would be transported by train to the ferry terminal at Mæl, the rolling stock loaded onto a ferry for the journey across Lake Tinnsjø, taken by rail down to Menstad, near Skien and thence by ship to Hamburg.

On 8 February, Tronstad informed Wilson that Sir John Anderson had been informed and that 'the responsible British authorities [i.e. the War Cabinet] have decided that in view of the importance of the matter, an attack should be carried out even if serious consequences for the local population may be involved'. Wilson noted that once Anderson's decision had been received, both General Hansteen and Torp were informed, and their consent was received almost straight away, within an hour.[47] Skinnarland was accordingly instructed that the heavy water – though not the plant equipment – should be destroyed, and that they should try to minimise the consequences for Norwegian civilians. Skinnarland replied on the following day that time was too short to mount an armed attack and that the only solution would be to sink the ferry or perhaps to blow up the train, warning that reprisals could be expected.[48] Haukelid, who was still in the area, discussed the options with his team. They settled on an attack on the ferry – there were too many risks involved in an attack on the train, as it would be well guarded and they could not be sure that they would be able to destroy the entire consignment. The best solution would be to sink the ferry half an hour after its departure, when it would be over the deepest point of the lake. After a reconnaissance trip during one of its journeys on 18 February, Haukelid concluded that explosives placed in the forepeak, near the bow, gave the best chance of ensuring that the ferry would sink quickly before the captain could beach it on the shore of the lake. Through contacts in the plant at Vemork (Alf Larsen and Gunnar Syverstad), they had been able to delay the tapping of the heavy water into drums to give them more time both to prepare the operation, and also to try to ensure that it would be shipped on a Sunday. On that day there would only be one ferry (so they would know which one to attack) and a probability that fewer passengers would be on board. Even so, some of the team had concerns about Norwegian casualties and the risk of German reprisals. Swallow passed their reservations to London and sought confirmation that the attack was necessary. This was quickly received. SOE also prepared a fallback option in case Haukelid was unsuccessful. They passed instructions for Chaffinch, in Vestfold, to send two trained men to Skien and prevent any special cargo from Rjukan being loaded at the port. This back-up party later complained bitterly that they were waiting, had marked down the ship which was to take the special cargo by sea to Hamburg, made their plans to destroy her, and had all their preparations ready but no special cargo had come…[49]

Remarkably, although the Germans had increased their vigilance and security measures in the area, they did not place a guard on the ferry before the heavy water consignment was loaded. Haukelid was accompanied by Rolf Sørlie (an engineer at Vemork who had already provided information and assistance), and a local man, Knut Lier-Hansen, when they went on board to plant the explosives. They were challenged by a night watchman, who fortunately was a patriotic Norwegian, and persuaded him that they were members of the resistance who had some illicit materials to hide. He showed them the hatch down into the bilges, which were below the waterline, and Lier-Hansen engaged him in conversation while Haukelid and Sørlie went down to do their work. The space was confined and there was nearly half a metre of water on the floor. The two detonators Haukelid was using had only 2 mm of clearance on their contacts, so it was an extremely difficult task – he described it afterwards as 'ticklish work'. Gunnar Syverstad's mother had been due to travel on the ferry the next day. Syverstad could not commit a breach of security by telling her to avoid making the journey at that time. He chose instead to dose her dinner the evening before with a very large amount of laxatives, which caused bad stomach pains and left her too weak to travel. Gunnar looked after her solicitously.[50] The following morning, the explosives worked effectively and the *Hydro* sank within five minutes. More than half the fifty-three passengers and crew were rescued by local boatmen, but fourteen Norwegians and four Germans were killed. The flatcars carrying the heavy water all sank, though a few containers holding less concentrated heavy water floated to the surface. They were salvaged and later shipped to Germany, together with some remaining low-concentration stocks totalling about 100 kilogrammes. Soon afterwards, Haukelid left for a break in Sweden. On this occasion, there were no German reprisals.

The sinking of the *Hydro* marked the end of Allied action against heavy water production in Norway. The equipment itself was dismantled in August and transported to Germany in September 1944. At the end of the war, there were attempts to recover it. Wilson was asked in May 1945 whether this would be feasible, because it was Norwegian property. He sought advice from the War Cabinet office and the MEW. They told him that most of the high-concentration electrolysis cells were in the Russian zone, but four of them were at Stadtilm, near Erfurt in the western zone. Since they would only be worth about £10,000, the MEW did not consider that they would be worth much effort – but suggested that Wilson inform the Norwegians, because they would be entitled to claim under the restitution of property formula.[51]

In October 1944, Tronstad, back in Norway on Operation SUNSHINE which was preparing to protect Norwegian strategic installations, confirmed the removal of the plant equipment from Vemork. However, it did not prove possible to establish where it had been sent, or how much progress the Germans had made in establishing their own source of production. Wilson asked him whether they could arrange for a director of Norsk Hydro to be evacuated to Sweden and questioned about this at greater length. He also asked about the possibility of kidnapping the German consul Erhard Schoepke, who, as a member of the *Wehrwirtschaftsstab Norwegen* (the War Economy Staff for Norway), was responsible for exploiting the Norwegian economy for German benefit, and had overseen the dismantling of the plant at Vemork. Tronstad doubted that either of these options would be worthwhile, commenting that Schoepke would not be in a position to add anything useful beyond what they already knew from other sources.[52] Wilson informed R. V. Jones at SIS, who agreed that there was no point in pursuing the project.[53] This was not the only time SOE considered the kidnap of a German in Norway. As Chapter 12 will highlight, in early 1945 they worked on a plan to kidnap Hans-Rudolf Rösing, the senior naval officer responsible for U-boat operations in Bergen. There were other plans, too, which did not get off the drawing board. For example, in December 1943, the SOE station Thrush Red recommended that kidnapping the Gestapo chief Siegfried Fehmer would help the fight against denouncers, and sought agreement for it, asking for confirmation that SOE would provide a pick-up and transport back to Britain. For good measure, they also enquired about a similar operation against Quisling and his equally unpopular lieutenant, Minister of Police Jonas Lie. SOE replied that this would not be possible. They agreed that Norwegian traitors should be taken, 'but it is too dangerous to take Germans unless they disappear without leaving any trace'. The resistance should judge whether the benefits of removing Fehmer were so great as to justify the reprisals which would follow. They doubted that there would be any benefit in kidnapping Quisling and Jonas Lie at that time. The matter was not pursued further.*[54]

The aftermath of the sinking of the Hydro
There was an unseemly aftermath to this operation because Haukelid's story was not initially believed. When he was put up for a DSO, Archie Boyle (A/CD, the Assistant to the Director) noted that Honours Board requirements meant that strict scrutiny was needed, doubted whether Haukelid's account of the action was truthful, and so informed Wilson. He observed that the report had been scrutinised by the security section of SOE dealing with Norway (BSS or Bayswater Security Section). They considered that it contained a number of inconsistencies, for example, questioning Haukelid's calculation that the ferry would sink within four or five minutes after the explosion.

---

* Jens Chr. Hauge, the leader of Milorg, worked out a plan for the kidnapping which would have involved using Ola Fritzner, a senior Norwegian policeman who was a friend of Fehmer. However, Fritzner refused to cooperate. (See Njølstad, *Jens Chr. Hauge: fullt og helt*, pp. 194–199.)

'It seems problematical whether a sausage of 8.4kg of 808 explosive would be sufficient to destroy a vessel if placed against the keel. Would it not need a very much greater charge to blow out a 0.6m square of the plates against the pressure of the water?' One of the Security Section staff, BSS/A, added that he had spoken to a Norwegian who was knowledgeable about icebreakers and the nature of their construction, describing how ships were designed and built so as to enable them to clear a path through the ice without damage; with stern ballast tanks flooded, enabling their bows to ride up over the ice. He said the principles involved were almost universally used on inshore lakes in Norway and cited *Hydro* as an example. He stated that the consequence was that the forepeak would be small, and that the plates in this part of the ship would be extremely strong and reinforced. Moreover, the fact that the ship was designed to ride up onto the ice would almost inevitably mean that it was improbable that the flooding of the forepeak would tilt the ship so much that she went down by the head. BSS concluded that the report struck them as one written by a man who had in fact taken no part in the operation, but had heard the general details of it, and was now attempting to claim credit for the sinking which either occurred in some other way, or was organised by another group of people.

Wilson defended Haukelid robustly: 'we regard this as a very typical Norwegian report and very much in keeping with others which we have had and which we know by our own observation to have been written by the man or men themselves'. Moreover, on the same day, Gubbins was informed that Selborne had read the complete report and considered it a very good account indeed! He wanted a copy to go to Lord Cherwell, the government scientific adviser, and another to Major Morton, Churchill's intelligence adviser. The aspersions on Haukelid's integrity were eventually seen off when advice was sought from Rear-Admiral Taylor (the head of SOE's naval directorate), who stated that he considered the various BSS criticisms of the story as based upon the supposed construction of the vessel to be unfounded. Haukelid was subsequently awarded his DSO.[55]

We now know that the Allies chose the right path in determining that the Manhattan project should concentrate on isotope separation to obtain uranium-235 from natural uranium, which enabled nuclear fission and the production of an atomic bomb. The Germans made the wrong choice. This certainly does not mean that the operations to prevent the production of heavy water at Vemork were a waste of lives and effort. At that time, the Allies did not have information which could have enabled them to conclude that the German approach was wrong. They had no choice but to take whatever steps were available to stop or slow down German research and development of all potential secret weapons. Indeed it might be argued that continuing Allied attempts to disrupt the production of heavy water may have encouraged the Germans to think that they were on the right track, and not to consider diverting resources elsewhere into what might have proved to be a more profitable line of research.

CHAPTER 10

THE TIDE STARTS TO TURN
1943–1944: PREPARATIONS
FOR LIBERATION

*Communist resistance groups are becoming more active in Norway ...
SOE state that they are in touch with certain communist groups around
Oslo, who have said that they are too short of supplies to engage in active
warfare. SOE have supplied them with small quantities of arms but
remain committed to send most to Milorg.*
ANTHONY NUTTING, NORTHERN DEPARTMENT OF THE FOREIGN
OFFICE, COMMENTING ON CONCERNS EXPRESSED BY THE BRITISH
LEGATION IN STOCKHOLM IN FEBRUARY 1944 THAT COMMUNIST
RESISTANCE IN NORWAY WAS INCREASING.[1]

*Certain arguments had been advanced in favour of recognising the com-
munist groups, and Colonel Øen raised this with the central leadership (of
Milorg). Their experience led them to believe that this would be an unwise
policy to follow ... FO, OSS and SOE agreed that no support of any kind
should be given to these groups, either directly or through Sweden.*
EXTRACT FROM THE SOE NORWEGIAN SECTION HISTORY.[2]

The first major change in Allied fortunes was the victory at the first
battle of El Alamein in July 1942, which was followed by landings
in French North Africa in November 1942. Rommel's Afrika Korps
was forced to retreat, and the Germans finally surrendered in North

Africa in May 1943. Soon after, the Allies landed in Sicily in July and took control of the island after a campaign which lasted six weeks. It would probably have been at this stage, with continued Allied concentration on the Mediterranean, that it started to become apparent to the Norwegians that Norway was unlikely to be high on the list for liberation. At the end of July, Benito Mussolini was deposed and the Italian government changed. On 3 September, the Allies made their first landing in southern Italy, and the Italian government surrendered. The main Allied landing took place at Salerno on 9 December. German resistance was stiff, and the Italian campaign lasted until almost the end of the war. These campaigns had their impact in Sweden, where there began to be changes in policy as it became clear that the Germans in some areas were on the retreat. In mid-1943 the Swedes agreed to set up secret training camps where Norwegians could be trained as policemen, who could take over in Norway after the liberation. The initial number was fifty, but by the end of the war the size of the force had risen to over 14,000.[3]

The role of Milorg in the liberation of Norway

In late 1942 and early 1943, the Norwegian High Command began to consider what sort of role Milorg should play in the future liberation of Norway, in whatever form that might take place. There needed to be agreement about the command structure, too. These issues were debated in London and then discussed at a meeting in Sweden in May 1943 between representatives from Milorg and the Norwegian High Command. Milorg agreed that its future activities would be determined by the Allied Supreme Command, through the Norwegian High Command, whose authority it accepted. Its role would be to prepare, train and arm units for assistance to an Allied liberation force, and to maintain law and order after the German surrender in Norway.

The consequence of this was that Milorg's involvement in sabotage actions would be restricted. Under the influence of its leader, Jens Chr. Hauge, it concentrated on improving its organisation and training, as well as developing a decentralised district structure. It had already been divided into fourteen districts (which later split into twenty-three) and further improved both control and security after earlier setbacks. Sabotage and raids would be carried out – but by groups operating from Britain against targets agreed by the Anglo-Norwegian Collaboration Committee (ANCC). This was a policy which was unlikely to appeal to war-weary young activists, impatient to be involved in opposing the occupiers. And it appealed to the communists even less.

Concerns about activities of the Communist resistance

While the Norwegian High Command was developing a closer relationship with Milorg, with policies which focused on more passive forms of resistance, the same was not true of the Norwegian communists. Although their numbers were small, they were well organised and disciplined. For much of the occupation, they kept their distance from other resistance groups. There were a few exceptions – Ole Halvorsen, the leader of SOE's Wagtail, was a communist who with other members of the group unsuccessfully tried to assassinate the collaborator Henry Rinnan in 1943. SOE's Razorbill, based in Bergen from September 1944, worked with both Milorg and the local communist organisation Saborg.[4] There were, moreover, several communist sabotage groups. The most prominent was the Osvald group, led by Asbjørn Sunde, which operated mainly in the Oslo region. Attempts at coordination with Milorg only rarely achieved anything. There were some exceptions, though. For example, when consulted, Milorg supported the attack by Sunde's group on the labour office in Pilestredet in Oslo in April 1943, in which Sunde himself was injured.[5] But in general, the Norwegian government advised Milorg against negotiating with communist groups.[6]

The latter carried on alone. Some of their acts of sabotage led to reprisals against the rest of the population. A group led by Sunde attacked a train near Drammen in October 1943, killing both Germans and Norwegians. The Germans arrested sixty hostages, and though the local population responded to their demands by endorsing an appeal to denounce such acts, they still executed five of them.[7] During the campaign to destroy labour records to prevent German attempts to force young Norwegians to mobilise, the communists also destroyed an office in Wergelandsveien in Oslo in May 1944. Three civilians were burned alive when the building was destroyed by fire, and another run down and killed by a vehicle driven by an escaping member of the group. When informing the Foreign Office, Wilson commented that Milorg had also selected the building as a target, but ruled out arson as they feared exactly what happened. 'The result, however, was satisfactory in that the records were destroyed.'[8] The communists were responsible for some very effective acts of sabotage, particularly an action in Oslo harbour in November 1944, which sank or badly damaged nearly 50,000 tons of shipping. They also put out of action the only loading crane in Norway which was capable of handling heavy tanks and artillery pieces.

Trygve Lie first brought up his concerns about communist sabotage with Collier in September 1942. At that time, he supported a passive policy on sabotage carried out by local resistance groups, and complained about the isolated sabotage activities of the communists. They needed to be coordinated, and moreover, this was not the right time to start such a campaign. He intended to raise the subject with the Russian embassy.[9] But his approach had no effect. Their sabotage continued.

Communist resistance activities continued to cause concern both in London and also in Stockholm. Worried that their activities were increasing, the legation there suggested to the Foreign Office that it might be worth asking the Norwegian government to take steps to initiate a more active resistance, and to instruct Milorg to cooperate with the communists. Observing that SOE were providing them with small amounts of arms, Nutting concluded that the differences between the communists and Milorg were too deep for this to be feasible. SOE also pointed to concerns of German penetration of the communists.

(Chapter 4 described how GC&CS were reading Abwehr reports of intercepted communist messages. SOE were presumably briefed about this in some form.) Nonetheless, Wilson thought that it would be worth asking Øen to explore this when he met the Milorg leadership in Sweden. Before he could do so, the Foreign Office learned that the communists had come out openly against the Milorg leadership, attacking them mainly for their opposition to intensified sabotage. Collier observed that Lie was not disturbed about this, as he would be pleased that Milorg were being pushed into an attitude of more positive opposition to German conscription measures. Nutting agreed, noting that the result of the campaign to oppose German mobilisation measures had encouraged Milorg to be drawn into closer cooperation with both the Norwegian government and SOE. 'There now appears at long last to be a fusion of effort and policy such as we have not seen before.'

It is not easy to reconcile the conflicting statements given at the beginning of this chapter about SOE support for the communist resistance. References in Foreign Office files are scarce, though recently released papers dated three months later contain some additional details confirming what Nutting was told.[10] No evidence is available in surviving SOE files to show how SOE may have delivered supplies to the communists, or in what terms they may have briefed the Norwegians about their activities.* Since Øen's meeting took place later in 1944, after these comments by Northern Department, it seems quite feasible that SOE had made deliveries earlier than that, but stopped when it became apparent that they would not be supported by the resistance leadership in Oslo. Although the wording of the SOE history supports that interpretation, there is insufficient evidence to make

---

* SOE did of course provide arms to communist resistance movements in several occupied countries such as Yugoslavia, Malaya and also to both EAM-ELAS and EDES, the communist and non-communist movements in Greece. The situation in Greece was much more complicated and very difficult for SOE to deal with effectively. The two resistance groups started fighting each other and their rivalry later developed into a civil war. Things in Norway were much more straightforward.

a judgement. Records also show that the Foreign Office considered making its own protest to the Russians in May 1944. They asked SOE to establish the extent to which the Russians might have been supporting or controlling communist sabotage attempts. SOE reported that there was 'no evidence of any Russian connection with this business' and the Foreign Office decided not to take it further. We know (from Venona reporting after the war – see Chapter 3) that there was indeed evidence, but SOE could not have been aware of it then.

Øen reported in June on his meetings with Milorg. They were indeed worried about the activities of the communists. They had no contact with them, and were worried about the extent of their ability to recruit disaffected young Norwegians, particularly those who might have gone into hiding to avoid labour mobilisation, the device used by the Quisling government in an unsuccessful attempt to provide as many as 75,000 Norwegians to the Germans for service on the eastern Front in Russia. These concerns, and those of the Norwegian government, gradually diminished over the next few months, not least once Milorg was itself more engaged in organising active resistance and sabotage.[11]

Wider issues in Anglo-Norwegian relations

The change of staff at senior levels and the establishment of the ANCC in 1942 had led to significant progress in improving relations between SOE and the Norwegian High Command. But the improvement went beyond that into other areas. Collier informed Eden in June 1943 that Lie had commented favourably on the greatly improved prestige enjoyed by Norwegians in Britain, to such an extent that Norwegian officers in Scotland preferred to be attached to British units, where they learned more and suffered less from personal jealousies, than to remain with Norwegian Army units.[12] Collier also wrote a 'very confidential' and flattering appreciation of the position and influence of King Haakon, the importance of his position as a rallying point for

Norwegians both at home and in exile, and the frankness with which he discussed the issues which concerned him. This gave Collier some valuable insights into current political issues, relations with Sweden (for King Haakon remained suspicious of King Gustav and Swedish motives) and the possibilities for post-war Atlantic collaboration.[13]

There were, of course, still difficulties. Air services remained a perpetually awkward issue, because it was never possible to provide sufficient aircraft to carry the large numbers of Norwegians who wanted to travel over to Britain, and probably frustrated the Foreign Office as much as it irritated the Norwegians. Nutting observed, 'Lie forgets that unless we put a hundred aircraft on the route, we won't solve the problem. One or two more won't do.'[14] There were tensions too when Lie sought Norwegian participation in third-party negotiations which affected Norwegian interests, such as the termination of German transit traffic through Sweden to Norway and the supply of Swedish locomotives to German-controlled Norwegian railways, or his reaction when he discovered that increased rates had been agreed for Swedish ships under charter to the British government, which could affect the interests of Norwegian shipping. An exasperated Orme Sargent commented that 'Mr Lie is becoming a nuisance and must not be encouraged.'[15] Lie was on rather firmer ground with his irritation at British obfuscation over Norwegian attempts to obtain materials for the rebuilding of industrial plant at Herøya and Rjukan, badly damaged by American bombing. These foundered because the Swedes would not grant export licences without Anglo-American agreement. The United States refused to agree, because it would be counter to Allied blockade policy, but the Foreign Office was not willing to divulge to the Norwegians that the Americans were the cause of the blockage.[16] The issue which caused greatest Norwegian concern, of course, was the damage inflicted by Allied bombing raids which caused what they considered to be unnecessary civilian casualties in Rjukan and Bergen, as examined in Chapter 9.

Special Forces headquarters: amalgamation of FO.IV and SOE/OSS
As planning for D-day developed, the staffs of both SOE and OSS grew, as did their workloads. It was eventually agreed in May 1944 that the directorate of SOE concerned with northwest Europe would be integrated with its OSS counterpart as Special Forces headquarters (SF HQ). This revived the question of whether the Norwegian section FO.IV should also be included – something which Tronstad had long argued for, but which had previously been resisted on the grounds of restrictive security. Work was being impeded since the Norwegian office was south of Hyde Park, while SF HQ was to the north of Regent's Park, some distance away. The only convenient meeting place was in the FO.IV flats in Chiltern Court, used mainly by the Linge Company. This led to serious congestion, with meetings having to be held not only in bedrooms, but also in kitchens and bathrooms too. In the end, common sense prevailed. When the Norwegian section of SF HQ moved to a larger building in Oxford Square in July 1944, it was agreed that FO.IV could also be accommodated there. Coordination improved significantly.

Preparations for liberation
Norwegians on both sides of the North Sea naturally wanted to see their country liberated as soon as possible. Some members of the resistance harboured unrealistic aspirations about how quickly this might happen. And Norwegian ministers in London could have been misled by the way in which Churchill (whose interest in Norway probably matched that of Hitler) flirted with the idea of making a landing in Norway. For example, he said to Nygaardsvold in September 1941, 'We should attempt the liberation of Norway at the earliest possible moment.' Later, he told him regretfully in February 1944 that 'we ought, of course, to have liberated Norway in the campaign of 1943'.[17] These were not mere musings. On more than one occasion Churchill directed the Chiefs of Staff to examine plans for an invasion of northern

Norway. He was particularly interested in Operation JUPITER, which he first raised in June 1942 and which envisaged a landing in Finnmark with a force of four divisions. The attraction of such an operation was that it would meet a request from Stalin to complement Russian activity in northern Norway, and do so in a place where the Russians would be able to provide air cover from Murmansk. This could help to offset the significant risks to the British fleet which would be supporting it. However, the Canadian appointed to oversee the planning, General McNaughton, concluded that it would be an extremely hazardous operation, 'only acceptable if politically the risks to be achieved were judged to be of the highest importance'. The plan was dropped. But to the dismay of the Chiefs of Staff, Churchill resurrected the idea in July 1943, suggesting it as a possible alternative or supplement to OVERLORD, the planned Allied landing in France. This time, it did not get very far and its consideration was crowded out by the pressure of other priorities. The Norwegians were aware of at least some of these ideas because they were invited to comment on the first paper in June 1942.[18]

It may have been partly for this reason – to maintain the idea of Norwegian liberation in a prominent position in the minds of the politicians and the planners – that Lie approached Eden in September 1943 with the request that Crown Prince Olav be appointed commander in chief of the Allied forces at some stage following their landing in Norway. Eden, who knew that Lie had already raised this with Roosevelt, replied that it would be difficult for him to be placed in charge of a force comprising troops from several different nations and led by professional soldiers, when important military operations were being carried out. He suggested instead that the crown prince might be appointed as head of the Norwegian military mission attached to the staff of the commander in chief. Eden put this idea to Churchill, who agreed.[19] In the event, it did not happen, though in July 1944 Olav was appointed commander in chief of all Norwegian forces. Increasingly, contingents of Allied forces earmarked for Norway were removed to support campaigns against the Germans in other parts of Europe. There were not enough to spare to allocate to a country whose strategic importance gradually diminished, especially once the major elements of the German fleet were sunk or badly damaged – although U-boats operating from Norwegian bases continued to pose a threat to Allied convoys. As 1943 wore on, it became clearer to the Norwegian government that the liberation of Norway was most unlikely to take place until much later in the war.

The operation by the Soviet Army to liberate the north of Norway, which began in October 1944, created a further problem for the Norwegians. As they retreated through Finnmark in front of the Russians, the Germans carried out a scorched-earth policy, driving out the entire population and destroying their houses and means of livelihood. This created considerable hardship, leading Lie to tell Collier that 1944 had been the worst year for Norway since the invasion in 1940. He asked whether the Allies could arrange a landing around Trondheim, in case the Germans pursued their scorched-earth policy further, warning that he would press this objective with the utmost vigour.[20] His request could not be met. Proposals for an expedition to Bodø, to cut off the Germans there, similarly foundered on a lack of resources. Matters were not helped by a lack of candour. The Chiefs of Staff were not willing to disclose to the Norwegians that they did not have the troops to make a landing in Norway and could not foresee when this might change. Eden asked the Chiefs of Staff to reconsider their refusal and wrote to Churchill on 24 December to gain his support. He wished to tell the Norwegians frankly – and very soon – what the constraints were not only for the immediate future, but also after the collapse of Germany. Churchill agreed, commenting that he regretted that nothing could be done until the Germans had surrendered. 'Once they have capitulated I should be loath to accept the military view that we could not send 2,000 troops to help the population defend themselves against stray German marauders who would be left. At any rate we can give them arms.'[21]

Planning: RANKIN

While resources were not available for a landing in Norway, contingency planning began as early as mid-1943 to anticipate how to deal with different situations which might arise in occupied countries as the war ended, particularly if it did so unexpectedly. The overall plan was codenamed RANKIN, and three different scenarios were envisaged. RANKIN A covered circumstances where German forces became so weak that reconquest was judged feasible – the least likely of the three options for Norway. RANKIN B dealt with the contingency of a German withdrawal from some areas, so as to concentrate forces elsewhere, which it was thought they might need to do after OVERLORD. RANKIN C described a complete German collapse. Forces were originally earmarked for RANKIN B in Norway, and responsibility for the reconquest of Norway was reassigned to Scottish Command under Lieutenant-General Sir Andrew Thorne. The Norwegians were not initially told about RANKIN B because of the need to preserve the security of OVERLORD before the invasion took place. They were only briefed on RANKIN C.[22] The decision to transfer responsibility to Scottish Command, further down the military pecking order and with less ability to debate directives issued to them from a higher command, caused significant Norwegian dissatisfaction. Hansteen observed to Lieutenant-General Frederick E. Morgan, then chief of staff to the General Eisenhower, Supreme Allied Commander, 'We know more about Norway than the British, and it is our country, so we should be enabled to comment at an earlier stage.'[23] Moreover, in the course of the summer of 1944, the forces allocated to Thorne gradually trickled away as they were reassigned elsewhere.* The Norwegians also found this hard to accept when they learned about it.

However, SOE were in a position to provide some significant support to certain elements of RANKIN, and contributed to the fairly tortuous

---

* Commenting on the problem caused by the serious lack of forces, General Bedell Smith, chief of staff to General Eisenhower, told him that he did not know what he would do if the German garrison in Norway fell apart.

process by which SHAEF (Supreme Headquarters, Allied Expeditionary Force) was attempting with Scottish Command to work out a feasible plan – a process made more complicated by changing political circumstances, shortages of resources, and limited knowledge among SHAEF planners of conditions in Norway. Wilson told Georg Unger Vetlesen, his OSS counterpart, that 'their general attitude is such as to make my somewhat remote Viking blood boil'. He was only slightly more moderate in a comment to Gubbins:

> I feel you are bound to agree that this plan has been drawn up without expert advice on political or topographical details. SF HQ have not been consulted by SHAEF in any way in regard to this plan, and were not even on the distribution list until I was informed by General Officer Commanding in Scottish Command that copies had been distributed. I am aware that it does not fall within the province of SOE to comment on the military and strategic aspects of these plans, but this seems to be a case in which SOE would be entitled to do so, on account of the accumulative experience and knowledge which it possesses.[24]

SHAEF's plan went through four drafts, was immensely detailed, and was finalised and put out on 10 July 1944, a month after D-day.

SOE concluded that if no regular Allied troops would be left for deployment to Norway, there would be an even greater number of tasks which SOE could perform. In preparation for this, they stepped up Norwegian training programmes so as to prepare and organise a larger resistance force. These programmes were extensive and built on previous experiences which had been shown to be effective, such as those of Gannet, which dropped into the Gudbrandsdalen area in November 1942. In four months, they ran eleven courses and trained fifty-nine men, as well as a few smaller teams who were intended to deal with traitors.[25] At the same time, SOE took advantage of the greater number of both British and American aircraft available and significantly increased the supply of weapons and other equipment, with well over a thousand sorties – ten times more numerous than in all the preceding seasons. There was an equally large increase in the number of deliveries by sea, with over 150 tons of arms and equipment despatched from the beginning of 1944.[26] It is estimated that by the end of the war, there were light arms available to equip some 30,000 men. When young Norwegians started to seek refuge to avoid labour mobilisation, it was agreed in August 1944 that Milorg should organise a series of five bases in the mountains where it was intended to assemble, arm, equip and train a force of up to 2,000 members in each. In the event, only three became operative – Elg, north-west of Oslo, Varg in the Setesdal mountains in the south and Bjørn, north of Bergen. Their complements had not reached the planned capacity by May 1945, but they were able to play an effective part following the German surrender on 8 May 1945.[27]

Special Forces headquarters issued a directive in September 1944, which noted that no Allied offensive operations were planned for Norway. Therefore no steps were to be taken to encourage the resistance movement to overt action, since it could not be supported. Resistance activity should be concentrated on preventing the Germans from pursuing a scorched-earth policy any further. Efforts were to be concentrated on providing protection to their likely targets, which were expected to be power stations, communications, public utilities (particularly ports) and industrial plant. Considerable effort was put into planning adequate protection against these eventualities. However, SOE was taking other measures as well. For example, from August 1944 onwards and with Swedish agreement they set up bases in northern Sweden, codenamed Sepals, to report German naval and military movements and provide weather reports. On occasion they sent fighting patrols across the border to interfere with the German withdrawal from Finnmark, though supply problems and poor weather made this difficult.[28] Sepals sometimes used SIS communications facilities, such as Brunhild, which had been set up in June 1943 north of Torneträsk on the Swedish side of the border (though without

Swedish knowledge).[29] Brunhild also operated a radio beacon to help Allied bombers returning from raids in Norway, such as the attack on *Tirpitz* on 12 November 1944.[30]

This did not mean that SOE abandoned sabotage operations. However, it changed its emphasis and concentrated on targets which were of more immediate value to the Germans, particularly those which supported German offensive capabilities such as fuel supplies, construction or repair facilities, weapons stores and factories such as those which made sulphuric acid which could be used in explosives or in batteries for U-boats.[31] However, as the campaign developed, Milorg gradually increased its influence over these joint operations. FEATHER II, an attack launched from Sweden on the Thamshavn railway in April 1944, was the last British operation to have been planned outside Norway,[32] although SOE remained responsible for authorising sabotage attacks proposed by the resistance.

Sunshine and Polar Bear

The plan for infrastructure protection, or counter-sabotage, was divided into six separate categories, of which Sunshine and Polar Bear were the most important. The objective of Sunshine was the protection of hydro-electric power installations in south-eastern Norway, while Polar Bear involved the protection of harbours throughout the country. The Sunshine party was led by Leif Tronstad. He commanded a party of eight officers including Norman Lind, an engineer who was one of only a handful of British members of SOE who deployed to Norway during the occupation. (The others included members of the Scale/Quaver party led by Joe Adamson and, separately, Ragnar Christophersen who jumped into southern Norway on 17 April 1945 with the Varg IV party.) They were dropped into Norway in October 1944 and linked up with Einar Skinnarland and former members of GUNNERSIDE. In the course of the next six months, they worked intensively to arrange protection of all the important plants by recruiting loyalists working in them, who concealed their weapons inside the buildings for use if the Germans showed signs of preparing to destroy their installations. Sadly, Tronstad was killed in March 1945 while interrogating a quisling official, when he was shot by the man's brother. He had been an inspirational leader who had not only played a key role in the planning of GUNNERSIDE, but also achieved much in building better cooperation with his British and Norwegian colleagues in SOE.

The ten Polar Bear parties were selected to cover the most important ports in Norway between Narvik in the north and the Swedish frontier. They were deployed between mid-January and May 1945, and were generally successful though one party had to be replaced when Åsmund Færøy of Polar Bear IV was arrested on 9 April, soon after his arrival.* The most outstanding achievement was that of Inge Steensland, assigned to Polar Bear VI E (East) to protect the ports of Moss and Fredrikstad. He devised and executed a plan to seize all the tugs operating from Fredrikstad, as the Germans were largely dependent on them for moving their shipping in Oslofjord. This was successful, and he arrived with eleven tugs and the salvage vessel *Uredd* in the Swedish port of Strömstad on 8 February 1945. Steensland returned to Norway, and on 20 April he brought out to Sweden the cargo ship *Aktiv* (650 tons) and the tanker *Denofa* (3,250 tons), which it was believed the Germans intended to use as blockships. His final action was to evacuate all of the local pilots to Sweden, in eight cutters, at the end of war. For these actions he was awarded the DSC.

Scale

Scale was an example of SOE's further contingency planning. The most significant element was Scale/Octave, whose aim was to place Allied representatives in the field at the earliest opportunity. It would constitute an Allied mission representing SHAEF through SF HQ, intended to help bring about the capitulation of the German armed

---

* Færøy unsuccessfully tried to hang himself but was released on 7 May and then participated again in Polar Bear work, helping to ensure that all demolition charges were removed from the harbour.

forces as soon as possible and to help Milorg to facilitate the arrival of Allied forces and supplies. It was to be led by Bjarne Øen. In the event, circumstances changed so much that it was cancelled. The task of another, Scale/Minim, was to represent SOE with SOE and OSS missions on all matters for which SOE were responsible to SHAEF, dealing with future plans involving military action in Norway launched from Sweden.

The only other Scale operation to take place was Scale/Quaver, led by Joe Adamson, who had been in SOE since 1940 and worked for Wilson as SN/Plans, responsible for planning. Its mission was to deploy to the Saltfjellet area of Nordland and contact local resistance elements. The objective was to report on southbound German troop movements, and to coordinate interference with their progress. Adamson and his party were dropped on 16 October. From the outset, the operation did not go well. They were dropped in broad daylight at 0900 because in view of the nature of the chosen landing site, a night drop was thought to be very hazardous. Wilson noted that the group would be willing to drop by daylight if the Air Ministry had no objection, while the RAF also preferred this timing to facilitate navigation.[33] There was no reception committee at the drop site, and Adamson injured his knee on landing and could not walk. He was captured by the Germans. The rest of the party were able to escape and make their way to Sweden. Adamson was able to convince the Germans that he was in the RAF. He was wearing army battle-dress with his parachutist's wings on the shoulder. As the German airborne forces were part of the air force and not the army, the German military may have chosen to accept his story that he had been an observer on an RAF aircraft when the captain ordered them to bail out after they had been hit. He was never interrogated by the Gestapo.* (There were precedents for this: the Welman driver Bjørn Pedersen, who was captured by the German Navy during an attack in Bergen harbour in November 1943,

---

* I am grateful to Nick Adamson, Joe's son, for this information.

was not landed in Bergen but was sent by them straight to the naval POW camp near Hamburg. This saved his life.) Adamson ended up in Germany in Dulag Luft Wetzlar, a transit camp for RAF prisoners. Earlier, while he was being interrogated in Oslo, SOE asked Coppersmith Blue whether there was any chance of rescuing him. They thought not.[34] Scale/Quaver was abandoned and there were no further operations mounted in the northern area. Adamson was released at the end of the war, and returned to Norway in time to join Wilson on his Scandinavian tour. Wilson later observed that Adamson's success in resisting German interrogation may also have been helped by the fact that he had been a member of the Oxford University Dramatic Society! He had already had to apologise to Boyle, assistant to Gubbins, for having failed to obtain written consent for Adamson to proceed to enemy occupied territory, and accepted responsibility for having been out-argued in allowing the operation to proceed in the first place.[35]

Jens Chr. Hauge meets SOE in London
Hauge, the head of Milorg, visited Britain twice, in August and November 1944. Before his arrival, SOE had not known his identity, which was a carefully concealed secret. On his first visit, in addition to extensive discussions with the Norwegian government, he met combined staff at SF HQ and attended a meeting of the ANCC. He also held discussions about protective measures against further German scorched-earth activities, and actions before and after the liberation. This included the capture and preservation of Gestapo and other documents, the planning for which Milorg had well in hand. Hauge also floated the idea of blowing up Gestapo headquarters in Victoria Terrasse by smuggling explosives into the cellar, though doubted that the time was right for such a venture. These productive exchanges reflected the closeness of the relationship which Milorg had now developed with SOE, who, following Øen's visit to Sweden in the summer, had already agreed to facilitate direct wireless communications between them. After Hauge's return to Norway, Milorg issued a directive to all

district leaders concerning actions to be taken in the event of a German surrender. On his next visit, Hauge discussed some of these subjects in greater detail, and agreed that action would be taken against a list of the most notorious Norwegian collaborators. There was also agreement that the RAF would make an attempt to bomb Gestapo headquarters in both Oslo and Kristiansand. The RAF attack on Victoria Terrasse on 31 December 1944 was unsuccessful. The Mosquitoes largely missed their target and seventy-eight Norwegians and twenty-eight Germans were killed, the worst single incident in Oslo during the war.[36] The plan to attack the Gestapo headquarters in Kristiansand was therefore dropped. Apart from this very unfortunate aftermath, the success of Hauge's visits reflected the extent to which Milorg and SOE interests had converged since the difficult days of 1941. Gunnar Sønsteby, the leader of the Oslo gang, also visited at the same time as Hauge. With Hauge's consent a directive was agreed for him, which specified that Sønsteby's Oslo detachment was to be held separate from local district organisation and remain available for special operations. The directive set out his priorities for sabotage both of industrial plant and Abwehr equipment such as direction finding vehicles which could be used against Milorg and SOE – or SIS stations, for that matter. It also specified the order of priority in which leading Norwegian quislings were to be assassinated, starting with Karl Marthinsen, head of the Norwegian police, who was killed in February 1945.[37]

Action against the railways
Milorg members had become increasingly frustrated by restrictions preventing them from taking action against the Germans. After the invasion of Normandy, SHAEF was reluctant to order sabotage against Norwegian railways, which might prevent Germans leaving to take part in the campaign in western Europe. They maintained this position despite representations from both the Commander in Chief of the Home Fleet (Vice-Admiral Fraser) and the Commander in Chief of No. 18 Group Coastal Command (Air Vice-Marshal Simpson) who

both wanted interference with internal railway traffic so as to drive the Germans to make use of sea routes. SHAEF argued that it might complicate attempts to liberate Norway when the time came. However, their position softened slightly when, in October, they agreed to some sabotage actions against the railways, as they acknowledged the benefit this could give to resistance morale. Soon afterwards, when fighting on the Rhine became bogged down, SHAEF decided that it would be desirable to try to limit German withdrawals from Norway. On 5 December they issued a directive calling for railway and road sabotage, which was intended to force all German traffic to proceed by sea, where it could be attacked by Allied warships, submarines and aircraft.[38] The effectiveness of this measure is not entirely clear, for German documents captured after the war cast some doubt on SHAEF's estimate that the rate of movement was reduced from four German divisions every month to just one. But it certainly made a significant difference. For much of the war there were seven divisions in Norway, increasing to thirteen by the end of 1943 and then to eighteen as the Germans withdrew from Finland. At this time, there were well over 400,000 German troops stationed in Norway, one soldier for every eight Norwegians. By the end of the war, there were eleven divisions left.[39]

Lie's visit to Moscow

In May 1944, Norway signed agreements concerning civil administration and jurisdiction in liberated territories with Britain, the United States and the Soviet Union. This permitted military authorities to retain control over administration as long as conflict persisted. In October 1944, the Russians moved into Finnmark in pursuit of the retreating German Army. The latter carried out a scorched-earth policy to try to slow down the Russian advance, enabling many German troops to avoid capture and escape southwards. The Norwegians sent a small force of several hundred men to support the Russians, later reinforced by two companies of the police troops which had been trained in Sweden. In November 1944, Trygve Lie visited Moscow for discussions about the Russian campaign, and was confronted by Vy-acheslav Molotov with demands for significant concessions over both Svalbard and Bear Island, which lies roughly halfway between Svalbard and the North Cape of Norway. This was an unexpected shock and on his return to London, Lie decided to discuss it with Eden before briefing his own government (see Chapter 1). The Norwegians stalled for a while, but the Russians returned to the charge and only finally dropped their claim over two years later, after the Norwegians made a robust rebuttal and put out a public statement to that effect.[40] Kirkenes was abandoned by the Germans and became the first town in Norway to be liberated on 25 October 1944. The Soviet Army advanced further into Finnmark, but stopped at Neiden, well short of Alta. Concerns that they might refuse to leave proved to be unfounded, and they withdrew from Norway in September 1945.

CHAPTER 11

HUNTING DOWN THE *TIRPITZ*
CHURCHILL'S OBSESSION

[After the attack by X-craft on Tirpitz] the first damage reports came from Raaby. They were the first he sent. Thereafter he and Ultra kept up a running commentary on the repairs to the wounded battleship. In fact, Raaby was to transmit daily for ten months ... [Following one air attack in April 1944], the navy had to depend entirely on Raaby for information on the progress of repairs. Follow-up attacks were attempted by the carriers for which Raaby, with utmost daring, transmitted hourly weather reports. All were frustrated and in July, Raaby having been forced to flee into Sweden, another agent from a safer place in Altafjord reported Tirpitz again on the move. A further large-scale attack was planned and this time, at my suggestion, we took Raaby with us in the Duke of York. *Alcohol meant no more to him than mother's milk and my mess bill soared.*

EDWARD THOMAS, INTELLIGENCE STAFF OFFICER ON *DUKE OF YORK*, ADMIRAL MOORE'S FLAGSHIP, DESCRIBES SOME OF THE ACHIEVEMENTS OF TORSTEIN RAABY, THE SIS AGENT WHO PLAYED THE MOST PROMINENT AND VALUABLE PART IN REPORTING ON *TIRPITZ*.[1]

Throughout the war, and particularly after it had moved to Trondheim in January 1942, Winston Churchill was almost obsessed with the threat which *Tirpitz* posed to both Atlantic and Arctic convoys. The heavily armoured sister ship of *Bismarck* was nearly 300 yards long and weighed over 50,000 tons. She carried a more powerful range of armaments than any warship in the Royal Navy. By May 1942, when *Tirpitz* had been joined by four heavy cruisers, *Hipper, Lützow, Admiral Scheer* and *Prinz Eugen*, they represented a very considerable threat to Atlantic and later Arctic convoys. The cruisers did not remain constantly in Norwegian waters. However, *Tirpitz* did, and by its mere presence tied down significant elements of the Home Fleet which could otherwise have been deployed to the Far East or elsewhere. Churchill took a very close interest in the progress of operations intended to sink the battleship, and constantly nagged the Chiefs of Staff, admirals and air marshals for information and for more operations aimed at destroying her. Between October 1940 and November 1944, *Tirpitz* was the target of twenty-four air and naval operations.[2] Many of these were bombing and mining operations carried out by the RAF and the Fleet Air Arm, some of them were carried out by naval submariners with assistance from SOE and some were planned by SOE. The intelligence provided by SIS on movements of *Tirpitz*, her status and battle readiness and the progress of repairs, was highly prized by both the Admiralty and the Air Ministry.

First steps against Tirpitz: Frodesley
After Theta had reported the arrival of *Tirpitz* in Norway in late January 1942, John Godfrey, the Director of Naval Intelligence, asked for ideas about how to destroy her. He suggested that possible schemes could include ruses for tempting or forcing *Tirpitz* to put to sea, where it could be engaged; making her berth unattractive while she was exercising in the Trondheimfjord; attacking the morale of the ships' company and also the judgement and determination of the German High Command. He copied the minute to SOE, saying he would welcome ideas from them. Nelson, then director, replied on 3 March that there might be a possibility of attacking *Tirpitz* by a special development of the idea for a one-man submarine. 'SOE is in fact working on the construction of a one-man submarine to be propelled like a bicycle by pedalling. It might be necessary to fasten the submarine beneath an

ordinary Norwegian fishing boat, which would go up the fjord near to the *Tirpitz* before releasing it.'This was given the codename Frodesley. Research seemed promising, and SOE thought that a prototype might be available for testing by the end of June.

Churchill took a close interest in the project, commenting and annotating approvingly the photographs and reports which he was shown. His interest was so great that Selborne, the minister, asked him whether he would like to watch some trials on Staines reservoir, near London.[3] Wilson discussed with Hambro, who had by then taken over from Nelson as director of SOE, whether his staff could be considered for the operation. He did so before he raised it with the Norwegian authorities, since he assumed that the operation would be carried out by British personnel. Hambro replied that all his staff were too busy, and after some internal wrangling, it was concluded that attack crews would be better drawn from the navy and that it would therefore be more suitable for Admiralty use.[4] The idea was eventually dropped.*

Few of Godfrey's other suggestions received much consideration. However, in 1943 some thought was given by SOE to the possibility of introducing an explosive charge in *Tirpitz's* berth during her absence, either by air, small submarine or by SOE. They hoped that since the berth was less likely to be well guarded when *Tirpitz* was at sea, it might be worth exploring further. In the end, once again, nothing came of it.

SIS intelligence on Tirpitz

Admiralty records suggest that from the time of her launch in April 1939 until her arrival in Trondheim in January 1942, *Tirpitz* was the

---

* The navy continued to develop the idea, which emerged as a midget submarine codenamed Welman. It was twenty feet long, with a one-man crew, a range of thirty miles and a 560lb warhead. However, the Welman was not considered very suitable, not least because it lacked a periscope and provided only very limited visibility. It was only used once operationally, in an attack on a floating dock in Bergen harbour in November 1943. This was not successful. Mountbatten, director of combined operations, nearly drowned when testing one in a London reservoir and arrived late and soaking for a meeting with Churchill at Chequers. See Foot, *SOE*, p. 89.

subject of just one SIS report, which described gunnery practice she had carried out off Sassnitz, east of Lübeck. During the time she was in Norway, until her sinking in November 1944, she was the subject of considerably more. For example, NID files contain details of 145 SIS reports about *Tirpitz*, most of which were graded B2, i.e. given a high degree of reliability. This list is far from complete, because it does not include many of the reports provided by coast-watching agents about her movements, or the weather reports which were sent regularly before bombing attacks by the RAF or the Fleet Air Arm. But they give a good idea of the extent of the comprehensive reporting which SIS was able to provide on *Tirpitz* and how far this complemented and added to Ultra reporting from GC&CS. Chapter 8 has already described the coverage provided by Magne Hassel in the Agdenes Fort, but it is also worth looking at some further examples to examine how, when *Tirpitz* moved north and used a series of different anchorages, SIS had to react quickly to establish adequate coverage of these sites. SOE also contributed quite regularly to intelligence reporting on *Tirpitz*. For example, Antrum (based near Ålesund) was asked on 4 March to provide a description of the anchorage which *Tirpitz* was using. It replied on 7 March that it was lying at Langstein in the Fættenfjord, off Åsenfjord, close in to the cliff wall, and that it was camouflaged with trees.[5]

Arctic convoys: the fate of PQ 17

The greatest damage caused by *Tirpitz* during the war occurred during an operation in which it did not take part, but where the threat of its imminent participation was sufficient to cause the Arctic convoy PQ 17 to be ordered to disperse. The history of this ill-fated convoy is well known and needs little description here. PQ 17 left Iceland for Murmansk on 27 June 1942. Ultra intercepts did not provide a clear picture of the intentions or movements of the German battle fleet, which might have included three further warships in addition to *Tirpitz* – *Hipper*, *Admiral Scheer* and *Lützow*. There were however undoubtedly signs that it was preparing to move to intercept the convoy. In the absence of confirmation that *Tirpitz* had remained in the Altafjord, Sir Dudley Pound, the Chief of the Naval Staff, ordered PQ 17 to disperse. As a result, fourteen of its thirty-seven ships were lost to German air attack, and a further ten to U-boats. Ultra later showed that *Tirpitz* had indeed sailed, but was recalled once it became clear how much damage was being done to the dispersed convoy by the German Air Force and U-boats. There was no need to involve the German battle fleet.[6] That *Tirpitz* could have caused so much damage, without even firing a shot, can only have increased Churchill's determination to ensure that it was disabled or destroyed as soon as possible. The pressure on SIS to provide intelligence on its activities increased even further.

Operation TITLE

TITLE was an operation intended to use two submersible chariots to deposit large warheads under the keel of *Tirpitz* while it was at anchor in one of the smaller fjords off the Trondheimfjord. This was one of the most imaginative, enterprising and daring operations mounted by SOE during the war, and it came very close to succeeding.

The idea for TITLE was first suggested in mid-June 1942 by Admiral Submarines, Sir Max Horton. He asked SOE about the possibility of using chariots to attack *Tirpitz*, which at that time was still at anchor off Åsenfjord, close to Trondheim. The original SOE plan involved sending a team and their equipment to a small island outside the fjord, and putting them on a local fishing boat. SOE sent a courier from Stockholm to put this request to the owner of a fishing boat which was thought suitable. This took time, but when the courier returned in early September, he reported that the owner had refused to consider their suggestion. Herluf Nygaard, the organiser of the SOE Lark station in Trondheim (not to be confused with the SIS Skylark B station, also in Trondheim), suggested sending a boat from the Shetlands instead, equipped with forged papers to get through the German security controls in the fjord. SOE was also given local advice that since a large number of commercial vessels and fishing boats which took cargo into Trondheim were not based in the port, there was a 75 per cent chance that their boat would get past the controls and gain access into Trondheimfjord. It was eventually determined to use *Arthur*, which Leif Larsen had stolen when *Nordsjøen* had sunk in heavy seas in October 1941, and then sailed back to Scotland. Larsen volunteered to lead the operation.

Leif Larsen (centre, wearing a cap) on board the *Arthur* in Scalloway. To his left are three of the most effective members of the Norwegian resistance: Bjørn Rørholt (then with SIS, in the white coat), Odd Sørli and Arthur Pevik (SOE). © Scalloway Museum

The preparatory research done for TITLE was meticulous. SOE agents collected information about everything which might affect the effectiveness of the charioteers. They gathered details of topography, meteorology (daylight and darkness, winds, temperatures, snow and frost), oceanography and also hydrography. This was particularly important as water density can vary at different temperatures. That could affect buoyancy, and the ability of the chariots to remain submerged at a particular depth. They also collected information about the warships anchored there and the nature of the booms which were protecting them – which cannot have been easy to obtain.[7]

There was still plenty of preparatory work to be done, to test the battery-driven chariots, to adapt *Arthur* to provide a hiding place for the six British seamen who were needed to carry out the attack (four chariot operators and two dressers to help them into their diving suits), to work out a suitable cargo to provide the pretext for their journey and to prepare all the false documentation needed to get them through the German controls. Nygaard, and Lark, provided much of the information and advice which was required. They also prepared plans to enable those involved to escape to Sweden afterwards. Peat was chosen as cargo for *Arthur* rather than fresh fish, as it would not be practical to arrange for supplies of fresh fish to be available daily. This would have been required if *Tirpitz* was not available in its berth and the attack had to be delayed. The problem with peat as an alternative was that it required a special permit from the supply commission, so that had to be arranged too. This meant that in all, seven different types of documentation had to be provided. Some of them were not available for copying, but fortunately on 23 September *Svalen* arrived in Shetland with most of those required, which provided suitable templates for the forgers. There were plenty of other last-minute problems also needing to be resolved. These required Odd Sørli, the original SOE contact in Trondheim, to coordinate most of the communications from Stockholm and then to fly back to Shetland to add to the final briefing of the *Arthur* crew and the briefing of the whole party about possible escape routes to Sweden. It was intended that the Norwegian crew and naval dressers should escape once the chariots had been launched. The attackers themselves were to try to get away and hide up and then escape, although it was accepted that the prospects of achieving this would be very small.

There was one final last-minute change. Since the operation had originally been planned, *Tirpitz* had left Trondheim to attack PQ17. After this sortie was abandoned, it moved to Bogenfjord, near Narvik. Larsen was intending to sail there. However on 23 October, *Tirpitz* was reported to have left. It arrived in Trondheim the following day. So Larsen had barely twenty-four hours to change the arrangements he had made and come up with a new plan. The trip itself was not without incident. There were engine problems, with a cracked cylinder which needed local tools to repair. These were found on the island of Hitra. The charging motor for the chariot batteries broke, and it was decided that the batteries would have to be used as they were. There were also encounters with inquisitive and potentially talkative fishermen who asked the crew some searching questions. The chariots were put on deep towing wires and *Arthur* successfully negotiated the security control. This was quite rigorous, though the German officer did not ask to see all their papers. However, he gave Larsen an anxious moment when he looked at the signature on one of the forged documents and commented that he knew the German officer who had signed it, but had not realised that he was in Ålesund. Also, to Larsen's relief, he did not inspect *Arthur* closely enough to notice the chariots, which were plainly visible in the clear water beyond the stern.*

Once past this check, it seemed to Larsen and his crew that they were now through all the obstacles and ready to mount the attack. But the Trondheimfjord channel is wide and subject to the vagaries of the weather. Conditions deteriorated and shortly after they rounded a point, *Arthur* ran into two large waves which cause the boat to rise on the crest and then sink sharply. They felt a bump as a chariot hit the propeller. One of the divers, Able Seaman Evans, went down and reported that both the towing cables had sheared at the point where they were attached to the chariots and that the chariots had sunk. So Larsen had no choice but to scuttle *Arthur* and escape. Unfortunately the unpredictable current later caught *Arthur* and she sank in shallows from which the Germans managed to salvage her. This unexpected misfortune meant that the party was unable to contact those who were standing by to help them to escape. The Norwegian crew and the British attack team split into two groups, with Norwegians in each, for the journey on foot to Sweden. This was not an easy passage, for the snow

---

* After the war, a Gestapo officer revealed that the German officer responsible for security in Trondheimfjord, Moller, had committed suicide as a result of the investigation which followed.

in places was three or four feet deep. There were also rivers to cross. One party called at a farm where the farmer's wife was very unfriendly. It was later discovered that she had reported them to the police. Soon afterwards they were challenged by two policemen, who attempted to arrest them. There was an exchange of shots. Evans was wounded, but the others were able to escape. They all managed to make their way to Sweden and then eventually back to England. However, Evans was harshly interrogated by the Germans and, together with the remaining survivors of the FRESHMAN operation, was shot at Trandum a couple of months later in January 1943.[8]

The new Admiral Submarines, Claud Barry, asked SOE to send a message to Lark thanking them 'for the most admirable work done on our behalf by all your people in Trondheim, at grave risk to themselves'. With a view to the next operation which was being planned, he added 'the fact that they are willing to continue to play their part should another occasion arise, is first rate and shows the fine spirit of the Norwegians'.[9] Larsen was awarded the Conspicuous Gallantry Medal for his part in TITLE, a medal which at that time was only given to naval ratings. He was told that this was the first time that it had been given to a non-British recipient.

Denham had reported from Stockholm in September 1942 that *Tirpitz* needed a refit. The battleship did not return to Germany for this, but remained in Trondheim while it was carried out. The main reason was that German anxiety about an Allied landing was again on the increase and Hitler remained very concerned about the defence of Norway.[10] *Tirpitz* stayed there until March 1943, when it moved back to the Narvik area. During this period, both Corona (in Oslo) and Scorpion (Trondheim) provided regular updates on the progress of repairs while *Tirpitz* was anchored at a large German naval base in Lofjord. On one occasion in January, in response to an urgent enquiry from SIS, Scorpion was able to provide rapid confirmation that *Tirpitz* was still moored there and had not left.[11]

Operation SOURCE

Very shortly after the failure of TITLE, planning began on another naval operation against *Tirpitz*. This was Operation SOURCE, originally envisaged as an attack against both *Tirpitz* and possibly also other capital ships in the Trondheimfjord. It was to use X-craft submarines, which were much larger than Welmans or chariots. They had a crew of four, with an intended range of over 1,000 miles, or 150 miles submerged. They were originally intended to go under an enemy ship in harbour, when a diver would be used to plant limpet mines on the hull of the vessel above. This idea was discarded in favour of using two large detachable side charges weighing two tons each, which would be dislodged and left on the bottom of the sea directly under the target vessel.

For transport, it was initially intended that some of SOE's fishing boats from the Shetlands base would be used, which would tow three X-craft to some of the outer skerries, or small uninhabited islands offshore from Trondheim. They would be left to operate independently thereafter. SOE's Lark station would be responsible for exfiltrating the crews to Sweden if they were unable to return to Shetland on their own. Odd Sørli was sent back in March 1943 for this purpose and set up Lark Blue.* However, the planning was bedevilled by technical problems. The Norwegian fishing vessels proved to be too small to tow the heavy X-craft except in a calm sea or with the wind abeam. Moreover, production of the X-craft was delayed, which limited opportunities for training. As the nights were getting shorter, the Admiralty decided to postpone the operation until the autumn, and also concluded that it would be better to use submarines, rather than fishing boats, to tow the X-craft. By then, there were six of them available for use, and *Tirpitz* had moved deep into the Altafjord. SIS resources in northern Norway

---

* The original Lark deployment had been disrupted when Nygaard and his wireless operator Hansen were arrested in December 1943. See Chapter 5.

at that time were so limited that it would have been more difficult to help the crews to escape to Sweden if that proved necessary.

Attack on Svalbard, September 1943

But before SOURCE could be launched, *Tirpitz* took part in its only offensive action of the war. This was an attack on the Allied weather stations on Svalbard. The Germans sent a large fleet, including not only *Tirpitz*, but also *Scharnhorst* and nine destroyers. They bombarded the buildings, destroyed coal depots and other facilities, and captured many of the Norwegians who were stationed there. The attack was of limited and temporary value, because the Allies restored a weather station on the island soon afterwards. The German fleet was not attacked during this sortie. Ultra had given indications of several different planned German operations, but it was not clear which was which. Once it was established that *Tirpitz* and *Scharnhorst* were involved in the attack on Svalbard, the Home Fleet set sail. But they were too late to make an interception. This illustrated again that Ultra and photo reconnaissance could not always be relied upon to give adequate warning of the movements of large German naval units from their Norwegian bases. It further emphasised the importance of extending the SIS coast-watching service in the area.

The attack by X-craft in the Altafjord

The six X-craft sailed from Scotland in mid-September. One was lost in unexplained circumstances on the journey north. It was therefore agreed that of the five others, three would attack *Tirpitz*, with one each going for *Lützow* and *Scharnhorst*. The one destined for *Lützow* was lost on the final stage of its journey. Of the remainder, only X-7 and X-6 were able to make their attack, which took place on 22 September. X-7 had considerable difficulty negotiating a way through the torpedo net, which extended all the way to the sea bottom, and succeeded by a lucky chance. The commander, Godfrey Place, dropped his charges and then found it even harder to get out through the net again. He spent about forty-five minutes trying to do so, and in the end only managed by a remarkable manoeuvre. He made contact with the net to make sure that he was as close as possible. He then went straight down, and blew his bow tank to full buoyancy so that he ascended as quickly as possible with the bow at a sharp angle upwards, while going at full speed. This enabled him, just, to get high enough to scrape over the net. The Germans did not notice this happening. However he was still in the area when the charges exploded and his submarine was damaged and sank.[12] X-6 attracted attention while negotiating the nets and came under fire but its commander, Donald Cameron, was nevertheless able to drop his charges by *Tirpitz* and scuttle the submarine. All four of his crew, and Place and one other crew member of X-7, were able to escape from their submarines. They were taken prisoner and sent to Germany. No other X-craft made an attack. X-5 was lost, while the fifth, X-10, was recovered by a towing submarine and returned to Britain. Place and Cameron were both awarded VCs.*

The damage to *Tirpitz* from the four large charges was extensive. The first indications came from Ultra in early October. An SIS report soon afterwards stated:

Ship lifted 1.5 metres by explosions. Upper bridge away, guns on after ship rendered unusable. On after deck especially, large dents and bulges. Engine room area particularly badly damaged. Ship unable to move under her own power. Engineers and stokers among casualties.[13]

SIS provided several more useful damage reports in the course of the next few weeks.[14] Upsilon in Tromsø also provided regular updates, reporting in early February 1944 that more than 22,000 bags of cement had been used to stop the leak. Steaming trials at a speed of 4 knots had resulted in a new leak, so delaying progress.[15] Repairs were carried out in the Altafjord and took six months to complete.

---

* This was not the only effective attack by X-craft in Norway. In April 1944, one penetrated Bergen harbour and sank a 7,500-ton merchant ship.

The problems experienced by X-7 in finding a way through the German torpedo nets were not expected, and they certainly interfered with her attack. There have been conflicting accounts about whether the Norwegian resistance provided prior intelligence through Denham, in Stockholm, about the depth of the nets, which was then rejected by Admiralty boom defence experts. Hinsley suggests that this was possible.[16] Upsilon certainly provided confirmation on 19 September that the number of nets had been tripled. It also provided their location, though made no mention of their depth.[17] It would have been a remarkable achievement for anyone to have obtained such detailed information from such a closely guarded area. We do know that Torbjørn Johansen, the brother of Einar who was actively involved in half a dozen SIS stations, was sent to the Altafjord to gather intelligence. He travelled north-east from Tromsø to Alteidet and cycled from there along Langfjord and Kåfjord, making notes and sketches of the anchorages and the boom defences of *Lützow*, *Tirpitz* and *Scharnhorst*. He also used a hydrometer to take measurements of the salinity of the water, while ostensibly out fishing. Upsilon II sent the maps and this information back to London via Sweden in August 1943 and they added significantly to intelligence available from a photo reconnaissance Spitfire operating from Vaenga in Russia.[18]

Sørli had spent eight months in Trondheim working for Lark and helping to plan TITLE, and a further ten months in 1943, first preparing for TITLE and then on other work after *Tirpitz* moved north. After his return to Britain, he was awarded the MBE (Military).

SIS operations against Tirpitz in the Altafjord and elsewhere in northern Norway

It was not a straightforward matter for SIS to establish stations in the north of Norway, apart from in towns such as Tromsø. The climate for much of the year is harsh, and it would have been difficult to establish hermit stations there. Communities were small, and strangers stood out. For this reason, SIS tried to send their agents back to their home areas, but it was not always practical. Distances between towns were great, and transport – except perhaps by sea – was often unreliable or unpredictable. Moreover, meteorological conditions often disrupted wireless communications. For example, on 24 September 1943 station Venus, in Finnsnes, reported that two warships and four destroyers had passed, going south. Due to the deplorable weather conditions which affected transmission, the message was not received by SIS until 14 October – far too late to be of any use.

An additional problem was that SIS had known from the spring of 1942 that the Germans were increasing the extent of their counter-espionage activities in northern Norway. Captain Hugh Trevor-Roper ran the Radio Security Service, otherwise known as Subsection Vw of the counter-intelligence Section V of SIS, studying the activities of the Abwehr and working closely with GC&CS. He reported the new measures which the Abwehr were taking, increasing telephone surveillance and arranging for two further direction finding squads to be made available. One would be based near Tromsø, the other in Kirkenes. They would be accompanied by a Y station, a signals intelligence collection unit gathering evidence of agent transmissions, which would be based at Lakselv airfield at Banak, used by the German Air Force. Trevor-Roper concluded that the move of *Tirpitz* was at least partly responsible for the development of this campaign.[19] It is not clear to what extent, if at all, SIS took account of these enhanced security measures when briefing agents destined for deployment to this area. Trevor-Roper also reported that the Abwehr was considering sending a party to occupy Bear Island to observe the passage of Allied convoys to Murmansk – though in the event this did not happen.

Some of the activities of Upsilon, the first SIS station to be set up in the Arctic Circle, were described in Chapter 8. Although it was disrupted by German arrests in the aftermath of the SOE Operation MARTIN, it survived in different guises, sending from different sites and using different codenames, until the end of the war. Upsilon operated alone until it was reinforced nearly a year later by Mu operating from Laukøya, about a hundred miles further north, and then station Lyra. Lyra operated from Porsa, in Vargsund, north of the Altafjord, nearly 300 miles north-east of Tromsø. Together with Upsilon, both these stations were able to obtain intelligence on *Tirpitz* when it was based in Kåfjord, off the Altafjord more than 200 miles north. Sometimes this was based on reports from agents, such as Torbjørn Johansen, who had visited the area; very occasionally it came from the codes used over the telephone employing cryptic language, and more often it came from a regular courier service which was operated between Alta and station Lyra. Both these stations had their difficulties. Mu had to close for a while when the Gestapo were active on a neighbouring island and captured some Norwegian agents who were working for the Russians. Mu undertook that in the event of the passage of a major warship, they would transmit a report whatever the circumstances. Fortunately that did not prove necessary, and they survived. Chapter 8 described how Lyra was captured, enabling the Germans to make a widespread series of arrests. They also forced the wireless operator to maintain contact with London for six months. Libra, in Kvitnes on Vesterålen, west of Harstad, was set up in late 1942. It was another station which was temporarily able to report on *Tirpitz* during periods when it was based in Bogen, close to Narvik.

But none of these were substitutes for a station on the Altafjord, which would be in a position to report significant activities relating to *Tirpitz* without delay once it established a more permanent anchorage in Kåfjord. SIS tried and failed three times to set up a station on the fjord. The fourth attempt was successful, when Torstein Raaby was landed by submarine in early September 1943. Raaby had worked for Russian intelligence in early 1942, sending reports from Tromsø.[20] He arrived in Britain in June 1943, and joined SIS straight away. Since he was already qualified as a telegraphist, he required little training. It was possible to send him back to Norway with minimal delay and he agreed to go to Altafjord.

Torstein Raaby, who reported on the movements of *Tirpitz*
from the SIS coast-watching station Ida. © NHM

Raaby was not a native of the Altafjord – he came from Andøya, several hundred miles south of Tromsø. Nonetheless he managed to establish himself in the small town of Elvebakken at the southern end of the fjord, not far from the anchorage of *Tirpitz*. German security was tight, and there was a large German garrison there with thousands of troops in the area. With the help of a friend, Karl Rasmussen, Raaby obtained a job as an assistant cashier with the road authorities. He was given responsibility for paying staff in different offices and locations in the area. He arranged the timings for doing this so that he was able to travel frequently, and at varying intervals, past the anchorage where *Tirpitz* lay. In order to build up further his reputation for carrying out an irregular routine, he simulated the behaviour of a drunkard. This helped to explain his absences from his office during working hours at times when it was particularly important for him to be operating his set. He sent his first transmission from station Ida on 11 November 1943. This meant that there were now seven SIS stations operating in the region: Ida near Alta, Lyra at one of the exits from the Altafjord, Mu on Nikkeby, Upsilon II in Tromsø, Valhall in Belvika on

Kvaløy, Venus in Finnsnes and Libra on Vesterålen. For the first time, SIS could feel confident that it had reasonably adequate coverage of German naval movements in northern Norway.

Raaby continued to provide regular updates on *Tirpitz*, which were much appreciated in London. The SIS progress report for March 1944 stated that Ida 'continues to send in extremely valuable information which in all cases has proved to be entirely reliable, exact and detailed'.[21] As the repairs to *Tirpitz* neared completion, the Admiralty began to prepare Operation TUNGSTEN, a carrier-borne attack using Barracudas of the Fleet Air Arm. Raaby provided much of the detailed intelligence required, including the locations of radar installations and anti-aircraft guns and high-tension cables, potentially damaging to low-flying aircraft. Prior to the operation, he also provided weather forecasts every two hours. This was an extremely important contribution, but also highly dangerous as it greatly increased the chances that Ida could be located by direction finding. The attack on 3 April caused considerable superficial damage, but the armour plating of *Tirpitz* was thick enough to withstand assault by armour-piercing bombs. Neither Ultra nor aerial reconnaissance was able to provide much information about the extent of the damage, to enable an estimate of how long she would be out of action. However, Raaby provided a series of detailed damage reports, starting on the day of the attack:

3 April. Local inhabitants extremely impressed by the bombing. No civilian casualties and very little civilian damage. Three direct hits. One on the foredeck, one on the afterdeck and one just before funnel, which has been damaged by fire.

4 April. She got more than three direct hits. You came in the nick of time, she had let go and was under way. She had two aircraft on board. Both are destroyed. Fo'csle badly gashed forward of forward turret, which appears to be pointing below the horizontal. All her guns were swung to port, but she still had a list to starboard.

13 April. *Tirpitz's* list is due to the fact that her pipes were burst and filled the cabins on the starboard side. The steam pipes for her engines were destroyed by fire. Impossible for the moment to define the condition of her engines.[22]

Raaby later confirmed that *Tirpitz's* engines had not been damaged.[23]

Tirpitz under attack by the RAF in Kåfjord, Alta. © NHM

SIS sent the following congratulatory telegram: 'Vice-Admiral in charge of the operation directs us to thank you on behalf of the fleet for supplying him with invaluable information and perfect weather.'[24] Not surprisingly, following the attack the Germans mounted an intensive investigation to try to find Ida. Raaby wanted to leave. However, further air attacks were being planned to prevent *Tirpitz* becoming seaworthy again. SIS explained this to Raaby, and left to him the choice of whether he should remain. He chose to stay while three further operations were being planned. None came to fruition, and Raaby finally left for Sweden in May.

On his return to Britain, Raaby was awarded the DSO.* Cordeaux arranged for him to meet the deputy director of naval intelligence, Ian

---

* The citation for this is contained in the appendix.

Campbell, and the flag officer, submarines, for dinner at the Savoy Hotel.[25] Shortly afterwards, he enjoyed another voyage to Norway to watch preparations from the Commander in Chief's flagship for a further air attack against *Tirpitz*, though it was prevented by bad weather. He did not remain long in Britain, returning to Norway in September 1944 to set up station Delfin in Kirkenes in the far north of Norway. After the Russians arrived in October, he moved the station to Vadsø and maintained independent contact with London. The Norwegian contingent under Colonel Dahl, which was attached to the Russian forces, was not permitted to have its own direct communications with London. So Dahl sought help from Raaby. He was not under Dahl's command, and was temporarily able to provide an alternative means of communication for him.*

In January 1944, when Raaby had been in place for several months and the SIS network in the north was flourishing, the DNI, Edmund Rushbrooke, wrote to defence minister Torp to pay a handsome compliment to the contribution of the agent network:

The reports from your agents in North Norway have been generally of a consistently high standard which is continually improving. This has recently been particularly evident in connection with the attack on *Tirpitz*.

Since the capture of the prisoners from *Scharnhorst* and the receipt of messages from British prisoners captured after the midget attack,† it has been possible to obtain almost complete confirmation of a large number of reports from your agents.

Knowing how hazardous their task must be and how much hard thinking must be put into the administration and maintenance of these sources, I thought that you would like to know that the reports have achieved this high standard and that they are of the greatest value.

---

* His training and wartime experience made Raaby well qualified to work as a radio operator on the Kon-Tiki expedition.

† Presumably arranged through MI9.

I would be grateful if my congratulations could be conveyed to the staff
concerned at your headquarters, and if possible to the sources concerned.

Torp showed this letter to Prime Minister Nygaardsvold and Foreign
Minister Lie.[26]

The break-up of Lyra in June 1944, when the Germans captured
a list of station contacts, was mentioned in Chapter 8. These events
had a very disruptive effect on coast-watching operations throughout
the north. Vali, a station which was being set up in Hammerfest, just
north of the location of Lyra, lost several agents to the Germans. It
never got on the air. Several other stations such as Mu and Vidar were
temporarily closed down. Concern about the German investigations
was also the reason why Libra, in Kvitnes, declined to become involved
in the rescue of Dean Arne Fjellbu (see Chapter 1). Many of Ida's contacts were also arrested. One of them was Karl Rasmussen, who had
helped Raaby to obtain his job as an assistant cashier. He was taken to
Gestapo headquarters in Tromsø, and committed suicide by jumping
out of a third-floor window. When the German investigation reached
Tromsø and some of the Johansen family were arrested, SIS was worried that the whole of their organisation in northern Norway was in
jeopardy. This would have been extremely damaging to their continued
coverage of *Tirpitz*. Fortunately, those arrested did not divulge the information the Germans wanted. Several replacement stations were set
up relatively quickly.

The contribution of Aslaug

Following Raaby's departure for Sweden in May, it was necessary to
set up another station to take over coverage of *Tirpitz*. This was Venus
II, in Moen, on the Målselv river south of Tromsø. Though a long way
from the Altafjord, it was operated by two telegraphists in close touch
with their colleagues in Alta, who provided them with a stream of
valuable intelligence. This worked effectively until it was raided by the

Germans following a successful direction finding operation.* The gap in coverage was very brief. In preparation for another air attack on *Tirpitz*, SIS needed to arrange further reporting of her anchorage. Anton Arild and Knut Moe were dropped by parachute in early September. It was intended that they should camp out in the open, in the snow on the mountainside above the fjord. Unfortunately, much of their equipment, including their tent and sleeping bags, was lost during the drop.[27] Nonetheless they made light of these difficulties and their station Aslaug came on the air with their first report on 13 September. This was just in time. Two days later a force of twenty-seven Lancasters, operating from Russia, dropped a series of enormous six-ton Tallboy bombs on *Tirpitz*. Despite the hindrance of a smokescreen, one Tallboy hit Tirpitz on the foredeck just behind the bow, causing extensive damage. Aslaug reported on this on 20 September. Knut Moe was known to the Germans from his previous work and was still being hunted, and there were nearly 30,000 Germans troops based in the neighbourhood. Nonetheless, he and Arild visited Alta at night to gather further intelligence. They provided detailed damage reporting, which significantly supplemented the rather patchy indications then available from Ultra.[28] The following is a good example:

1 October. We have been in Kåfjord and visited our source. He sees 'T' every day and is known as a solid and reliable man.† Damage is as follows: she got a direct hit on the starboard side which made a hole from the bow towards the stern seventeen metres along. The hole is both above and below the water line and is so large that motor boats could go in. Neither the turrets nor forepart of the ship is under water, neither have they been under water, but just after the attack the ship had a list to

---

* The wireless operators were Aslaug and Olaf Ellefsen, a married couple. Aslaug was pregnant when the station was raided, and while her husband escaped to Sweden, she was captured. The Germans never discovered that Aslaug was herself a very capable operator. She was sent to Oslo and gave birth to their son in captivity.
† That is, Tirpitz.

starboard and the fore part of the ship was low in the water. How much it was difficult to see because of the fog.* Ship is now on an even keel but it is still down by the head.[29]

When Admiral Karl Dönitz was informed that it would take nine months before *Tirpitz* would become seaworthy again, he decided that the battleship would no longer be used as a warship. Instead, '*Tirpitz* would be used merely as a floating battery in defence of northern Norway.'[30] The Germans were beginning to prepare their evacuation from the northern part of Norway, so it was necessary for her to be moved south. She was patched up and, on 15 October, limped slowly out of the Altafjord and down to an anchorage at Håkøya, an island close to Tromsø. Shortly after her arrival, the berth chosen was found to be unsuitable owing to varying depths under the hull. However, a change was considered to be too difficult, so it was decided to fill up the main hollow under the midships section until there would be only six feet of water under the keel at low water. This work was started on 1 November, but had not been completed by the time she was sunk.[31]

Aslaug reported her departure, and when Egil Lindberg, from station Vidar, confirmed that she had arrived in Tromsø shortly afterwards, SIS instructed Arild and Moe to close the Aslaug station and return to Britain via Sweden. Both were later awarded the DSC.[32]

The sinking of Tirpitz

Once *Tirpitz* had moved back to Tromsø, the ship was once again within range of RAF bombers operating from Britain. She was attacked by Lancasters from 9 and 617 squadrons on 29 October. Low cloud over the target hampered their attack and the ship was not hit, though a near miss damaged one of the engines and caused some flooding. A further attempt was made on 12 November by aircraft from the same squadrons. This time, the weather was fine and clear. German

---

* From fires and German smoke generators.

defences were not prepared. Although the smokescreen units had been moved from Kåfjord to Tromsø, they were not ready on the day of the attack. Nor was there any German fighter protection, although this was repeatedly requested from the moment it became clear that another attack was being launched. There have been conflicting accounts of the reasons for this, but it seems likely that poor communications were the main contributory cause. Additionally, GC&CS noted that German aircraft at Bardufoss airfield (where an entire fighter group was based) had been at cockpit readiness since 0826, shortly after the first Lancaster was reported to be in the area. They were prevented from taking off for an hour, first because Lancasters were flying over their base, and then because of the possibility that the airfield itself was a target for the RAF. The first fighter did not take off until 0925, barely fifteen minutes before the attack started. So the Lancasters were able to make their attack without interference. They achieved several direct hits and *Tirpitz* capsized; 971 seamen, about half of the crew, were killed.[33]

Egil Lindberg was operating his station Vidar from the attic above the mortuary where dead German sailors were being brought in. He sent the following message: '12 November. *Tirpitz* capsized after a series of hits. Part of the ship's side and the keel are above the water.' He noted afterwards that the telegram took only two minutes to send, but the searching Germans very soon arrived in the area with three direction finding vehicles.[34]

The capsized wreck of the *Tirpitz*. © NHM

Reactions and consequences

Once the Lancasters started landing and the news of *Tirpitz's* sinking had been confirmed, Air Marshal Harris immediately informed Churchill in Paris. Churchill was quick to congratulate him, and to inform both Stalin and Roosevelt. He further commented to Roosevelt that 'it is a great relief to us to get this brute where we have long wanted her'.

The main immediate consequence of the sinking of the *Tirpitz* was that the navy was at last able to release a number of ships for deployment to the Far East. The author of the SOE Norwegian section history, who was understandably partial, noted that another consequence was that SIS had to forego its stranglehold on priorities, and SOE operations became of equal importance. Because by this time Shetland was carrying out almost all of SIS's operations, this equality of priority did not make much of a change to allocation of transport resources, and came too late to provide much benefit to most SOE operations.[35]

After the end of the war Admiral Otto Ciliax, the Commander in Chief of the German Navy in Norway, said 'of the measures Great Britain took ... in Norway, the most effective were the air attacks ... against convoys ... The enemy appears to have obtained news ... from agents and a very effective communications system'.[36] While SIS certainly played a valuable role in reporting on convoy movements, presumably Ciliax was not aware of their achievements against his warships, and particularly *Tirpitz*.

CHAPTER 12

SOE SABOTAGE AND DISRUPTING THE U-BOATS

1944: DIVERSIFICATION OF OPERATIONS

I would like to thank you for the valuable and gallant assistance which your organisation has rendered to the anti-U-boat effort, particularly in Norway.

LETTER TO GUBBINS FROM VICE-ADMIRAL JACK MANSFIELD,

ASSISTANT CHIEF OF THE NAVAL STAFF, U-BOATS AND TRADE,

14 JUNE 1945.[1]

The anti-U-boat campaign

Although SOE had first become involved in the campaign against them as early as February 1943, no significant sabotage attempts were made against U-boat targets in Norway until August 1944. This was surprisingly late, given how much damage U-boats had already inflicted in the Battle of the Atlantic. It took time for an effective campaign to be developed. In early 1943, British knowledge of German equipment and methods was fairly limited, so early planning was quite broad-brush and rudimentary. What targets or types of targets would offer the best chance of affecting the U-boat campaign as a whole? Thought was given to interfering with supply bottlenecks, and attacking key personnel, with a view to eliminating them. The Admiralty helped to refine SOE's thinking. They doubted that the interruption of utility services to U-boat bases would have much effect. They were most interested in interference with torpedoes and batteries, food and fuel oil – and direct attacks on submarine crews. 'It is considered that interference with the amenities provided for submarine crews would have a serious effect on their morale. The assassination of Admiral Dönitz and/or the blowing up of his headquarters in Lorient in France would profoundly affect the morale of U-boat crews and the efficiency of U-boat operations.'[2] (In the event, of course, neither of these ambitions was achieved.) The initial reaction of SOE was that torpedoes would be too well protected, and that interference with batteries and attacks on oil supplies and key men in the submarine campaign could do the greatest damage.

Planning in Norway was also restricted by the lack of any specific information which could be of operational value. In March 1943, a meeting to assess prospects in both Norway and Denmark concluded that there were no targets in either country for which completed plans existed. There were thought to be approximately fifteen submarines lying in bases in Trondheim, Bergen and Narvik but German security was, not surprisingly, so tight that it was impossible to get near them. Various other possibilities were considered over the next few months – factories manufacturing batteries in Oslo or near the naval base in Horten; interference with small coastal vessels carrying torpedoes from the factory at Horten to their bases; more specific information about the locations of U-boats and their crews which might enable some of them to be attacked and finally the feasibility of attacking repair bases in Bergen and Trondheim if they proved to be less closely guarded. None of these proved to be immediately viable. It was not until August 1944 that the first serious attack was made.*

SOE's campaign against U-boats in Norway was given added importance when the flotillas based in France moved there after the Allied invasion, leaving Norway as the only base on the Atlantic coast capable of continuing U-boat warfare. The Anglo-Norwegian Collaboration Committee (ANCC) noted evidence of German intentions both to remain in Norway and to extend U-boat operations following

---

* There is a gap of eighteen months in SOE records of the Norwegian anti-U-boat campaign, and therefore very limited information about their activity during this period.

the deployment to Norway of Condors and other large reconnaissance aircraft capable of mounting shipping patrols. They also took into account that during the previous few months, significant additional supplies of fuel had been sent there. It was calculated that by the end of April 1944, there was a stock of some 150,000 tons of all types of fuel which was widely dispersed and well defended.[3]

This nonetheless represented a weak point on which SOE could concentrate. On 17 August 1944, Milorg blew up the oil storage depot at Son, on the Oslofjord, destroying 4,700 tons of diesel and special fuel for U-boats. The depot burned for five days. In the course of the next few months there were another thirty attacks, which destroyed millions of litres of oil of different types, mainly by using explosives, but sometimes by contamination. Perhaps the most spectacular was the destruction of Shell storage facilities in Oslo, containing 360,000 litres of fuel oil, by the Linge Company in January 1945, while a local Milorg group used sugar to contaminate 100,000 litres in Honeføss in September 1944. Two successful attacks were also made against factories producing concentrated sulphuric acid (used in batteries) near Lysaker in July and September 1944.[4] Commander Firth, responsible for the Admiralty's campaign against U-boats, was very complimentary about the effect of these operations. At a meeting to discuss the campaign in Norway, he asked about the possibility of making attacks on the bases themselves in Bergen and Trondheim – and also Horten, a transit port where U-boats carried out final checks, testing and in some cases deep dives before departure. Wilson explained that the bases were all closely guarded and that SOE could not do anything by direct attack against the pens in Bergen and Trondheim. However, he noted that Sønsteby, the leader of the Oslo gang, was back in Oslo and was paying particular attention to Horten. This led to a remarkable piece of sabotage by Hjalmar Berge, who worked in the torpedo store there. He planted explosives which on 21 January 1945 blew up 184 torpedo warheads and fifty-three tons of charges and other U-boat stores, as well as barracks and workshops, killing one German and injuring several others. SOE noted proudly that as a result, the Germans had only five live torpedoes left in south-east Norway at the end of the war.[5] Berge, who took refuge in Sweden, was awarded the King's medal for courage.[6]

In view of the impracticality of arranging direct SOE attacks against U-boat bases, Firth raised the feasibility of concentrated bombing of Laksevåg in Bergen and Nyhavna in Trondheim, though air experts present were not hopeful of success. They were largely right. As already highlighted, the attack in October 1944 did little damage to the Bergen base, but caused plenty of civilian casualties, many of them in Holen primary school, close to Laksevåg. A further attack in January 1945 by Lancasters, using the same enormous Tallboys which had sunk the *Tirpitz*, damaged only one of the six heavily reinforced U-boat pens. Consideration was given to attacks on subsidiary bases, such as Kristiansand. Wilson pointed out that SOE had not been able to work up any local organisation there because of the SIS embargo on SOE activities. The record of the meeting noted somewhat acidly that this comment 'attracted the usual remarks'.[7]

Plan to kidnap Captain Hans-Rudolf Rösing

SOE's anti-U-boat campaign did not concentrate only on sabotage as the means of decreasing their efficiency. In January 1945 Firth suggested to SOE that they should consider organising the kidnap of Captain Hans-Rudolf Rösing, who had been Captain U-boats West in France, responsible for U-boats deployed to the Atlantic. After the fall of France, Rösing and many of the U-boats under his command were transferred to Norway. He was thought to be based in Bergen. At this time, the Admiralty was concerned about indications that the Germans were increasing the number of U-boats which they were producing, so such a target might deserve a higher priority. Firth had earlier discussed the possibilities for attacking the U-boat base and staff in Bergen with Louis Pettersen, a longstanding SOE agent operating in the Bergen area. Since October 1943, he had played an important part in providing intelligence about the U-boat pens in Laksevåg and in exploring the potential for sabotage operations against U-boats. Pettersen returned to Bergen by sub-chaser on 18 January to research further the idea of a kidnap.

The detail contained in the SOE enquiry about this possible kidnap (imaginatively codenamed Operation TIGER) showed how well informed they were about the movements of Rösing and his staff. Some of their information drew on interrogations of prisoners of war, but it is evident that most of it came from GC&CS. Unfortunately, despite extensive searches, Pettersen and his colleagues were unable to locate Rösing. The identities of U-boat crews were extremely difficult for them to establish. Pettersen reported that they had two contacts in German naval circles but neither of them had been able to confirm Rösing's presence in Bergen. He asked whether SOE were really certain that he was there. SOE replied that they had information that the crews of his flotillas were based in Melkeplassen, a large camp near the U-boat pens at Laksevåg. Pettersen noted that he had not yet been able to develop a contact at Melkeplassen. The war ended before they were able to take this project any further. Pettersen was later awarded an OBE. The SOE citation stated that his work had been of the greatest possible value to the Admiralty's anti-U-boat committee.[8]

The warm letter of appreciation from Vice-Admiral Mansfield to SOE deserves to be repeated in full:

> I would like to thank you for the valuable and gallant assistance which your organisation has rendered to the anti-U-boat effort, particularly in Norway.
>
> I well know the losses which have been suffered and the dangerous and arduous work which has been undertaken to interfere with U-boats and their facilities in harbour. Apart from the tangible results (such as the destruction of large quantities of diesel oil, of the torpedo store and workshops at Horten ... and of the U-boat battery acid factories in the Oslo area) the intangible results on U-boat morale and the feeling of insecurity which you engendered have been of the greatest value. The other multitudinous activities not specifically aimed against U-boats, such as destruction of communications, continually pinpricked the

enemy and made his operating conditions more difficult. Although I realise that this has been only a small part of their duties as a whole, nevertheless I would be grateful if you would convey to all concerned, particularly to Lieutenant Colonel J. S. Wilson OBE, the warm appreciation of the Navy on their fine efforts.[9]

Intelligence reporting on U-boat movements

It has sometimes been suggested that either SIS or SOE agents provided specific intelligence about the movements of U-boats which enabled them to be intercepted by the Allied forces shortly after leaving Norwegian ports. No documentary evidence has been found in British or Norwegian archives to support this hypothesis. The absence of evidence is not of course conclusive – and both services certainly tried hard enough. For example an SIS team was landed in December 1944 near Bergen, to set up station Pommac and report on U-boat movements. No contact was established, and they asked to be evacuated because of threats to their security.[10] But given the importance of U-boats as targets, it would be remarkable if any SIS or SOE agents involved in the reporting of such traffic had not revealed their activities after the war if their efforts had proved to be successful. We know that Louis Pettersen had managed to infiltrate the U-boat pens in Bergen for sabotage purposes, but there is nothing to suggest that he was able thereby to obtain intelligence about U-boat movements, which would have been among the most closely protected German secrets. The limited reports which are available from either service are of a fairly basic nature. For example, an SIS report of June 1943 which was graded C5 (i.e. of low reliability) stated that German naval personnel in Trondheim had sabotaged fourteen (or, according to another informant, twenty) of their own U-boats. Crews considered that their training was insufficient and the hazards of U-boat service were too great. NID commented that they had no confirmation of this, and considered it implausible.[11] There is though plenty of evidence of the extent to which GC&CS was able to provide reporting which predicted U-boat movements in and out of port. This would have been a far more reliable and useful source of intelligence, especially when it was timely. The remarkable achievements of the submarine HMS *Venturer* are a case in point. *Venturer* had a busy few months. While on a special operation in northern Norway, it had chanced upon *U-771* and torpedoed it on 11 November 1944. It returned to the same area on the following night, landing and caching five boatloads of supplies for SOE at a deserted spot at Mefjord, on Sørøya, near Alta.[12]

On 9 February 1945, just outside Bergen, *Venturer* successfully attacked and sank *U-864*, a large submarine carrying Japanese and German scientists and engineers as well as a large quantity of mercury and military equipment back to Japan. On 5 February the Admiralty had recommended a patrol area which included two routes known to be used by U-boats operating from Bergen, advising that *Venturer* should concentrate on the one near Hellisøy.[13] GC&CS had already picked up a series of messages concerning escorts for *U-864* on previous voyages in and out of Bergen. These described the route which she would take or where and when she would rendezvous with escorts. On 8 February, the day before *U-864* was sunk, they intercepted another message giving the location of Hellisøy for a further rendezvous with an escort and specifying the time at which the escort would be available. It was in that area that *U-864* was intercepted. The remarkable feature of this engagement is that it was perhaps the only one in the war where the attacking submarine intercepted, tracked and sank another submarine while remaining submerged and using just hydrophones and echo ranging (without sonar, whose ranging pings would have alerted the German submarine) to assist with locating the exact position of the target it was attacking.[*14]

---

[*]   HMS *Tribune* had also attacked a German submarine on 6 September 1940 when both were submerged, and reported an explosion shortly after it had fired a torpedo. But the captain only observed a small amount of evidence of wreckage afterwards and no German submarine was reporting missing in the operational area on that date. *Venturer* was sold to the Royal Norwegian Navy after the war, and remained in service as *KNM Utstein* until 1964.

Problems with effectiveness of air supply drops

Chapter 9 described the difficulties of navigation over snow-covered terrain in Norway at night, a problem which was exacerbated by inadequate maps. It was also noted that the GUNNERSIDE party had been dropped some twenty miles away from where the reception committee was waiting for them, and that this was in accordance with an arrangement reached between the pilot and Rønneberg before departure. These were not the only problems with navigation and, following the GUNNERSIDE incident, Wilson suggested to the ANCC that Norwegian pilots and navigators should be attached to 138 squadron and used on flights to Norway. This did not prove straightforward, for the Air Ministry was reluctant to comply with the request. Wilson therefore produced a list of nine examples where serious mistakes had been made. These included an incident when Andreas Fasting, the agent accompanying Odd Starheim, had landed on the edge of a precipice and an accompanying container had ended up on a mountain over half a mile away across the valley. Another one created serious problems for the Raven party when the party landed over ten miles from their agreed dropping place, and it took them eight days to work out where they were. Pheasant were slightly more fortunate, because they landed only four miles from their designated landing site, but that still presented significant difficulties for them in deep snow in the mountains in winter. Following an attempt to drop Chaffinch, the pilot reported that there were no lights to be seen – but the reception party stated that lights were shown throughout the period when the drop was scheduled, and that the aircraft had passed directly over them twice at a height of 500 metres. The difficulties of navigating in such unfamiliar terrain in difficult winter conditions were not underestimated, but these incidents were judged to be too many.

It eventually proved possible to persuade the Air Ministry to change its mind, and some Norwegians were posted to Tempsford, the main base for clandestine flights to occupied Europe, and used on flights to Norway. The first, in the summer of 1943, were Per Hysing-Dahl and Egil Sandberg. Their arrival led to some improvement, but there were still accidents. For example, of the four SOE parties which were dropped in Norway to undertake railway sabotage in support of OVER-LORD, two experienced significant problems. In October 1943, three members of the Grebe party landed in a lightly frozen lake and were drowned. The Fieldfare party (which included Joachim Rønneberg, who had led the GUNNERSIDE party), refused to jump on their first attempt in November 1943, because after circling for twenty minutes the pilot could not find the pinpoint where they were to be dropped. They were finally successful in March 1944 – though landed nearly ten miles from their reception point and lost some of their food in a lake. Not least because of very poor weather, a limited resupply did not prove possible until July, and they were forced to subsist on short rations in the mountains for the rest of the year, until they were able to make their attack on 5 January. The poor diet and insufficient food took its toll on Rønneberg, who became ill and was later forced to return to Britain for treatment.[15]

The Oslo gang

William Mackenzie, SOE's historian, wrote with reasonable justification that NORIC (Oslo), generally known as the Oslo gang, led by Gunnar Sønsteby 'had some reason to think itself the best team of saboteurs in Europe'.[16] The gang does not seem to have been formed as the result of any conscious decision either in London or in Oslo, but its members just gradually coalesced around Sønsteby. Indeed, Wilson took issue with a post-war account of its development, which rather misrepresented the manner in which it had been recognised by SOE. He commented, 'No! Sønsteby received a personal message from Colonel Wilson shortly after his report of the formation of the detachment was received, giving full approval to his action and plans.' Later, these were developed further when Sønsteby was given a very detailed directive in December 1944, after he and Hauge had visited Britain at the same time.[17] SOE's Norwegian section history described Sønsteby as the most intelligent, most efficient and most productive agent in Norway, noting that 'he looked a most ordinary man until he smiled'.[18]

Following an earlier visit to Britain, Sønsteby parachuted back into Norway in November 1943 with Knut Haugland, a member of the Swallow party which had supported GUNNERSIDE. It was originally intended that he would continue to assist with courier routes to Sweden and provide general assistance, but he gradually formed a group comprising some of the most outstanding members of the Linge Company, including Max Manus, Gregers Gram, Edvard Tallaksen and Birger Rasmussen. Tallaksen and Rasmussen had recently carried out the very successful attack on the smelter at Eydehavn near Arendal, which produced large quantities of silicon carbide for the manufacture of abrasives in Germany. SOE informed Churchill that this was expected to interrupt production for six months.[19]

From the spring of 1944 onwards, Sønsteby was responsible for a remarkable range of successful sabotage attacks. One of the first was an operation to disrupt Quisling's plans for labour mobilisation, intended to provide Norwegian troops for the German eastern front in Russia. Quisling's earlier and more limited attempt in February 1943 had been obstructed by a mixture of passive resistance and sabotage of labour offices, which included support from the communist resistance. His second attempt was more ambitious and aimed to recruit 75,000 Norwegians by announcing a labour draft whereby those selected would then be enrolled into the military. Resistance operations were directed against labour offices and their record-keeping facilities, including IBM punched-card systems. On the day before young Norwegians were scheduled to register for the draft, Sønsteby was contacted by Jens Chr. Hauge and asked to blow up a labour office in Akers Gate just three hours later. The reason for the short notice was that Hauge could find no else to do the job. It needed to be done in daylight so as to provide time for word to spread of the outcome before the draftees turned up the following morning. Sønsteby rustled up Gram and Manus to support him, carried out a very limited reconnaissance and obtained an office key from a contact in the Labour Ministry. His basic plan worked perfectly, and the office was destroyed.

The success of this and similar sabotage operations crippled the attempts at wide-scale mobilisation and very few young Norwegians were drafted. Many more chose to avoid being picked up by the police by taking refuge in isolated areas in the forests or mountains. This created logistics problems for Milorg, who had to find means of feeding them all. Their difficulty was exacerbated by the decision of the Quisling government to cancel the ration cards of those who did not answer the summons for the draft. This would have made it practically impossible for Milorg to feed all of those who were in hiding. So Sønsteby was asked to steal a large consignment of ration cards which was being delivered from a printing plant. He achieved this discreetly and effectively by hijacking the lorry. Milorg were then able to hold the Minister of Supply to ransom. They informed him that the cards would be returned if he rescinded his instruction that no ration cards would be issued to those who had avoided the draft. This was done, though the Quisling government later put out a press release saying that the cards had been stolen by criminals, and announced a temporary ban on alcohol and tobacco rations. Their intention was to turn the population against the resistance and damage morale, but they were outwitted when the clandestine press quickly published the real story and no reputational harm was done. Sønsteby did however admit that another of his operations had an unwelcome consequence. He tried to blow up the headquarters of the official responsible for the draft. The attack was only partially successful – but largely destroyed the stock of the business next door, which was one of a limited number of Norwegian outlets licensed to sell wines and spirits. That would have had a much more serious effect on morale...

One of the key wartime products for both British and German industries was ball bearings, manufactured in Sweden and elsewhere in Scandinavia by SKF, a Swedish company. A major British success had been Operation RUBBLE, when in January 1941 George Binney succeeded in smuggling nearly 20,000 tons of ball bearings out of Sweden on five Norwegian merchant ships. To give some idea of the value of this consignment, the Ministry of Aircraft Production calculated in March 1943 that 100 tons of ball bearings would be sufficient to build about 75 per cent of the airframe work on about 1,200 Lancasters and about 60 per cent of the airframe work on about 1,600 Mosquitoes.[20] The success of RUBBLE could not be repeated because of German naval interference, but Britain continued to import smaller quantities of ball bearings from Sweden using both aircraft and MTBs, which could carry up to fifty tons each. The Germans also procured ball bearings from Sweden and Norway, but in 1944 Allied diplomatic pressure gradually reduced the amount they were able to obtain from Sweden.[21] SOE then turned its attention to Norway, and in November and December 1944, the Oslo gang carried out successful operations against three SKF subsidiaries in Oslo, Drammen and Larvik, rendering all three factories unusable.[22]

From the range of what SOE calculated to be twenty-two major operations carried out by Sønsteby and the Oslo gang in the last few months of 1944, three in particular are worth highlighting. In August, they attacked and destroyed an aircraft repair shop at Korsvoll in Oslo which contained more than twenty Messerschmitt airframes, 150 aeroplane engines and a wealth of auxiliary equipment such as grinding machinery and tools. This was not straightforward, because their two previously unsuccessful attempts had caused the Germans to reinforce the guards on the building. In September, they completed the work of Peter Deinboll at Orkla, by destroying the last of the special locomotives which were used to transport pyrites from the mine down to the quay. This locomotive, damaged in a previous attack, had been brought to Oslo for repairs which were just completed. Finally, and perhaps most difficult of all because it was so heavily guarded, only two days later they attacked the weapons factory at Kongsberg, south-west of Oslo. The factory manufactured Bofors anti-aircraft guns and also repaired large field guns. With the help of local Milorg members, one of whom had cleverly smuggled over fifty kilograms of explosive inside the plant, they breached the defences and destroyed one large field gun, four Bofors guns and the two lathes which were necessary for their manufacture – and badly damaged the structure of the building as well.[23]

All of these sabotage operations were carried out without incident or German retaliation, though employees were occasionally brutally interrogated in attempts to obtain information about those responsible. However, two members of NORIC lost their lives in a separate incident. In November 1944, Edvard Tallaksen and Gregers Gram were lured to a meeting where they expected to meet two disaffected German soldiers whom they hoped might help them to subvert German troops.* It was a trap. In an exchange of shots when the Gestapo tried to arrest them, Gram was killed and Tallaksen injured. He committed suicide in prison.

This was a bad time for SOE. In the same month Peter Deinboll, who had been responsible for several attacks on the Orkla pyrite works, was killed when the aircraft bringing him back to Norway disappeared and was presumed to have crashed near Oslo. Others who had supported the work of the Oslo gang were also arrested by the Germans. There were even larger setbacks in southern Norway for SOE – and SIS as well. The Sandpiper station and Tomtit wireless operator were arrested in November 1944 and, following a series of raids, Milorg lost some 400 members through arrests in Arendal, Mandal and, to a lesser extent, in Kristiansand.[24] At the same time, the Germans arrested people working for the SIS stations Otto and Makir in the same area[25] and SOE's Osprey was forced to go into hiding.[26] The situation deteriorated to such an extent that Sønsteby confided to Max Manus that unless there was an invasion or the war ended by Christmas, the

---

* It was later established that the two Germans were actually deserters who had carried out some small acts of sabotage but were then given away by another German whom they met. They were forced to keep the meeting with Gram and Tallaksen so as to identify them, but were shot the following day. (TNA, HS 2/193.)

resistance might as well give up its work.[27] However, German successes did not continue at the same rate and things quickly improved. Milorg made an excellent recovery in the south and six months later their armed strength was 1,000 armed and trained men with arms available for another 300.[28]

The well-camouflaged site of the SIS station Makir, operated by Oluf Reed Olsen. © NHM

Manus, Gram and BUNDLE

Manus and Gram continued their shipping sabotage activities, code-named BUNDLE, in 1944 with both success and frustration. In February Gram attacked a newly launched patrol vessel in Oslo harbour with limpet mines. It sank in shallow water and was unserviceable for several months. In June, as they had noticed that security was less tight when no ships were in harbour, the two spent several days in hiding under a quay in the harbour. Then they planted seven limpet mines on the 13,000-ton troop ship *Monte Rosa*, shortly before she sailed. They did not explode, most likely because the anti-removal fuses did not work and the limpets were probably washed off, so the ship survived. The early versions of these mines were quite frequently ineffective, a source of considerable frustration to those who had run great risks to attach them.

Chapter 7 outlined how Gram and Manus, in particular, had an unconventional attitude to military discipline. The consequence of this was that they sometimes had a rather uneasy relationship with Wilson, who did not always appreciate their blunt – though quite understand- able – complaints about the ineffectiveness of armaments such as lim- pets, or imaginative suggestions such as that SOE should develop small torpedoes which could more readily and safely be deployed against German shipping in harbour. Of one specific complaint, Wilson wrote to Tronstad in August 1943, 'I am aware that the general tenor of their letter probably arises out of a somewhat misguided sense of humour. On the other hand, they must be made to realise that they are sol- diers in the Royal Norwegian Army, and not freelance journalists.'[29] On another occasion, when SOE in Stockholm intervened on behalf of Manus concerning a more personal matter, Wilson did not hold back. 'You are in no position to judge in a matter of this kind... I wish you clearly to understand that as CO of the Norwegian section such matters are decided by me personally. I do not make hasty decisions and I expect my orders to be accepted and carried out.'[30]

Far from being downcast by negative reactions from London, and with help from several colleagues, Manus was inspired to devote considerable time and energy into developing a home-made torpe- do himself. The welding was done in a building in Oslo, where the Germans had requisitioned the whole house except the room where they were working. This made moving the torpedo around a dangerous business – they were twice stopped and checked at a road block when carrying one, an experience which Manus later described as 'unpleas- ant'. A series of prototypes were developed and transported more than sixty times in all, and at some risk, to fjords for testing or use against German ships. There were many setbacks and disappointments, when the torpedo did not run straight or changes in the expected salinity of the water affected its buoyancy. Eventually, in August 1944, Manus and Roy Nielsen (another member of the Oslo gang) launched a torpedo from a range of sixty yards against a German destroyer in Moss Sound. It exploded on the stern and caused sufficient damage to put it out of service for seven months – a remarkable achievement.[31]

Donau in the Oslofjord before it was sunk. © NHM

Manus had been in Stockholm when Gram was killed. He returned bent on revenge and determined to sink a large German ship, choosing the *Donau*, a 9,000-ton troopship, which had long been a target for him and Gram. He pursued this objective despite being under considerable nervous strain, as correspondence with SOE made clear. Security was extremely tight, and German guards were shooting indiscriminately at any objects floating in the fjord. In January 1945, Manus and Nielsen bluffed their way into the harbour and launched an attack from under the quay where *Donau* lay alongside, planting nine limpet mines. For good measure they attached their remaining mine to the stern of the 2,000-ton *Rolandseck*, also carrying troops. *Donau*, which was carrying 1,500 soldiers, including five companies of Alpine troops with full equipment as well as horses and other material, sank in the Oslofjord and many soldiers and horses drowned. *Rolandseck* was put out of action for months.

Donau, sunk with limpet mines in the Oslofjord by Max Manus
and Roy Nielsen in January 1945. © NHM

Wilson wrote a heartfelt and understanding letter of congratulation to Manus:

> I have realised very fully what you must have felt when you heard of Gregers' loss. For this reason I can appreciate to the full that the action in which you were lately engaged ranked very high in your mind and in your heart, as a proper revenge for your comrade. Apart from this, the blow you have struck is one of the biggest that has been carried out by a single man anywhere, and you may take a very legitimate pride in the fact that BUNDLE has definitely done its job.[32]

Manus was awarded a DSO.

Railways

The reluctance of the Supreme Headquarters Allied Expeditionary Force (SHAEF) to permit railway sabotage in the summer and autumn of 1944, though poor for morale, did not hold up the active training programme for NORIC members based near Aviemore. The only glitch was caused by a newly appointed stationmaster at Aviemore who forbade the use of his line for any future exercises. On being informed of this tiresome inconvenience, Wilson instructed the commanding officer to go and see the general manager of Scottish Railways, an old friend of his, and request that the facility be restored forthwith. This duly happened.[33] It was not the only time that Wilson, who was born in Jedburgh in the Scottish Borders, used his Scottish connections to SOE's advantage. And it may not be a coincidence that the name of his birthplace, Jedburgh, was used as the codename for SOE and OSS operations to drop small groups into parts of occupied Europe, mainly France, to carry out sabotage and guerrilla warfare operations against the Germans.

At the end of October, and in the face of continued pressure, SHAEF relented and agreed to a limited number of sabotage attacks being carried out against the main Norwegian railway routes. It recommended that these attacks should concentrate on the lines from Oslo to Bergen and Trondheim. In the face of some sustained German resistance as the Allied offensive approached Germany, they changed their mind in early December and requested a sustained operation against German road and rail transport throughout Norway. The subsequent campaign lasted until April 1945, and included more than forty major attacks, as well as plenty more sabotage on a smaller scale. There were some spectacular successes. On 13 January 1945, Woodlark destroyed the Jørstad bridge, leading to the destruction of a German troop train, the death of some seventy soldiers and the closure of the line for a fortnight. Grebe blew up three bridges, with similar results, while Fieldfare destroyed a bridge over the Rauma river which disrupted traffic for three weeks. Since the Special Air Service (SAS) had very few trained skiers, Wilson also decided to send in a platoon of trained Norwegian Army paratroopers to launch an attack north of Trondheim (Waxwing). This they did successfully. In March, Milorg went one better, coordinating an attack in southern Norway which involved over a thousand men, destroyed ten important bridges, countless sections of railway line as well as switching equipment, and prevented any traffic for more than four weeks.[34] SHAEF were very appreciative of the effectiveness and the significance of these actions, as their assessment in Chapter 13 will highlight.

A successful railway sabotage operation to slow down the rate of German troop withdrawals from Norway in March 1945. © NHM

There were plenty more significant sabotage actions carried out by the Oslo gang. For example, Sønsteby was also responsible for the destruction of the German railway authorities headquarters in Oslo. He consulted the architect of the building so as to establish the size of the charge required, and used sixty pounds of dynamite to destroy the building and bury all its records. He told Wilson later that he had not consulted Hauge beforehand 'because he would have thought it to be an impossible idea'.[35]

OSS and the American contribution

The spring of 1943 saw the beginning of the integration of OSS with SOE in the European theatre. Their influence, combined with the friendly disposition of other influential American commanders, was pivotal in arranging the loan of the three submarine chasers used by SOE in the Shetlands. Mackenzie observed, 'it can be said without irony that this was practically all that the USA contributed to subversive war in Norway'.[36] This may seem a somewhat harsh judgement, but it reflects the fact that by the beginning of 1943 SOE and SIS had reasonably well-established organisational structures in Norway, and two years of experience of clandestine operations there. Both they, and General Hansteen, were apprehensive about the possible consequences of introducing another untested service into Norway. At a meeting in January 1943, Hansteen told Lieutenant Colonel Ellery Huntington of OSS that the Norwegians were already working closely with both SOE and Combined Operations, and there were also the very delicate activities of SIS agents to be considered. He suggested that it might be better if OSS devoted their efforts to the northern part of Norway. Following representations from the Admiralty, who were concerned to protect the position of SIS, the Chiefs of Staff went further. They considered that Norway was already sufficiently well covered by existing organisations. They were unwilling to agree to yet another service operating there independently, so specified that OSS assistance would be welcome, but only as long as their activities were conducted through

SOE and subject to the agreement of the Norwegian High Command. Gubbins informed Colonel David Bruce of OSS accordingly, and the Americans accepted this condition.[37] They arranged for the training of 120 American officers and men with Norwegian backgrounds in three Norwegian-American operational groups, whom they planned to bring over to Scotland for training in the Highlands. They also established Westfield, an office in Stockholm tasked to develop operations in Norway as well as elsewhere in the region. A memorandum of understanding to that effect was signed with Wilson on 23 October 1943.

In the event, and despite their initial enthusiasm, it proved impossible to work out any substantial operational tasks for OSS in Norway, and so their active involvement was limited. There was one American deployment to Trøndelag in March/April 1945, involving a detachment of the Norwegian Special Operations Group (NORSO), commanded by Major William Colby, who later became director of the Central Intelligence Agency (CIA), on Operation RYPE (Norwegian for grouse). They were tasked to parachute in and destroy a section of the railway line running through this area, so as to slow down German troop movements. Their arrival was delayed by poor weather. They also sustained serious losses when a B24 aircraft crashed into a mountain and another dropped its agents on the wrong side of the Swedish border. Colby eventually succeeded in blowing up a bridge near Tangen, and then another section of the line near Snåsa.[38] A separate American attempt to become involved in intelligence work also came to nothing. This was Kitten, the plan for an OSS Mission to deploy to Norway in close collaboration with the intelligence service FO.II to obtain information which would be useful in the Allied occupation of Germany and – again with FO.II – to conduct counter-espionage activities against the German intelligence services.[39] Their attempts were initially frustrated by what the SOE Norwegian section history candidly described as natural prejudices, and the Westfield office in Stockholm did not work as effectively as it might have done because of what one of their own officers considered to be misconceptions regarding its original purpose, poor leadership by the officer in charge and an indifferent attitude on the part of their London headquarters.[40]

Despite their operational disappointments, the Americans none-theless proved to be valuable Allies in other respects. They participated actively in planning, and a succession of effective officers, particularly the widely respected Georg Unger Vetlesen, were participants on the ANCC. They also provided prodigious quantities of weapons and equipment to supplement the limited allocations which had previously been available because of the demands of the armies in France. Equally important, from late 1944 onwards, they were able to provide sufficient aircraft to make a substantial difference to supply bottlenecks.

Wireless stations

The statistics describing the growth of SOE wireless stations in Norway reflect an impressive story of a fairly steady increase, though the num-bers fluctuated from time to time following German disruptions. SOE calculated that there were just two sets in use in early 1941, sixteen in 1943, and that in the spring of 1944 work was going on in over twenty districts, with one or more wireless sets operating to the UK from each of them. Among the stations then working, three were in the Oslo neighbourhood and carried Milorg traffic. German interception and direction finding would no doubt have given some indication of the extent of this traffic. This makes it difficult to understand how a German report was submitted to the High Command in January 1945 stating categorically that Milorg was no longer in communication with London! SOE does not appear subsequently to have been able to find out why this happened.[41]

Although some wireless operators were able to live clandestinely in towns, most of them endured a hard life in remote locations in huts in the forest or the mountains, and were regularly short of food when air supplies all too frequently failed to arrive. SOE calculated that during the occupation 110 wireless operators worked in the field, of whom sixty were trained in the UK, forty-three were trained in Norway, and seven in Sweden. Twenty of them were captured, of whom nine were killed, one escaped, three were released on liberation while the remainder, with the exception of Johnny Pevik who was killed in jail, were later freed from prison camps.[42]

Chapter 1 described how the SIS station Cygnus sent King Haakon a Christmas tree in 1943. An SOE wireless station near Moss did something similar, sending a Christmas message to Churchill in December 1944:

> To his Excellency Mr Churchill
> We congratulate you and wish we had your strength to sweat, weep and bleed. We will try to do our best. Axel

This was forwarded to Desmond Morton, Churchill's personal assistant who liaised with the intelligence agencies. There is, disappointingly, no record of any reply.[43]

CHAPTER 13

'LUKKET PÅ GRUNN AV GLEDE'
'CLOSED BECAUSE OF JOY'
– THE FINAL STEPS TO FREEDOM

SIGN IN AN OSLO BOOKSHOP WHICH CLOSED
TO MARK THE LIBERATION OF NORWAY.

Attempts to alleviate the situation in northern Norway

The situation in northern Norway became more desperate in early 1945, with growing devastation as a result of the continuing German scorched-earth policy. Trygve Lie explored further means of achieving Allied intervention. First, he sought public British support and sympathy. He requested that British ministers mention Norway in speeches and commend her contribution. Eden asked his Cabinet colleagues to help, and several did.[1] Eden himself also obliged a few days later in a speech in Parliament on 16 January when, referring to Norway and Holland (where starvation was also prevalent), he said,

> they are two countries that set perhaps some of our allies something of
> an example in political unity, two countries which have contributed to
> the fullest extent in their power to the Allied effort, and I think that the
> House would wish that at this time of their greatest travail, a message
> from us should go to the people to tell them that everything that is in our
> power to alleviate their suffering will be done and that we shall not forget,
> either now or in future years, the glorious part that they have played.[2]

Public statements alone were of course insufficient to cause any change in policy. The Norwegian government continued to search for ways to stimulate the Allies into changing their attitude and invading northern Norway. This was partly, as Lie candidly admitted to Collier, because he wanted to provide the Norwegian government with an alibi for use with Norwegian public opinion after the war. He asked Collier for assistance in arranging a conference with the director and deputy director of Military Intelligence (Generals Sinclair and Peake respectively) to discuss the possibility of military action. Victor Cavendish-Bentinck, the chairman of the Joint Intelligence Committee, pointed out that Sinclair and Peake were not competent to discuss military possibilities in such circumstances. He recommended that the Norwegians should be advised to approach SHAEF instead, as this responsibility fell within their competence. The Foreign Office Northern Department countered that to do so would suggest to Norwegians that they were not being taken seriously. It proposed that Eden should meet Lie, ask him to submit his proposal to SHAEF, but also request a copy of the details, so that the Foreign Office could study the political aspects while SHAEF looked at the military considerations. Eden did so on 13 January.

Lie provided a very detailed plan prepared by the Norwegian High Command. Its purpose was mainly to provide humanitarian assistance in Finnmark. It would include large elements of the Norwegian brigade in Scotland, as well as part of one of the Norwegian squadrons serving in the RAF.[3] Eden observed, 'we can hardly refuse to allow the Norwegians to use their own forces on behalf of their own folk'. General Thorne of Scottish Command, who was to become Commander in Chief of British Land Forces in Norway, passed the plan to SHAEF, and Crown Prince Olav took a copy to Washington to discuss with the Americans – though the American Chief of Staff General Marshall made clear that he considered this to be a British, rather than an American, problem.[4] However, as with previous attempts to encourage a landing in Norway, the Norwegian plan foundered on the attitude of the Chiefs of Staff. They put forward a range of objections, noting that it would entail diversion of naval and air units required to counteract the U-boat offensive, that SHAEF would be unable to provide a maintenance commitment and that the allocation of shipping would place an extra burden on Allied resources when naval resources were already in short supply. Finally, they pointed out that it remained the case that the Allies simply had insufficient forces to be able to support the Norwegians in such a move. The Chiefs of Staff calculated that even in the event of a German collapse, it would take weeks before they would be able to divert adequate forces to Norway to assist with the process of disarmament.[5] It would be necessary to rely heavily on Milorg. At the end of January, when the Chiefs of Staff consulted SHAEF about briefing the Norwegians on this problem, Eisenhower decided that they should only be given a limited explanation about the nature of the Allied difficulty. The Chiefs of Staff asked the Foreign Office to discourage the Norwegians from pursuing their idea.[6]

Large quantities of medical, fuel and building supplies, as well as foodstuffs, were delivered to northern Norway during this period. The Ministry of War Production calculated in February that 5,183 tons of relief supplies had already been delivered, but this was only a small part of what was needed.[7] Not surprisingly, the British failure to do more to provide assistance to northern Norway, however understandable in the face of the resource issues which they could not adequately resolve, cast something of a shadow over Anglo-Norwegian relations during this late stage of the war.

As the Allies advanced into Germany in the spring of 1945, there remained much uncertainty about what might happen in Norway. In particular, there were concerns right up until the last days of the war about *Festung Norwegen* – the possibility that the eleven German divisions remaining in Norway might continue to fight even after the army in Germany had been defeated. On 3 May at a meeting in Flensburg, Böhme and Lindemann (German commanders in chief in Norway and Denmark respectively) and Terboven (*Reichskommissar* in Norway) all spoke for continuing the war. This might have been intended as a bargaining counter for use by Dönitz in negotiations with the Allies. Hauge, who had his own contacts with German headquarters, had reported to London a fortnight earlier that both Böhme and the naval commander Admiral Ciliax had told Terboven that they could not guarantee the loyalty of their troops.[8] Nor was it known how far Sweden would be willing to become involved in supporting Allied operations in Norway or even in temporarily giving up its long-standing neutrality and entering the war. Military staff talks with the Swedes did eventually take place, but they did not get very far. Britain remained unable to offer the Norwegian government any reassurance about the support which would be available if Germany did decide to fight on in Norway. At a meeting on 5 April, Churchill told Nygaardsvold that he could not promise any diversion of Allied resources if that happened, and could only undertake that the Allies would continue the war until Norway was liberated.

SOE operations

Wilson chaired a meeting at Special Forces headquarters (SF HQ) on 9 January to assess the current state of the Norwegian resistance. He emphasised the importance of maintaining their morale and the danger to any secret organisation of a prolonged period of inactivity. He pointed out that there were thought to be as many able-bodied male Germans in Norway as there were able-bodied male Norwegians – approximately 250,000. This meant that the balance of armed strength remained very much in the German favour.[9] In fact, as Wilson acknowledged after the war, estimates varied and he considered that SHAEF's calculations of enemy forces in Norway had been too low. It transpired that the total number of Germans in Norway, including military, security and police forces and a small number of civilians, was actually over 365,000. Wilson also referred to the dangerous situation in the north, particularly around the Kirkenes area. Without referring to the political complications, he simply said that the government was thinking of transferring the Norwegian brigade there to protect Norwegian interests and show that something was being done, but plans were held up because of the strength of German naval forces in the area.[10]

Although many members of the resistance had to bide their time, waiting for the order to move into action, their morale would have been lifted by the continuing series of effective sabotage operations. Attacks continued against shipping, as well as loading cranes, railway lines and bridges, fuel supplies and factories linked to the production of war materials, as well as equipment, clothing and other supplies. One of the most imaginative was the sabotaging of more than twenty shells of 88mm anti-aircraft ammunition at a store at Gvepsborg (near Rjukan) in February 1945, which was carried out by members of the Sunshine counter-sabotage group. The shells were unobtrusively doctored so that they would explode immediately when fired. Sunshine reported that they had been evenly distributed among 200 tons of ammunition transported to Oslo and Horten. Wilson sent Sunshine a message of congratulations a few days later, informing them that the German anti-aircraft guns at Horten had been put out of action during an RAF raid there on 23 February, and he assumed that their work was responsible for this achievement.[11] It was shortly after this, on 11 March, that Leif Tronstad and Gunnar Syverstad were killed when they were interrogating a quisling official. Tronstad was replaced in command by Jens-Anton Poulsson, the leader of the Grouse/Swallow party which supported FRESHMAN/GUNNERSIDE, who had been in charge of Moonlight (one of the subordinate Sunshine teams tasked to protect Norwegian strategic installations against German destruction).

A further preparatory measure, the Scale/Minim operation, was implemented in December 1944 with the posting of Henning Nyberg from the SOE Norwegian section to Stockholm. His role was to assist with the training of Norwegian police troops, who could be deployed into Norway as soon as the Germans capitulated, in an operation known as BEEFEATER. This did not work as Wilson had hoped, because Nyberg was not permitted access to any of the BEEFEATER units – apparently because it was being treated as a bilateral matter with the Swedes. Nyberg also judged that it was a sign that the Norwegians wanted to be able to 'run their own show', perhaps not surprisingly by this stage of the war.[12]

The Anglo-Norwegian Collaboration Committee (ANCC) did not meet for nearly four months between December 1944 and April 1945 because several of the Norwegian members were abroad. Øen planned to be absent for three weeks, but was away for three months. By this time it may not have been thought to matter too much, because there were few difficult issues to resolve and operational reports were still being circulated. However, Wilson noted that it caused unfortunate results, because Øen held the balance between the military and Milorg elements of FO.IV, which coordinated their activity. Things did not run quite so smoothly in his absence.[13] Øen was able to complete some complicated and protracted negotiations with the Swedes over the establishment of bases on Swedish territory and the transport of operational stores. Furthermore, to the considerable surprise (perhaps even consternation) of Wilson and the SOE hierarchy, he visited Norway, meeting the Milorg leadership and a range of district leaders. Escorted by Sønsteby, he inspected a fully armed and equipped resistance unit at Odal, north-east of Oslo in one of the larger Milorg areas, and then went to Kongsberg, where he met Tronstad and other members of the Sunshine party.[*14]

---

* Sønsteby commented after the war that this visit 'seemed almost foolhardy to me, but that wasn't my affair'. He also noted that he had long been in touch with Øen's family in Oslo, who had greatly helped him by harbouring radio operators and other 'dangerous' visitors. (Sønsteby, *Report from No. 24*, p. 170.)

Bjarne Øen, the head of FO.IV, the Norwegian counterpart of SOE. © NHM

Sønsteby's last coup

On 2 May 1945, Sønsteby carried out one of his most important operations – and one of the most brazen. He organised a group of eleven
members of the Oslo gang to bluff their way into the Ministry of
Justice and the police headquarters and to remove more than two and
a half tons of documents from them, including some from the office of
the Justice Minister Sverre Riisnæs, which he was shown by a cooper-
ative secretary. Many of them were in a safe weighing more than half a
ton on the second floor. Remarkably, the group were able to manhan-
dle it downstairs. Their raid was just in time, because some documents
had already been burned. The material which they rescued was to
prove of considerable value in the trials of Quisling and NS collaborators held after the war. Wilson described it as 'a haul of the utmost
importance'.[15] After the liberation, Sønsteby was awarded a richly
deserved DSO.

SIS activities

By January 1945, SIS had forty-two stations in Norway, of which half were sending in what it assessed as being good or valuable intelligence, mainly on convoy and shipping movements. Of the other half, some were in the process of establishing themselves, some were closing down because of security or other concerns, some had not been able to make contact and two were under German control. It is worth looking at a representative sample of their activities. Delfin, manned by Torstein Raaby, was operating from Vadsø, near Kirkenes. At that time SOE had no communications equipment available, so Delfin was relaying back to London all messages from the Norwegian military mission liaising with the Russians in northern Norway. This service was stopped on 18 January, following the Russian refusal to permit the transmission of encyphered traffic to London.[16] In addition to sending in regular and valuable reports on the military situation in the Tromsø area, Gudrun was relaying instructions from the Norwegian High Command to the local population for action in the event of compulsory evacuation. Because of security concerns, the agent manning Libra, together with his family and seventeen others including an SIS Synnøve agent, was evacuated by a naval whaler from Kvitnes, in the Lofoten islands. Frey, south of Ålesund, continued to be one of SIS's 'most regular and valuable convoy reporting stations'. An attempt to establish Ulva snear Bergen had not succeeded because of the discovery by the Germans of an SOE arms dump near the site of the intended station. The agent, Erling Lunde, was arrested in the widespread search which followed. SIS admitted that his brother was an SOE agent, an indication that some security lessons still remained to be learned. Njord, in Hurum on the Oslofjord, manned by the redoubtable Hans Clifton (an outstanding SIS agent of long standing), sent in its 600th message: 'He continues to send in first class shipping intelligence.' Lyra (in Finnmark) and Reva (near Bergen) were two German-controlled stations which continued to be active. SIS observed that despite the sinking of *Tirpitz* on 12 November, Lyra had sent in a message more than a month later accusing SIS of leaving him in the lurch. They judged that the Germans were still trying to obtain details of the organisation in Tromsø – though they did not persist for very much longer.[17]

During the last few months of the war the Germans remained very active – and effective. Gubbins told the Foreign Office that they were still working hard to suppress Norwegian activities, and had put out a notice saying that they would shoot any Norwegian serviceman who landed with or without uniform.[18] They were very successful against SIS during this period, capturing a series of stations, including Leporis III and Mani in Trondheim, Sabor in Stavanger, Turid in Ålesund, Roska in Florø and Corona, Thor II and Olga in Oslo. Most of the operators survived, though members of Roska, Corona and Sabor were shot when resisting arrest. Other stations were forced to close and evacuate, either because some of their agents were arrested, or because of other security alerts in the area. These included Frey, Glaur and Njord. Following the capture of Olga, Clifton was told to leave Njord and take refuge in Sweden. However, making light of the risks, he returned a few weeks later and established another station, Lillemor, in the same area.[19]

Liberation

After Hitler committed suicide on 30 April 1945, the end of the war came quickly. Hitler was replaced by Dönitz, who authorised General Jodl to sign an unconditional surrender on 7 May, which would come into force on 8 May. General Thorne established radio contact with General Böhme and sent Brigadier Hilton to negotiate the German surrender at a meeting later the same day at his headquarters in Lillehammer, north of Oslo. Böhme accepted the following morning, 9 May. He may have been taken by surprise by the speed of the unconditional surrender, and would certainly not have been aware of the very limited forces which the Allies could have made available to enforce the surrender terms if he had chosen to fight on.

SOE had also been taken somewhat unawares by the speed of developments, and SF HQ was slow to send out definite and immediate orders to Norway. Milorg themselves reacted quickly to the statement made by Churchill on 6 May about the imminent cessation of hostilities, and took that as the signal to start to come out of hiding and take their positions to prevent any last-minute German attempts at demolition or sabotage. They made contact on 7 May with the German headquarters in Lillehammer, north of Oslo, to discuss their intentions. The Wehrmacht eventually accepted that Milorg could make a valuable contribution to maintaining law and order. There were nonetheless a series of tense meetings across Norway as similar discussions took place elsewhere – usually between a Milorg commander in some sort of makeshift uniform with a small group of bodyguards and a senior German officer backed by a large staff. Fortunately, discipline prevailed and there were no significant incidents. Terboven committed suicide. Norwegian police battalions and some of the Sepal groups moved into Norway at the same time, supplemented a few days later by airborne troops and further special forces detachments. The German surrender, and the subsequent disarmament and repatriation of German troops, was more peaceful than even the most optimistic forecasts.

Crown Prince Olav returned to Oslo on 13 May with some members of the Norwegian government. King Haakon returned, amid enthusiastic scenes of joyful celebration, on 7 June, five years to the day since he had left Tromsø. Some of the NORIC detachment acted as his bodyguard as he returned to the palace. On 9 June, 15,000 members of Milorg, and others who had assisted the resistance, paraded in front of the King and his family together with Jens Chr. Hauge and Colonel Øen. On 28 June, 205 members of the Linge Company and sixty crew members of the special naval unit which had manned the sub-chasers paraded in front of King Haakon. The following day they had a final inspection in front of Colonel Wilson, marking the formal end of their collaboration with the British, and were dismissed. Members of Milorg were finally stood down on 15 July.

The Linge Company on one of their final parades in Oslo
before being stood down in July 1945. © NHM

The aftermath

In the months after liberation, SOE spent much time trying to find
out what had happened to those of its agents who had been captured
or killed by the Germans. A total of 530 men had been recruited into
the Linge Company, of whom 245 were on active service on 8 May 1945.
Fifty-one had been killed by the Germans, and six had died on training or while in Britain. There were eight men initially unaccounted for,
of whom seven were later released from prison. It was not initially possible to establish the fate of the eighth, Johnny Pevik, a long-serving
member of the Linge Company, who had carried out numerous courier trips to Trondheim. He went back to Norway on Wagtail, whose
mission was to kill the notorious collaborator Henry Rinnan. Pevik
was captured in November 1943, badly tortured (by Rinnan, among
others) and hanged without trial in Trondheim in November 1944.[*20]
A notable survivor was Jan Herman Linge, the son of Martin Linge,
who was dropped in January 1945 with the task of killing a collaborator

---

[*] The Gestapo officer Gerhard Flesch, who ordered the hanging of Pevik, was himself executed
by the Norwegians in Trondheim in 1948. Pevik's brother Arthur was also a member of the
Linge Company and took part in several operations, including Sønsteby's removal of eviden-
tial material from the police and Ministry of Justice described above. He was among those
who eventually helped to establish the fate of his brother.

near Eidsvold. He was captured and subjected to a lengthy interrogation, during which the Germans asked him about Joe Adamson, suggesting that they may still have had suspicions about both of them. However, his story was believed, and he was sent to a POW camp in Germany. He escaped in late March, was rescued shortly afterwards by American troops and returned to Britain in time to join the last Linge Company detachment returning to Norway on 14 May.[21]

After the final parade and disbanding of the Linge Company, Wilson travelled around the country visiting the sites where some of the major operations had taken place and meeting both former resistance members as well as those who had supported its work. The diary of his trip contains some noteworthy details and personal insights. For example, he visited the Hardanger plateau where the FRESHMAN gliders were to have landed and saw the hill where the Eureka transponder had been placed. 'It was still functioning four months previously, and should be a museum piece.' Sønsteby took him on a tour to see the aftermath of some of his sabotage in the Oslo district, where in all thirty-five actions were undertaken. He was struck by the extent of NORIC's careful reconnaissances and simplicity of action. Haugland took him to the Rikshospital and the scene of his escape, pointing out bullet marks in the walls. His escape had been almost miraculous. One of the Gestapo fired six shots at him from a range of five yards, but had missed every time as his arm was shaking with fright. He also visited Måløy, where Martin Linge had been killed in 1941. Finally, when he was in Trondheim, he visited the cathedral and was told that one of the rooms in the tower had housed a wireless set and even an illegal printing press![22]

Within days of the liberation Eric Welsh and other officers from SIS and FO.II were back in Norway to check up on the welfare of their agents. The final SIS progress report of early June noted that they had met and accounted for members of sixteen stations who had been caught by the Germans and who had survived captivity. Only those from Leporis III were, at that stage, unaccounted for. All the remaining stations closed down by the end of May, with the exception of Gudrun, which remained open a little longer to act as a link with northern Norway.[23]

Acknowledgements

Eisenhower, the Supreme Allied Commander, wrote to Gubbins on 31 May to thank him for the valuable contribution made by SOE in developing an effective resistance across occupied Europe. He observed that there had never previously been a war where resistance forces had been so closely harnessed to the military effort. He added:

> I consider that the disruption of enemy rail communications, the harassing of German road moves and the continual and increasing strain placed on the German war economy and internal security services throughout occupied Europe by the organised forces of resistance, played a very considerable part in our complete and final victory. In Denmark and Norway, the commanders concerned have already reported on the great help which they have received from the resistance forces in maintaining law and order during the early stages of the liberation … Finally, I must express my great admiration for the brave and often spectacular exploits of the agents and special groups under control of SF HQ.[24]

In July, SHAEF produced a comprehensive assessment of the impact of SOE operations in Norway. This paid SOE a handsome compliment for their work, noting that until December 1944 it had been SHAEF policy not to interfere with troop movements which might reduce the German garrison there. It added:

> However, in December 1944, the importance of German forces in Scandinavia increased as they became one of the few remaining sources of reinforcement. SOE were therefore directed to hinder the evacuation of German forces from Scandinavia to the greatest extent possible.

Action in Norway was designed to force the enemy to take the sea route from Trondheim, where they could be attacked by allied naval and air forces. The results were striking and resulted in a reduction in the rate of movement from Norway from four divisions to less than one division per month. A number of transport vessels ... were sunk ... The striking reduction in the flow of troops and stores from Norway early in 1945 undoubtedly had an adverse effect on the reinforcement and reforming of units which the enemy had to undertake for the battles east and west of the Rhine.*[25]

This was heartfelt recognition of a significant achievement.

---

*   Chapter 10 explained that there is some doubt about the accuracy of SHAEF's estimate of the reduction which railway sabotage caused to German troop movements – though not about its impact.

CHAPTER 14

RETRIBUTION, RECOGNITION AND COMPENSATION
THE AFTERMATH

What did the resistance achieve in Norway?

S ome historians have been quite dismissive of the effectiveness of SOE in meeting Churchill's picturesque challenge to 'set Europe ablaze', observing that the organisation made little progress in fomenting the sort of revolution which such an instruction might have been expected to produce. Others note, perhaps rather more to the point, that until the eve of D-Day in June 1944, SOE lacked a clear strategy setting out the ultimate purpose of stimulating resistance. Directives to SOE for specific operations could come from Combined Operations Headquarters, Admiralty, Air Ministry or elsewhere. However, much of its tactical direction was provided by the Ministry of Economic Warfare (MEW), whose purpose was to disrupt the German economy by supplementing the usual means of warfare in order to promote the Allied war effort. But our knowledge about the relationship between MEW and SOE, and of the extent to which SOE thereby supplemented Britain's economic war effort, remains frustratingly limited.[1] Historians have yet to examine this important aspect of the war.* We have little information about the intelligence which the MEW received from occupied Europe, and how they

---

* There is an unpublished PhD thesis by Nechama Janet Cohen Cox, *The Ministry of Economic Warfare and Britain's Conduct of Economic Warfare* (King's College London, 2001), but she excludes from her study the work of SOE in sabotage operations.

used it to develop strategy and work out which targets could be most effectively attacked by sabotage rather than by other more traditional means such as bombing. Although SOE's Norwegian section history describes in some detail its relations with the Foreign Office, SIS, Combined Operations and naval authorities as well as other government departments, it does not mention MEW (with whom, of course, it shared a minister) at all in this context. It merely acknowledges that after the end of combined operations on the Norwegian coast, SOE collaborated closely with General Hansteen and the MEW in working out policies to reduce Norwegian industrial production for German benefit, without unduly endangering Norwegian morale, life or property.

It has therefore generally only been possible to consider specific examples where the MEW provided tasking and requested SOE to take action to destroy the means of production or to prevent the export of specific minerals of value to the German war effort. And the MEW was certainly quick off the mark to identify some of its Norwegian targets. Before SOE had even been established and before the German conquest of Norway was completed, the MEW wrote to the Admiralty in May 1940 to identify six plants producing or refining ferro-alloys such as nickel, tungsten and molybdenum. It wanted production to be disrupted and asked whether the Admiralty could arrange this through naval action. SOE took over the tasking and successfully disrupted production at most of the sites. It was unable to attack the molybdenum mine at Knaben, but contributed at least by providing details of intelligence about the deep snow conditions which guided the Mosquito pilots of RAF 139 squadron when attacking it at low level with limited success in March 1943.

It took time for both SOE and SIS to develop productive working relationships with their Norwegian counterparts: both sides had plenty to learn about the art of developing mutual trust and working together. In particular, we should not underestimate the seriousness of the problems caused after the second Lofoten raid, when Anglo-Norwegian relations in the resistance field reached their nadir. But this setback provided the necessary impetus which led to the creation of the Anglo-Norwegian Collaboration Committee. It provided a model for effective cooperation which was never really matched elsewhere. Thereafter, SOE's Norwegian operations ranged from spectacular achievements, of which the sabotage of the heavy water plant at Vemork was the most outstanding, to a profusion of the workmanlike and effective. The most significant element of these, once SHAEF lifted its embargo and permitted operations to take place, was the extensive sabotage of the railway system which greatly slowed down the rate at which German troops were able to be transported out of Norway to provide reinforcements elsewhere. But during the last nine months of the war, other extensive operations mounted partly by SOE but mainly by Milorg, against fuel dumps, arms depots and factories, played an important part in degrading the German capacity to wage war. Eisenhower made a telling comment when he observed that there had never previously been a war where resistance forces had been so closely harnessed to the military effort – and he was, after all, the one best placed to judge.

It is rather easier to evaluate the contribution of SIS and its agents in Norway. Its main task was to provide intelligence on the movements and status of German warships and marine traffic. Operational and actionable intelligence about ships' movements (being time-sensitive) would have been the most valuable, and probably the most difficult, to obtain. After an understandably slow start while it began to establish networks, SIS began to earn approval for the extent and quality of its coverage from both Godfrey and his successor as DNI, Rushbrooke, as well as from senior admirals in the Home Fleet.[2] We cannot judge very precisely the extent to which its reporting assisted in the sinking of merchant traffic, because its contribution was often complemented by Ultra reporting and aerial reconnaissance. Sometimes too, specific reporting could not be acted upon because of poor weather or the lack of availability of naval or air assets to attack suitable targets. But Ole Snefjellå's comment, that Welsh had credited Crux with responsibility for reporting which led to the sinking of twelve ships, provides a fair indication of the sort of success which SIS achieved – even if he suspected that Welsh's estimate was somewhat exaggerated. And while SIS agents might have valued the praise from admirals, had they known about it, they would surely have appreciated more the comment of an officer in the Naval Intelligence Division who had seen daily evidence of the quality of their reporting, and who later wrote:

> One of the most remarkable successes in Naval Intelligence in the last war was the reporting of the *Tirpitz* and other big ships from Altafjord, Trondheim and other ports in Norway. So reliable was this service ... that the OIC [Operational Intelligence Centre] had complete faith in their accuracy and regularity.[3]

SIS also provided a range of reporting on coastal and port defences, as well as airfields. It was much less successful in providing political intelligence, on which the chairman of the JIC, Cavendish-Bentinck, commented quite disparagingly. SIS did not consider this to be a high priority – but the deficiency was anyway to some extent remedied after XU, established in Norway but later supported from Britain by FO.II and with training provided by SIS, began to provide reporting.

Norwegian intelligence organisation XU picture – prisoners
from Grini prison camp doing hard labour. © NHM

There are also other factors to take into consideration – particularly those which helped to support Norwegian morale, and the will of the vast majority of the population to continue to endure their isolation, privations and the continuing threats of German oppression or forced mobilisation, whether they were involved in passive or active resistance. The activities of SOE in this respect, many of which were quite well publicised, certainly played their part in strengthening morale. On the Norwegian side, the roles of King Haakon, and of the BBC, which broadcast not only his speeches but provided regular news (as well as specific messages for the resistance) were of paramount importance. And the Norwegian government, after an uncertain start, managed to strike an effective balance in maintaining the confidence of Milorg in Norway (helping to ensure that it accepted reasonable strategic direction from Allied commanders) and asserting itself with the British sufficiently to be able to exercise a degree of control over the conduct of much of the war in Norway. There were significant exceptions early on, before trust and an adequate degree of coordination were established. Even then there were still occasional problems caused by Allied initiatives such as the bombing of Vemork. Although the Norwegians complained, they usually took these setbacks in their stride and did not allow them to affect relations too much or for too long. Eden's compliment with which this book begins was not hyperbole. It was an acknowledgement of the contribution of a government whose pragmatism and tolerance stood favourable comparison with the other governments in exile.

Retribution

After the war the Norwegian government, which had reintroduced the death penalty, brought to trial the most prominent members of the Quisling government and collaborators on charges of treason. The prosecution sought the death penalty in fewer than 100 cases. The death sentence was handed down in thirty of them, and carried out in twenty-five, which included Quisling, as well as Henry Rinnan and other members of his gang who betrayed resistance members.

Thousands more Norwegians were convicted of lesser crimes and sentenced to terms of imprisonment, though the appetite for such punishments gradually diminished. Twelve Germans, including Gestapo officers Siegfried Fehmer and Gerhard Flesch, were also executed by the Norwegians for war crimes.

The British authorities also launched a series of exhaustive investigations to establish who was responsible for the murder of the British troops involved in FRESHMAN and other commando raids, as well as the Norwegian and British crew of MTB 345 who were captured while on a naval mission off the coast and shot shortly afterwards. All of them were wearing naval uniform. They achieved some results, especially when dealing with those involved in FRESHMAN. Erich Hoffmann and Werner Seeling, who brutally tortured and murdered four badly injured prisoners in Stavanger prison on November 1943, were found guilty. Seeling was shot in Oslo, while Hoffman was hanged in Hamburg. Friedrich Wilkens, the Gestapo chief in Stavanger who might also have been complicit in those murders, was killed by Norwegian SIS agents when he was taking part in the capture of Sabor in April 1945. General Karl von Beeren, and his subordinate Erwin Probst, were charged with killing the fourteen commandos who were shot one by one outside Slettebø camp. Von Beeren was acquitted while Probst, who had commanded the detachment which carried out the killings, died of cancer before he could be brought to trial. Oscar Hans was sentenced to death by a Norwegian court for supervising the shooting of more than three hundred Norwegians, including the prominent trade unionists Viggo Hansteen and Rolf Wickstrøm in September 1941. His sentence was commuted, but he was then tried by a British court for the killing of five commandos from FRESHMAN, as well as Able Seaman Evans, at Trandum in January 1943.* He was once more

---

* British ambassador Sir Laurence Collier commented in June 1947 that the greatest adverse public reaction to a war crimes trial in Norway was that which greeted the minority recommendation of some of the judges that Hans should be acquitted, on the grounds that he was not aware that he was carrying out orders which had no justification in law. This led to the commutation of his sentence. (FO 371/66068.)

sentenced to death, but again the sentence was commuted. Hans Wilhelm Blomberg was found guilty and executed for the killing of the crew of MTB 345. It did not prove possible to identify those responsible for the killings of the commandos involved in MUSKETOON and CHECKMATE, who died in German concentration camps. General von Falkenhorst, who remained in command of German troops in Norway until 1944, was tried by a joint British-Norwegian court on a charge of implementing Hitler's Commando order and insisting that commandos should be handed over to the SD (the Nazi Party's intelligence service, *Sicherheitsdienst*) for execution within twenty-four hours of their capture. He was sentenced to death, but this was later commuted to twenty years' imprisonment.

Recognition

During the war, the most outstanding achievements of SOE and SIS agents were generally recognised soon after the completion of their operations. After the liberation, both SOE and SIS worked hard to ensure that the most deserving of the remainder of their agents received suitable recognition in the form of medals, certificates of commendation or mentions in despatches. Scrutiny was exacting, and many recommendations were turned down. Nonetheless, one very embarrassing mistake occurred. In September 1945, Wilson recommended that Leif Larsen, the most successful skipper of transport from the Shetlands to Norway, should be awarded a DSO to add to the DSC, CGM and DSM and bar which he had already received. This was approved and cleared with the Norwegian government. It was gazetted in November 1946 and details of the citation were also published in Norway. Admiral Horve, the commander in chief of the Norwegian Navy, then informed Collier (by now the British ambassador in Norway) that of the four expeditions with which Larsen was credited in the citation, no fewer than three had been carried out by another officer, Ingvald Eidsheim, who was only going to receive a mention in despatches. This was accurately described as 'an unholy mess'. Collier and Wilson, together with other former senior members of SOE, agreed that Larsen deserved a DSO. However, the SOE officers did not think that Eidsheim's level of performance had matched that of Larsen, so it would not be fair either to Larsen or to other Norwegian officers if he were to be given a DSO as well. They suggested the award of a bar to his DSC instead. Horve, who initially thought that Eidsheim should be awarded a DSO too, changed his mind on receipt of a letter from Wilson and supported this suggestion. This was challenged by Collier, who insisted that Eidsheim deserved a DSO. The problem took well over a year to resolve. Eventually Sir Robert Knox, secretary of the Honours Committee, wrote to Rear-Admiral Mansergh, the Naval Secretary, setting out the arguments for both decisions, but without making a recommendation. One's heart warms to the no-nonsense Miss S. Harbottle, Mansergh's secretary, who summarised this letter succinctly and concluded: 'Submit for approval that in the circumstances the Admiralty recommends that Eidsheim be awarded a DSO'. Mansergh commented meekly 'concur'. The Embassy asked Horve to convey an apology to both officers for what had happened. They received their awards from Collier at a ceremony on 20 July 1948, when other members of SOE were also decorated.[4]

SOE also consulted Milorg about the provision of awards to members of the resistance. The list which they agreed contained a remarkable range of people. It included those involved in aggressive resistance activities and some of those who supported them, as well as those doing propaganda work – such as Roy Nielsen (also involved with Max Manus in the sinking of the *Donau*), who was killed in April 1945 and received a posthumous certificate of commendation. There is space to mention only a small representative sample. There were those such as Per Frivik, Ottar Mjærum, Leif Strenge Næss and Arne Solum. These were members of the group established in the NS-controlled State Secret Police (Stapo) early in 1942 that warned of measures being planned against the resistance, which Milorg was thereby often able to circumvent. They were awarded the King's medal for courage. Arthur

Ørstenvik, part of a group in Ålesund, built a secret cell in the bathroom of his house which was used by wireless operators for two and a half years, though it was situated only a few hundred yards from a German barracks in an area subject to frequent searches. They played an important part in arranging the evacuation of ship's crews and sabotage parties. He also helped in the rescue of Leif Larsen and the surviving crew of the *Bergholm* in 1942. Ørstenvik received the King's medal for service. Harald Risnes, who returned to Norway in October 1944, trained some 240 men in the Bjørn West base near Bergen. The Germans attacked it on 26 April 1945. Risnes drove them off after an engagement lasting six days, losing seven men and killing more than one hundred Germans. This was the largest action between the Norwegian resistance and the Germans. On 9 May Risnes took his group into Bergen to take over military duties after the German surrender. He was awarded an MC.

The list also acknowledged the achievements of some remarkable women. Among her other achievements, Gudrun Collett was responsible for establishing a system to provide food for members of the resistance in Oslo – an arrangement which lasted from the end of 1942 until the liberation. She arranged distribution through the (legal) Danish Help aid organisation, which was allowed to supply food to children and old people in Oslo. Their accounts were devised (and falsified) in such a way that Germans could not trace the final destination of supplies. Her illegal depots were established in some twenty different hospitals which it was permitted to supply. After she came to German attention, she evaded capture by lying for hours under a veranda in winter wearing only her nightdress. She had to leave immediately for Sweden.* She received the King's medal for service. Collett was assisted by Valborg Hammerich, the widow of a Danish admiral killed in an

---

* Max Manus provides a vivid description of his chance meeting with Gudrun Collett as they were both on their way to the border, when she was 'tramping vigorously up the track with a suitcase in her hand and a smart leopard-skin coat slung over her arm'. Manus, *Underwater Saboteur*, pp. 162–163.

RAF raid on the Gestapo headquarters in Copenhagen. Hammerich was the leader of Danish Help and worked with Collett to divert large quantities of supplies to resistance members who would not otherwise have been able to carry out their work. She also supplied many of the dependants of men in prison, sending them parcels every month. This was done in defiance of Gestapo orders. She received a certificate of commendation. Kari and Kolbein Lauring were both members of a resistance group who carried out sabotage and propaganda work in the Oslofjord area. The Germans surrounded their house at dawn on 4 April 1945 and tried to force entry. Kolbein fought them off with a pistol and hand grenades. Kari kept him supplied with ammunition and rang Max Manus and others to warn them of the danger, enabling them to escape. She continued to resist until after Kolbein had escaped through a back window. The Germans broke in and arrested her, but she remained silent during interrogation. Her citation noted that by her prompt and brave actions she had saved many lives. She received the King's medal for courage.[5]

Among staff who worked in London, Roscher Lund and Nagell were awarded the OBE.[6] SIS arranged for Roscher Lund's medal to be presented to him by Menzies.[7] Øen, who had earlier been given an OBE for his work in Canada in forming the first Norwegian fighter squadron, was awarded a CBE. The late Leif Tronstad was awarded a certificate of commendation, which, unlike most other marks of recognition, was one that could be awarded posthumously. Wilson, who had been awarded the OBE in 1943 after GUNNERSIDE, was awarded the Order of St Olav in 1944 and later given a CMG. Welsh had been awarded the Order of St Olav in November 1943.[8]

Compensation

There were, not surprisingly, many claims for compensation after the war. One of the most remarkable came from Einar Sandvik, a fisherman from the island of Leka, some seventy miles north of Trondheim. He approached the British consul in Trondheim in October 1945 to describe the help which he had provided to six British air crew in September 1940. They had been flying in two Swordfish, operating from the aircraft carrier *Furious*, which made forced landings on Leka after carrying out an attack in the Trondheimfjord. The crews destroyed their aircraft and sought help from local Norwegians to try to get back to Britain. Sandvik told the consul that he had given them his fishing boat, a 38-foot fishing smack which was his only means of livelihood, for which they provided a receipt. This was signed by one Sub-Lieutenant Poynter, and listed the names of the crew. Sandvik was later imprisoned by the Germans for assisting the enemy. He sought 1,000 Norwegian kroner* in compensation for the loss of his boat.

The embassy informed the Foreign Office, observing that if the facts which Sandvik had provided could be established, then the claim which he was making seemed a very reasonable one, in view of the service which he had rendered and the risks which he ran in doing so. They passed the details to the Admiralty, which confirmed that Sandvik's story was correct, and that the crews were members of the Fleet Air Arm. They contacted Poynter, who explained that owing to a series of mishaps the boat had been intercepted by the German Navy five days after they had set sail.† They were sent to Germany and spent the rest of the war as POWs. He added that they were grateful to Sandvik and to other local Norwegians who had also provided food and fuel. The Admiralty asked the Foreign Office to arrange to pay Sandvik the compensation which he had sought, and to send him a suitable letter of thanks.[9]

In this history we have looked at many instances of the courage, ingenuity, resourcefulness, endurance and sometimes sheer stubbornness shown by individual Norwegians who risked and sometimes lost their lives in their campaign of resistance against the German occupation.

---

* Allowing for inflation, worth about £2,000 at 2019 prices.
† One of the pilots was Henry Deterding, son of Henri Deterding, the former chairman of Royal Dutch Shell, who had married a prominent Nazi and moved to Germany after his retirement. This connection did not appear to affect his son's treatment in prison.

Some of their achievements, such as FRESHMAN/GUNNERSIDE, are well known. Others, such as those of the SIS coast-watchers, were equally important though less widely publicised. But the example provided by Sandvik illustrates a wider point. The resistance campaign could not have hoped to succeed if it had not also been supported by many thousands more Norwegians, almost all unacknowledged, whose individual contributions may have been small but who collectively made an incalculable difference to the outcome of the fight for freedom.

APPENDIX

DSO CITATIONS FOR BJØRN RØRHOLT AND TORSTEIN RAABY

M edal citations are sensitive documents. It did not often occur in wartime that other government departments were consulted when awards were being considered. However, SIS was in an unusual position. It was employing foreign agents to collect information required by the Admiralty and was recommending the award of a significant honour. So it is not surprising that Menzies chose to seek validation from the Admiralty before proceeding.

Menzies wrote on 28 May 1942 to Rear-Admiral John Godfrey, the director of naval intelligence:

I enclose a recommendation for the award of an honour to Second Lieutenant Bjørn Rørholt, of Norwegian army, whom you have met. Although this officer is in the army, we have employed him on work which was of benefit almost exclusively to the Admiralty and I think the recommendation could most suitably be made through that Department. Also, you are in the best position to judge the value of the information for which this man has been responsible, and you may wish to endorse my recommendation. The attached statement goes into some detail concerning the work of this organisation, and I would be grateful if its circulation within the Admiralty could be limited.

The covering note for the citation states:

Second Lieutenant Bjørn Rørholt RNA, proposal for award of decoration.
A fairly extensive ship reporting organisation has been built up by this
department on the Norwegian coast and it is understood that for some
time past it has been providing information of considerable value to
NID. The agent chiefly responsible for setting up and operating this
organisation is the above-mentioned officer and it is largely due to his
initiative, enthusiasm and above all personal courage, that the success
obtained is due. A short account of his Norwegian missions is attached.
He comes from a well-known Norwegian service family, his uncle being
the late director of military intelligence in the Royal Norwegian Army
and his services were given to us for reasons of patriotism and not for
the sake of material reward. He is now in this country and it is not
possible to employ him again on this work although the organisation
that he has built up remains. There is therefore no security objection to
giving some recognition of his services, although the reasons for any
honour awarded could not be made public. It is accordingly proposed
that Second Lieutenant Rørholt be awarded a very high honour. Such
an award, in addition to being earned for his own unselfish and gallant
service, would be a tribute and encouragement to the many other Norwegians who are serving our organisation with equal devotion but of
whom Second Lieutenant Rørholt has proved the most successful.

The SIS citation reads:

In February 1941, an attempt was made to establish an intelligence group
in Trondheim. Great trouble was experienced in obtaining contact with
this group but in May 1941 satisfactory communications were set up. It
was later discovered that this contact was entirely due to the initiative
coupled with technical qualification of the highest order, of Lt Rørholt.
For seven months, operational information of the highest order was sent
to this country until the organisation was broken up by the Germans. At

the time of the arrests in Trondheim, Rørholt was in Oslo. An attempt was made to arrest him in his father's house, but after an exchange of shots he escaped over a garden wall. (We have since learned that a German soldier on watch in the garden had to go back to find a ladder in order to scale the wall over which Rørholt had just jumped, hence the escape.)

Before leaving for Sweden, Rørholt spent ten days in Oslo making plans for his colleagues to escape from prison and perfecting plans for a new organisation. On his arrival here on 13 October 1941, his wireless experience was placed at our disposal, and his criticisms and suggestions have been invaluable in improving our sets and methods of using them. After September 1941, when the Rørholt organisation broke up, we were without radio communications with Trondheim. Late in January, we were urgently requested to re-establish contact with this area without delay. Regardless of the consequences, Rørholt immediately volunteered to go. His first trip was unsuccessful. The log of the voyage, however, provides details of engine problems, the need to use sail instead, the lack of a serviceable W/T set and the consequent decision to return to Shetland and come back in a more serviceable boat. It provides further witness to the undaunted courage, resourcefulness and initiative of this man. Eight days later he was again returned to Norway, and this time was successful in reaching Trondheim, where he immediately set up an organisation for watching the movements of German warships. This organisation has been and is still functioning successfully. His adventures in Trondheim rival the most exciting of the 'thrillers'. For example, on the occasion when he entered Agdenes Fort in the guise of an insurance agent, he offered policies to German officers in addition to reconnoitring the area with a view to installing an illicit W/T station. This station has now been successfully installed close to the Fort and is providing most valuable information. During this time, Rørholt also visited Oslo and Narvik in an attempt to organise groups there. When contact with this country was successfully established and the new groups working satisfactorily, he returned here after an absence of three months as his continued presence in Norway might have compromised his associates. He arrived here on

9 May 1942, bringing with him most valuable information and suggestions for further work in Norway. He is at present actively engaged in the preparation and furtherance of these schemes.

Torstein Raaby

On 19 August 1944, Menzies wrote in similar terms to Rear-Admiral Edmund Rushbrooke, Godfrey's successor as DNI. On this occasion, he did not refer to Raaby by name, but used the alias Pettersen which Raaby had adopted for his mission to Norway.

I do not normally trouble you or your department about honours and awards to my agents since the Honours and Awards Committee is in most cases the appropriate body to approach. I feel, however, that if I am to ask – as I now propose to do – for the award of a DSO, the application should have the support of the service department concerned. Both you and also I think the Vice Chief of Naval Staff* and Commander-in-Chief Home Fleet† will be fully aware of the work that Second Lieutenant Pettersen of the Royal Norwegian Army accomplished in establishing a reporting service that covered the *Tirpitz*. You will know, too, that he took his life in his hands in accepting this mission.

Although it may be true that many of my agents have run similar risks and have been in my service longer, I feel nevertheless that the special nature of Pettersen's work and his courage in remaining at his post after the first attack when he knew full well that the enemy were on his track, do single him out for special reward. I would ask you, therefore, to consider whether my suggestion that he should be granted the DSO might not be forwarded with the support of yourself or a member of the Board of the Admiralty. I enclose a memorandum citing Pettersen's services and should add that I have in writing the agreement of the Norwegian Commander in Chief‡ to such an application being made.

---

* Vice-Admiral Neville Syfret.
† Admiral Sir Henry Moore.
‡ Major-General Wilhelm Hansteen.

The citation read:

Second Lieutenant Pettersen, 26, first arrived in this country in June 1943 and entered our service at once. Directly he was trained he was sent by submarine to the north of Norway as one member of a team of W/T operators which we proposed to set up in that area, in an attempt to control enemy fleet movements to and from Altafjord. Pettersen was given the most important and also the most difficult task of establishing a station at the actual German base. He was not a native of that part of the world but nevertheless succeeded in establishing himself at Elvebakken at the southern end of the Altafjord. Elvebakken is a small place and security measures there are naturally very strict. He obtained an appointment as second cashier with the road authorities and he so arranged the details of payments at the various sites that he was able to travel continuously and at irregular intervals by car past the *Tirpitz*. In order to build up further his reputation for carrying out an irregular routine, he managed to acquire the reputation of being a drunkard. This helped to explain his absences from work during working hours at times when it was especially important for him to be at home operating his W/T set.

It was about two months after landing that Pettersen was able to start operating but from November 1943 onwards his reports have been of very great value. From the start they have dealt with movements of the German fleet units, the state of repairs of the *Tirpitz*, and the probable date of her readiness for sea. From February 1944 onwards he provided most valuable information on which the plan for the Fleet Air Arm attack on the *Tirpitz* was largely built up. This included detailed information concerning radar, aircraft, high tension cables, and the position of flak in the neighbourhood. Finally it was arranged that Pettersen should take an active part in the actual attack by providing two-hourly weather reports prior to the attack, the question of the weather at the actual position of the anchorage being a vital element in the operation. Pettersen carried out this work with the greatest success though the danger to himself in sending a message every two hours from his home can be imagined. As a result of the attack there was an intense search by the Germans for the wireless station in that area which they believed must exist, and Pettersen told us that he would have to try and escape. However, a second attack on the *Tirpitz* was then in contemplation and after consultation with the Admiralty we explained the situation to Pettersen and left the choice to him. He decided to stay on and he remained there while three further operations against the *Tirpitz* were in preparation. None of the operations materialised, but from the station's point of view they were fraught with considerable danger. Pettersen finally left for Sweden in the middle of May.

Although Pettersen has only been in our service for twelve months he can be credited with the greatest individual success achieved by any of our agents. The establishment of a resident W/T reporting agent in the Altafjord area in proximity to the main anchorage is a task which we had been attempting without success ever since this German base was first established. We had almost reached the conclusion that the sparseness of the population combined with the intensity of the enemy's security measures made the problem insoluble. It was only finally solved as a result of Pettersen's exceptional courage and resource combined with his natural flair for the collection of intelligence. Pettersen is now in the UK and has been able to have some useful interviews with members of the Admiralty staff and Commander in Chief Home Fleet. He will be leaving again shortly for Norway to carry out a further mission on our behalf.[1]

ACKNOWLEDGEMENTS

I am grateful to Arnfinn Moland and Ivar Kraglund, who sowed the seed which developed into this book when we met at a conference in London a few years ago. It has been a privilege to be able to tell this remarkable story.

I have had much valuable support from the Gerry Holdsworth Special Forces charitable trust, the Hjemmefrontmuseum in Oslo, and the Department of War Studies at King's College London.

Ingrid Winther Øyslebø has given me a great deal of assistance – not just in carrying out research in Norwegian archives but also in her preparation of the maps we have used. She was, too, a source of much good humour. My long-standing friends Haavard and Marianne Martinsen have shown me much generous hospitality on numerous visits to Oslo.

I also wish to thank the staff of the National Archives, and to Ivar Kraglund, Frode Færøy, Sigurd Stenwig and Hanne Rollag in particular at the Hjemmefrontmuseum, all of whom dealt with my innumerable requests with considerable patience. Olivia Beattie and Steph Carey at Biteback Publishing have been a great source of patient and helpful advice.

I am grateful to Norges Hjemmefrontmuseum and the Scalloway Museum for permission to use their photographs.

I am also grateful to a range of people who have helped me in a wide variety of ways, by giving me advice or making helpful suggestions, reading my drafts and painstakingly helping to improve them, lending me rare books or generally providing encouragement. They include Nick Adamson, Mats Berdal, Antony Beevor, Gill Bennett, Mike Goodman, Nick Hills, Tom Kristiansen, John Lunde, Stephen Mallet, Joe Maiolo, Bill Moore, Alastair Noble, Russell Pullen, John Ranelagh, the late Olav Riste, Mark Seaman, Patrick Salmon, Michael Smith, Duncan Stuart, Leif Tronstad Jr, Stephen Twigge and the late Carl Wallin.

Finally, I am – as always – grateful to my wife Nonie for her patient support and forbearance.

ENDNOTES

Chapter 1: An Introduction, pages 1–26

1   Extract from *The Times*, 24 May 1945. The National Archives (henceforth TNA), FO 371/47509.
2   The problems faced by the Norwegian government on arrival in Britain are vividly described in J. Nygaardsvold, *Norge i krig: London 1940–1945* (Oslo: Tiden Norsk Forlag, 1983), J. Sverdrup, *Inn i Storpolitikken 1940–1949* (Oslo: Universitetsforlaget, 1996) and O. Riste *London-Regjeringa: Norge i krigsalliansen 1940–1945, Volume 1* (Oslo: Det Norske Samlaget, 1973).
3   Patrick Salmon (ed.) *Britain and Norway in the Second World War* (London: HMSO, 1995).
4   The details of this extraordinary story are well described in R. Pearson, *Gold Run* (Oxford: Casemate, 2017).
5   Bjørn Rørholt, *Usynlige soldater: Nordmenn i Secret Service forteller* (Oslo: Aschehoug, 1990), p. 127.
6   Norges Hjemmefrontmuseum (hereafter NHM), FO.II 8.5 – Daea 0002. SIS monthly progress report, September 1943.
7   NHM, SIS monthly progress report, December 1943.
8   TNA, FO 371/24828.
9   Conversation with Haakon Lie, 5 July 2005; also Avon papers Birmingham University, letter from ambassador to Moscow Sir A. C. Kerr to Eden, 20 November 1944, AP SCA 44 19. Kerr had been told of Molotov's demands in the strictest confidence by Rolf Andvord, Norwegian ambassador to Moscow. Lie also briefed Jens Chr. Hauge, head of Milorg, the Norwegian military resistance organisation, in Stockholm on his way back to London. Olav Njølstad, *Jens Chr. Hauge: fullt og helt* (Oslo: Aschehaug, 2008), pp. 207–208.
10 TNA, Sargent minute, 19 February 1944, FO 371/43248.
11 TNA, despatch from Collier, 5 January 1943, FO 371/36876.
12 See Tony Insall, *Haakon Lie, Denis Healey and the Making of an Anglo-Norwegian Special Relationship 1945–1951* (Oslo: Unipub, 2010).
13 Margaret Cole and Charles Smith (eds), *Democratic Sweden* (London: New Fabian Research Bureau, 1938).
14 Riksarkiv (hereafter RA), Box 71 G8E.2/38.
15 For example, a report of 17 March 1918 entitled 'The position of the working classes and the Socialist movement'. TNA, MUN 4/3590.
16 Alan Judd, *The Quest for C: Mansfield Cumming and the Founding of the Secret Service* (London: HarperCollins, 1999), pp. 457–458, quoted by Gill Bennett, *Churchill's Man of Mystery* (Abingdon: Routledge, 2007), p. 49.
17 Keith Jeffery, *MI6: The History of the Secret Intelligence Service 1909–1949* (London: Bloomsbury, 2010), pp. 279–280. See also Michael Smith, *Foley: The Spy Who Saved 10,000 Jews* (London: Biteback, 2016), pp. 217–243.

18 The papers provided to Benjamin Vogt, Norwegian minister in London by Basil Thomson, head of Special Branch, describing Zachariassen's arrest, interrogation and deportation are in RA, Boks 481 Rets A1.6.

19 This was reported in *Aftenposten* on 17 December 1920, quoting a speech by Lloyd George in the House of Commons the previous day and subsequently reported by the legation. TNA, FO 337/90.

20 For further details, see Tony Insall 'Britisk sikkerhetstjeneste og mistenkte norske bolsjeviker i mellomkrigstiden', *Arbeiderhistorie*, Årbok for Arbeiderbevegelsens arkiv og bibliotek (Oslo: LO Media, 2009).

21 William Mackenzie, *The Secret History of SOE: The Special Operations Executive 1940–1945* (London: St Ermin's Press 2002), p. 21. The first four chapters of Mackenzie's book provide a detailed account of the establishment of SOE.

22 Klugmann's file in TNA (HS 9/1645) gives much of the background to this remarkable story. See also John Cripps, 'Mihailović or Tito? How the Codebreakers Helped Churchill Choose', in Michael Smith and Ralph Erskine (eds), *Action This Day* (London: Bantam, 2001), pp. 237–263.

23 See, for example, David Stafford, *Britain and European Resistance Movements 1940–1945* (London: Macmillan 1983), Chapter 5.

24 RA, Nagell papers, box 3.

25 F. H. Hinsley, *British Intelligence in the Second World War, Volume 1* (London: HMSO, 1979), p. 100.

26 R. V. Jones, *Reflections on Intelligence* (London: Heinemann, 1989), Chapters 10 and 11. Michael Smith, *Foley*, pp. 141, 143, 207–208.

27 NHM, SIS progress reports, June and July 1944.

28 Conversations with Haakon Lie, 5 and 18 July 2005. Lie had a wide reputation for being a good friend of Israel. See, for example, Hilde Henriksen Waage, 'How Norway Became One of Israel's Best Friends' *Journal of Peace Research*, Vol. 37, No. 2 (March 2000), pp. 189–211, which describes Bryhn's initiative in arranging for Norway to sell heavy water to Israel in 1958, a most controversial issue both at that time and afterwards.

29 TNA, Langmo's SOE PF is HS 9/886/2.

30 TNA, SOE history in Norway, HS 7/174.

31 TNA, HS 7/174. The paragraph has been annotated 'No trace of this exists'. HFM, Wilson, unpublished history, p. 24.

32 TNA, PREM 3/139/4.

33 Rob Smith, *Radio Times*, February 1973.

Chapter 2: The Resistance Begins, pages 27–54

1 John Kiszely, *Anatomy of a Campaign: The British fiasco in Norway, 1940* (Cambridge: Cambridge University Press, 2017), p. 110.

2 Ibid., pp. 83–85 and pp. 110–112.

3 See, for example, the examination by Major General Francis Davidson, director of military intelligence from 1940 to 1944, of Norway as a case study of intelligence failure to heed the lessons for future intelligence work. Liddell Hart Military Archive, Davidson 4/3.

4 Basil Collier, *Hidden Weapons: Allied Secret or Undercover Services in World War II* (Barnsley: Pen & Sword, 1982), pp. 65–70.

5 TNA, HW 12/251, report No. 79679 of 4 April 1940.

6 TNA, letter from Menzies to Hankey, 14 April 1940, PREM 1/435.

7 TNA, report No. 80 of 11 April, 1940. Halifax described this as 'a very valuable report'. FO 1093/206.

8 TNA, letter from Hankey to Wilson, 29 April 1940, PREM 1/435.

9 TNA, Menzies letter to Jebb, 31 March 1940, FO 1093/206.

10 Hinsley, *British Intelligence in the Second World War, Vol. 1*, p. 115, quoting T. K. Derry, *The Campaign in Norway* (London: HMSO, 1953), pp. 16–18.
11 TNA, CX 0114 of 25 January 1940, FO 1093/206.
12 TNA, FO 1093/206.
13 Hinsley, pp. 108–109.
14 Hinsley, p. 119, also quoted by Kiszely, p. 103.
15 TNA, PREM 1/435. See also Michael Goodman, *The Official History of the Joint Intelligence Committee* (London: Routledge, 2014), pp. 69–75.
16 TNA, report 78644, HW 12/249.
17 Olav Riste, 'Intelligence and the "Mindset": The German invasion of Norway in 1940', *Intelligence and National Security* (2007), Vol. 22, No. 4, p. 527.
18 TNA, despatch by Halifax, 12 June 1940, FO 371/24833.
19 TNA, minute by Collier, 14 June, FO 371/24833.
20 TNA, despatch by Eden, 28 December 1940, FO 371/24828.
21 TNA, letter from N. F. Hall, MEW, to Admiral Taylor, Admiralty, enquiring about possible naval action to deal with these minerals, 3 May 1940, HS 2/239.
22 Rørholt, *Usynlige soldater*, pp. 29–30; Ragnar Ulstein, *Etterretningstjenesten i Norge: Amatørenes tid, Vol. 1* (Oslo: Orion, 2008), pp. 23–25 and 28–35.
23 Rørholt, pp. 142–143; Jeffery, *MI6*, p. 376.
24 RA, letter from Welsh, 16 December 1941, Nagell box 3.
25 Sverre Midtskau, *London svarer ikke* (Oslo: Ernst G. Mortensen, 1968), pp. 60–69.
26 TNA, letter from Godfrey, 18 November 1939, ADM 223/851.
27 TNA, post-war summary, written by Godfrey in November 1947, ADM 223/475.
28 TNA, letter to the Vice Chief of Naval Staff, 28 July 1940, ADM 223/851.
29 TNA, HS 2/241–242.
30 TNA, Cheese, HS 2/150.
31 Interview with Carl Wallin, family records.
32 TNA, minute by Chaworth-Musters, 3 November 1940, HS 2/128.
33 TNA, evaluation of SOE activities in Norway, HS 7/178
34 TNA, HS 9/1553/6.
35 TNA, minute of 5 August 1940, HS 2/240.
36 TNA, HS 8/321.
37 TNA, HS 7/174.
38 TNA, minute from Churchill to Morton, 20 January 1941, PREM 3/409/7.
39 TNA, Mallet letter to Hopkinson, Private Secretary to Cadogan, 5 February 1941, FO 371/29408.
40 TNA, Hopkinson to Mallet, 21 March 1941, FO 371/29408.
41 TNA, Warner minute, FO 371/29408.

Chapter 3: 'Dangerous Rivals', pages 55–74
1 TNA, HS 7/174.
2 For an entertaining account of these manoeuvrings, see Jebb's biography by Sean Greenwood, *Titan at the Foreign Office* (Leiden: Nijhoff, 2008), pp. 85–101.
3 Mackenzie, *Secret History of SOE*, p. 95.
4 Ibid.
5 TNA, paper by Godfrey, 3 April 1941, ADM 223/851.
6 Jeffery, *MI6*, p. 374.
7 TNA, Menzies to Nelson, 5 February 1942, HS 8/321.
8 Ibid., pp. 354–356.
9 TNA, HS 2/150.
10 TNA, Scott minute, 15 May 1942, FO 1093/155.

11 TNA, HS 8/321.
12 NHM, FO II.8.2 F3.
13 NHM, SIS progress report late March 1943.
14 HS 9/892/7.
15 NHM, Wilson history, p. 102.
16 TNA, correspondence between Cordeaux and Campbell, DDNI, September 1944, ADM 223/481.
17 NHM, SIS progress report. October 1944.
18 Kristian Ottosen, *Theta, Theta* (Oslo: Universitetsforlag 1983), p. 56, quoted by Ian Herrington, *The SIS and SOE in Norway 1940–1945: Conflict or Cooperation? War in History* (2002), Vol. 9, No. 1, p. 101.
19 TNA, HS 7/182.
20 TNA, HS 2/184.
21 TNA, HS 2/161.
22 NHM, FO.II 8.2 E5.4.
23 RA, Nagell box 3.
24 TNA, ADM 223/884.
25 NHM, report on German direction finding and interception system against illicit transmitters, August 1945, FO.IV box 21.
26 Ragnar Ulstein, *Etteretningstjenesten i Norge* (Oslo: NHM, 1994), p. 24.
27 NHM, Roscher Lund report, *Hovedtrekk i etteretningstjenestens utvikling*, p. 10, NHM 283.
28 TNA, report from Haugland, 22 September 1943, HS 2/173.
29 TNA, HS 7/175, appendix M: W/T communications.
30 TNA, report by Wilson to the SOE security section, 12 April 1943, HS 2/151.
31 NHM, SOE box 25.
32 NHM, FO.IV box 40, report on German direction finding and preventive measures.
33 See for example Nøkleby p. 147, giving details of comments from Einar Johansen (Upsilon) and Bjørn Rørholt (Lark).

Chapter 4: Cracking Abwehr Codes, pages 75–94

1 Henry Stimson and McGeorge Bundy, *On Active Service in Peace and War* (New York: Harper, 1948).
2 For further detail, see C. Andrew, *For the President's Eyes Only: Secret Intelligence and the American Presidency from Washington to Bush* (London: HarperCollins, 1996), pp. 68–69.
3 TNA, Rees to Denniston, 15 November 1941, HW 14/22.
4 Ibid.
5 See for example, message to Denniston, 11 December 1941, TNA, HW 14/24
6 TNA, minute to Denniston, 16 January 1942, HW 14/27.
7 TNA, HW 19/266. Intercepted Norwegian communist messages. There are 250 reports in this file, based on intercepted Abwehr telegrams.
8 The Venona messages have also been released to the National Archives, and provide some fascinating glimpses of the range of intelligence activities carried out by Soviet MGB and GRU officers in Stockholm in the later stages of the war. The bulk of the messages date from 1944, and they are available in TNA on HW 15/14, HW 15/40, HW 15/41 and HW 15/42.
9 D. McLachlan, *Room 39: Naval Intelligence in Action 1939–1945* (London: Weidenfeld & Nicholson, 1968), p. 406. Also see F. H. Hinsley, *British Intelligence in the Second World War, Vol. 2* (London: HMSO, 1981), pp. 176–177.
10 H. Sebag-Montefiore, *Enigma: The Battle for the Code* (London: Phoenix, 2000), pp. 92–93.
11 F. H. Hinsley and A. Stripp, *Codebreakers: The Inside Story of Bletchley Park* (Oxford: OUP, 1993), p. 2.
12 Hinsley, Vol. 2, p. 174.
13 Sebag-Montefiore, *Enigma*, pp. 83–86.

14 Ibid., pp. 132–136.
15 Ibid., pp. 167–171.
16 Sebag-Montefiore, pp. 224–229.
17 TNA, HW 14/26.
18 Hinsley, Vol. 4, p. 72.
19 Different dates are given for the breakthrough in hand cyphers, but this is used by Hinsley, Vol. 2, p. 677. In a footnote in Vol.1, p. 120, he states that it was broken in December 1940, but this must be an error as it had already been widely used by then. TNA, ADM 233/792, containing the first part of the Naval Intelligence Division history, gives the date as 14 April 1940. The GC&CS files are silent on this point.
20 TNA, ADM 233/792.
21 A sometimes used variant of this acronym is 'Intelligence Sections Oliver Strachey'. This is given by Peter Twinn in his chapter on the Abwehr Enigma in Hinsley and Stripp (eds), *Codebreakers*, p. 123. Twinn worked with Dilly Knox, who later broke the Abwehr machine code. Mavis Batey, who also worked with Knox, in *Dilly: The Man Who Broke Enigmas* (London: Biteback, 2009) p. 141, puts it the other way around and states that it was officially referred to as Illicit Signals Oliver Strachey. This seems a more likely interpretation. But however the acronym is decrypted, its meaning is perfectly clear.
22 TNA, generic description of the HW 19 archive for ISOS and ISK, contained in the introduction to the hard copy file series. A similar figure is given in ADM 223/793, German agents' traffic.
23 TNA, HW 19/316, notes on the history of ISOS.
24 Hinsley, Vol. 4, p. 44.
25 TNA, HW 19/324. No record has been found to show whether Øverby did prove to be identical with Holte.
26 TNA, HW 19/331. Reports and correspondence of Captain Hugh Trevor-Roper with Strachey.
27 TNA. ADM 223/792.
28 Hinsley, Vol. 2, pp. 677–678.
29 TNA, KV 4/8. History of Camp 020.
30 Hinsley, op. cit. p. 678.
31 TNA, ADM 223/792.
32 TNA, letter from Philby to Vesey, 26 June 1946, KV 3/113.
33 TNA, HS 7/31.
34 TNA, HW 19/324.
35 Correspondence between Liversidge and Roscher Lund, November and December 1944, HFM, FO.II 8.2 E3.1a.
36 Letter from Cordeaux to Roscher Lund, 27 November 1944, HFM, FO.II 8.2 E5.4.
37 TNA, HW 19/331.

Chapter 5: German Success, Near Misses and Failures, pages 95–140
1 M. R. D. Foot, 'SOE in the Low Countries', in Mark Seaman (ed.) *Special Operations Executive: A New Instrument of War* (London: Routledge, 2006), p. 83.
2 TNA, KV 3/7. Reports on the Abwehr up to March 1942. KV 3/4 contains an updated version of this report, completed by J. C. Curry in August 1942. There are a number of generally small discrepancies between the details contained in these reports or similar histories and the individual subject files. In such circumstances, I have tended to rely on the subject file because it was compiled contemporaneously, except in a small number of instances where common sense dictates otherwise.
3 Ulstein, Vol.1, p. 83.
4 Whatever papers SOE had on Johansen – and there are references to them on Security Service files – have not been released either in the HS 9 series containing personal files, or

elsewhere. The main Security Service case file in TNA is KV 2/371, and there are summaries with some limited additional information on KV 4/8, a history of Camp 020. Many of the papers on KV 2/371 have been redacted, although the file register gives a few further details.

5   TNA, Milmo case study, March 1943, KV 3/75.
6   RA, Nagell papers, box 12.
7   TNA, Milmo case study March 1943, KV 3/75.
8   http://www.wwiinorge.com/our-stories/kristian-fougner/
9   Order from Vice-Admiral Wells, office of Admiral Commanding Orkney and Shetland, 10 March 1943. TNA, HS 8/790.
10 TNA. Sætrang's personal file has not been released. However, there are detailed references to his investigation in TNA on KV 3/7, KV 3/76–77 and KV 4/8.
11 TNA. Wallem's case file in TNA is KV 2/3282. There are also some further details on KV 3/7, describing Abwehr history up to 1942.
12 TNA. Larsen's case file in TNA is KV 2/2628, and there are further details on KV 4/15.
13 This provides an example of discrepancies between two different files. KV 2/2628 shows that the original information drawing attention to Larsen came from Norwegian counter-intelligence. The entry in the Camp 020 history, KV 4/15, attributes the tip off to ISOS, which cannot be correct.
14 TNA, WO 141/3/5. There are also references to him in KV 4/248. There is a file on Hagn's case in the Riksarkiv, Boks 481, Rets A.1.
15 TNA. Brodersen's case files in TNA are KV 2/447–451, and there is also a brief history on KV 4/14 which contains additional material. CRIM 1/1604 describes preparations for his trial at the Old Bailey.
16 His case files in TNA are KV 2/1303–1306; see also KV 3/7.
17 Vera Eriksen's case file in TNA is KV 2/14. There is a detailed account of Eriksen's explanation of her background in Hinsley, Vol. 4, pp. 323–325.
18 TNA, KV 2/20 (Lund) and KV 2/21–22 (Edvardsen).
19 There is no case file for Øien or Hanssen. Details in TNA are on KV 3/7.
20 There is no case file for this operation, but there are details in TNA on KV 3/7, KV 3/76–77 German espionage objectives in Britain since 1939, and KV 4/8.
21 The case file in TNA is KV 2/727, and there are also substantial details on KV 3/7.
22 There are no details available about Hammerun, apart from a brief reference in TNA on KV 3/7.
23 TNA, KV 2/553–554.
24 TNA, KV 2/1164.
25 TNA, KV 2/2246–2249. There is also an account of his release, and of an interview conducted with him by the Norwegians, among the Nagell papers in the Riksarkiv, box 10.
26 The Camp 020 history in TNA, KV 4/14, notes that in 1943 Hansen was the only one of sixty-five people admitted to Camp 020 who had entered Britain illicitly.
27 TNA, KV 2/1936. See also HO 382/374 for consideration about his continued detention. There are also details on KV 3/77, KV 4/8 and KV 3/5. Some of Hansen's story is also described by Hinsley, op. cit. p. 345.
28 The case file on Fanger in TNA is KV 2/2142.
29 TNA, KV 4/14.
30 TNA, KV 3/75.
31 TNA, HS 2/136.
32 TNA, HS 2/149 Anchor.
33 TNA, Harmer minute, 23 November 1942, KV 2/829 Tor Gulbrandsen.
34 TNA, KV 2/826.
35 Hinsley, *British Intelligence in the Second World War*, Vol. 4 (London: HMSO, 1990), p. 336.
36 It seems as though the idea to take Gulbrandsen back to Norway on Operation SUNSHINE, to protect Norwegian strategic installations, may have originated with Leif Tronstad. See

Njølstad, *Professor Tronstads Krig 9. april 1940–11. mars 1945* (Oslo: Aschehoug, 2012), p. 344, also HS 2/167, the interrogation of Gulbrandsen.

37 TNA, KV 2/289.

38 Details of this protracted saga are contained in TNA on KV 3/75, KV 2/2260 (Lark), HS 2/243 (Interrogation reports), HS 2/170–171 (Sunshine) and HS 9/1114/3 (Nygaard's PF). It is also described by Christopher J. Murphy, *Security and Special Operations: SOE and MI5 during the Second World War* (London: Palgrave, 2006), pp. 99–101, 103, 106–109 and 130–131. See also Njølstad, op. cit. pp. 231–233. While Tronstad was briefed by Wilson on the progress of the investigation of Nygaard, there are no grounds for believing that he was able to intervene on his behalf. Nygaard himself wrote an account of the investigation after his escape, but not the *Vinmonopolet* incident, in *Tortur, flukt og gisler – til tross* (Trondheim: self-published, 1982). See also Rolf Dahlø, *A Typical SOE Story: The Unknown Warriors of the Norwegian Resistance* (London: Createspace Independent Publishing, 2017), an account of how he found that his father was Evald Hansen, Nygaard's wireless operator.

39 NHM, SIS progress reports, September and October 1944.

40 NHM, SIS progress report.

41 NHM, Report by Mack, 3 June 1945, FO II.8.5 – Daea 0005 Stasjonsrapporter: Otto II, giving details of his deployment.

42 Anyone interested in learning more might start with J. C. Masterman, *The Double-Cross System* (London: Granada, 1979). Masterman was the chairman of the committee, so was well placed to describe how it worked. Ben Macintyre, *Double Cross: The True Story of the D-Day Spies* (London: Bloomsbury 2012) gives a very readable update.

43 Tore Pryser, *Svik og gråsoner: Norske spioner under 2. verdenskrig* (Oslo: Spartacus, 2010), p. 113.

44 TNA, Harmer minute to Robertson, 18 April 1943, KV 2/1068.

45 Hinsley, op. cit. p. 298. It was therefore possible for two Asts to have agents in the same place without either being aware of it.

46 TNA, KV 4/47, report on the operations of E1AS in connection with the Norwegians, Danes and Dutch in the later part of the war.

Chapter 6: Secret Alliances Take Effect, pages 141–170

1 TNA, 10 September 1941, PREM 3/328/11B.

2 Winston Churchill, *The Grand Alliance* (London: Cassell, 1950), p. 551.

3 Henry Denham, *Inside the Nazi Ring: A Naval Attaché in Sweden, 1940–1945* (London: John Murray, 1984), pp. 84–86. See also ADM 233/489, NID history of Scandinavia, which was written by Denham.

4 Rørholt, *Usynlige soldater*, p. 62.

5 Ottosen, *Theta, Theta*, photograph of document opposite p. 125.

6 TNA. The main papers describing this are on PREM 3/328/11B. There are also details on ADM 223/464 and ADM 223/489, where Denham states that he had encouraged the First Lord of the Admiralty to intervene with Churchill. See also FO 371/29433, where some additional documents have recently been released, showing that Northern Department were for some time unaware of the involvement of Eden and Churchill.

7 TNA, correspondence between Eden and Churchill, 22–23 September 1941, PREM 3/328/11A.

8 TNA, FO 371/32837.

9 TNA, HS 2/231.

10 TNA, ADM 223/851.

11 TNA, FO 371/36875.

12 David Garnett, *The Official History of PWE: The Political Warfare Executive 1939–1945* (London: St Ermin's, 2002), p. 168

13 TNA, FO 371/29431.

14 TNA, FO 898/241.

15 TNA, FO 371/29435.

16 TNA, FO 371/29431.
17 Ibid.
18 Garnett, *The Official History of PWE*, p. 204.
19 TNA, HS 2/126.
20 Garnett, p. 204.
21 Thomas Barman, *Diplomatic Correspondent* (London: Hamilton, 1968), p. 104.
22 TNA, HS 2/236.
23 TNA, report by Manus and Gram on impressions of the Home Front, 26 May 1943, HS 2/191.
24 TNA, HS 7/174.
25 TNA, SOE reports for the Prime Minister, July to September 1943, HS 8/250.
26 TNA, Leaflets for Norway. FO 898/447.
27 TNA, FO 898/63.
28 TNA, HS 2/178.
29 TNA, PREM 3/409/7.
30 TNA, HS 2/225.
31 TNA, FO 371/29422.
32 TNA, FO 371/32829.
33 TNA, HS 2/127.
34 TNA, HS 2/138.
35 This was set out in some detail by Wilson in a long-term policy paper of 21 September 1942. TNA, HS 2/128.
36 TNA, PREM 3/409/7.
37 TNA, PREM 3/409/3.
38 Ian Herrington, *The Special Operations Executive in Norway 1940–1945: Policy and Operations in the Strategic and Military Context* (Unpublished PhD thesis, 2004), pp. 93–94. There is a slightly different explanation of how Milorg's letter reached Britain in Sverre Kjeldstadli, *Hjemmestyrkene, Hovedtrekk av den militære motstanden under okkupasjonen* (Oslo: Bokstav og Bilde, 2011), p. 84.
39 TNA, HS 2/231.
40 Ibid.
41 TNA, FO 371/29446.
42 TNA, FO 371/29417.
43 TNA, FO 371/32823.
44 TNA, HS 2/161.
45 TNA, Menzies to Loxley, 24 September 1942, FO 371/32825.
46 TNA, HS 2/129.
47 TNA, FO 371/29421.
48 Ibid.
49 TNA, FO 371/32823.
50 TNA, HS 2/196.
51 TNA, FO 371/32827.
52 TNA, HS 2/129.
53 TNA, HS 8/937.
54 NHM, FO.IV box 55.
55 TNA, FO 371/26596. A few months later Ruge was moved from Königstein to a camp in Toruń, in Poland.
56 TNA, FO 371/29416.
57 TNA, FO 371/36876.

Chapter 7: SOE's Successes and Setbacks, pages 171–212

1 TNA, HS 2/136.
2 TNA, HS 8/790.
3 TNA, HS 8/822. Fleming later became famous as the author of the James Bond novels.

4   TNA, HS 2/177.
5   NHM, SIS progress report, February 1943.
6   Berit Nøkleby, *Pass godt på Tirpitz!*, pp. 46 – 47.
7   Rørholt, *Usynlige soldater*, pp. 447– 448.
8   Oluf Reed Olsen, *Two Eggs on my Plate* (London: Companion Book Club, 1954), pp. 41–89.
9   TNA, HS 9/892/7.
10   TNA, HS 7/175.
11   TNA, HS 2/234.
12   TNA, HS 2/229. Neither the identity of the agent, nor of the incoming party, is recorded here.
13   TNA, HS 7/175.
14   M. R. D. Foot, *SOE*, p. 72.
15   TNA, HS 2/167.
16   TNA, HS 7/174.
17   TNA, HS 2/162–163. Merkesdal's personal file, HS 9/1023/2, contains no relevant information beyond his training report.
18   TNA, HS 9/781/1 and HS 2/162–163.
19   TNA, HS 7/280.
20   TNA, HS 9/1553/6.
21   TNA, HS 2/150.
22   TNA, HS 2/150.
23   TNA, HS 9/1406/3.
24   TNA, HS 2/182.
25   TNA, HS 2/180–183.
26   TNA, HS 9/1603/3.
27   Max Manus, *Underwater Saboteur* (London: William Kimber, 1953), p. 30.
28   TNA, HS 2/191.
29   TNA, HS 2/208–210.
30   TNA, HS 2/11. Pyrites were used for the manufacture of sulphuric acid, a key chemical for many industrial processes.
31   TNA, HS 2/134.
32   TNA, HS 9/413/5.
33   Security Service 'lessons learned report', 20 August 1942, TNA, HS 2/136.
34   Ibid.
35   TNA, Wilson minute to Gubbins, 14 June 1942, HS 2/154.
36   RA, Letter from Nagell to Hansteen, 18 May 1942, Nagell papers, box 10.
37   TNA, HS 2/155.
38   TNA, HS 2/136. The last sentence was a reference to operations which were envisaged against Norwegian informers and agents provocateurs working for the Germans.
39   TNA, HS 2/243.
40   Ibid.
41   TNA, HS 8/790.
42   Kristian Ottosen, *Natt og tåke. Historien om Natzweiler-fangene* (Oslo: Aschehoug, 1989), p. 387 and p. 385.
43   NHM, SIS progress report, April 1943.
44   TNA, HS 2/161. A fuller version of the story of Baalsrud's escape is graphically told by David Howarth in *We Die Alone: A WWII Epic of Escape and Endurance* (London: Lyons Press, 2016), also in Norwegian as *Ni liv* (Oslo: Cappelens Forlag, 1955). Baalsrud is one of a small number of SOE Norwegian agents (others are Gunnar Sønsteby, Ingvald Johansen and Tor Gulbrandsen) for whom there is no personal file in TNA.
45   TNA, HS 2/234.
46   TNA, HS 2/161.
47   TNA, 2-147-8.

48 TNA, HS 2/232.
49 Sverre Kjeldstadli, *Hjemmestyrkene*, pp. 252–254.
50 TNA, HS 2/229 and HS 2/170.
51 TNA, HS 9/1178/7.
52 TNA, HS 2/200.
53 Arnfinn Moland has carried out extensive and well-documented research on this subject, published in *Over Grensen? Hjemmefrontens likvidasjoner under den tyske okkupasjonen av Norge 1940–1945* (Oslo: Orion, 1999). British records are less than complete. For example, the files for Chaffinch and Goldfinch are not among those which have survived and been released to the National Archives.

Chapter 8: The SIS Coast-Watchers, pages 213–250

1 TNA, KV 3/77.
2 NHM, SIS progress report.
3 Rørholt, *Usynlige soldater*, pp. 337–338, and Ulstein, Vol. 3, p. 196.
4 Nøkleby, *Pass godt på Tirpitz*, pp. 148–150.
5 TNA. The Gullfax and Johanna messages are on HW 40/76. This file contains material about German exploitation of SIS and SOE codes and cyphers. Rørholt pp. 477–478 contains an account of the end of Corona.
6 F. H. Hinsley, *British Intelligence in the Second World War* (four volumes, London, 1979–1988).
7 Edward Thomas in Salmon, *Britain and Norway in the Second World War*, pp. 121–128.
8 Jeffery, *MI6*, p. 375.
9 Herrington, *SOE in Norway*, footnote, p. 197.
10 TNA, ADM 223/851. See also Hinsley, Vol. 2, p. 200.
11 Ulstein, Vol. 2, p. 57.
12 Hinsley, Vol. 2, p. 203.
13 TNA, ADM 223/464.
14 Nøkleby, pp. 40–41.
15 Jeffery, p. 519.
16 RA, Nagell, box 15.
17 Account by Ole Snefjellå of his involvement in SIS operations in occupied Norway. Eric Welsh papers in private possession of the family.
18 Nøkleby, p. 46.
19 TNA, ADM 223/851.
20 Nøkleby, p. 45.
21 NHM, FO.II 8.2.F3.
22 NHM, SIS progress report.
23 Nøkleby, p. 162.
24 RA, Nagell, box 15.
25 See Bjørn Rørholt, *Amatørspionen 'Lerken'* (Oslo: Hjemmenes, 1985).
26 Hinsley, Vol. 2, p. 530.
27 NHM, SIS progress reports February and May 1943.
28 Hinsley, Vol. 2, p. 536.
29 MTB 631 ran aground during the attack. It was later salvaged and used by the Germans as S631. https://www.uboat.net/allies/warships/ship/17167.html The action itself is described (though without reference to Erica's intelligence) by Jon Rustung Hegland, *Angrep i skjærgården* (Oslo: Dreyer, 1989), pp. 55–59.
30 NHM, FO.II 8.5 Daeb 0004.
31 Dag Christensen, *En spion går i land: brødrene Snefjellås utrolige innsats på norskekysten under krigen* (Oslo: Damm, 1988), p. 136.
32 Ulstein, Vol. 3, p. 137.
33 Nøkleby, p. 120.
34 TNA, ADM 1/30535.

35 Ibid.
36 NHM, SIS progress report. See also Reed Olsen, *Two Eggs on my Plate*, pp. 159–185.
37 Rørholt, p. 142. Ulstein, Vol. 2, p. 137.
38 NHM, SIS progress report.
39 TNA, ADM 1/27180.
40 RA, Nagell box 3, letter to Graur, 4 June 1943.
41 NHM, SIS progress report.
42 TNA, ADM 1/30535.
43 NHM, SIS progress report.
44 Nøkleby, pp. 144–145.
45 NHM, SIS progress reports March–December 1943.
46 NHM, SIS progress report.
47 Christina J. M. Goulter, *A Forgotten Offensive: Royal Air Force Coastal Command's Anti-shipping Campaign, 1940–1945* (London: Cass, 1995), p. 353.
48 Thomas, in Salmon, p. 126.
49 Christensen, p. 229.
50 NHM, SIS progress report.
51 Ulstein, Vol. 2, pp. 98–101.
52 Goulter, pp. 150–151.
53 Ibid., p. 193.
54 NHM. SIS progress reports, May and November 1943.
55 Goulter, pp. 204–205.
56 Hinsley, Vol. 3, part 1, p. 256.
57 Ulstein, Vol. 2, p. 127.
58 NHM, FO.II 7.4 –HMP 201.0 contains an example of this agreement.
59 NHM, FO.II 8.2 E5.
60 NHM, FO.II.2 S.2. Cordeaux letter of 28 February 1943.
61 Ibid. Cordeaux letter of 20 March 1943.
62 NHM, Roscher Lund report on intelligence work during the war, p. 92.
63 NHM, FO.II.2 S.2. Cordeaux letter of 19 January 1944.
64 Ibid.
65 Sverre Bergh and Svein Sæter, *Spion i Hitlers rike* (Oslo: Damm, 2006). Bergh is the only XU agent who has publicly commented in detail about his activities on behalf of XU. There is also an account in Arnold Kramish, *The Griffin: The Greatest Untold Espionage Story of World War II* (Boston: Houghton Mifflin, 1986). See also Michael Smith, *Foley*, pp. 250–252.
66 Letter from Rosbaud to Sam Goudsmit, 16 July 1961, Samuel A. Goudsmit papers, Box 28, Folder 44, Niels Bohr Library & Archives: http://repository.aip.org/islandora/object/nbla%3A248880#page/27/mode/1up. I am grateful to Mike Goodman for drawing my attention to this correspondence.
67 NHM, FO.II 8.2 E5.4
68 NHM, FO.II 8.2 E3.1a.
69 The website wwiinorge.com mentions two more students, Øivind Holt and Frithjof Thingstad, who were both studying in Munich and also worked for XU.
70 RA, Nagell box 3.
71 NHM, FO.II 8.50001.
72 Account by Ole Snefjellå.
73 Nøkleby, p. 146, Rørholt, p. 485 and Ulstein, Vol. 2, pp. 50–55.
74 TNA, HS 2/135.
75 TNA, HS 2/135. Rørholt, pp. 322–328 and 466.

Chapter 9: Operations FRESHMAN and GUNNERSIDE, pages 251–286
1 TNA, HS 9/1603/3.

2   The development of the heavy water plant at Vemork, and the French operation to smuggle the stocks to France, are well described in N. Bascomb, *The Winter Fortress: The Epic Mission to Sabotage Hitler's Atomic Bomb* (London: Head of Zeus, 2015), pp. 3–16. See also Njølstad, *Professor Tronstads krig*, p. 30.

3   Rørholt, pp. 64–65, Bascomb, p. 23 and Jeffery, p. 375.

4   TNA, minute by Ismay to Sir John Anderson, 4 September 1941, CAB 126/330.

5   TNA, minute to ACAS, 3 December 1941, CAB 126/330.

6   TNA, meeting of the German target committee, AIR 20/4772.

7   Jeffery, *MI6*, p. 375.

8   Tronstad diary 24 December 1941, quoted by Njølstad, p. 127.

9   TNA, AIR 8/1767 and HS 2/184.

10 NHM, Wilson history, pp. 71–72.

11 TNA, letter from Wilson to COHQ, 14 November. HS 2/184.

12 TNA, HS 2/184

13 TNA, DEFE 2/219.

14 TNA, DEFE 2/224.

15 There is a good account of the complex nature of this part of FRESHMAN and the use of gliders in Ion Drew (ed.), *Silent Heroes: Operation Freshman and Others* (Stavanger: Hertevig Akademisk, 2011).

16 TNA, HS 2/184.

17 TNA, HS 2/153. Jakobsen escaped to Sweden shortly afterwards, and was debriefed in London in January and February 1943.

18 NHM, Wilson history, p. 72.

19 Ibid., p. 73.

20 in TNA (HS 9/774/8)

21 (HS 9/689/6)

22 Gunnar Myklebust, *Tungtvannssabotøren: Joachim H. Rønneberg, Linge-kar og fjellmann* (Oslo: Aschehoug 2012), pp. 118–119.

23 TNA, HS 2/185.

24 Ibid.

25 Ibid.

26 Jens-Anton Poulsson, *The Heavy Water Raid* (Oslo: Orion, 2009), p. 122.

27 TNA, HS 9/774/8.

28 TNA, HS 2/185.

29 TNA, HS 2/173.

30 TNA, CAS to Field Marshall Dill, Joint Services Mission Washington, AIR 8/1767.

31 TNA, minute from Wilson, 10 March, HS 2/190.

32 Ibid.

33 TNA, HS 2/186.

34 TNA, Wilson minute 10 August 1943, HS 2/187.

35 TNA, HS 9/1279/5.

36 TNA, AIR 8/1767.

37 TNA, HS 2/187.

38 TNA, HS 9/1436/4.

39 TNA, letter from Collier, AIR 2/8002.

40 See, for example Njølstad, *Tronstad*, pp. 281–282.

41 TNA, Tronstad to Hansteen, 30 November 1943, HS 8/955.

42 TNA, German target committee meetings. AIR 20/4772.

43 NHM, Wilson history, p. 75.

44 TNA, air attacks in Norway. AIR 2/8002.

45 Bascomb, p. 277–279.

46 TNA, HS 2/188.

47 TNA, CAB 126/171.
48 TNA, HS 2/188.
49 TNA, HS 7/175 appendix H.
50 Bascomb, p. 303.
51 TNA, HS 2/189.
52 Njølstad, p 396.
53 TNA, HS 2/188.
54 TNA, HS 2/234.
55 TNA, HS 2/188.

Chapter 10: The Tide Starts to Turn, pages 287–306

1   TNA, 18 February 1944, FO 371/43221.
2   TNA, HS 7/174.
3   Ibid.
4   Herrington, *SOE in Norway*, p. 341 and p. 346.
5   Kjeldstadli, *Hjemmestyrkene*, p. 280. Morten Conradi and Alf Skjeseth, *Osvald. Storsabotøren Asbjørn Sunde* (Oslo, Spartacus, 2016), pp. 97–99.
6   Kjeldstadli, p. 163.
7   Tore Gjelsvik, *Norwegian resistance 1940–1945* (London: Hurst, 1979), p. 127.
8   TNA, FO 371/43223.
9   TNA, FO 371/32825.
10 TNA, minute by Galsworthy, 30 May 1944, FO 371/43223.
11 Ibid.
12 TNA, FO 371/36886.
13 TNA, FO 371/3674.
14 TNA, FO 371/36886.
15 Ibid.
16 TNA, FO 371/43228.
17 T. K. Derry, *A History of Modern Norway 1814–1972* (Oxford: Clarendon, 1973), p. 388 footnote.
18 For a detailed consideration of this, see the papers by H. P. Wilmott and Einar Grannes in Salmon, *Britain and Norway in the Second World War*, pp. 97–108 and 109–118.
19 TNA, PREM 3/328/11A.
20 TNA, FO 371/43242.
21 TNA, PREM 3/417/5A.
22 TNA, Warner to Collier, 18 July 1944, FO 371/43259.
23 Paal Frisvold, in Salmon, p. 200.
24 TNA, Wilson to Gubbins, 20 June 1944, HS 2/223.
25 Ibid. A number of operational files do not exist in TNA. Several of them, such as Gannet, Chaffinch and Goldfinch, would have described the training of specialists intended to deal with traitors.
26 TNA, HS 7/178.
27 TNA, HS 7/180.
28 TNA, HS 7/174.
29 Nøkleby, *Pass godt på Tirpitz*, p. 121.
30 Bjørn Rørholt, *Usynlige soldater*, pp. 444–445.
31 TNA, directive from Wilson, 31 July 1944, HS 2/235.
32 Arnfinn Moland, in Salmon, p. 148.
33 TNA, HS 2/130.
34 TNA, HS 2/215.
35 NHM, Wilson history, pp. 105–106.
36 TNA, HS 9/679/4, HS 7/174 and Wilson history, p. 163.
37 TNA, HS 2/204.

38 Mackenzie, *The Secret History of SOE*, p. 671.
39 https://www.axishistory.com/books/134-campaigns-a-operations/campaigns-a-operations/2085-number-of-german-divisions-by-front-in-world-war-ii
40 For more details, see Tony Insall and Patrick Salmon (eds) *The Nordic Countries: From War to Cold War, 1944–1951*, DBPO Series I, Volume IX (London, Routledge, 2011), passim.

Chapter 11: Hunting Down the *Tirpitz*, pages 307–330
1 Salmon, *Britain and Norway in the Second World War*, pp. 125–126.
2 Patrick Bishop, *Target Tirpitz: X-craft, Agents and Dambusters – The Epic Quest to Destroy Hitler's Mightiest Warship* (London: Harper Press, 2012), p. xxvi.
3 TNA, PREM 3/191/1.
4 TNA, HS 2/179.
5 TNA, HS 2/141.
6 The most balanced account of Pound's decision to order the convoy to disperse, based on the intelligence which he then had available, is probably contained in Hinsley, Vol. 2, pp. 214–223. See also Jonathan Dimbleby, *The Battle of the Atlantic: How the Allies won the War* (London: Penguin, 2016), pp. 289–312.
7 TNA, HS 8/785.
8 TNA, HS 2/202–203.
9 NHM, SOE 35a, TITLE reports.
10 Hinsley, Vol. 2, p. 526.
11 NHM, SIS progress reports.
12 Roderick Bailey, *Forgotten Voices of the Victoria Cross* (London: Ebury Press, 2011), pp. 201–202.
13 TNA, ADM 223/87.
14 Hinsley, Vol. 3 part 1, p. 261–262.
15 NHM, FO.II 8.5 Daea 0006.
16 Hinsley, Vol. 2, pp. 529–530.
17 Ulstein, Vol. 2, p. 182.
18 NHM, Progress report for September 1943. Ulstein, Vol. 2, pp. 181–182.
19 TNA, HW 19/331.
20 Ulstein, Vol. 2, p. 37.
21 NHM, SIS progress reports.
22 TNA, ADM 223/87.
23 Hinsley, Vol. 3, part 1, pp. 275–276.
24 NHM, FO. II 8.5 Daeb 0004.
25 NHM, FO.II 8.2 E5.4 E5.4
26 Rørholt, p. 260.
27 NHM, FO.II 8.5 Daeb 0001.
28 Ulstein, Vol. 3, pp. 68–69.
29 TNA, ADM 223/87.
30 Bishop, p. 340.
31 TNA, HW 11/36.
32 NHM, FO.II 8.5 Daeb 00001.
33 TNA, ADM 223/51. Report on the sinking of *Tirpitz*.
34 NHM, FO.II. 8.5 – Daea 0006.
35 TNA, HS 7/174.
36 Hinsley, Vol. 3 part 2, p. 495.

Chapter 12: SOE Sabotage and Disrupting the U-Boats, pages 331–352
1 TNA, HS 2/2.
2 Ibid. SOE planning paper, 20 February 1943.
3 TNA, HS 2/236.

4 TNA, HS 7/178, appendix J.
5 TNA, HS 2/2. See also 'Norges dristigste sabotør', *Militær Historie* (2018), No. 1, pp. 4–10.
6 TNA, HS 8/407.
7 TNA, HS 2/2.
8 TNA, HS 9/1177/1 and HS 2/249.
9 TNA, HS 2/2.
10 NHM, SIS progress report January 1945.
11 TNA, HS 8/766.
12 TNA, ADM 1/30052 and ADM 199/1813.
13 TNA, ADM 199/1815.
14 TNA, HW 18/384.
15 TNA, HS 2/138, HS 2/132 and HS 2/234. See also Myklebust, *Tungtvannssabotøren*, passim.
16 Mackenzie, *The Secret History of SOE*, p. 665.
17 TNA, HS 2/204.
18 TNA, HS 7/174.
19 TNA, PREM 3/408/1.
20 TNA, FO 371/36872.
21 John Gilmour, *Sweden, the Swastika and Stalin: The Swedish Experience in the Second World War* (Edinburgh, Edinburgh University Press, 2012), pp. 104–107 and pp. 124–125.
22 TNA, HS 7/174 and PREM 3/408/1.
23 TNA, HS 7/174 and HS 7/178. See also Sønsteby, *Report from No. 24*, passim.
24 TNA, HS 7/174.
25 Rørholt, *Usynlige soldater*, p. 470 and p. 472.
26 Herrington, unpublished PhD, p. 343.
27 Manus, *Underwater Saboteur*, p. 168.
28 TNA, HS 7/174.
29 TNA, HS 2/191.
30 TNA, HS 2/192.
31 TNA, HS 2/193.
32 Ibid.
33 NHM, Wilson history, pp. 171–172.
34 Mackenzie, p. 671.
35 NHM, Wilson history, p. 145.
36 Mackenzie, p. 662.
37 TNA, HS 2/219.
38 Mackenzie, p. 659. See also John Prados, *Secret Crusader: The Secret Wars of CIA Director William Colby* (New York: OUP, 2003), pp. 29–34.
39 TNA, HS 2/134.
40 TNA, report by Lieutenant. Commander Georg Unger Vetlesen, 7 July 1944, HS 2/7.
41 TNA, HS 7/174.
42 TNA, HS 7/175.
43 TNA, HS 2/234.

Chapter 13: 'Lukket på grunn av glede', pages 353–366
1 TNA, CAB 66/60/22.
2 TNA, FO 371/47528.
3 Tønne Huitfeldt, in Salmon (ed.), *Britain and Norway in the Second World War*, p. 235.
4 TNA, PREM 3/328/11A.
5 Ibid.
6 TNA, FO 371/47505.
7 TNA, letter from Ministry of War Production, 12 February 1945, FO 371/47515.
8 Sir Peter Thorne in Salmon, pp. 213–214.

9   TNA, HS 2/234.
10 NHM, Wilson history, p. 164.
11 TNA, HS 2/170.
12 TNA, HS 2/215.
13 TNA, HS 7/174.
14 TNA, HS 2/138.
15 TNA, HS 2/204.
16 For the background, see TNA, FO 371/47506.
17 NHM, FO.II 8.2 E5.4.
18 TNA, HS 8/197.
19 NHM, FO.II 8.2 E5.4.
20 TNA, HS 2/212.
21 TNA, HS 2/243.
22 TNA, HS 9/1603/3.
23 NHM, FO.II 8.2 E5.4 E5.4.
24 TNA, HS 8/379.
25 TNA, HS 8/378.

Chapter 14: Retribution, Recognition and Compensation, pages 367–378
1   Neville Wylie in Seaman, *Special Operations Executive*, pp. 171–172.
2   See, for example, a letter from Menzies to Rushbrooke of 13 August 1943. TNA, ADM 223/851.
3   McLachlan, *Room 39*, p. 38.
4   TNA, HS 9/892/7, HS 9/473/1 and ADM 1/30743.
5   TNA, HS 8/407.
6   NHM, FO.II HMP D1.1 HMP D1.1 and TNA WO 373/108/963.
7   NHM, FO. II – 8.2 – HMP D 1.1 HMP D 1.1.
8   NHM, FO.II 8.5 Daeboo04.
9   TNA, FO 371/47523 and ADM 358/265.

Appendix: DSO citations for Bjørn Rørholt and Torstein Raaby, pages 379–384
1   TNA, ADM 223/475.

SELECT BIBLIOGRAPHY

There has been a considerable number of books written about this subject, or important parts of it. I have only included here those books which I have cited in the text, or consider to be especially relevant.

Barman, Thomas, *Diplomatic Correspondent* (London: Hamish Hamilton, 1968)

Bascomb, Neil, *The Winter Fortress* (London: Head of Zeus, 2016)

Beevor, J. G., *SOE: Recollections and Reflections 1940–1945* (Bodley Head: 1981)

Bennett, Gill, *Churchill's Man of Mystery: Desmond Morton and the World of Intelligence* (Abingdon: Routledge, 2007)

Bergh, Sverre and Sæter, Svein, *Spion i Hitlers rike* (Oslo: N. W. Damm & Søn, 2006)

Berglyd, Jostein, *Operation Freshman: The Hunt for Hitler's Heavy Water* (Solna: Leandoer & Ekholm, 2006)

Bishop, Patrick, *Target Tirpitz: X-craft, Agents and Dambusters – The Epic Quest to Destroy Hitler's Mightiest Warship* (London: Harper Press, 2012)

Collier, Basil, *Hidden Weapons: Allied Secret or Undercover Services in World War II* (London: Hamilton, 1982)

Conradi, Morten and Skjeseth, Alf, *Osvald: Storsabotøren Asbjørn Sunde* (Oslo: Spartacus, 2016)

Conway, Martin and Gotovich, José, *Europe In Exile: European Exile Communities in Britain 1940–45* (New York: Berghahn, 2001)

Cookridge, E. H., *Inside SOE: The Story of Special Operations in Western Europe* (London: Arthur Barker, 1966)

Croft, Andrew, *A Talent for Adventure* (Upton upon Severn: Self-Publishing Association, 1991)

Denham, H. M., *Inside the Ring: A Naval Attaché in Sweden 1940–45* (London: John Murray, 1984)

Foot, M. R. D., *Memories of an SOE Historian* (Barnsley: Pen & Sword Military, 2008)

Foot, M. R. D., *Resistance: European Resistance to the Nazis, 1940–1945*, 2nd edn (London: Biteback, 2016)

Foot, M. R. D., *SOE, 1940–1946* (London: Bodley Head, 2014)

Gilmour, John, *Sweden, the Swastika and Stalin: The Swedish Experience in the Second World War* (Edinburgh: Edinburgh University Press, 2011)

Gjelsvik, Tore, *Hjemmefronten: den sivile motstand under okkupasjonen 1940–1945* (Oslo: Cappelen, 1977)

Goulter, Christina, *A Forgotten Offensive: Royal Air Force Coastal Command's Anti-Shipping Campaign, 1940–1945* (London: Frank Cass, 1995)

Haukelid, Knut, *Skis Against the Atom* (Minot: North American Heritage Press, 1989)

Hinsley, F. H. and Stripp, Alan (eds), *Codebreakers: The Inside Story of Bletchley Park* (Oxford: Oxford University Press, 1993)

Hinsley, F. H., *British Intelligence in the Second World War: Its Influence on Strategy and Operations, Vol. 1* (London: HMSO, 1979)

Hinsley, F. H., *British Intelligence in the Second World War: Its Influence on Strategy and Operations, Vol. 2* (London: HMSO, 1981)

Hinsley, F. H., *British Intelligence in the Second World War: Its Influence on Strategy and Operations, Vol. 3, Part I* (London: HMSO, 1984)

Hinsley, F. H., *British Intelligence in the Second World War: Its Influence on Strategy and Operations, Vol. 3, Part II* (London: HMSO, 1988)

Hinsley, F. H., *British Intelligence in the Second World War, Vol. 4: Security and Counter-Intelligence* (London: HMSO, 1990)

Howarth, David, *The Shetland Bus* (London: Thomas Nelson and Sons, 1951)

Howarth, David, *Escape Alone* (London: Armada, 1989)

Insall, Tony, *Haakon Lie, Denis Healey and the Making of an Anglo-Norwegian Special Relationship 1945–1951* (Oslo: Oslo Academic Press, Unipub, 2010)

Insall, Tony and Salmon, Patrick (eds), *The Nordic Countries: From War to Cold War, 1944–1951, Documents on British Policy Overseas Series I, Vol. 9* (London: Routledge, 2011)

Jeffery, Keith, *MI6: The History of the Secret Intelligence Service, 1909–1949* (London: Bloomsbury, 2010)

Jones, R. V., *Most Secret War: British Scientific Intelligence 1939–1945* (London: Coronet, 1979)

Jones, R. V., *Reflections on Intelligence* (London: Mandarin, 1989)

Kersaudy, François, *Norway 1940* (London: Arrow, 1991)

Kiszely, John, *Anatomy of a Campaign: The British Fiasco in Norway, 1940* (Cambridge: Cambridge University Press, 2017)

Kjeldstadli, Sverre, *Hjemmestyrkene: Hovedtrekk av den militære motstanden under okkupasjonen* (Oslo: Bokstav og Bilde, 2011)

Kramish, Arnold, *The Griffin* (Boston: Houghton Mifflin, 1986)

Lie, Haakon, *Krigstid 1940–1945* (Oslo: Tiden Norsk Forlag, 1982)

Mackenzie, William, *The Secret History of SOE: the Special Operations Executive 1940–1945* (London: St Ermin's, 2002)

McLachlan, Donald, *Room 39: Naval Intelligence In Action 1939–45* (London: Weidenfeld & Nicolson, 1968)

Mann, Christopher, *British Policy and Strategy towards Norway, 1941–45* (Basingstoke: Palgrave Macmillan 2012)

Manus, Max, *Underwater Saboteur* (London: William Kimber, 1953)

Masterman, J. C., *The Double-Cross System 1939–1945* (London: Granada, 1979)

Midtskau, Sverre, *London svarer ikke* (Oslo: Ernst G. Mortensen Forlag, 1968)

Moland, Arnfinn, *Gunnar Sønsteby 24 kapitler i Kjakans Liv* (Oslo: Orion, 2004)

Moland, Arnfinn, *Over grensen?: Hjemmefrontens likvidasjoner under den tyske okkupasjonen av Norge 1940–1945* (Oslo: Orion, 1999)

Munthe, Malcolm, *Sweet is War* (London: Gerald Duckworth, 1954)

Murphy, Christopher J., *Security and Special Operations: SOE and MI5 During the Second World War* (London: Palgrave Macmillan, 2006)

Myklebust, Gunnar, *Tungtvannssabotøren* (Oslo: Aschehoug, 2011)

Njølstad, Olav, *Jens Chr.: Hauge – fullt og helt* (Oslo: Aschehoug, 2008)

Njølstad, Olav, *Professor Tronstads krig 9 april 1940–11 mars 1945* (Oslo: Aschehoug, 2012)

Nøkleby, Berit, *Pass godt på Tirpitz! Norske radioagenter i Secret Intelligence Service 1940-1945* (Oslo: Gyldendal, 1988)

Nygaardsvold, Johan, *Norge i krig: London 1940–1945* (Oslo: Tiden Norsk Forlag, 1983)

Ottosen, Kristian, *Natt og tåke: Historien om Natzweiler-fangene* (Oslo: Aschehoug, 1989)

Ottosen, Kristian, *Theta, Theta* (Oslo: Aschehoug, 1983)

Pearson, Robert, *Gold Run: The Rescue of Norway's Gold Bullion from the Nazis, April 1940* (Oxford: Casemate, 2015)

Poulsson, Jens-Anton, *The Heavy Water Raid: The Race for the Atom Bomb 1942–1944* (Oslo: Orion, 2009)

Preisler, Jerome and Sewell, Kenneth, *Code Name Caesar: The Secret Hunt for U-Boat 864 During World War II* (London: Souvenir, 2013)

Reed Olsen, Oluf, *Two Eggs On My Plate* (London: Companion Book Club, 1954)

Riste, Olav, *London Regjeringa I: Prøvetid* (Oslo: Det Norske Samlaget, 1973)

Riste, Olav, *London Regjeringa II: Vegen heim* (Oslo: Det Norske Samlaget, 1979)

Riste, Olav, *The Norwegian Intelligence Service 1945–1970* (London: Frank Cass, 1999)

Roberts, Adam (ed.), *Civilian Resistance as a National Defence* (Harmondsworth: Penguin, 1969)

Rørholt, Bjørn, *Amatørspionen 'Lerken'* (Oslo: Hjemmenes, 1985)

Rørholt, Bjørn, *Usynlige soldater: Nordmenn i Secret Service forteller* (Oslo: Aschehoug, 1990)

Sæter, Einar and Sæter, Svein, *XU I hemmeleg teneste 1940–1945* (Oslo: Det Norske Samlaget, 2007)

Salmon, Patrick (ed.), *Britain and Norway in the Second World War* (London: HMSO, 1995)

Salmon, Patrick, *Deadlock and Diversion* (Bremen: German Maritime Museum, 2012)

Seaman, Mark (ed.), *Special Operations Executive: A New Instrument of War* (London: Routledge, 2006)

Sebag-Montefiore, Hugh, *Enigma: The Battle for the Code* (London: Orion, 2000)

Skodvin, Magne, *Krig og okkupasjon 1939–1945* (Oslo: Det Norske Samlaget, 1990)

Smith, Michael, *Foley: The Spy Who Saved 10,000 Jews*, 2nd edn (London: Biteback, 2016)

Sønsteby, Gunnar, *Report from No. 24* (Fort Lee, New Jersey: Barricade, 1999)

Stafford, David, *Britain and European Resistance 1940–1945* (London: Macmillan, 1980)

Sverdrup, Jakob, *Inn i storpolitikken 1940–1949* (Oslo: Universitetsforlaget 1996)

Tennant, Peter, *Touchlines of War* (Hull: University of Hull Press, 1992)

Ueland, Asgeir, *Shetlandsgjengen: Heltene i Nordsjøen* (Oslo: Kagge, 2017)

Ulstein, Ragnar, *Etterretningstjenesten i Norge 1940–1945 Bind 1 Amatørenes tid* (Oslo: Orion, 2008)

Ulstein, Ragnar, *Etterretningstjenesten i Norge 1940–1945 Bind 2 Harde år* (Oslo: Orion, 2008)

Ulstein, Ragnar, *Etterretningstjenesten i Norge 1940–1945 Bind 3 Netten strammes* (Oslo: Orion, 2008)

Unpublished PhDs

Cox, Nechama Janet Cohen, *The Ministry of Economic Warfare and Britain's Conduct of Economic Warfare* (King's College London, 2001)

Herrington, Ian, *The Special Operations Executive in Norway 1940–1945: Policy and Operations in the strategic and political context* (De Montfort University Leicester, 2004)

INDEX